SEDUCED BY HITLER
The Choices of a Nation and the Ethics of Survival

Adam LeBor and Roger Boyes

SOURCEBOOKS, INC.
NAPERVILLE, ILLINOIS

Published by Sourcebooks, Inc.
P.O. Box 4410, Naperville, Illinois 60567-4410
(630) 961-3900
FAX: (630) 961-2168

First edition published 2000 in the United Kingdom as *Surviving Hitler* by Simon & Schuster UK Ltd. North American edition published 2001 by Sourcebooks by arrangement with Simon & Schuster UK Ltd.

Where it has not been possible to trace copyright holders, the publisher will be happy to credit them in all future editions of the book.

Library of Congress Cataloging-in-Publication Data

LeBor, Adam.
    Seduced by Hitler : the choices of a nation and the ethics of survival / by Adam LeBor and Roger Boyes.
        p. cm.
    Includes bibliographical references and index.
    1. Germany—Politics and government—1933–1945. 2. National socialism—Moral and ethical aspects. 3. Informers—Germany—History—20th century. 4. Military occupation. 5. Political persecution—Germany—History—20th century. I. Boyes, Roger. II. Title.

DD256.7 .L43 2001
943.086—dc21

                                                                        00-066162

Printed and bound in the United States of America
RRD   10   9   8   7   6   5   4

For my father, Maurice LeBor, one of many thousands who volunteered for the Royal Air Force so that Britain would survive Hitler.

—*Adam LeBor*

To the memory of Professor Zygmunt W. Kuligowski who did more than survive.

—*Roger Boyes*

They trudged up the street, their women in a whispering knot behind them, and now there was mud on their shining shoes. They came to the tangle of bodies and then moved closer together. The living looked at the dead and the dead stared back at them and there was no sound on the hill....But this was not their guilt, the leading citizens of Ohrdruf explained. They had never shot a man, or used a club. Yes, they were of the same political faith as the executioners. They prospered from the work of these slaves. This camp was in their town but they had never come here before this. Therefore, the leading citizens say, they were blameless.

—James Cannon, *European Stars and Stripes* staff writer,
on the forced visit of local Germans to Ohrdruf,
a sub-camp of Buchenwald, after its liberation
by U.S. troops in April 1945

Contents

Acknowledgments

Adam LeBor

Thanks first of all to my agent Laura Longrigg for her faith in *Seduced by Hitler* and her dedication to ensuring its publication. I am grateful to the editorial staff of Simon and Schuster, past and present, for their patience and cogent editorial advice: Helen Gummer, Ingrid Connell, Catherine Hurley, and Katharine Young. At *The Independent*, my thanks go to foreign desk editors Leonard Doyle and James Roberts, for their tolerance of a foreign correspondent who corresponded little while this book was being written, as well as to my colleagues John Lichfield, Imre Karacs, Andrew Tuck, and Clare Longrigg. The same is true of my editors at the *Jewish Chronicle*: Ned Temko, Jenni Frazer, and Gerald Jacobs. In the United States, our gratitude also goes to Hillel Black and Alex Lubertozzi at Sourcebooks, Inc., for their continuous enthusiasm and sharp-eyed editing.

The genesis of this book was in Paris. There my gratitude goes to Adrian Brown, for his lengthy and repeated hospitality, as well as Chantal Agueh, Patrick Bishop, Alex Chester, and Nicholas Farrell who all contributed as they knew best. Much of the manuscript was written in Budapest, where I am grateful to numerous friends and colleagues, especially Bori Dornbach. At the Budapest International Press Centre, I greatly appreciated the good humor and support of my fellow journalists Chris Condon, Simon Evans, Jim Lowney, John Nadler, and Mark Milstein. Special thanks are due to Erwin Tuil, for his detailed research into the history of the Netherlands under Nazi occupation and knowledge of Dutch language sources. Others who have helped with knowledge, expertise, and their time include: in Budapest, Agnes Csonka and Dominic Strauss. In Britain: the staff of the Holocaust Educational Trust, Cathy Galvin of *The Sunday Times* magazine, Rudy Kennedy, Lawrence Yusupoff, and Dan Korn of 3BM television. In the United States: Elsa Moravek de Wagner and Charlotte Opfermann. In Germany: Professor Ernst Hoffmann and Klaus Lang of *Süddeutsche Zeitung* magazine. In Israel: Esther Hakim, Laszlo Devecseri, and the late Hansi Brand. In Turkey: Andrew Finkel. Special thanks also to Barry Brown for the four volumes of documents on the Third Reich, to Compuserve for the provision of a complimentary Internet account and to the Holocaust mailing list (h-holocaust@h-net.msu.edu) for many valuable leads and insights.

I am grateful also to the staff of the following archives and libraries for their assistance in locating documents and expertise. In London, the British Public Records Office, the Imperial War Museum, the Wiener Library and the Jewish Chronicle library. In Washington, D.C., the U.S. National Archives, and in Jerusalem, the Central Zionist Archives and the Yad Vashem Holocaust Museum. Finally, in Britain, my chief researcher Barbara Wyllie continued her tradition of excellence in unearthing many precious historical documents that highlighted the dilemmas, and horrors, of the Nazi era. Doubtless there are some who have helped me with ideas and inspiration whose names I have unintentionally omitted; to everyone I say thank you.

Roger Boyes

I would like to thank dozens of Germans, Poles, and Hungarians who in their different ways survived Hitler and who were ready to talk to me about their experiences. It was important and impressive for me to understand how these people—many of them little more than children during the war—not only survived but also reconstructed their lives afterwards, often under very difficult circumstances. The members of the Auschwitz club in Warsaw, for example, taught me much about the nature of choice in extremis.

My gratitude also goes to Rita Abraham, Marek Edelman, Arnold Mostowicz, Hersh Fischler, Michael Pinto Duschinsky, Leni Riefenstahl, and Simon Weisenthal.

Very special thanks for Dorte Hunecke, Philip Boyes, Kaja Burakiewicz, and, of course, Farida Kuligowska, who made everything possible.

Introduction

This is a personal book about the intimate secrets of a closed society, about daily life within the Third Reich and the countries and people who came under its domination. It is a book about choices, choices made by those who lived under Nazi rule, and their consequences. It examines freedom for movement within the moral—perhaps immoral is a better term—maze of the Third Reich. *Seduced by Hitler* focuses on the German-speaking lands but also examines countries occupied by the Nazis, as well as the ambivalent responses to Hitler by neutral nations.

It is personal not only in its subject matter but also in its conception. Both authors lived and worked for many years in Communist and post-1989 Eastern Europe and came to understand how, in the nooks and crannies of a splintering authoritarian system, a delicate civil society could grow and flourish. The Soviet bloc was never totalitarian in its full-blown sense; nor indeed was it ever really a homogenous bloc. All empires, and Reichs, must to some extent tailor their regimes to prevailing circumstances.

Life under Nazi rule in Nordic Denmark, where the King remained on his throne and Parliament continued sitting, was far easier than the terror state in Slavic Poland. Hungary's Goulash Communism was always far more tolerable than food rationing in Ceausescu's Romania. Even at their most extreme—the Stalinist show trials, the Gulags, the murder of priests, private farmers, and dissidents—or intrusive, the Communist police states left some breathing space. There was scope for independent thought and action. Out of the failures of the economic system and the vagaries of political leadership—which even when swaddled by a dense propaganda blanket could not be concealed from an alert population—came a clear sense of the limits of power.

The corruption of politicians and bureaucrats and the everyday compromises needed to survive provided a certain moral elasticity. It could never be said, even in the darkest days, that there were no choices. There was always choice; not always between finely contoured options, rarely between unambiguous good and hell-scorching evil, but it was possible to deliberate on a problem and settle on the least detrimental course.

As we watched friends and acquaintances struggle with these choices—whether and when to emigrate or stay at home, whether to take a promotion or turn it down—so our admiration grew. Few residents of the United States or Western Europe face such moral quandaries. We began to wonder whether academic work on closed societies had really taken into account the complexities of everyday life. If the closely monitored inhabitants of Communist states could flex their ethical muscles, then surely those who lived under Hitler's Third Reich were also confronted with daily choices. The millions of words written on the Nazi era only seldom considered the individual freedom, the room for personal negotiation available to Hitler's citizens. Instead, historians have mainly reconstructed a world inhabited only by victims and criminals. As a result, the most important questions about everyday life in Nazi dictatorship have not been adequately confronted. What choices were available? Why were they not exercised? If fear inhibited honorable action, when did this fear ebb?

This is a book, then, about possibilities. Scholarly writing about power and authority in police states has so far been based on a very narrow definition of power; the ability to compel citizens to do something against their will. In these terms, the power of Communist and National Socialist leaders was near absolute; the machinery of state terror was such that almost everyone could be forced into some form of compliance through fear. But not everyone could be forced into total compliance all the time. For power did have its limits, and the reason is plain; even in a closed society or a police state, power is always more than the threat of force. It is a balance between terror and consensus. That balance has to be adjusted according to circumstances. *Seduced by Hitler* examines the moral conflicts within the Third Reich, the choices opened up in that shifting balance.

The vast majority of ordinary Germans—if they were not Jewish, handicapped, Communists, or Jehovah's Witnesses—were more or less safe from the clutches of the Gestapo. They had to be careful, and a small single act of outright defiance could lead to devastating punishment. The journalist Aleksander Kulisiewicz was sent to Sachsenhausen concentration camp after publishing an article with the title "Heil Butter!—Genug Hitler!" ("Salute butter!—Enough Hitler!") One Catholic priest was executed for telling a joke (see chapter 1).

There was, however, no inevitability of punishment for the ordinary German for the countless acts of nonconformity to which the secret police did not respond. There were practical reasons for this. The Gestapo was small. The Gestapo—the *Geheimstaatspolizei*—had 40,000 officials watching a country of eighty million. By contrast, the East German Communist Stasi employed 102,000 agents to control only seventeen million. The comparison, made by Simon Wiesenthal, is not a watertight one; the Nazis had other monitoring institutions apart from the Gestapo, and the Stasi had over four decades to develop.

But the point is important. There was one Gestapo officer for every two thousand people, while the Stasi had an agent for every 166 people. The East Germans could reckon with a strong possibility of an informer being present at every dinner party. The inhabitants of the Third Reich could, by and large, eat in peace. The Gestapo's main targets were the declared opposition: Communists, Socialists, non-German minorities—above all the Jews, but also Roma (Gypsies)—and the churches.

Perceived weaknesses—homosexuality, marriage to a Jewish spouse—were exploited; the draconian laws that could be applied in the mere possibility of this happening helped bring about conform-ist behavior.

For the most part, though, ordinary Germans were left alone. The Gestapo was too busy dealing with those considered a real threat to the Reich. "Many Gestapo officers, as long-time police-men, also understood the need to be sensitive to popular opinion when dealing with ordinary citizens who posed no real threat even if they had been caught committing a minor offense," writes Eric Johnson in a comprehensive study of Gestapo influence.[1] Hence, by applying leniency or pressure depending on the situation and the offender, the Gestapo officers coated Nazi terror with a legalistic gloss that helped legitimize their activities in the eyes of a largely faithful German populace.

The informer network was equally small. In the city of Duisburg in 1937, there were only twenty-eight paid informers, in Würzburg, just twenty-two. The police system survived on voluntary denun-ciation, of which there was no shortage. Germans, to some extent, terrorized themselves. A mother in one village denounced a neigh-bor for listening to Radio Moscow, after the neighbor had told her that the name of her missing son had been read out on a Russian prisoner-of-war (POW) list.

In fact, so numerous were the denunciations on trivial and personal matters—such as disputes between neighbors that had no relation at all to either national security or Jewish matters—that in 1934 the Interior Ministry demanded that those who made "thoughtless, invalid complaints" be prosecuted them-selves. This atmosphere of accusation fostered some truly bizarre situations. One family held a proxy funeral for their son who had been reported killed on his submarine, even though they knew, from committing the criminal offense of listening to the BBC, that he was alive in a POW camp. After the funeral, the mourners invited trusted guests home, told them the truth and celebrated with champagne. Terror there was, and fear too, but fear of a Gestapo that was always present in the background rather than on an intrusive day-to-day basis. It was a force that could, once alerted, potentially destroy a life in an instant. Truly a time when the main thing to be feared was fear itself.

There were, according to a study by historian Bernward Dörner, two principle types of denouncer: those motivated by personal grudges and those acting out of supposedly ideological rectitude.[2] Under the Heimtücke laws of March 1933 and December 1934—which protected the Nazi party and state from slander—one witness was sufficient. The result was a flood of denunciations during the early years of the Reich. Dörner gives an example of a tipsy twenty-five-year-old salesman telling a joke a little too loudly in a Krefeld hotel restaurant. "On the first of January, there will be a new law on putting fibers in clothes. It is not going to work. You know why? Because some of the fiber comes from the spider webs in the brain of Hitler, some of it comes from the web of lies woven by Goebbels, and some of it from the medal ribbon on Göring's chest. That leaves just the bad threads worn by the German people." An SS-man at a neighboring table overheard the joke and hit the salesman. After showing his SS-pass, he insisted that the unfortunate wag accompany him to a police station. The fate of the salesman is unknown. But this was December 1936, in the early years of enthusiasm for Hitler's reign.

As denunciations poured in, it became evident in the years that followed that there was little chance of action being taken against those denounced. There were moments when the police machinery would spring into action, but even when the Gestapo acted, it was usually after a long delay. German women were liable to arrest for sleeping with Polish forced laborers (and the laborers themselves were hanged). In a local community, there was no shortage of denunciations from neighbors, janitors, or jealous rivals, but the sheer force of the punishment made the police hesitate before acting; for the disruption to the community had to be weighed against any notional reward for vigilance. That is the true meaning of the statistic: two thousand inhabitants for every one Gestapo officer.

The police had to reach an accommodation with the population it was monitoring. The informer system was, if anything, the weakness rather than the strength of the Gestapo. The secret police who dutifully wrote down every detail of a case based, perhaps, on nothing more than neighborhood gossip found itself diverted from its major tasks. Above all, it was receiving information largely from the working and lower-middle classes. There were very few informers in the aristocracy and the upper middle class. As a result, the Gestapo was taken by surprise by the July 20, 1944, plot to kill Hitler, although hundreds of conspirators were in the know.

Moreover, the Nazis' anti-Catholicism fostered important social inhibitions among religious believers against dealing with the Gestapo. One Nazi party member is quoted as saying: "Anyone who denounces a priest should be beaten to death." In Catholic regions, this was a fair expression of public opinion. For ordinary Germans then the terror was not stark, and it only rarely figured in their daily lives. The regime had to accept David Hume's insight: "Nothing appears more surprising to those who consider human affairs with a philosophical eye than the easiness with which the many are governed by the few; and the implicit submission with which men resigned their own sentiments and passion to those of their rulers."

The Scottish philosopher goes on to say: "When we inquire by what means this wonder is effected, we shall find that, as force is always on the side of the governed, the governors have nothing to support that opinion. It is therefore on opinion only that government is founded; and this maxim extends to the most despotic and most military governments, as well as to the most free and most popular...."

For "opinion," one should read "consensus." The Nazi leaders acknowledged the need to react to, as well as shape, public opinion. The 1943 Rosenstrasse protest—when the German wives of arrested Jewish men marched through the streets of Berlin in defiance of the regime—illustrated the domestic vulnerability of the Nazis. Concessions were made quickly; none of the marchers was arrested, and their husbands were released. By 1943, the Nazis simply could not afford to alienate the many friends and relatives of Jews married to Germans. Stalingrad had fallen, Germany was being bombed. Maintaining morale was of more importance than deporting Berlin's last remaining Jews.

The Nazi leadership, startled by the protest, realized there were other issues to consider. What if a brutal suppression of Rosenstrasse triggered other outbreaks of civil disorder? How far would it spread? Loyalty to a regime that was faltering militarily could be spread thin at times of defeat and misery. Strategic and domestic imperatives overrode the ideological aim of deporting more Jews. There were cracks, if not fissures, in the Nazi totalitarian edifice. In those spaces was room for maneuver. The Third Reich could be a nervous government, infected by Hitler's memory of 1918 when, in his view, discontent on the homefront led to the defeat of Germany. A premium was placed on making ordinary Germans happy, or at least diverting their discontent with leisure cruises, cars, and cheap holidays.

This weakness at the heart of the police state was grasped by those Germans who chose to think and act. Consider the case of the thousands of hidden Jews dubbed "submarines," or "U-boats." They lived underground in Nazi Germany, often in Berlin, the heart of the Third Reich. They were hidden in cellars and attics, sometimes in cupboards and closets, by their non-Jewish friends and neighbors. Not for a few hours, or a couple of days, but for months, sometimes years at a time. Every minute of those long years put the German hiders, and any family members living with them, at risk of arrest by the Gestapo and an almost guaranteed trip to a concentration camp. The Jews had to be fed, clothed, and cared for through complicated and extremely dangerous logistical operations. If there were several thousand of these so-called U-boats, many thousands more Germans were needed to run the networks of people to feed and house them.

And one of the biggest dangers the hidden Jews faced was denunciation if they ever dared venture out into the streets. Denunciation, not just from Germans, but from other Jews, forced into working for the Gestapo to spot and denounce their fellow Jews in exchange for their own lives. The U-boats are an example of civil disobedience, low-scale resistance that made a difference and saved lives. The Rosenstrasse demonstration not only saved lives, but effected a change in Nazi policy toward those previously destined for the camps.

Yet, there was only one Rosenstrasse demonstration. Most German Jews were not saved by an underground network of sympathizers. Most of them were killed in the camps. The political culture of Germany was indeed saturated by anti-Semitism, yet the dominant theme seems to have been anti-Jewish brutality carried out by a minority and regarded with apathy by the majority, rather than the rabid, universal hatred demanded by the propaganda machine. The Nuremberg laws of 1935, which drove the Jews to the margins of German society, caused no uproar. There was more opposition to the anti-Jewish pogrom of *Kristallnacht* (the Night of Broken Glass) in November 1938, when Jewish synagogues were burned and Jewish businesses destroyed. But even that was born out of German distaste for disorder and destruction, rather than pro-Jewish sympathy. This moral paralysis has to be explained. The simple fact is that even though the mass of German people had ethical choices, they ignored them.

The organized German resistance was an extremely marginal phenomenon. Extravagant figures have been cited for the number of Germans arrested for opposition activities (Shareen Blair Brysac, a chronicler of the Red Orchestra Group, says that 800,000 Germans were jailed for active resistance during the twelve years of Hitler's rule), but this is largely sleight of hand. Communists, whether they were active or not, fell quickly into the Gestapo net after their party was banned. Social Democrats were sent to the early concentration camps—11,687 in 1936—but many were released after a few months. After 1937, Communists in Germany concentrated on survival; Social Democrats on building up an information network with party colleagues in exile. The churches, with the exception of a few outspoken priests, avoided direct confrontation with the regime. Many parishes in Germany still boast that they were instrumental in saving individuals (though rarely Jews). But they also employed slave laborers to dig graves, maintain rapidly growing cemeteries, and to help out in monasteries. The Catholic and Evangelic Churches argue that requests for slave laborers actually saved lives. The survivors we talked to give mixed reports about this supposedly humanitarian action; many seem to have lived in cold, difficult conditions.

There was no single resistance movement in Germany. The so-called *Kreisauer Kreis* did, however, manage to bridge some differences between army dissidents, social and liberal democrats, and churchmen. The critical energy for a decisive push against the regime developed only in the dog days of the war when the tide of battle was quite evidently turning against the Germans. The daring plot to kill Hitler in July 1944 showed that the coalition of resistance was, at last, able to come up with an alternative. It was an overdue act of imagination, as well as courage: the ability to envisage a postwar, post-fascist Germany. Above all, however, it was an act of despair by conservatives. There was no place for Communists in their ranks, for they feared a Soviet-controlled Germany.

Great men and women did emerge from these groupings. Some of their stories are told in *Seduced by Hitler*. Many were executed or broken, seeming to confirm the postwar German hypothesis that an act of rebellion was tantamount to an act of martyrdom. They were good Germans who died so that the rest of the country could be absolved. Heroic biographies have been manipulated: the role of the communist resistance fighters in the Red Orchestra was minimized in West Germany, while the suspect nationalism of the July 20 plotters was overstressed in East Germany. Since German unification, historical writing on resistance has attempted to correct these imbalances and restore some personality to courageous people who have become little more than political chess pieces. But the fundamental issue has still not been addressed: why only such a small minority of Germans was prepared to make difficult choices.

There could be choices, too, for the victims of the Third Reich. But in their case, the balance between terror and consensus was dramatically different. The situation of a Dortmund housewife was a macabre world away from the dilemma of Roman Frister, inmate in a concentration camp. Frister, a Polish Jew, was required to possess a cap, which had to be duly removed at the morning roll-call. The punishment for not having a cap was death. Frister's cap was stolen, and so he stole somebody else's. The capless prisoner was executed. Should Frister have died instead? To what extent did he share in the guilt for the other man's death?

In the camps, the imbalance between "crime" and consequence was such that it is difficult to compare the ethical dilemma of ordinary Germans with those facing ordinary Jews. The moral maze is almost too complex for modern minds, but we try nevertheless to chart a way through it. In our interviews with Holocaust survivors, we have come across extraordinary tales that highlight the ethical dilemmas of life under the Nazis but which lack enough necessary information to reach a proper rounded judgment. Consider, for example, the SS-man called Zirpins who was delegated to the Lodz ghetto to increase the flow of gold and jewelry to the Reich. Degussa, the Nazi smelting company, was impatient for more material, so too was the Reichsbank. Zirpins set up search gangs of Jews within the ghetto who knew the location of, or who could unearth, hidden valuables.

As the war stumbled to a close, the leader of one of the gangs disappeared—deported, it was assumed, to Auschwitz. But he survived. After the war, however, he reemerged under a different name as a precious metals dealer in Germany (and a close associate of the man who was later to become the head of the German-Jewish community, Ignatz Bubis).

Do we condemn this man for his past? Did he, to use a rather emotive phrase, sell his soul? Or did he use his influence not only to guarantee his survival in future prosperity but also to save Jews in the ghetto, to help them escape, protect them (perhaps in return for jewelry)? There are no fixed moral categories. It is pointless to ask whether he was a traitor or a hero since in wartime it is sometimes possible, or necessary, to be both.

Seduced by Hitler examines the darkest and most compromised Nazi microcosm: that of the wartime Jewish leaders who were corralled and terrorized into helping the Nazis prepare for the deportations to the camps. For some Jews, such leaders were heroes, who tried—albeit in vain—in the most terrible circumstances, to save some Jews by sacrificing others. Yet the surviving testimonies of many Holocaust victims condemn them as traitors. Can we now, with hindsight, judge Mordecai Rumkowski, self-styled Jewish ruler of the Lodz ghetto, who worked with the Nazis to ensure Lodz's factories were highly productive and so assisted the German war effort? Or Budapest Zionist leader Rezso Kasztner who made a deal with Adolf Eichmann to ensure safe passage to Switzerland for 1,685 chosen Jews, many of them his friends and family, at a price of one thousand dollars each, while hundreds of thousands remained behind? In the end, Rumkowski's empire and his privileges counted for nothing. He, too, perished in Auschwitz. Kasztner survived the war, only to be killed in Israel by fellow Jews who saw him as a collaborator.

All of these very different biographies and dilemmas are connected by what we call survival ethics, choice under pressure. The personal compromises, the corruption, the abandoning of professional or social codes, all this was done in the name of naked survival. German workers, the generals, the housewives could find ways of justifying their behavior. "There was no choice," is what elderly Germans now tell visitors from another age. Survival was the highest good. The life-threatening implications of defying or disobeying the regime were emphasized to the point of distortion.

The survival ethic places the preservation of life on a higher level, beyond a normal moral spectrum.

This view, however, manipulates or misrepresents history. The confusion of Nazi rule and of war, the fuzzy chain of command, and the friction between institutions carved out possibilities not only for survival but for ethical choice. Naturally, some people, having understood that they had significant room for maneuver, still made the wrong choices.

Hans Safrian, the Viennese historian, explains that, even at the very hub of the repressive state, there was scope for initiative. "No bureaucracy can operate on a basis that people simply obey orders. There are guidelines and given strategies. But it is up to individual bureaucrats what they do with this power. The SS, in particular, functioned in this way....Personal initiative—in the right direction of course—was an unbelievably high value in the SS."[3]

This rule demolishes the Adolf Eichmann defense (put forward at his trial in Israel) that he had no choice but to obey orders. The orders were vague and left space for interpretation. Eichmann, however, used his bureaucrat's freedom to perform overzealously rather than to exercise mercy. Safrian believes that, in 1944, Eichmann had a critical choice and chose to kill rather than to save. "It was a time when a few Nazi leaders were trying to enter talks with the Allies who were ready to use the Jews as an entry ticket. Eichmann in Hungary had large scope in his decisions. The message from above was: 'Take it easy for now.' Eichmann went ahead anyway and sent the people to Auschwitz."

The case of Oskar Schindler, who saved Jewish workers in his factory, is intriguing because it demonstrates that even a weak man—a womanizer, liar, and gambler—can use his weakness to do good: he can lie and gamble for human lives. The message of Schindler was interesting for contemporary readers and filmgoers accustomed to a black-and-white presentation of wartime heroism. The degree of risk to Schindler, however, is still not entirely clear. Making Schindler into a hero is legitimate, but the mythmaking needed to develop the man's character as a film hero—to make him into a contemporary hero—clouds the essential fact that he did not do very much. The effect of his actions was great but the energy deployed in the life-saving deception was modest. Many entrepreneurs, in other words, could have acted like Schindler without placing themselves in great personal danger.

Or consider the case of the Göring brothers, Hermann and Albert. Like Schindler, Albert Göring was an industrialist, in his case, working for Skoda. He was an active anti-Nazi who expended much effort, at some personal risk, to save Jews and other anti-Nazis. But he had few scruples about taking valuable paintings in return for helping a Jewish family. Big brother Hermann, who was building up a private art collection by other even cruder methods, protected Albert. Parallel lives provide useful insights, but they can also distort our judgment. Guarded by Hermann, what risks did Albert really take? The frightened microcosm of the ghetto, the dictates of an occupying army, the self-deception of those who collaborated with the regime in the hope of buying freedom or safety: this is a world without moral compasses.

Among businessmen and industrialists, Albert Göring and Oskar Schindler were the exceptions. Usually, as the officially sponsored historians now trawling German company archives demonstrate, there was not even a flicker of interest in saving or improving the quality of life. The possibilities were there, but they were only rarely exploited. There were a few exceptions, such as the scientist and industrialist Robert Bosch, of the IG Farben chemical combine. He demonstrated what one man could do, safely and effectively, within the Third Reich to protect and save lives. After his removal from IG's top management, the firm was to become a by-word for mechanized industrial slaughter, with its own dedicated concentration camp at Auschwitz.

How much did ordinary Germans know of Auschwitz? Most were more geographically removed from the killing field than Schindler and generally were excluded from Eichmann's tight loop of official secrecy about the Holocaust. But German society was nonetheless relatively well-informed. Foreign broadcasts penetrated the Reich. *Feldpost*, the soldiers' correspondence from the front, often contained important information about the course of the war. Soldiers returning home on leave or hospitalized—military sanatoriums have always been hives of information in wartime—told stories to relatives, lovers, friends, and each other. Tens of thousands of Reichbahn employees knew about the massive logistical scope of deporting millions of Jews. Word of mouth was a powerful factor and, unlike in Soviet Russia, there were no serious inhibitions to exchanging information within the extended family circle. Few knew everything, millions knew something.

The ability to exercise choice does not require perfect knowledge; it is enough to possess a basic ethical code in order to judge behavior. It was not necessary to be aware of gas chambers in Auschwitz in order to see that German Jews—the neighborhood tailors, doctors, shopkeepers, and lawyers, once trusted members of society—were being treated systematically like animals. Nor did it take much political sophistication to see that Nazi leaders were enriching themselves, that institutions were being corrupted.

The central question then is why this information was cast aside. A number of explanations have been put forward. The most current, and most radical, was advanced by Daniel Goldhagen the author of *Hitler's Willing Executioners*: that Germans were historically programmed for anti-Semitism and that ordinary Germans therefore experienced little anxiety about contributing to the machinery of the Holocaust. There are more traditional explanations. One is that Germans inherited a culture of servility to state authority, allowing the most fragile of all defenses: "We were only obeying orders." The third strand emphasizes repression and terror. Certainly anti-Semitism, whether preprogrammed or cultured by the Nazis, was a factor. As late as 1941, a resistance hero such as Carl Goerdeler, the mayor of Leipzig who was executed by the Nazis, was talking of the need for a separate state for the Jews.

There is no single, all-purpose explanation of the Holocaust. We do believe, however, that insufficient work has been carried out on the motivation of ordinary Germans in either ignoring or cooperating with the mass deportations and murder. Certainly, part of this was rooted in the widespread willingness of Germans to profit from the plight of the Jews, both personally and commercially.

The historian Richard Grunberger records that a Berlin Jewish doctor, having witnessed the deportation of his mother and sister, was then forced to show a Nazi official around his flat (he was reprieved from deportation because of his mixed marriage). Finding himself at last in the grand bourgeois milieu to which he had always aspired, the Nazi official became visibly excited. "All my life I have dreamt of furniture like this!" he exclaimed, before taking possession of the contents.[4]

Business and commerce exhibited the same moral vacuum. Shorn of any humanitarian considerations, provided with a slave labor workforce that did not have to be fed, let alone paid, IG Farben and much of German industry responded enthusiastically to the opportunity to literally work its workers to death, thus increasing profits to previously unimagined heights. In 1944, in Nazi-occupied Budapest, the authorities had to issue a decree calling for a halt to the flood of petitions from Hungarians who wanted to take possession of confiscated Jewish-owned businesses and shops.

Across the Third Reich there was, in short, a massive collapse of moral and civic values. We believe that this can best be described as a process of seduction. Hitler was a political seducer, versed in the seducer's art. The Germans, in turn, allowed themselves to be seduced. Ethical options can be blurred by irrational emotions. The crime of passion is still a fixed feature in some penal codes. That is why we have chosen the image of seduction. Hitler refined the seducer's art, spinning arguments worthy of John Milton's serpent and binding the German people to a personal relationship with the Führer. A personal, rather than a political connection: Germans were capable of becoming angry with their Führer and then forgiving him as he forgave them. It was seduction for the machine age; an attempt to create a sense of belonging at a time when there were few reliable reference points. The Führer's will did not replace individual will, but it made it easier to dodge morally based decisions. For seduction suggests a willingness to be seduced, a readiness to suspend disbelief.

There has never been such a popular German leader as Hitler. His hold on the German people endured years of chaotic leadership, bungled military campaigns, and corrupt economic management. This was more than politics, it was personal—less political support than near-religious love and adoration. Women wrote to him in the thousands, declaring their devotion. (Ironically, those who appeared too fixated on the Führer were liable to be arrested by the Gestapo.) They wept with joy and ardor when he spoke at Nuremberg. Those rallies, with their flaming torches and searchlights raking the sky, were organized as acts of worship: the individual self, with all its doubts, fears, and complexes, knew instead the joy of psychic surrender, of sublimation into the Germanic nation, with its sacred mission to Aryanize Europe.

Thomas Mann in his passionate essay of May 1945, "Germany and the Germans," compared the relationship between Hitler and the Germans with that between Faust and Mephisto. Nowadays, this seems too crude an explanation, the cliché of the Devil's pact. Mann traced a readiness to accept a Hitler-led police state to a historically conditioned submissiveness. "The German concept of freedom was always directed outwards, it was understood as the right to be German, only German and nothing beyond that....It was a sense of militant serfdom. National Socialism took this mismatched relationship between external and internal freedom and projected it onto the idea of world slavery led by a people as unfree as the Germans."

Our view of the relationship between Hitler and his people leans less heavily on a national will to be dominated and to exercise domination. That seems to us to present Germans in too passive a light. Seduction, combining myth and very down-to-earth, practical considerations, thus seems to us a more appropriate metaphor.

Hitler positioned himself as a central, and then the only significant, figure in the German body politic. This involved a shrewd sense for the weakness of the system and an understanding of the kind of profound fears and resentments that mobilized a society which has lost its bearings. In 1930, Germany shifted from a chronically unstable democracy to a mode of presidential government. The Reichstag saw its authority shrinking away, and a succession of chancellors (Brüning, Papen, Schleicher) were drawn into an increasing dependency on Reichspräsident Paul Hindenburg. Hitler was able on the one hand to exploit the popular distaste for western, "un-German" democracy and, at the same time, the feeling that ordinary Germans were losing their say.

The critical moment was the second Reichstag election in November 1932, the last election before Hitler came to power. The National Socialists lost more than two million votes and were left with 33.1 percent of the vote (down from 37.4 percent in July). By contrast, the Communists surged forward and seemed almost as strong as the Social Democrats. The concern was that the mass unemployment of 1932–33 would sweep the Communists into power and unleash a red revolution. Social Democrats, conservatives, big business and estate owners, and ultimately Hindenburg himself came to see a Chancellor Hitler as a less dangerous option than the postponement of new elections. Postponement of elections would have violated the constitution while nominating Hitler stuck to the letter of the law. Hitler chose the correct words, promising work and bread to the unemployed, the elimination of class warfare (and its "parties"), and a "new German Reich of greatness and honor."

The takeover was a masterstroke of political maneuver, and the November 1933 election results were more than a manipulation— they were an expression of relief. Popularity rose and fell in subsequent years, at least until the defeat at Stalingrad when Hitler's standing and credibility as a commander and as a seducer started to slip into long-term decline. Between 1933 and 1935, Hitler managed to tap into ancient myths and make himself appear as a man of destiny. This, as we demonstrate in this book, is perhaps the most important component in the process of political seduction. Only men of destiny, with tasks preordained by history (if not the ancient Nordic gods themselves), can credibly demand that their followers surrender to him the space in which personal moral decisions are taken.

At the Nuremberg rally of September 1934, Hitler spun the mythic web: "Just as previous invasions from the East were halted in Germany, so this time our people is a dam against the flood that is threatening Europe's prosperity and culture." Two years later, also in Nuremberg, he was declaring the Spanish civil war as an omen of an evil era, a Bolshevik danger to Christian history.

History had chosen Hitler to lead the struggle, and since the Germans too had chosen Hitler, they could again feel as if they were on the winning side. An underlying theme of writers in the Weimar Republic, trying to make sense of a world in which money had become worthless, was the need for a political messiah. "Where will our people find their Führer?" wrote the German essayist Paul Ernst in 1929. "I hear no voice, see no figure," said Gottfried Benn in the same year. It was not immediately clear that Hitler would be the savior. In February 1933, which was after Hitler was already chancellor, Reinhold Schneider was speculating in his diary over where a Führer could be discovered. He surmised that such a figure could be found only in the higher ranks of the army. By 1936, however, there was no longer any doubt: Hitler had not only engineered a political victory, he had won the hearts of Germans.

Most recent writing on Hitler seems to assume a fixed relationship between the Führer and his people. Since there were no pre-elections and no opinion-poll sampling, it is certainly difficult to measure the fluctuation in the relationship. There was, however, dynamism: it was a process of seduction, of continued wooing and conquest rather than a single act. On the basis of *Sicherheitsdienst* (SS Intelligence) reports—the tailored but essentially accurate reporting of the public mood—one could construct a temperature chart for the Third Reich, showing the dips and rises in popularity. Certainly popularity rose steeply until 1937–38, and it remains a common assertion—not only among revisionist historians—that had Hitler been killed in 1938, there would to this day be statues in his honor throughout Germany.

There is no uniform measure of popularity. Soldiers reacted differently from civilians; the brutalization of the army in the East probably led to faster disillusionment than on the homefront where everything was being done to keep morale high. The main problem for the regime's leadership was the growing distinction made between Nazi chiefs (*bonzen*) and Hitler himself. The mythmaking protected him from some of the worst outbreaks of unpopularity, at least in the civilian population, while Göring, Goebbels, and assorted *gauleiters* (provincial governors) increasingly became the butt of bitter jokes and complaints. The popular mood was in flux, and the regime—or at least the older Nazis and World War I veterans like Hitler himself—was sensitive to opinion. The assumption that World War I had been lost by disaffection and weakness at home rather than by the fighting men colored the judgment of these Nazis. Those parts of the machine manned by technocrats with little memory of World War I—the *Reichshauptsicherheitsamt* (Reich Central Security Office, including the Gestapo) was run by men in their thirties—were less bothered by unpopularity.

Even so, there was a heightened awareness that the regime was vulnerable. This influenced a range of policies—the use of women in the workforce, the distribution of food, the encouragement to plunder Jewish property—and was the subject of many nervous conversations in the leadership. The regime was in some respects frightened by its own population—this is a phenomenon we also witnessed in the Communist world—and the fear gave a degree of bargaining power to ordinary people. Some did say, "no."

The Berlin police chief, away from his office during the November 1938 *Kristallnacht* pogrom, was enraged at the breakdown in law and order and harangued his subordinates for failing to prevent the destruction. He would, he said, have ordered his officers to shoot the looters. Such examples refute the arguments of those who say there was no choice.

How were Germans seduced? They were offered the chance of social mobility, of bettering themselves. They were presented with a vision of the modern, a dream of technological perfection. At the same time, the regime paid tribute to the traditional and offered security to those within the *volksgemeinschaft*, the racially based community of "true" Germans. There was space to thrive within this closed society, and Hitler understood this better than most of his satraps. The dream was marketed, packaged, and sold: the seducer's art was also the persuader's science. The German people became consumers. But consumers have certain powers: the power of non-purchase, of boycott, of uninterest. The Germans did not, for the most part, exercise these options.

The victims of Hitler—Jews, leftists, Roma, and other non-conformists—were of course not so much seduced as raped. There the question, "Why did you not say no?" does not apply. The pace and the passion of seduction applied only to those within the *volksgemeinschaft* of "true" Germans. Hitler accelerated politics and planned and realized factories, motorways, extravagantly huge buildings, and architectural follies within a few short years. The sense of speed blurred the sense of choice. To say "no" was to step in the way of progress.

For Hitler's victims, acceleration meant that a German-Jewish Social Democratic politician like Ernst Heilmann could be at the height of his parliamentary powers in 1931 and, by 1933, be forced by SS thugs in Oranienburg concentration camp to crawl on all fours and bark like a dog. Heilmann exercised choice—he spoke out against National Socialism in the most public form available—and was then denied choice.

The seduction metaphor then has only limited value in extremes. Even so, there were attempts at wider wooing: to persuade sympathizers in occupied countries to share in the largesse of the Reich, to persuade the blonde and the Nordic, such as the Danish and the Dutch, to enter the *volksgemeinschaft*. Attempts were made to seduce politicians, indeed whole nations.

Seduced by Hitler is about different kinds of survival—from mere existence to profitable comfort—and different levels of choice. We have tried to provide some answers to the puzzling questions about compromise and corruption in closed societies. It has been difficult to make our points about moral desertion without minimizing the horror of the Reich. There is something tasteless about declaring that "only" a few Germans waged personal resistance against Hitler. Our interest is not to debunk heroes and reduce everybody to "ordinary" status. On the contrary, we searched for the heroic amongst the ordinary in order to understand better the concept of political conformity.

The Israeli psychologist Dan Bar-On, who runs encounter groups for children of Nazi criminals and the children of their victims, tells the following story: the daughter of a commander of an *Einsatzgruppe*—an operational group involved in Holocaust massacres—asked him what he thought of Daniel Goldhagen's book about German anti-Semitism. Its straightforward thesis, of an ingrained German anti-Semitism had given her bleak comfort as she attempted to understand why her father had killed so many, so readily. The woman broke down in tears. "I could have lived with my father's deeds if he had committed them as an anti-Semite. But if this explanation is not enough, then I have to carry on struggling with the enormity of his cruel crime—I need a sensible, rational explanation."

Her dilemma is both a personal and universal one. Why did some Germans kill in the Third Reich? Why did others refuse? What could they have done, and what did they do? This is not just a question of history: the massacres in Rwanda and Kosovo, the killings in East Timor and Chechenya show these questions still need to be answered. The complexities of ordinary people living under murderous regimes must be studied and understood to see how the extraordinary came to pass.

Chapter One

From Cradle to Grave

"The only people who still have a private life in Germany are those who are asleep."

—Robert Ley, director of the German Labor Front

"A stranger passes through a village and sees the weathervane being taken down from the church steeple. He asks the workmen, 'Are you putting a new one up?' 'Oh no,' the workman replies. 'We're replacing it with a civil servant. No one knows better which way the wind is blowing and how to turn.'"

—Popular joke told during the Third Reich

The secretaire was a fine piece of furniture, tall and handsome with a roll top and walnut inlays. It was only after a year or so that we found the hidden compartment—opened by placing pressure on both sides of a flat surface and then tipping it up. In it we found an old letter written in spidery Polish. Why it should have been concealed was not clear from the contents—a rather dry communication from a clothing manufacture in Litzmannstadt, Lodz as it is now known—but the date was interesting: 1940. That was after the German invasion of Poland, before the setting up of the ghetto. We had little doubt that the recipient of the letter, Nathan Majman, was Jewish—his name and the context of the letter made it plain enough—and that he was the owner of the secretaire. It was also a safe assumption that he lost his furniture soon after storing the letter. We had bought it in a Düsseldorf antique shop and tried to retrace the route of the secretaire. There was nothing very remarkable about the search; the 1990s was the decade when the wartime dispossessed attempted to find and reclaim their paintings, their gold, their houses, and their pasts.

Throughout Germany and central Europe, newly opened up by the fall of communism, search teams were at work, trawling through archives and property registers. Antiquarians were on their guard. Ours too. At first, he claimed to have bought the piece from a Rhineland widow. Later he admitted it came from a North German dealer. We followed the paper trail from shop to dealer from dealer to shop. It seemed like a small but significant victory when we managed to travel in time to 1947. A Hamburg "collector"—in fact another dealer—had bought the secretaire from a formerly well-to-do coffee importer living in the suburb of Blankenese.

That is when the trail ran cold. We never did find Mr. Majman. The leap from postwar to wartime desperation had to be made intuitively. Long-standing Hamburg residents told us how furniture, furs, and valuables from "the East"—that is, for the most part stolen from Jews—ended up in the port. The resulting picture brought us only a little closer to Mr. Majman, but it did reveal something about the corruptibility of ordinary Germans in the Third Reich, their readiness to profit from misfortune.

Public auctioning of Jewish goods in Hamburg began during 1941—between three and four thousand giant containers of furniture and clothes abandoned by those Jews lucky enough to emigrate. Hamburg was Germany's main embarkation point for America and Britain. Priority was given to bidders who were young, unmarried couples, or Germans who were likely to return to the Fatherland. Public institutions also benefited; the local tax authorities bought office furniture, the Hamburg library bought up the abandoned private book collections, the city art gallery bought paintings. The profits landed in a Gestapo account held with the Deutsche Bank.

Public auctions of Jewish goods were held on every working day between February 1941 and April 1945. Forty-five cargo ships full of belongings stolen from deported Dutch Jews provided rich pickings for the bidders who soon extended well beyond the original qualifying groups. The goods poured in from all corners of the expanding Reich. There would be complaints if there were not sufficient possessions formerly owned by Jews to pick over and select. The contents of 72,000 apartments in the East—Jews sent to Auschwitz—were loaded onto trains and sent to central collection points in German cities. Jewish slave laborers sorted through the property and then sent it for auction around the country. Essen received 1,928 freight wagons, Cologne 1,457, Rostock 1,023, Hamburg 2,699. Mr. Majman's secretaire, we believe, became German property at one of those auctions.

Frank Bajohr, who has researched the "Aryanization" of Hamburg, calculates that more than a hundred thousand people in the city alone, "ordinary Germans," directly profited from the Holocaust.[1] The Hamburg librarian Gertrud Seydelmann remembers how Germans felt as if they had won the lottery: ration cards were still being honored, there were no serious shortages, husbands were returning from the East laden with meat, wine, and clothes, and then luxury goods were offered at basement prices. "Simple housewives were suddenly wearing fur coats, dealing in coffee and jewelry, had fine old furniture," recalls Seydelmann. "It was the stolen property of Dutch Jews who, as I found out after the war, were already on their way to the gas chambers. I didn't want anything to do with it."[2]

A process that had begun in 1933 with individual purchases of Jewish property snowballed into what Bajohr calls, "one of the biggest changes of ownership in modern history, a massive robbery in which ever more sections of the German population participated." A systematic ransacking of Jewish homes began in 1938 and stretched well beyond Hamburg. Tax officers were declared responsible for deducting a 20 percent wealth tax on Jewish families. "Tax officers are now in the front line of the battle of the National Socialist empire against Jewry," said the *Steuerzeitung* (the "tax newspaper," required reading for Hitler era accountants) bursting with pride. As the ghettos took shape in the East and the deportation gathered pace, so the furniture trade flourished. Removal companies—such as Kühne und Nagel, now an international moving firm—profited from the so-called "M-Aktion" (M, for Möbel, meaning "furniture" and Aktion, or "operation"). Nazi institutions claimed first right to the furniture. Alfred Rosenberg, minister for civil administration in the East, made the first bid in December 1941 for desks and office equipment for his bureaucrats. Some of the biggest furniture transports came from Belgium and Holland, especially from Antwerp where many Jews had stored their belongings.

After the war, Jewish restitution claims were rejected. The documentation was said to fall under the realm of tax secrecy. Under the German archive law, these documents have to be sealed for eighty years. Only a few tax offices such as the Oberfinanzamt in Cologne have started to cooperate. Many Third Reich tax officials continued to work in the same capacity in postwar Germany, and so there was no rush to open the files. The inventories that have been released are comprehensive, itemizing every last spoon and kettle. The auctions announced in the newspapers drew large crowds in the exhibition halls of Cologne and the central slaughterhouse in Düsseldorf. As the war drew to a close, perhaps three out of every ten German households had at least one stolen item.

There were explanations for this—German cities, including Hamburg, were heavily bombed, and households needed to replenish their stocks—but no excuses. What had happened to a nation once proud of its civil service, its rectitude? The Germans—and we use the term carefully to incorporate the Prussians, the Bavarians, the Swabians, the Hanseatic, and all the tribes of the still young nation-state—looked down on others, the French, the Italians, the Poles for their corruption and their perceived lack of moral fiber.

The Allied bombing of German civilians provides a clue, but no more. The worse the bombing, the more likely Germans were to see themselves as victims. In war, there are informal hierarchies of victimhood; stronger, or better-off, victims feel no solidarity, only distaste, for weaker victims. Moral categories are blurred—the highest good is survival on the best possible terms.

This evolution in attitudes began far earlier than the bombing or indeed the outbreak of war. It was the very essence of the totalitarian system, the key seduction technique of the Nazis—to fudge the issue of personal responsibility to make everyone accountable to the Führer and no one accountable to himself. The oddity of the Nazi dictatorship was its recognition of consumer demands. This does not tally with any familiar definition of a totalitarian state. Yet stimulating consumer demand was an important component of early Nazi economic policies. German citizens were also consumers who had to be satisfied. The middle class had increased their savings by the mid-1930s—recovering from the desperate times of the hyperinflation—and were given opportunity to spend on cars (whose output tripled between 1933 and 1938) and other consumer durables.

There is still a heated discussion among economic historians as to whether the economic recovery was spontaneous, the result of a predictable cyclical shift, or induced by Nazi policies. Structural changes were on their way throughout Europe and in Germany too. Low-paid and unskilled jobs were giving way to white-collar employment, and joblessness was dropping. The result was that there was more money to spend, more consumer choices.

The Nazi economists shaped these choices. Tax breaks allowed Germans to buy their cars; they received grants to repair the roofs of their houses and to buy household goods. Those who got married under Nazi rule were offered loans of up to one thousand reichsmarks (RM) to buy furniture. By the end of 1933, 183,000 loans had been taken up. It would be, however, an exaggeration to say that the Nazis invented a form of consumer fascism. Hitler's Germans were never offered a grand choice between products; they had far less influence over competing policies. But the early Nazi focus on consumer demand ensured that the government's ability to meet popular expectations became a measure of the regime's legitimacy.

That created a special dynamic within Nazi society. It meant that a citizen-as-consumer had a degree of bargaining power with the authorities, a potential platform for protest. And it meant that the leadership was obliged to be alert to all fluctuation in the popular mood when consumer shortages began to set in.

The American political sociologist Ted Gurr answered the question, "Why do men rebel?" by developing the concept of Relative Deprivation.[3] The dirt poor, he argued, rarely rebel. Populations in political turmoil are usually those who previously enjoyed a substantial period of prosperity. When that prosperity tapered off, expectations continued to rise. The gap between these rising expectations and deteriorating living standards was (and is) a cause of domestic political violence.

The Nazis understood this danger, and the latent fear of the regime can be found reflected in its policy toward women, food, and consumer products. Hitler, it is fair to say, did not think like an American sociologist. He could compare for himself the mood in August 1914—a grainy photograph shows him in Munich as war is announced—and the sour, revolutionary mood of November 1918. An increasingly prosperous, self-confident state felt truly united in August 1914, perhaps for the first time. Four years of war—not only the bitter, pointless trench warfare, but also the long queues and hunger at home—set Germans at each other's throats. Hitler's analysis—as a former soldier in the trenches—was that World War I had been lost on the homefront. In order to be successful, the Nazi movement had to woo the German consumer in a way that he (and, in particular, she) wasn't during the First World War.

The queues, high prices, and poor harvest created a surliness that rapidly turned the population against the government and the war. "The war events are being followed with only passing interest because of the food shortages," said a Berlin police report in 1915. "The position of women in relation to the war is 'peace at any price.'" In 1914–15, the potato steadily replaced bread, or war-bread (kriegsbrot), as the staple. By 1916–17, potatoes, too, had become scarce, and the turnip, the steckrübe, became the basis for soup, coffee, and many other normal foodstuffs. It served as main dish, vegetable, and even dessert. In 1917, a Hamburg woman wrote to her son on the front: "It is sad here, no potatoes, flour, or bread for five weeks....[O]ne goes hungry to bed and wakes up hungry." By February 1917, even the *steckrüben* were rationed.

Since there was a massive exchange of information between the war zones and the homefront—29 billion letters and parcels were sent over four years, and every day ten million letters were dispatched to the front—the anger of the wives infected the soldiers. Nothing sapped military morale quite as much as grumbling and the rise of the black market at home. Society collapsed at all levels. Schools had to be shut because of the cold—only the rich had sufficient coal—and, in any case, children played truant in order to stand in the lines. Illness spread: 175,000 died of influenza in 1918. But it was food that stirred passion, that dictated the rhythm of everyday life: the ban on baking cake, the orders to butchers to sell only to people from the neighborhood, the rationing of milk for infants.

Hitler was determined that the German people should not suffer again in the same way. A sense of prosperity at home had to be linked to perceived success on the battlefield. Better than most of the Nazi leadership, Hitler knew how uneasy Germans were about a new war. The buoyant spirit of August 1914 was missing. As long as a war signified hunger for Germans, wars could not be won. Blitzkrieg was popular because it seemed to bring early and low-cost success. It broadened rather than narrowed the base of prosperity. Conquests abroad translated quickly into better living standards.

"The formula reduced to its simplest expression was Loyalty is bought through a Full Stomach," writes historian Birthe Kundrus. "[T]he National Socialist leadership was determined to spare the 'German,' 'Aryan,' 'racially pure' members of society every hardship and to reduce to a minimum unavoidable restriction....[F]oodstuffs and raw materials were drawn from the occupied countries."[4]

The connection between occupation abroad and consumption at home comes through clearly in a letter of a director of IG Farben in Kirovgrad in occupied Ukraine. "We are sending to Reich wheat, sunflower seeds, sunflower oil, and eggs. My wife writes to me that sunflower seed oil is available again on the ration cards. I can say with some pride that I was substantially involved in that."⁵

The preparation for war naturally entailed sacrifices for the consumer. Civil production had to be switched to military production, consumption and buying power curbed in order to keep inflation under control. Rationing was the best method available to the Nazis, and ration cards were issued right at the beginning of the war for food, clothing, coal, and shoes. But the popular memory of World War I was that rationing made the rich richer and the poor poorer. Cards were not honored and goods were swept under the counter to reappear on the black market.

Hitler was determined that this time rationing should be perceived as equitable and efficient. Workers in heavy industry or performing heavy physical labor were awarded an additional ration—a move that brought approval from the working class. Prices and wages were put under comprehensive state control—there was to be no repeat of World War I inflation. Black-marketeering was subject to draconian punishment, which kept it more or less under control until the final year of war, when the state distribution channels buckled.

The Sopped reports from 1939–40 suggest that public opinion accepted the slight drop in living standards associated with rationing. Just as Ted Gurr speaks of relative deprivation, so we can use the term "relative satisfaction" for the German mood. War made everyday life more difficult, but it also held out the prospect—as long as the Wehrmacht could report victories abroad—of greater prosperity.

The non-Jewish Germans were infinitely better off than German Jews, and they felt that the so-called *volksgemeinschaft*, the racially based community of "true" Germans, would thus enjoy indefinitely privileges and protection from the Nazi leadership. Jews were given only restricted rations, and meat, fish, white bread, unskimmed milk, butter, fats, chocolate, cake, coffee, and tea steadily slipped off their list of entitlements. There was no economic rationale for this discrimination (immaculately chronicled in the diaries of Victor

Klemperer⁶). The point was to make the Jews feel worse and the non-
Jewish Germans feel better. On the whole, this worked; such anti-
Semitic policies were designed not to stir up ancient hatreds of the
Jew (as Goldhagen would have it) but to make the average German
feel superior at a time when, objectively, his life was getting worse.

In the same spirit, recycling measures were introduced, ostensibly to push Germany along the road to economic self-sufficiency.
This device, adopted in World War I, as well as World War II,
certainly had no particular economic impact. Its real purpose was
psychological: to create a sense of community of shared participa-
tion in the war effort. Even today, elderly Germans, some of whom
stuff their cupboards with old string as they were told to do in the
Third Reich, still remember warmly the recycling, fuel-saving, and
housekeeping aspects of the Nazi era. It was one of the hidden links
that subtly connected the regime with its citizens. The *volksgemeinschaft* was substantially better off in World War II than in World
War I. Only in the winter of 1944–45 did the average German diet
fall below the nutritional minimum of 1,800 calories a day. By then,
of course, the seductive appeal of Hitler had almost evaporated.
Shortages of coal and wood, price increases, uncovered ration cards,
the dislocation caused by the bombing raids: all this demonstrated
to Germans that the regime had failed as a material supplier.

It is possible then to chart the satisfaction levels of the Third
Reich and to see how, at each stage, the relationship shifted between
leader and led. Each shift brought new choices, new possibilities to
influence the regime, but also risks and danger. In January 1933,
when Hitler became Reichskanzler, there were six million unemployed. By 1936, there was full employment. "Crying need and
mass hardship had generally turned into modest but comfortable
prosperity," is how the shrewd historian and journalist Sebastian
Haffner sums up those three years.⁷

The fact is, people had expected worse of Hitler. Even the most
enthusiastic supporter was rational enough to distinguish between
Hitler the brilliant demagogue of the Depression and a potential

leader making complex decisions. And the lukewarm followers, the nervous middle class, had expected terror on a dramatic scale when Hitler came to power. Instead, the bloodbath promised by the SA (*Sturmabteilung*, Hitler's brownshirted "army" of thugs who helped him rise to power through violence and intimidation) and the Night of the Long Knives (in which Hitler disposed of his political enemies in one bloody weekend in 1934, including the leadership of the SA, which was effectively replaced by its own more ruthless faction, the SS) did not take place. Prominent politicians of the Weimar republic were locked up in camps and brutally beaten—but sooner or later most of them were released.

"In short," concludes Haffner, "everything was very bad but nevertheless a little less bad than anticipated. Those who, rightly as it would turn out, were saying, 'All this is only the beginning,' were apparently proved wrong when during 1933 and 1934 the terror slowly died down to give way, during 1935–37, to the 'good' Nazi years, to almost normal conditions, only slightly disturbed by the continued existence of the now less-crowded concentration camps."

German workers shifted their allegiance in huge numbers from the Social Democrats and the Communists to Hitler after 1933. "This grateful amazement entirely dominated the mood of the German masses during the 1936 to 1938 period and made anyone who still rejected Hitler seem a querulous fault finder."[8] By April 1939, Hitler was able to tell the Germans: "I overcame chaos in Germany, restored order, enormously raised production in all fields of our national economy....I succeeded in completely resettling in useful production the seven million unemployed who so touched all our hearts....I have not only politically united the German nation but also rearmed it militarily...."

It was easy to accept such a speech at face value. There was no need to suspend disbelief because the facts, broadly speaking, were correct. The price of that "restored order"—the labor and concentration camps, the almost total marginalization of Jews, the steady brutalization of society—was secondary. War stirred apprehension.

But as we have seen, Hitler remained master of the popular mood, adept at purchasing loyalty.

There was nothing spontaneous about Hitler's reading of the Germans. In some ways, the combination of Hitler, Goebbels, and the various monitoring institutes (including the *Sicherheitsdienst*, or SS intelligence) was a precursor of the focus groups and opinion poll policy-making of the present day. The winter of 1935–36, despite Haffner's comments, was not easy. Wages were at the 1932 level, food prices had risen (officially by 8 percent) since 1933. Some foods had gone up by 50, even 150, percent. The Berlin police reported a hostile mood in the city because of the shortage of butter, cooking fat, and meat. The food queues were growing longer, the prices higher; policemen monitored the sale of butter.

Carl Goerdeler, mayor of Leipzig, was appointed Reichs Commissar of price surveillance. Goerdeler was not alone in seeing the problem: the competition for foreign exchange was torn between the money needed to buy raw materials for rearmament and the funds needed to buy fats. The solution, said Goerdeler, was to give priority to food. A devastating report sent to Hitler in October 1935 said Germany was faced with a choice. It could either return to a market economy, put new emphasis on exports, and curb the rearmament program or accept that it was a non-industrial economy with a reduced standard of living. This was the beginning of Goerdeler's road toward becoming a member of the resistance to Hitler, a position he adopted less out of moral repugnance than out of criticism of Hitler's wrong-headed economics. Yet Hitler understood all too readily, and although he marginalized Goerdeler, he also intervened with Reichsbank chief Hjalmar Schacht—who would be awarded near dictatorial control over the economy—to ensure the availability of foreign exchange for oil seed imports to produce margarine.

Step by step, Hitler removed the venom from the food lines and restored the population's sense of confidence in him. The popular trust did not extend to other members of the Nazi leadership. The Germans were more concerned with the inequitable distribution of food than the objective shortages. The so-called *volksgemeinschaft* was supposed to lift Germans above German Jews into a position of material privilege awarded by the Führer on the basis of race. But the sustaining myth of the *volksgemeinschaft* was that all would be treated equally, or at least justly, within the community. That is how leading Nazis became the butt of continuous public criticism while the Führer—apparently living a spartan life in the service of his people—was raised above his cronies. Already in 1940, informers of the *Sicherheitsdienst* of the SS were reporting that Germans in the food lines distinguished between *buttervolksgenossen* and *margarine-volksgenossen*—"butter comrades" and "margarine comrades." At the time, both butter and margarine were still available, but the price of butter was far higher. Discontent and dismay was reported in 1942 that "the wife of Reichsmarschall Göring invited seventy to eighty wives of generals for coffee and cake, and the table creaked under the weight of luxurious foods."[9]

The company run by August Nöthling—"supplier of wines, fine delicatessen, and poultry"—delivered food to high-ranking party members and generals in Berlin. There was never any question of ration cards, though the products were rare. Interior minister Wilhelm Frick, for example, had twenty-five pounds of chocolates, 264 pounds of poultry, and more than twenty-five pounds of game delivered to his home.[10] August Nöthling was so essential to the luxurious eating habits of the elite that he felt immune, indeed an honorary member of the club. After Stalingrad, Hitler ordered tough action—"irrespective ranks or standing"—against any Nazi leader pursuing an extravagant lifestyle. But when the prosecutors of this edict decided to act against Nöthling—the complaints in the queues had become too frequent and too harsh—"rank and standing" counted for rather more than a passion for clean living.

Wilhelm Frick sought an audience with Hitler who agreed that "every woman has to take what she can in these difficult days." Foreign Minister Joachim von Ribbentrop refused to answer police questions about his dining habits. The agriculture minister blamed his cook for the large shopping bills from Nöthling. All the ministers blamed Nöthling for persuading their wives to purchase unnecessary groceries. Nöthling, dubbed Tüten August ("Shopping August") by Berliners, was interrogated. Hellsdorf, the chief of the Berlin police—who was also a customer—said it was outrageous that Nöthling behaved as if he were above the law. Nöthling was fined, but he appealed, saying that he was ready to go to court and disclose the names of his customers. The investigating judge—also one of his customers—decided, not surprisingly, to jail him. In January 1943, he was placed under arrest. In May 1943, the grocer to the Nazis hanged himself in his cell. At the end of 1943, presumably as a kind of compensation, the Nazis offered a posthumous medal, the War Service Cross. His widow refused.

Such stories presented a stark contrast to the lot of the ordinary German who was becoming increasingly dependent on "balcony pig." This was a somewhat inflated term for a rabbit which had become the main secure source of meat. The Reich's Association of German Rabbit Breeders became an influential body, the key to making Germany independent of meat imports. Naturally, the rabbits were bred according to the principles of racial selection; a fat rabbit previously known as the Lorraine Giant was patriotically renamed the Silver Germania but ended up in any case on the dinner table. Stuttgart had 520 registered rabbit breeders in 1940 and well over a thousand by 1943. Rabbits were bred in parks to provide meat for hospitals. Earnest speakers declaimed on the ethical, educational, and economic virtues of Nazi rabbit husbandry. Every member of the family was allowed one rabbit. Extra rabbits had to be surrendered to the authorities. "Such measures," records the Canadian historian Martin Kitchen "gave rise to endless denunciation by neighbors, secret slaughtering, hidden hutches and bribery of the authorities with a choice piece of illicit meat."[11]

As the food supply chain broke down, appetites turned to cats—known, perhaps inevitably, as "roof rabbits." According to the suggestions of the Leipzig nutritional research center, cats could be delicious with nettle soufflé or with daisy salad. The strangest eating frenzy came in the winter of 1943 when the Berlin Zoo was hit in a bombing raid. Many hundreds of Germans discovered that it was possible to eat crocodile tail—which tastes like the food the crocodile has been last fed on, usually chicken or fish—buffalo, and antelope. Dead elephants were used to make soap. A panther, escaping the flames, ran as far as Lützow Platz, where it was shot and eaten shortly afterwards. Not surprisingly, there was little popular enthusiasm for tales of Nazi food orgies. The process of seduction demands a degree of secrecy, and so it was that reports of the fine lifestyles of the Nazi elite were continuously censored or, if criticism was voiced too loudly in public, punished.

Jokes about the foibles of the Nazi leaders provided a safety valve, but they were dangerous for the tellers (see "That Joke Isn't Funny Anymore," p. 36). The public illusion had to be maintained: the Führer looked after his people. If they felt neglected or cheated, the response was, "If only the Führer knew." Just as in the Soviet Union, where average citizens could not believe that Stalin knew about the reality of the terror and the purges. But, of course, the Führer, like Stalin, did know exactly what was going on. And he tolerated a high level of corruption among the elite. Cases that came to light were sometimes investigated. The Nazi auditors' office (*Reichsrevisionsamt der NSDAP*) dealt with thousands of cases. There was, for example, Gauleiter Hans Schimm in the Bavarian Ostmark who diverted funds from job creation schemes into constructing a hunting lodge set in four thousand hectares of estate, complete with a trout farm. Funds from the building companies of the Deutsche Arbeitsfront were used to subsidize the houses of Nazi leaders. Those who could be helpful in giving contracts, such as Hitler's adjutant Julius Schaub, were given valuable presents. In another case, some of the money stolen from Poles and Jews was deposited in a bank in Poznan. Only Gauleiter Arthur Greiser had access to the account. When auditors tried to check the account in October

1944—the war all but lost—they met a wall of silence. They were given no access to figures or receipts, and the staff reported sick or (most unusual at this state of the war) were given leave.

That Joke Isn't Funny Anymore

Telling anti-regime jokes in the Third Reich was a risky business. The penalty was death. On July, 28, 1944, the People's Court sentenced Father Josef Müller to be hanged for telling the following joke:

> *On his deathbed, a wounded soldier asked to see for one last time the people for whom he had laid down his life. The nurses brought a picture of the Führer and laid it on his right side. Then they brought a portrait of Reichsmarschall Göring and laid it on his left. Then, he said, "Now I can die like Jesus Christ, between two criminals."*

Humor is a safety valve in a dictatorship. There are few other outlets for dissent, and anti-regime jokes even act as a form of therapy, giving the joke-teller a feeling, however transitory, that he has, in his own way, somehow stood up to and mocked the authorities. The authorities are largely powerless to stop the spread of anti-regime jokes or the quips with which wits dubbed certain aspects of the Third Reich. Margarine, for example, was known as "Hitler Butter," and sterilization (often compulsory) was known as the "Hitler Cut."

By the time that the hapless Catholic priest was denounced for his joke, the old anti-Semitic wisecracks had become pointless. The Jews were plainly not responsible for the dismal state of Germany. The Nazis were. In the early stages of the war, the jokes were aimed mainly at the vanity and the unsavory lifestyle of the Nazi chieftains. The racial ideology was mocked. The perfect German? "Blond as Hitler, slim as Göring, tall as Goebbels." There was some cynical anticipation in the jokes circulating in 1940. "Two friends are talking. 'When the war is over,' says one, 'I plan to make a bicycle tour around Germany.' The friend replies, 'Fine, what will you do after lunch?'"

The social historian Hermann Glaser first heard the following joke in 1941:

> *An SS man says to a Jew in a concentration camp, "You will die today, but I will give you one last chance. I have a glass eye. If you can tell which one, I will spare you."*
> *The Jew looks at the SS man and says, "It is the left one, sir."*
> *"How did you guess?"*
> *The Jew replies, "It looked more human."*

"Such jokes were for us a little bit of resistance," says Glaser. They were always a bit more than that. First, they provided a snapshot of the level of popular awareness about the dangers posed by Hitler. If Germans could joke in 1940—when the invasion of France suggested that the Germans were unbeatable—that the country could shrivel rather than expand, then there must have been healthy skepticism about the regime's credibility. If Germans were joking about Jews in concentration camps in 1941 that also suggests a wider-than-admitted knowledge about the mechanics of the Holocaust.

As the Wehrmacht's victories halted under the onslaught of the Red Army, and the death notices mounted in the newspapers back home, jokes began to circulate about the army's military performance. A mock communiqué about the battle of Stalingrad said, "Valiant German soldiers captured a two-room flat with its own kitchen, toilet, and bathroom, and despite fierce counterattacks by Soviet bandits, managed to retain two-thirds of it."[12]

The foibles of Nazi leaders provided rich material for humorists. Ernst Röhm, leader of the SA brownshirts, who was executed in the 1934 Night of the Long Knives, was a notorious homosexual. After his death, this joke proclaimed: "Now we can understand his recent address to young people that 'Out of every Hitler Youth a Storm Trooper will emerge.'"

But it was the vain, hugely fat and puffed-up Göring, head of the Luftwaffe, with his mania for uniforms and self-awarded medals, who was the favorite butt of numerous Nazi jokes:

> *A water main bursts in the Air Ministry basement. Göring calls his secretary—"Fetch me my admiral's uniform immediately!"*

> *One night, Emmy Göring wakes up at an early hour and sees her husband with his back to her performing a strange dance with his "baton." Asked by his wife what exactly he is doing, he replies: "I am promoting my underpants to overpants."*

Even wry Jewish humor found a new outlet in the madness of Hitler's rule:

> *Cohen and Greenbaum are sitting on a park bench in Berlin in 1933, shortly after the Nazis took power.*
> *"You know, Cohen, despite everything, do you realize that we are living history, here, real history?"*
> *"Is that a fact?" asks Cohen. "Personally, I wouldn't mind trying geography next time."*

Five years later, after *Kristallnacht*, the two friends meet again:

> *"Did you hear the sad news?" asks Cohen. "Our friend Goldberg has died."*

"Well," replies Greenbaum, "if he got a chance to better himself..."

Very few people were executed for telling jokes, but publicly expressed anti-regime humor was the subject of many denunciations to the Gestapo. This has made it possible to chart the public mood, from mockery to cynicism and, finally, bitter criticism.

The Nazi party had no form of internal democracy, no institutionalized ways of expressing different interests. As a result, the movement became a conglomeration of cliques and clans. Personal loyalty to the clan chief was the key binding element, and this loyalty was rewarded with patronage and promotion. It was a system—if that is not too grand a word—that encouraged nepotism. Each branch of the clan created its own slush fund. In Hamburg alone, there were more than three hundred trials against Nazi members on charges of fraud and embezzlement. But this was a small fraction of the real number of corruption cases—most bubbled below the surface, and cases came to court only when one particular clan had lost out against another. The self-enrichment reflected not only the chaotic situation of the party and its naturally criminal element but also a more general attitude in society. The Nazis trawled among the victims of society—those who had been made redundant, served time in prison, gone bankrupt and/or were unemployable war veterans—and played on their sense of victimhood.

German scholar Christoph Schmidt, in a psychological analysis of the "Old Guard" of the Nazis, found that 30 percent believed that their personal, social, and financial woes had resulted from persecution for their beliefs. "They describe, in almost crazed terms, a world of permanent prosecution and disadvantage inflicted on them by a hostile environment."[13] These attitudes converted, on coming to power, into a feeling that society owed them a debt. It was a short step from that point to making the party into a self-help organization, to right perceived wrongs through self-enrichment. The Nazis thus mirrored the victimhood of German society and the party's response—a self-righteous greed—was also partly the response of ordinary Germans.

Britain's Army of Blackmailers

Those Germans unable or unwilling to oppose or obstruct the Nazis sometimes found the choice made for them—by undercover agents of the British Special Operations Executive (SOE) operating inside the Third Reich. The SOE was founded by the British during World War II. Its agents operated behind Nazi enemy lines, in conditions of great peril. Their brief was to cause chaos and sabotage, as Churchill instructed them to "set Europe ablaze." Declassified wartime intelligence files at the Public Records Office include a fascinating list of eighty-four individuals, mostly living in Berlin, whom British intelligence believed could be induced to aid the Allies, sometimes through conviction but mainly through bribes, coercion, or direct threats of violence. This secret—and dirty—war was not fought by Marquis of Queensberry rules, or even according to the Geneva Convention.

The dry title of "Operative List of Personalities" belies the wealth of fascinating details about those named. But it illustrates the extensive reach of the SOE inside the very heart of the Third Reich. A complex network of informers and agents for Britain was operating at some of the highest levels of German society, among army officers, aristocrats, and industrialists. SOE's informers in anti-Nazi circles were supplying a stream of tidbits and information to London headquarters.

Together with information from sympathetic neutral diplomats, these pieces of an intelligence jigsaw, once collated, gave invaluable insight into the fractures and fault-lines that lay below the surface of Nazi society and offered a myriad of opportunities for influence, disruption, further information gathering, and sheer mischief-making.

The eighty-four names on the list ranged across all sectors of Nazi society, from publicans to bedmates of Nazi leaders. No. 2 was a comedian, Erich Carow, with his wife, who like several individuals, had a shady legal record. Anyone already convicted of a criminal offense was particularly vulnerable to rearrest and thus blackmail as well. Carow, a popular comic and theater owner in Berlin, had good connections with some SS officers who were regular customers. The recommended method of approach was "threats and blackmail." Owners of public establishments such as theaters or pubs were ideal targets for the British agents. The flow of customers brought the proprietors into touch with a wide cross section of the public, often including Nazi officials, who liked a night out as much as anyone else, and such premises were useful meeting places for clandestine assignments. The pub owned by no. 6, Herr and Frau Baarz, "frequented by influential people mostly party and political," was a natural target. The Baarz couple should be approached with a "mixture of threats and promises. Consider a threat of physical violence sufficient," the report notes.

Some of those on the list were known as anti-Nazis and were better cajoled than threatened. Promises of a rosy future and a promising career once Germany was liberated from Hitler were more effective with individuals such as no. 15, a Herr Meissner, who "could be approached through his wife Hilda. Does not like Nazis. Promise of personal amnesty, bribes, and job in eventual German puppet government." Captain Schmelzer, no. 18, also listed as an anti-Nazi fared less well, perhaps because of his right-wing views. "Former cavalry officer and right-wing conservative. Method of approach threats and attempt on family or frame-up."

Nor was the list politically correct, as the listing for no. 27, Herr Rehn, a theater director shows: "Good connection in society. 'Pansy' and consequently easy to get hold of." Several actors and actresses appear on the list, presumably as there was considerable bed-hopping between theater stars and the Nazi leadership. Hermann Göring's second wife Emmy was an actress, and Goebbels' many affairs with film and stage stars were well known. On one occasion, Hitler even intervened to prevent a divorce between Goebbels and his wife, because it would not have been good publicity for the man in charge of the Third Reich's propaganda. Maria Paudler, no. 30, was an actress with "very good connections with Nazi leaders. Slept with practically all of them." No. 31, Miss Erica von Thellman was a fellow thespian. "Comes from a little better set than no. 30," the report notes laconically. "Family good, father was a colonel in the Hungarian army. Approach bribery."

The more serious or important prospects for influence had longer biographies. There were several possible approaches dreamt up for using no. 33, Frau von Coler, who was related to Himmler's wife and worked for the Nazis in Romania. At the same time, her daughter was believed to be having an affair with Himmler. This was a far more serious prospect than tittle-tattle from bars and actresses. "Method of approach bribery, personal amnesty, and threats. Always broke, very clever and smart. Good connections through her sister Mrs. Manzel. Both were former society prostitutes in Berlin. Her daughter is very pretty and is a mistress of Himmler. An attempt on daughter would be useful." The daughters of no. 38, the anti-Nazi and half-Jewish Countess Wedel, were also considered suitable prospects: "The first two are normal, but the latter is a lesbian...all girls are good-looking and are very ambitious and, as quarter Jews, are only tolerated. Threats and promises."

Away from the sexual peccadilloes of the Nazi glitterati and back on the streets, something as commonplace as a garage could prove immensely useful in clandestine operations, as a hiding place for people or documents. Which is where no. 68, Herr Adolf Baude, came in. "Garage proprietor always in need of money, does not like Nazis as his wife was Jewish. Very greedy and egotistic, garage useful. Method of approach physical violence and promises." And so the list goes on—no. 72, Herr W.L. Frieske, a former wholesale butcher who could be bribed or threatened to sabotage Berlin's meat supplies, or no. 75, Herr Otto Banse, who owned a rubber stamp shop—equipment of vital importance when forging documents—and who should be bribed.

SOE agents were prepared to exploit any human foible: sexual, financial, moral, or political, even the Jewish ancestry of their targets in their drive to defeat the Nazis. The "Operative List of Personalities" does not provide a very edifying view of human nature, but, then, neither did the Third Reich.

※ ※ ※

As the party expanded its membership, so it became a vehicle of social mobility. To get on, you joined the party. And in many cases, to get rich, you also signed up. Samuel Huntington has argued that the tendency to use political office to amass personal wealth increases in societies with limited scope for advancement.[14] This certainly seems to apply to the Third Reich. An authoritarian dictatorship like the Nazi regime stifles real possibilities of control. The Nazis abolished parliament and all chances of parliamentary investigation, they politicized the judiciary, they scratched away the power of the *rechnungshof* (the auditors office), and the press danced to Goebbel's flute. Police detectives working for the fraud squad (established in 1938) known as the "*Reichszentrale zur Bekämpfung von Korruption*" soon stumbled against the limits of their power. On the scent of a massive corruption scandal in the construction of the *westwalle* (the defensive line on the western frontier), the fraud squad opened hundreds of investigation cases. But the general building inspector quickly put an end to that. All the corrupt building companies were obliged to pay a "voluntary" contribution of RM500,000 to the winter aid fund, and the cases were quietly dropped. Hitler's fear of open disgruntlement about profiteering was decisive. The fraud squad rapidly lost its meaning.

The pursuit of corruption took on a more serious edge only in the autumn of 1943. This may have been due to Hitler's obsession with the "November syndrome," the idea that a demoralized homefront could provoke defeats on the battlefield. The driving force behind this (brief) anticorruption crackdown appears, however, to have been Heinrich Himmler. The head of the SS was at the very hub of the corrupt power network—it was through him that bonuses and subsidies were passed on to high party officials and army generals—and he had become personally wealthy. But he seemed to be playing a political game, perhaps building up his profile for the postwar years. Certainly there was nothing systematic about the manner in which he cracked down. One SS officer would be punished for profiting from the "Aryanization" of a company while another officer would be supported. Like much of domestic policy in the war years, orders were flawed and contradictory. This, in theory, should have given Germans opportunities to exploit the confusion not only in the interest of survival and personal advantage but also to take ethical stands in ordinary life.

Instead, honesty—measured not only in strictly biblical terms but in the sense of reasonable, dignified behavior—came to be viewed as an act of stupidity. The scope of Aryanization was so wide, the sums involved so large, the party members from the top to the bottom of the ladder felt that a chunk of the profits were theirs by right. In Thüringen, the *gauleiter* took a 10 percent cut on every Jewish property sold under duress. The money was used to fund pensions for the "old fighters"—the founding generation of the Nazis—and as start-up capital for companies run by party members. In the Saarpfalz, the cut was as much as 40 percent, which was paid into a special account.

Corruption is seductive in so far as it gains legitimacy by enveloping as many people as possible. Even before the deportations, thousands of non-Jewish Germans profited from their privileged position in the most hypocritical way, offering anxious Jews the possibility of selling their property for sums well below the market price. The erosion of values is easily illustrated by how two German institutions, the police and the insurance companies, cooperated for mutual profit at the expense of the Jews. The standing of the Berlin police had gone up and down since the nineteenth century, but by the 1930s, it was, broadly speaking, trusted and respected. A policeman was (and remains) a *beamte*, a civil servant with generous pension and housing benefits. And the insurance companies played an influential part in the unification of Germany and the creation of a social welfare state. Then, as now, Germans were the most heavily insured people in the world.

Yet in the 1930s, the Berlin *kriminalpolizei* entered into a systematic fraud with the insurance companies. To wriggle out of their obligations to pay for damaged Jewish property and looting of Jewish shops, Berlin detectives were regularly bribed to find false witnesses from the criminal milieu. The witnesses would testify that they have been persuaded by Jewish shop owners to ransack and plunder in order to cheat the insurers. The result was that insurance companies were relieved from their obligation to pay, while Jews were charged with insurance fraud (charges that could be dropped if appropriate bribes were paid), and Berlin policemen augmented their incomes.

The corruption and compromises of everyday life could have—should have—created a new bargaining environment. The transactions of ordinary people were often corrupt. The regime was personally corrupt, ready to make compromises to secure a quiet and easier time. But this was an era almost devoid of heroism. There is, of course, no moral duty to be a hero or a martyr. But there was scope for action within a narrower code. Wilhelm Kruzfeld, for example, was a Berlin policeman who pulled out his gun and threatened to shoot at looters trying to destroy a synagogue on *Kristallnacht* (the Night of Broken Glass), November 9, 1938. Nothing happened to his career as a result. He was, after all, merely performing his professional duty as a policeman to protect life and property.

It was a similar process that persuaded professional groups to resist the blandishments of the regime when it tried to create a uniform pension plan. It was perhaps the seductive ploy with most impact. The scheme was put together after a series of conversations between Hitler and Robert Ley, leader of the German Work Front (DAF) which had replaced the trade unions as the country's social arbiter. Hitler, after the invasion of France in 1940, knew that not every war could be waged as blitzkrieg. To make the expansion of the Reich work, he needed a vision for the Germans at home. He had none. *Mein Kampf* was not *Das Kapital*. It did not challenge established thinking. It had no economic or social component worth the name. There was a vague commitment to egalitarianism, though not, of course, the Bolshevik version. He agreed with Ley that the Germans should be given a social plan that encompassed health care, housing, wages, training, social insurance, and pensions. "Germany's war aims," said Ley, "are not imperialist but social." Germans should feel they were fighting for a better, more modern, more protected Germany that would make credible the demand for sacrifices. The brief was passed on to the Institute for the Study of Labor which produced a plan for postwar Germany.

Hitler As Tax Dodger

Hitler had a passion for Mercedes limousines and tried, unsuccessfully, to persuade his cash-strapped party to pay for one. Eventually, Hitler got his Mercedes as a gift, perhaps from Helena Bechstein of the piano dynasty or from the car manufacturer himself. (Hitler later claimed to have sent his own designs to Mercedes in Stuttgart.) The car was the heart of a row with a Munich tax man who could not understand how Hitler was able to live such a good lifestyle—by the late 1920s, he was living in a nine-room apartment in Munich—on such a low declared income. According to the research of Wolf Schwarzwäller, Hitler received his first tax warning in May 1925. He was ordered to submit a declaration for 1924 and the first quarter of 1925. Grudgingly, he replied: "I had no income last year and earned nothing in the first quarter. I have been living on bank loans." He claimed that the Mercedes was also bought on credit.

For the last quarter of 1925, he submitted a declaration. Net income: 11,231 marks. Professional expenses: 6,540 marks. Interest payment to bank: 2,245 marks. Taxable: 2,446.

The car, he said, was needed for his work as a political author, as was his private secretary—Rudolf Hess, who earned three thousand marks a month—a bodyguard, and a chauffeur. "I have neither property nor capital. I don't smoke or drink, my meals are eaten in the most modest of restaurants," he complained to the tax office. The tax man did not believe him, disallowed half his expenses, and continued to pursue him. In 1933, when Hitler came to power, the tax demands dried up, and one can safely assume the career of a certain tax inspector took a downward turn.

But the taxman was on to something. By 1929, Hitler's tax declaration no longer claimed deductions for interest payments. Somebody, presumably, had paid off his debts. *Mein Kampf,* written in prison (where he lived a very cushioned life thanks to his various patrons), was given as his main source of income. His cut was high—15 percent—but the sales figures were initially modest. In 1925, he sold 9,273 copies, and turnover only picked up in 1930, when he sold 54,006.

The book made Hitler a millionaire, but he had to wait for the cash to roll in. 1933, sales exploded to 854,127 and, until 1944, never faltered. There was also a blurring of Hitler's personal fortune and party funds—so much so the party was beginning to ask questions in 1925 about the true source of his income. It was jewelry from Frau Bechstein—an emerald necklace with platinum and diamonds, a ruby set in platinum, a diamond ring of 14-carat gold—that served as security for a loan of 60,000 Swiss francs which allowed Hitler to buy the *Völkischer Beobachter* newspaper.

The paper later became a party asset, and it is clear that Hitler did not personally profit, although he cashed in with unusually high fees for his articles and the reprinting of his speeches. Other money earners for Hitler included the clever use of copyright. Every time his photograph or image was used on a postage stamp, some cash came his way. Albert Speer remembered seeing Hitler receiving a fifty million–mark check—worth about $150 million today—for postage stamp rights. It is assumed there were several such payments.

Speeches collected in book form also generated a good income. Hitler had a soft spot for hustlers like his personal photographer Heinrich Hoffmann who made money for both of them by selling reproduction rights to Hitler's watercolors. Once scorned by gallery owners in Vienna, these paintings were in big demand after Hitler came to power. Hoffmann became one of several art scouts for Hitler, searching and buying up paintings for his personal pleasure.

In 1936, Hitler complained to Speer that the building work on the Eagle's Nest, his holiday home in the Bavarian mountain village of Berchtesgaden, was costing him a fortune. "It's all so expensive—I've used up all the income from my book." That was a lie. He was earning up to two million marks a year tax-free from *Mein Kampf,* and at the time of his suicide, he had seven million marks waiting to be collected from the publisher's bank account. An estimated 100 million marks a year was paid into a special Hitler account by industrialists during the twelve years of the Third Reich. The fund administrator was Martin Bormann. He took Eva Braun shopping for clothes and jewelry, paying with money drawn on the slush-fund account. He also bought property for Hitler in the Alps and paid off the mortgage on Hitler's Munich apartment.

Hitler's millions no longer exist. After the war, his fortune was regarded as a Nazi asset and appropriated by the Allies, along with his art treasures. Those works not returned to their rightful owners were held by the Americans until 1951 and then placed under the supervision of the Bavarian finance ministry. The state of Bavaria owns Hitler's former home in the Alps and all rights to *Mein Kampf.*

※ ※ ※

The result, seen from a distance of more than sixty years, was quite sensible. There was a stress on improving productivity with mass production (the techniques borrowed from Henry Ford) and modern management. The idea of class struggle was to be replaced by a social partnership between capital in labor (albeit within the *volksgemeinschaft*). Better health care and better conflict management would also play their part in boosting productivity. The institute opposed the wartime restrictions on the free movement of labor. After the war, weighted wages would attract workers to jobs most needed to be filled—farm workers and coal miners would get paid more than clerks because of the central imperative of food and energy.

Pension reform was at the heart of the proposals—and it is precisely this issue that shows how it is possible to opt out of a supposedly totalitarian agenda. No particular bravery was needed, merely determination to change a directed policy. Pensions based on accumulating contribution throughout a working life were yielding pitiful survival sums for old people. Ley's experts proposed that pensions and sickness benefits be paid out of general revenues and that pensions be indexed to the cost of living. "The justification was distinctly Bismarkian," says Martin Kitchen, "in that it was argued that generous pensions would result in a grateful people who would redouble their efforts to help the state."[15] The pension would be available only to the *volksgemeinschaft*—not to the antisocial, the work shy, the handicapped, or the "racially inferior." It would, however, break new ground—workers who had been unable to pay into pension funds because of unemployment could now reckon with a reasonable pension. Blue and white collar workers would be treated equally. Germans—that was the theory—would be gripped by a new sense of community.

Civil servants resisted, though. They rightly calculated that their special standing in German society was about to be undermined. And so, in an act of professional self-interest, they refused to comply, opting out of the Nazi pension reform scheme. Other groups followed suit—businessmen and the self-employed merely saw a scheme that would cost a great deal and offer them little protection. The infighting continued for months and ended with the regime accepting that some groups in the *volksgemeinschaft* could rule themselves out of the Nazi blueprint. As the tide of war turned, the issue became irrelevant: old-age pensions were the last things on the minds of soldiers freezing on the eastern front or their wives at home scrambling to make ends meet. But the message was clear—a nonpolitical interest group could, by means of arguing and lobbying, opt out of Nazi policies.

Chapter Two

The Führer and His People

"Everything the HJ [Hitler Youth] preaches is a fraud. I know this for certain, because everything I had to say in the HJ myself was a fraud,"

—*German youth, Karlsruhe, 1942*

In 1946, William Emker was a young man stationed with OMGUS (Office of the Military Government of the United States) in Berlin. Out of curiosity, he visited Hitler's Reichskanzlei, inspecting the bomb damage and shuffling through the scattered papers. The Russians wanted to use the metal filing cabinets and had tipped the documents onto the floor. Emker picked up a letter addressed to "My dearest Führer" and pocketed it. Over the subsequent months, Emker traveled twenty or twenty-five times into the Soviet sector, entered the Reichskanzlei by a side entrance, and stuffed bags full of letters to the Führer into his briefcase. For the most part, they were love letters, duly registered by the chancellery staff, never shown to Hitler, and stored in metal cases. Some of the senders were reported to the Gestapo. Most were treated with contempt. The letters were addressed to "My sweet one," "My dear sugar sweet Adolf," "My hotly loved dear heart," and were of remarkable intimacy. Friedel S., writing from Hartmannsdorf on April 23, 1939, begged the Führer to father her child. There were thousands of such letters. "I want to eat you up with my love," wrote one woman. "You are looking for a woman, I need a man," said another.[1]

Some of these women were plainly demented with loneliness, with the burden of running a household while their husbands were on the front. But the underlying point of these love letters is that they represent the triumph of Hitler's dictatorial style: he wanted to bind all Germans to him personally, to circumvent and ultimately destroy mediating institutions. The traditional family structure, already eroded by the Weimar years, was rendered increasingly outmoded by war and the absence of men. The Nazi party simulated a defense of the German family while actually concocting policies or tolerating behavior that eroded it. Hitler set out to supplant the personal, physical love of a husband with an immaculate love of the Führer. By the same token, children were to be given an ersatz Father. Not only the Hitler Youth, but also a whole system of elite schooling loosened ties with parents and brought up many thousands of children according to supposedly manly and Germanic standards, equipping them to be the future leadership of the Reich.

The seductiveness of this system illustrates the ease with which Hitler attempted to remove one of the key pillars of civil society: parental influence over the personal upbringing of their children. Some 17,000 children were educated at thirty *napolas* (national political educational institutions). In addition, there were thirteen Adolf Hitler schools and, in Bavaria, a *reichsschule* of the Nationalsozialist Deutsche Arbeiterpartei, the NSDAP. All mimicked British public schools (called "private schools" in the U.S.) and added, for good measure, a strong flavor of army cadet college. They were almost universally popular with pupils. "We had a great time," recalls Count Manfred Nayhauss, "I had ten pairs of shoes and different uniforms, training suits all provided by the state with a minimal contribution from my mother of seventy-five reichsmarks, including five reichsmarks pocket money."[2]

The schools laid great stress on tests of courage. "In Napola," remembers Hardy Krüger, "you had to jump from a ten-meter board into a cold swimming pool. But in the Adolf Hitler School, I had to swim under the ice of a Berlin lake for ten meters."[3] The Adolf Hitler school pupils considered themselves the future elite. "I assumed that after the Final Victory, I would be made, at least, the *gauleiter* of Moscow," jokes Krüger who in fact became an actor.

The children were selected on the basis of racial purity, party recommendation, and physical fitness. Parents were usually more than happy to have their sons sent to such schools because the quality of normal education had slumped. Male teachers had been called up, funds had been diverted, and by the time the bombing raids started, regular school life was completely dislocated. Hitler took a personal interest in the special schools—the headmaster of the Adolf Hitler school was the only teacher to have regular audiences with him. Plainly, Hitler saw the need for an elite, fast-lane form of education. Although this is an uncontroversial position in Britain and France, in postwar Germany, such schools became taboo, firmly identified with the Nazis.

The positive memories of these schools' graduates suggest that Hitler knew which emotional buttons should be pressed: how to give boys back their childhood and at the same time, subtly prepare them for party service. The party demanded a quid pro quo from the parents. Once a pupil was enrolled, he could not be removed from the Adolf Hitler school by his parents. Holiday time disappeared. Letters home were strictly rationed. Step by step, mothers and fathers were banished from the lives of their children and familial loyalty was transferred to the teacher, to the school, and to the Führer.

The Hitler Youth, on a broader level, tried to achieve something similar. Yet, it was never a wholly popular organization and, as a way of bonding children to the regime, was notably less successful than the Bund Deutsche Mädel, which managed to stimulate and encourage many girls and make National Socialism seem like a shared adventure. The Hitler Youth carried the dead weight of compulsory service. From 1936, membership was obligatory, and even before this time, there were less-than-subtle appeals. Fathers of Hitler Youth refuseniks received warnings at work. As a result, many boys were pressed into membership by their parents. In the mid-1930s, many Hitler Youth members—up to 30 percent in some towns—also belonged to illegal youth organizations, above all the banned "Bündische."

Our experience with the FDJ (Free German Youth) of Communist East Germany suggests that there are built-in limits to the seductive appeal of youth organizations in authoritarian societies. On a trip to Erfurt in the early 1980s, FDJ activists told us how, when travelling to meetings, they would put on second shirts over the distinctive blue blouses of the movement—they were embarrassed by their membership, even though it was all but compulsory and presented officially as a patriotic duty.

There were ways of distancing oneself from the Hitler Youth, just as there were from the FDJ. Some chose a dramatic form of protest which could almost be classed as armed resistance. The Edelweiss Pirates, or Navajos, set themselves in open opposition to the Hitler Youth, picking fights with them and mocking them. The politics of the Pirates was unclear. Some came from the pre-Nazi youth organizations, some from Catholic households. A few ran wild and would, under different circumstances, be described as juvenile delinquents.

A Hitler Youth newsletter in Cologne reported in September 1936: "Every youth wearing a colorful checked shirt, short trousers, boots with socks rolled over the top should be regarded by the Hitler Youth as a Navajo."[4] They were part of youth subculture, in the manner of Teddy boys and rockers, and, as such, they were concerned more with the aesthetics of resistance than with the substance.

Edelweiss Pirates were not necessarily fierce opponents of the Nazis. Their high point came in the last years of the war. Schools were closed or bombed out. Youth were being called up, food was short, dance bars were shut. Parental authority, deliberately eroded by Hitler, was by then nonexistent. Many youths were living with distant relatives or strangers. The case of the Steinbrück group shows how the categories of resistance are often blurred by war (see "The Steinbrück Group—Heroes or Criminals?" opposite). The Pirates were an intriguing but marginal phenomenon, most active in the turmoil of the bombing raids when black marketeers, desperate fugitive slave laborers, and army deserters created a wild subterranean society in the cities. Even so, they vented the anger and displeasure of a working class youth that was gradually waking up from the spell placed on them by Hitler.

The Steinbrück Group— Heroes or Criminals?

Hans Steinbrück, born in 1921, grew up in an orphanage. A successful youth leader as a teenager, he applied in the early years of the war to work in the Gestapo. Before the Gestapo had made a decision, however, he presented himself to friends and acquaintances as a fully fledged agent. He was arrested for fraud and sent in 1943 to a labor camp outside Cologne from where he emerged as a successful defuser of unexploded bombs.

Toward the end of that year, he slipped out of the view of the police and lived with his girlfriend in Cologne. He set up a group that collected an arsenal of weapons and looted bombed-out houses—as many as five a night. In September 1944, his gang managed to steal a ton of butter—with a black market value of RM120,000. They used money to buy weapons and munitions.

The gang grew quickly, including young deserters and members of the Edelweiss Pirates. The youth were fascinated by Steinbrück's vision of occupying an island on the Lido-See Lake outside Cologne and defending it from the Nazis, to create their own world separate from the war. Steinbrück's hideout, however, was discovered, and his girlfriend was arrested. Together with a dozen members of his gang, he decided to storm Gestapo headquarters in Cologne to free her. The attack failed, although Steinbrück shot an SS man and sprayed bullets at a column of Hitler Youth members. Steinbrück and his gang were arrested soon afterwards and publicly hanged on November 10, 1944.

▩ ▩ ▩

If these youths, streetwise but denied any real access to information, could defy the regime, why couldn't other sections of society? Why was there no serious opposition in the universities, for example? Professors, after all, have a commitment to values independent of any regime—to knowledge, truth, the integrity of research. Yet university professors and lecturers found themselves swept along by the Nazis; the Gestapo was not needed to keep most academics in line. Lecturers and researchers were enthusiastic supporters of Hitler, largely out of self-interest, but also partly because they had themselves paved the way for the intellectual revolution represented by the Nazis. The Nazis could draw on over four decades of research by historians, anthropologists, geographers, biologists, and scientists from other disciplines to justify their creed.

The swift corruption of Jena University is one case among many. In 1862, the social Darwinist Ernst Haeckel was awarded the university's chair of zoology. He was a member of the Society for Racial Hygiene and argued for the elimination of handicapped children. In 1925, six years after Haeckel's death, the National Socialist German Workers' Party, the NSDAP, was demanding that Jews be banned from Jena University. There was no great resistance to such initiatives. By 1930, Nazi sympathizers were being called to chair crucial departments. Hans Günther made his inaugural speech as professor of the university on "The Causes of the Racial Collapse of the German People." Hitler and Göring were in the audience. In 1934, Karl Astel, a former sports teacher, was appointed professor for breeding science. In a note to Himmler, he wrote: "Jena University should become the SS University." And so it was that the university spread its tentacles through society.

Jena biologists became involved in the development of biological "defense" weapons; the Jena anatomist Hermann Voss had an agreement with the Gestapo to stand by the guillotine in occupied Poznan and secure skeletons and "Jew" skulls for research. Jena University surgeons were involved in the forced sterilization program. The psychiatrist Rudolf Lemke was a loud proponent of castration for homosexuals. Remarkably, some of these academics became professors in East Germany after the war. Research based on data gathered in atrocious ways became the foundation of postwar scientific achievements. That was precisely the intention, and not only at Jena. Scientific research was wrapped up in a way that would justify heavy Nazi funding. It put itself at the disposal of the regime. So who was seducing whom? Why did not more scientists question the ethical basis of the research? What had happened to the idea of a university?

Perhaps the most shocking desertion of ethical standards was carried out by medical professionals. There were many brave doctors in the Third Reich; some saved Jews, others saved the handicapped. But far more doctors participated in or, at the very least, tolerated killing programs that ran directly counter to the Hippocratic oath. The sterilization program was applied to all those diagnosed as schizophrenic, addicted, blind, dumb, or heavily alcoholic. Such a diagnosis was elastic and served the convenience of doctors as much as the ideology of the regime. Ernst Lossa, for example, was sent to an orphanage in 1939 at the age of ten. A few months later, he was transferred to another home because of his "learning difficulties." The young boy tried to organize a protest by his fellow inmates and was transferred again to another Bavarian clinic. There the children were being placed on a special withdrawal diet (*entzugskost*) devoid of fat or vitamins. The doctors claimed it would change the children's behavior. The point, however, was to kill them. Ernst Lossa broke into the clinic pantry to feed himself and other patients. In 1944, caught in the pantry, he was diagnosed as an "asocial psychopath" and was killed with a morphine injection.

Trust in doctors eroded quickly as the so-called T-4 euthanasia program gathered pace. News of euthanasia leaked out, and increasingly, mothers and fathers began openly to protest at the institutional abduction of their children. A Führer order of August 24, 1941, responded to these protests by suspending T-4 in Germany. Seventy thousand people had already been killed under the program. But even after the Führer order, the doctors continued killing, essentially by starving their inmates: 130,000 died in this way. There were two postwar consequences to this action. The first was that Germany became one of the leading scientific authorities on malnutrition and food withdrawal; the doctors' notes proved valuable. The second was a concerted attempt to restore the tarnished image of the medical profession: sixty-five German films featuring brave doctors were made between 1946 and 1959. There was, however, no compensation available for the families of victims, and the issue was barely discussed in public.

The manner in which the professions and other sections of society prostrated themselves before Hitler turns the stomaches of present-day observers. But naked opportunism does not explain everything. Civil society existed in the Weimar and Wilhelmine years. It was weakly developed, but there were, nonetheless, dozens of autonomous institutions, hundreds of charities and volunteer organizations, honest articulation of interests, respect for education, and social mobility. Yet all these appeared to crumble like ancient pillars eaten by termites as soon as Hitler came to power.

Our experience in Communist Eastern Europe reinforces the importance of the idea of "civil society" as a counterpart to an authoritarian regime as a breeding ground of social, political, and economical alternatives. The dissidents and nonconformists of the Cold War years drew their inspiration from flimsy democratic and revolutionary traditions of previous eras. The values of civil society provided citizens with a choice and helped to educate a new elite ready to lead when communism imploded. Why could not a similar parallel universe come into being in the Third Reich? The range of responses to authoritarian rule—as the work of the German historian Detlev Peukert illustrates—can fall well short of organized armed resistance. It is civil society that allows one to imagine ways of expressing discontent without necessarily seeking to overthrow the regime. Peukert talks of *resistenz*—the reservations about a regime arising from a personal code of belief and behavior.[5]

One can express *resistenz* by demonstrating a lack of enthusiasm, by withdrawing from the collective, by restricting as far as possible all social interactions within the confines of the trusted milieu. The second category of behavior is dissidence and nonconformity. Dissidents create their own social space, they go beyond the pure passive form of inner emigration and try to establish contacts with like-minded citizens. Protest means publicly aired confrontation: a worker talking back to his boss, a nurse disapproving of a doctor's treatment of a patient. Resistance, in our full-bodied use of the term, suggests planned action against institutions and personal representatives of the regime.

Peukert's classifications make it easier to see how representatives of different groupings in the Third Reich had the possibility of criticizing or even—through passive, Schweikian, foot-dragging obstructions—prevent an obviously wrong or immoral decision. There were resisters, and we do not intend to minimalize their actions; they often paid with their lives. But the shadow side of this small minority of brave opponents is the comprehensive pattern of social conformity, of active acceptance. This chapter attempts to show how workers were so convincingly seduced by Hitler that lesser forms of opposition barely figured in their ethical vocabulary.

"Whoever can conquer the streets, can conquer the masses and thereby conquers the state," said Goebbels in 1926. The streets referred to were the streets of Berlin, and the SA brownshirts, stirred up by Goebbels, were ready to take their case into the traditional worker districts of Wedding, Spandau, and Moabit. The early Nazis were heavily outnumbered by the left-wing groupings, the Social Democrats and the Communists. Goebbels took aim at the Communists, seen as being more vulnerable than the Social Democrats. Even so, the Communists polled two million voters in 1925, against 280,000 for the Nazis. Goebbels' idea was to show workers that they had an alternative, a "national socialism" rather than a socialism stirred from Moscow.

"Now we have two possibilities," said Goebbels after Nazis had yet again been given bloody noses. "Either to give up, and thus to lose forever the party's political appeal to the proletariat or to strike out with resumed and redoubled force...to challenge Marxism."

But Goebbels' premise—conquer the streets and you conquer the masses—was false. The street battles did radicalize some of the younger workers, did send older Germans looking for a party that could guarantee law and order, and did raise the profile of the Nazis, dramatizing the political choices. The German working class, however, needed more than Goebbels' violent street theater to abandon their long–standing allegiances to the left, above all to the Social Democrats.

The left-wing British historian Timothy Mason, in a seminal essay on the German working class, summarized the Nazi wooing and containment of the workers in four words: *angst, belohnung, zucht,* and *ordnung*—fear, reward, discipline, and order.[6] Without minimizing the use of terror, we believe that Hitler's success in winning over the working class was due to a sophisticated reward system, that sufficient numbers of workers were seduced to neutralize resistance. The Nazis understood that the working class was highly segmented, different according to region and industrial sector (there was a huge gap, for example, between the mentality of a Bavarian Catholic truck driver or a Berlin seamstress). Dividing the workers rather than "conquering" them became one of the central goals of Nazi social policy, as well as the guiding principle of the Gestapo.

The workers in the Third Reich have long been a riddle to historians. The workers, and their parties, Communist (KPD) and Social Democrat (SPD), were the only force in the 1920s and 1930s that could have blocked the rise and hegemony of the Nazis. Until the last year of the war, the regime managed to secure the active or passive support of many sections of the middle class and the various elites. That support fluctuated: the farmers were restless between 1938 and 1940, the educated middle class was upset with the pogroms of November 1938, and there were constant bureaucratic conflicts. But the loyalty of these and other skeptical Germans was won, or bought, and organized resistance was confined to the nooks and crannies of society. The workers may have shifted allegiance from the leftist parties to the Nazis, but their defection should be seen as a temporary loan to the new party.

The dominant theme of the 1920s was the unbridled power of capital and of speculators, the feeling that ordinary people were vulnerable to the unaccountable maneuvering of the wealthy. (Indeed, one could argue this remains a dominant concern providing the legitimacy of the postwar East German state and fueling modern Germany's opposition to globalization.) Those who believed the Nazis would seal them from *wucherkapital*, wild exploitative capitalism, were to be quickly disappointed. The role of capital was strengthened rather than sapped by the Nazis. The question then is, Why was there no massive protest from within the working class? Why did the working class—the most aggrieved sector of society—not launch at least one major challenge to the regime?

A Communist True Believer

Professor Ernest Hoffmann was not seduced by Hitler. He looked to Moscow and Marxism, rather than Nuremberg and Nazism. Hoffmann joined the KPD, the German Communist Party, in 1930 at the age of eighteen. It was a time of absolutes, of left or right, when the weak democracy of the Weimar republic crumbled. For Hoffmann, like many young anti-fascist Germans, the Communists offered the only alternative to Hitler. His father had been a prominent Social

Democrat editor and politician, but the Social Democrats were too bourgeois, too compromised, to take on the Nazis.

The KPD, then the most powerful Communist Party out-side Russia, stood for revolution, with Moscow behind it. Like the Nazis—and the Social Democrats—the Communists were more than a political party: the KPD was a com-plete, self-contained cultural and political world. Its front and subsidiary organizations included, for example: the Revolutionary Trade Union Opposition, the paramilitary Red Front Fighters League, the Communist Youth League, and even the Community of Struggle for Red Unity in Sport. In 1931, the KPD boasted 246,525 members and many more supporters and sympathizers, particularly in Berlin. Many cadre members had studied in Moscow, where they were trained in sabotage, military techniques, and organizing revo-lution. As Weimar collapsed, taking world capitalism with it, it seemed that Germany could soon become the world's second communist state.

"The reason I became a Communist in 1930 was that the world economic crisis had just started with the Wall Street Crash, and the Nazis were the second strongest party in Germany. In the Soviet Union, there was no crisis and no fascist party. Another reason was that I saw a Communist demonstration with Ernst Thaelmann [KPD leader, later killed in Buchenwald concentration camp] at its head. I had never seen him, except on posters. He made a deep impression on me, as somebody in whom you straightaway have complete confidence," said Professor Hoffmann.

His warnings to his father were unheeded, he recalled. "When Hitler came to power, I told my father that the Social Democrats would be persecuted as well as the Communists. I asked him what they would do. He said that everything was prepared, but it was too early to talk about it. After the Reichstag fire, I asked him again, and he said, 'Now it is too late.'"[7]

In 1932, Hoffmann left his hometown of Wuppertal and enrolled at Cologne University to study natural sciences. He spent most of his time organizing Communist youth groups, sometimes even debating with his Nazi foes. "It happened sometimes, it was quite dangerous. I was invited to Nazi meetings, to discuss things, although some other comrades went and were beaten up. One meeting that I went to I was refused entrance because I didn't have one mark. A week later, I met a Nazi on the street. He told me that I was very lucky, because they would have killed me in the cellar."

On Good Friday 1933, Hoffmann fell into the hands of the Nazis. His brother was also arrested and taken to a remand prison. But Hoffmann was taken to one of the dreaded jails run by the SA, the brownshirts, where prisoners were often beaten to death. Hoffmann was beaten and tortured, accused of fomenting Communist revolution with his brother.

"They beat me all over. They told me my sister had been arrested and they would beat her to death if I did not confess. They held a gun to my head. I thought I should say something, so I invented two people, fictitious communist organizers. At midnight, I was sent to the police station. A police officer had been ringing up the SA prison every hour demanding to know my whereabouts. He saved me practically."

Two days later, together with his brother and his wife, Hoffmann left for Berlin and joined the Communist underground. Later, they discovered that the family had been denounced by the sister of an SA member who had a crush on Hoffmann's brother. In Berlin, Hoffmann was a leader of the Youth League's underground network, charged with overseeing contacts between the committees spread throughout Germany and running the network of safehouses for Communists coming to Berlin. One operative was a banana-seller, Hoffmann recalled. Contact was made by a special pass-phrase, or by showing a certain newspaper.

"I was responsible for finding rooms where people could sleep illegally or where we could meet and have discussions. I would find rooms from neighbors who were sympathetic. Maybe they would have a typewriter, but the neighbors would ask, 'Who is typewriting all day?' The housewardens were responsible for reporting anything like that. The Nazis were successful in winning over large numbers of German people to spy on them."

Life in the Communist underground was difficult and extremely dangerous. One slip could mean the difference between life and death. In Wuppertal, Hoffmann had run into an SS leader while carrying a pile of illegal Communist newspapers which, luckily, were wrapped up. "He immediately recognized me and embraced me. He was drunk. He said, 'We need people like you, come along with us.' I said I couldn't, because I had party orders, and I showed him the pile of newspapers. 'That's right,' he replied. My heart stopped beating, but I acted correctly, and I saved my life."

In October 1933, Ernest Hoffmann was finally caught and arrested. In prison, he was aided by the Communist underground, which operated in both the concentration camps and prisons. He eventually fled to France, then Britain, where he arrived in 1938, one of many left-wing German refugees. The KPD and the Social Democrats were no match for the sheer ruthlessness and violence of the Nazis. Germany's once-mighty left-wing and labor movement collapsed, but Ernest Hoffmann did not give up his Communist ideals. After the defeat of the Nazis, he returned to Berlin. He stayed in the German Democratic Republic (East Germany), even after the Berlin wall was built in 1961, to build the workers' state for which he had struggled for so long.

There are many modern examples of workers rebelling against authoritarian regimes. As journalists, we witnessed the outbreak of strikes in Poland throughout the 1980s, pushing the Communist regime to the very brink. In Poland, too, organized labor was penetrated by agents, independent union leaders were arrested and jailed; in 1970 and 1981, workers were gunned down by armed representatives of a workers' state. During World War II, Dutch workers mounted large and sustained strikes. Black workers in South Africa turned to armed rebellion, burning a factory and attacking police units. Yet the protest of German workers in the Third Reich was scattered and individual.

Historian Timothy Mason sums up the problem. "Why did three hundred workers (a whole department in a big plant) go on strike, but not three thousand (an entire factory, a mine, a dockyard)? Why were there enough cases of refusal to work and indiscipline to amount to a 'genuine wave of sabotage,' and also many individual acts of sabotage, but no deliberate mass destruction of production machinery?"[8]

We could go further. Workers in the Third Reich were plainly unenthusiastic about attending official Nazi demonstrations, including the May Day assemblies. We saw how Polish workers, living under strict martial law, transformed May Day marches into vivid anti-regime protests, ripping down red flags and plunging into street battles with the feared Zomo riot police. Why did the Germans not undertake similar action?

A straightforward answer is that the scale of terror was different. The Gestapo was a much more vindictive force in the factories than the secret police of the later communist or apartheid regimes. The small labor camps, the so-called *arbeitserziehungslager*, were attached to major industrial companies. The scholar Heinz Hoehne has calculated there were 165 such camps. Arrests were continuous. They were on a small scale but regular, part of the rhythm of the factory. The aim was to induce suspicion of one's workmates on the shop floor, to break up links between potential resistance groups. It was focused terror made possible by the institutional repression of working-class parties and the trade unions.

The Nazis made it plain from the outset that they intended to eliminate labor unions since they were regarded as the cradle of Marxist class struggle. The idea of establishing a separate national social movement came from two sides. Reinhard Muchow, head of the Nazi NSBO, wanted to create a unified union: eight million workers, under one umbrella, speaking with a single voice. Trade union leaders had come to a similar conclusion. But unlike Muchow—who wanted some muscle for workers in the emerging totalitarian state—they saw a single structure being the only way to save the principle of workers' representation. Hitler was not convinced. His aim was to make class warfare redundant, but both the NSBO and the Social Democratic union organizations came from an assertive, combative tradition. Like Robert Ley, he knew that the "best, most fanatical, and strongest critics of National Socialism" were grounded in the union movement.

Hitler's initial plan was thus to place the unions under the command of a *reichskommissar*, preferably someone with Social Democratic credentials, such as August Winnig, a bullish building worker who had shown some sympathy for the Right. Muchow believed he had a better idea for wooing the workers. May Day 1933 should be declared a workers' holiday, thus fulfilling a long-time ambition of the Social Democratic workers' movement. This was a typical seduction technique of Hitler and Goebbels: to hand the workers a triumph and at the same time plot to take away their power. On April 16, Muchow presented to Hitler the timetable for the emasculation of the free—that is, Social Democratic—union movement.

Hitler approved, though he had no intention of fulfilling Muchow's ambition to be at the head of the new movement. Hitler had earmarked Ley, an ex–World War I pilot and a brilliant organizer with a foul temper. No contemporary speaks well of Ley— partly because of the pain of a war wound in his head, he was a heavy drinker and had an unpredictable personality. Ley, however, was to be one of the beneficiaries of a party reorganization. Rudolf Hess had been proclaimed deputy party leader in April 1933 with—on paper, at least—wide-ranging powers. In practice, that power ebbed away from, rather than flowed toward, Hess. Ley's promotion was the first sign of this: Hitler omitted making Ley subordinate to Hess and, in essence, awarded Ley his own little empire. The struggle between the mystic Hess and the alcoholic Ley was to be one of the running battles at the top of the regime.

May Day was a victory for the seducer's art. Beginning in the early morning, the radio broadcast worker songs, worker plays, and worker essays. Around ten million people were on the move—the biggest demonstration ever staged in a non-communist state. For the first time, managers and entrepreneurs could be seen marching arm-in-arm with blue and white collar workers ("workers of the forehead and the fist" in the Nazi jargon). Not all the workers had been brainwashed. On their way to the Tempelhof, the sprawling aerodrome in the center of Berlin, two workers stopped off to relieve themselves in a *pissoir*. As a contemporary reported, they looked at each other and, in a few gruff words, decided to break away from the overregulated proletarian parade and head home. They were amazed by the numbers of swastikas fluttering from the windows in working class areas.[9]

The next morning, at ten o'clock sharp, the SA brownshirts and the SS stormed into the offices and banks of the Social Democratic unions and arrested union officials. Files and accounts were carried away in trucks. They were needed to support trumped-up corruption charges against union leaders for abuse of union funds—a crude attempt to turn popular anger against worker leaders. Funds, said Ley, had been used to finance Marxist parties. In one hour, the operation was over: the union movement had been decapitated with barely a squeak of protest. Ley and Muchow decided that all unions should join an "action committee." Two hundred thirty-nine union associations joined up by May 5, 1933.

The DAF (Deutsche Arbeitsfront), an umbrella organization for all industrial workers, was up and running in the same month. The speed of the action, but also the sharpness of the rhetoric was almost revolutionary. The point of the DAF was to end class warfare, yet it used, initially at least, the muscle-flexing vocabulary of militant socialists. Indeed, many employers wondered what had hit them. "Those industrial magnates still in power should watch their language, otherwise they could find themselves swept aside with force," said a DAF functionary in Muenster. The DAF distributed questionnaires on the shop floor asking for information about wages and working conditions. First wage demands were lodged—for a pay hike in the building industry—and Ley started to talk of the need of a minimum wage. But the intention was clear: to radicalize the workers and offer them a credible alternative, not only to Social Democratic unions, but also to the Social Democratic Party (SPD) itself. By June, the Social Democratic Party was banned, and the DAF started to transform itself from a union-like organization with hierarchies built on the shop floor to a mass organization in which everyone was merely a member.

Terror and seduction, the fatal attraction of Hitler. The propaganda machine created a new world, a virtual reality, which could be barely recognized by ordinary workers. "It sounded good, yet somehow it seemed to be happening to somebody else," said one steel worker looking back at 1933 from the perspective of 1947. In most car factories, there was full employment; furniture shops were enjoying record sales; cinemas and theaters were flourishing. In 1933, three hundred thousand more marriages were registered than in 1932—an achievement chalked up to Hitler. In November 1933, the number of unemployed dropped to 3.7 million. That was 2.2 million less than at the beginning of the year. The number of people in work rose by 2.5 million in the same period. That is, the number of the unregistered unemployed, the great gray region, was also falling.

There is no doubt that fear hugged the shop floor. The practice of *sippenhaft*—arresting family members of a suspected resistance worker—was a powerful inducer of conformity. According to historian Arnold Sywottek's estimate, more than a hundred thousand Communists were killed by the Gestapo during the twelve years of the Third Reich; many more were arrested.[10] That was only a tiny fraction of the working class, but it was enough to persuade prudent workers that they should, at all costs, avoid being labeled "Marxist." There was nothing cowardly about this approach, but workers distinguished between the Gestapo, the SA on the streets (seen as a provocation even to workers who were non-Communists), the SA wearing police armbands, and the Prussian police.

There were two chief forms of resistance: one, being a member of the Communist underground and risking one's life; or two, protesting within the factory against the management about wages or working conditions. The underground stayed underground, knowing that to openly support a strike or a "go-slow" would attract Gestapo attention and mean almost certain destruction of their political cells. This level of resistance concentrated on survival, the passing on of information, and endless strategy discussions about when and how to act once Hitler was fatally weakened on the battlefield. Communists were jailed and killed and were replaced.

The spontaneous strikes were, however, treated more mercifully by the Gestapo, which understood—sometimes, at least—that the protesters were targeting the management rather than the regime. At least until 1938–39, there was no certainty that a striker would be jailed or sent to a concentration camp. There were cases of the Gestapo issuing warnings or even putting some pressure on managers to make concessions. The war and the effective millitarization of the workplace naturally changed that. The coercive mechanism functioned along the uncertainty principle: the fear of arbitrary action (threatened, rather than actual, punishment) set the tone.

Historians make a distinction between the neutralization of the workers—the smashing of organized structures—and their integration into the *volksgemeinschaft*, seducing them into sharing the values of the regime. Much hinges on this question. Tim Mason has argued, for example, that worker resistance was in its very essence political. Such strikes as occurred were not aimed at employers, he says, but at the Nazis, and when employers and workers colluded (buying labor peace by raising wages), they did so in a way that undermined the regime. The Nazis thus failed to integrate—we would say "seduce"—the workers and remained vulnerable to their own fear of a working-class uprising.[11]

This, in turn, created a domestic dynamic that made war inevitable. The problem with Manson's and similar renderings of the German working-class predicament is that it still fails to answer the question of why, as Hitler's power weakened, there was no large-scale revolt. Our interpretation is that Hitler's seductive skills far outweighed the impact of coercion. He recognized that there was no single working class. Many workers were striving toward the middle class. Class solidarity had been destroyed in the Depression. Hitler offered something quite new: the image of an organized work and leisure society in which hard work and loyalty was rewarded in a completely modern manner.

The DAF was the perfect vehicle for this strategy. Under its wings, the Nazis' prime seductive devices, *Schönheit der Arbeit* (Beauty of Work) and *Kraft durch Freude* (Strength through Joy), were set up and dangled in front of a disoriented but ultimately grateful workforce. The former promised better working conditions, the latter state-sponsored leisure and recreation. Ley and Goebbels have been painted as practitioners of the black arts, the very embodiment of evil. In fact, they were, for the most part, modern politicians, willing to take risks, adaptable, aware that image was often more decisive in politics than reality. It was clear to both men that class conflict could not be wished away; rather, the image of the working class had to change.

Others in the regime agreed but gave the plan an overly literal interpretation. Albert Speer became the nominal leader of the "Beauty of Work" campaign aimed at giving a new face to factories. The logic seemed to be: scrub the dirt from the workers, and they will behave differently; abandon old neighborhood and factory loyalties. National Socialism was to be the home of the aspirational worker, the man who wanted to get on. "Bring Spring into the Factories" was the slogan. Sports fields and gardens were laid around smoky steel works. Inside day-rooms were installed, outside window frames were painted, and swimming pools were dug. In line with American productivity studies, it was ruled that "Good Lighting Means Good Work," and Siemens and AEG profited accordingly, decking out shop floors with neon. The arrival of war enforced a change of slogan, "Good Lighting Despite the Blackout," but not a change of philosophy.

The Nazis were continuing a benign tradition begun in the nineteenth century. In Britain, too, there was a garden city movement. One such site was established in Port Sunlight near Liverpool at the initiative of the industrialist Lever, and Bournville, a model workers' estate, was started by the Cadburys near Birmingham. Alfred Krupp began building worker estates in the 1870s. In 1890, a garden city was begun in Dresden, designed by Heinrich Tessenow, the teacher of Albert Speer.

But "Beauty of Work" was too clumsy a device to seduce workers. The pressure still on workers to boost productivity and clean lavatories did not alter the situation—rather, it seemed like an excuse not to pay higher wages. Above all, *Schönheit der Arbeit* had become a bureaucracy. Its inspection teams viewed 70,000 factories, made recommendations, handed out praise, and, on occasion, took bribes for failing to notice cesspits or flaking ceilings. *Schönheit der Arbeit* was treated with the same kind of skepticism that greeted clean-up campaigns in Soviet Russia in the 1970s. Work, quite simply, was not supposed to be beautiful.

The resistance of the workers to "flowerpot socialism" carried over at first to *Kraft durch Freude* (Strength through Joy), or KdF. The scheme was copied from the Italian Fascist system of *Opera Nazionale Dopolavoro* established as early as 1925. Its aim was to create a leisure culture for the workers, a culture that was not independent of the factory or the *volksgemeinschaft*. KdF was divided into four main departments—after hours entertainment, mass tourism, sport, and night classes. Quickly, KdF emerged as the most popular element in the German Workers Front, and while it may not have seduced every German worker, it did conjure up a new world of opportunities. Workers were told that National Socialism, more than the encrusted Wilhelmine structures or the chaos of Weimar, offered social mobility, the chance of improvement. And it offered physical mobility, the opportunity to travel, often for the first time, to Bavaria or the Black Forest.

By 1935, the first worker cruises were being advertised to Madeira or the Norwegian fjords. Very swiftly, KdF developed into the first modern, mass package tourism concern, with RM880 million earmarked between 1934 and 1942 to subsidize tourism. A three-day tour to admire the blossoming gardens around Lake Constance was offered for RM7.90, including train travel from Munich, lunch, and a boat ticket. A seven-day Christmas break in the Black Forest was RM34, all inclusive. The annexation of Austria in 1938 yielded yet more possibilities for travel to the Tirol, to Salzburg, and to Carinthia. Mussolini's Italy was ready to provide a link between state travel companies, and ordinary Germans discovered Lake Garda, which has remained a popular destination for German tourists.

The foundations for Germany's postwar mass tourism industry were laid in the 1930s by KdF. Millions traveled on the KdF ticket, and it ballooned into the world's biggest travel company. In 1939, 8.5 million Germans took KdF holidays. Many of them would now be called weekend breaks. Short trips to the Oktoberfest in Munich were, for example, much favored by the coal miners in the Ruhr. The most spectacular feature of the KdF program was the cruise ship. Cruising had been previously regarded as a preserve of the wealthy leisured class. Suddenly, foundry workers and their wives were sitting on the deck chairs of the *Sierra Cordoba* which wound its way from Hamburg to Palermo. The *Admiral* steamed up to Helgoland, the

Oceania to the fjords, the sparkling white *Robert Ley* to the Canaries. "Our workers on Madeira!" shouted the *Völkischer Beobachter*.

Goebbels and his propaganda artists naturally inflated the importance of these cruises. Perhaps 1 percent of the total work-force took to the sea, but it was spun into a gossamer dream. The wives of workers saved up throughout the year and someone who had just returned from a cruise was the talk of the canteen. Apart from the *Robert Ley* and the *Wilhelm Gustloff*, most were chartered tubs, but there were films on board, organized parties, deck sports, plenty of beer, four to six meals a day, a doctor and dentist on call. And, of course, Gestapo and *Sicherheitsdienst* agents: at least two full-time officers on every cruise, dutifully cataloging the social and sexual antics of the passengers since there was little if any politics discussed. KdF trips, not just the cruises, were often a time of sexual adventure. Returning workers were teased they had lost too much *kraft* because of too much *freude*.

The general assessment of KdF travel was summed up by a Berlin working woman, no starry-eyed Nazi fanatic: "It was our first real holiday. With the *Oceania* run by Hapag. Before, only the rich could do that, it cost three hundred, four hundred marks. And we paid only fifty-four marks for a week. Six meals a day, lots of courses at lunch. Served by uniformed waiters. No propaganda speeches, not many wearing party badges, and really no politics on board. Instead there was music, dancing, new films, and lectures."

The SPD in exile warned that "the solution of social questions can be avoided if the workers are offered more honor instead of more wages, more *freude* instead of more free time, more petit-bourgeois self-regard instead of better working conditions." That was said with a bitter note: the Nazis had seduced the workers away from the Social Democratic Party.

As in all seductions, there were broken promises. Ley, for example, pledged that workers would be given three to four weeks holiday, but vacation time rarely edged above two weeks. A holiday complex was build on the island of Ruegen—huge concrete silos on four miles of beach capable of offering 350,000 holidays a year. But the war ensured that the complex was never completed—the empty buildings are still there, windswept caverns. When the war started, the cruise ships still traveled—but as hospital ships ferrying the wounded back to Germany. Even so, the Nazis had acted with some innovative brilliance, creating a new kind of leisure travel positioned somewhere between the spa cures of the bourgeoisie and the no-cost weekend walk in the forest. Workers were not just bought or bribed, they were lured into a world as fake but as fascinating as Santa's grotto. That was enough to keep the workers on their side long after the *Robert Ley* had made its last trip to Tenerife.

Chapter Three

The Führer and His Women

> *"Darling can I come to you soon? Do you doubt my love? Today I had such a strong longing for you,"*
> — *German housewife, Eva K., author of a letter to Hitler on July 22, 1940*

War has always been viewed as a man's world. But in a war as general, as total as Hitler's war, women were destined to be more than passive supporters of their absent husbands. Around 500,000 women served in the German army, not including nurses and doctors. In 1944, for example, 160,000 young women worked as anti-aircraft gunners, fixing the sights and loading the guns. Others operated searchlights. The Germans were not alone in using women. Britain and above all the Soviet Union (which had 800,000 women under arms) were ready to deploy women in ancillary jobs.

The significant feature of the German woman, however, was her proximity to atrocity. The biographies of female concentration camp guards—and women married to SS troopers, who occasionally visited their husbands at some of the most horrible sites—shows that women faced some of the same moral dilemmas as men. At home in the Reich, women were remarkably well informed about the massacres on the *ostfront* (eastern front). Usually, this translated not into a rejection of war but merely into concern about the physical safety of their husbands. Forced and slave laborers, living in abysmal conditions, were marched to work through their villages and towns. It did not take much political knowledge to realize these pitiful workers (many of them women) were being deployed so that Hitler did not have to force German women to work.

The Nazis, haunted by the November 1918 syndrome—the collapse of morale on the homefront—were determined to cushion women as long as possible. The question is whether this cushioning represented some form of moral compromise. German women directly benefited from the miseries of the occupied East and thus gradually came to realize—perhaps through personal contact with forced laborers—that the war entailed crimes of terrible magnitude. The war was making criminals of their husbands. Yet, there were only sporadic protests, the most prominent of which was the Rosenstrasse demonstration (see "The Rosenstrasse Protest," below). This demonstration, by German women whose Jewish partners had been arrested, forced the regime to change its policy. But the protestors' agenda was personal and specific, it was not directed at the wider policy of genocide against the Jews. Other forms of female protest, even loosely organized, could have prompted concessions. The terror of being sent to Ravensbrück was not very pronounced, except among prostitutes and women actively dealing on the black market.

The Rosenstrasse Protest

In February 1943, the German authorities launched the final mass roundup of Jews still living in Berlin. Among the several thousand Jews arrested by the Gestapo and the SS were a group of between seventeen hundred and two thousand men. Separated from the other detainees, they were taken to a building in central Berlin: Rosenstrasse 2-4, a welfare office for the city's Jewish community.

These men were also marked for extermination. But they had to be dealt with more carefully than most. They were married to German non-Jews, and many had quite highly placed German relatives by marriage. Goebbels, who was *gauleiter* of Berlin, as well as propaganda minister, realized that this group's German family connections meant they could not just be transported en masse to the death camps of Poland by the usual brutal methods. The plan was to separate these two thousand or so on the fiction that they would be sent to "mere" labor camps—instead of Auschwitz, their real ultimate destination—to defuse any possible protests. Either way, Goebbels would achieve his ambition of a "Jew-free" Berlin in time for Hitler's birthday that April, without any repercussions.

But the German wives thought otherwise. By 1943, much of the German population was aware, in broad terms, that something horrific was happening to the Jews in the East and to those being sent there. The wives and other relatives of the detainees began to gather outside the Rosenstrasse building, first in handfuls, then in hundreds, and eventually, in the thousands to protest the detention. Their demands were simple: they wanted their husbands back.

Thus began one of the most remarkable events of the Third Reich: the only mass public protest against the German authorities. In the epicenter of the Third Reich, the women protestors took on the Nazi leadership and Goebbels himself. The women protestors were unorganized, unarmed, and not members of opposition or resistance groups. The protest continued for day after day, as their numbers grew. By the end of the week, word had spread across Berlin about the Rosenstrasse protest. It was becoming the talk of the city and had to be ended.

Goebbels had two options: either shoot or arrest the protestors, or release the men. Certainly, the machinery was in place to kill or round up the women demonstrators. But the repercussions could have been serious. It was one thing for the Nazi state to cleanse ethnically Germany of its Jews, who had been demonized, marginalized, and excluded from society for a decade. It was quite another to round up thousands of German housewives in public. There was a high risk that more arrests would trigger more protests, and the situation would spin out of control. Even a dictatorship needs a measure of consensus from its subjects.

Goebbels could not, then, afford to see morale inside Germany dip further. Coming shortly after the defeat at Stalingrad, the turning point of the war, the Nazi leadership needed to keep up morale on the homefront. There was also the question of the secrecy of the Final Solution. The womens' protests were drawing unwelcome attention to the fate of Germany's Jews. The protest was reported on the BBC. So Goebbels released the Jewish men held at Rosenstrasse. He even ordered the return of twenty-five who had been sent already to Auschwitz. The Nazi leadership believed their release was a temporary delay in ridding Berlin of its Jews. But Goebbels and Hitler were wrong: nearly all of the Rosenstrasse detainees survived the war.

The courage of their wives and the fortuitous timing after a major defeat for the Nazis helped save the Rosenstrasse detainees. But the protest took place in an intersection of German society where the Nazis' had an uncertain grip— marriages between Jews and Germans. The Jews were enemies, but their German spouses were not. Berlin was not occupied Poland, where all family members could be sent to the gas chambers. Goebbels pondered this question in his diary entry of March 7, 1942, where, after recounting yet again the "need" to clear Europe of its Jews, he considered what he described as "a large number of exceedingly delicate questions. What with those related to Jews? In-laws of Jews? Persons married to Jews? Evidently, we still have quite a lot to do and undoubtedly a multitude of personal tragedies will ensue within the framework of the problem."

The bureaucrats came to the rescue. Nazi racial doctrine defined two degrees of *mischlinge* (individual of mixed race). Those of the first degree, or half-Jews, had two Jewish grandparents, but did not practice Judaism or have a Jewish spouse. *Mischlingen* of the second degree, or quarter-Jews, had one Jewish grandparent.

Mischlingen lived in a twilight world of legal compromise, in a system designed to deal with black and white. They remained non-Aryans under the Nuremberg laws but, in general, were not deported or exterminated.

Ironically, it was the Nazi obsession with the purity of German blood and its supposed virtues that helped save those who were excluded from the *volksgemeinschaft*. William Stuckart, the official who helped draw up the Nuremberg laws, was opposed to deporting the *mischlingen* because that would mean a loss of German blood, even if mixed with Jewish. "I have always considered it dangerous biologically to introduce German blood into the enemy camp. The intelligence and excellent education of the half-Jews, linked to ancestral German heritage, makes them natural leaders outside Germany and therefore very dangerous, he said.

Or just more confident. The Rosenstrasse protest was a unique event, but it illustrates that the Third Reich responded to public protest. Its policies, even of extermination, could be modified by well-timed pressure. As historian Nathan Stoltzfus, author of *Resistance of the Heart: Intermarriage and the Rosenstrasse Protest in Nazi Germany*, notes, the "history of intermarriage is substantial additional evidence that the Nazi dictatorship backed down when it encountered overt mass protest...that it relented, in small numbers, even on the issue constituting the core of its ideology."[1]

※ ※ ※

Women were the first to spot the yawning gap between the myth of the perfect Aryan, blonde, soft, baby-producing German mother and the wartime reality of food and soap shortages. There was a revolutionary potential in women, but it was never tapped. Women barely figure in the annals of the German resistance (the most prominent exception being the Munich student Sophie Scholl, executed for distributing an anti-Nazi leaflet), and the few brave women who sheltered Jews are heavily outnumbered by the hordes of female denouncers. The fundamental point is that women found enough in the regime to satisfy them, that the Nazis, for all their apparent misunderstanding and manipulation of the female sex, discovered ways of keeping women out of the political arena or upholding their loyalty to the Führer. The theme of our book is the exercise of choice in a dictatorship. Germans do not deny they were seduced by Hitler, for the seduction of a nation is such a broad brush concept that it diminishes personal responsibility; they gave way to the Führer in a momentary lapse, the Führer was "irresist-ible." But our intent is to examine in detail how this seductive pro-cess worked—which policy and which maneuver dulled the senses of which section of society. One has to search for explanations why people do not act against tyranny.

German women were only rarely subjected to Gestapo terror; they were not frightened into subservience. As in the case of the industrial workforce (see preceding section), they were cautious, aware that the Gestapo monitored publicly expressed complaints, and this in turn undermined gender solidarity. But there were many pockets of trust, areas where women could meet and talk freely. The ideology of the Nazi regime was so replete with contradictions, its attitude toward women so lacking in confidence, that choices could be made, decisions could be resisted or changed.

Instead, some German women still look back to the Third Reich as the best time in their lives. Eva Sternheim-Peters, a mem-ber of the Nazi Bund Deutsche Mädel, or BDM (League of German Girls), recalls in her memoirs, published in 1987, that "in the forty years since the end of the Hitler dictatorship, I have never felt so intensely, never functioned as such a free, politically aware creature, never had such political responsibility." She was not writing as a dyed-in-the wool National Socialist, but as someone who was given early managerial power of a kind not previously (and indeed not subsequently) accorded to women. As a sixteen-year-old girl, Sternheim-Peters was responsible—without adult supervision—for the organization of a Jung Mädel camp, a collection of more than a hundred primary school–aged children. She organized the daily routine, arranged parents' evenings, musical and theater performances, parties, and expeditions. It was then when she realized, "[W]hen it came down to it, women can do as much as men." Other BDM activists make similar comments: "It was then that I developed into an independent person."[2]

All this happened in spite of, rather than because of, a Nazi program. The Nazi system on the surface seemed to emphasize the role differences between men and women, with women firmly confined to the kitchen and the bedroom. The reality, however, was that differences merged. The sociologist Mario Erdheim notes that army recruits have to go through a process of feminization. "Behind the walls of the barracks, the recruit has to learn roles normally associated with women: precision in making beds, polishing, and cleaning. He has to ask himself several times a day if he is properly dressed, if the creases of his trousers sit properly."[3] Nowhere was this more apparent than in the SS, with its undercurrent of homoerotic ritual, its elaborate loyalty to the person of the Führer, which transcended marriage vows. Women, for their part, became more self-reliant, more "manly." War makes single mothers out of millions of women, and their competence in handling finances or household repairs reflected a more general sense that it was possible to live independently of men.

The Nazi influence on women's organizations was more significant when it came to creating rituals, touching on cultural nerves, building the mystique of a closed, even elitist, society. Neither Hitler nor the Nazis were much interested in furthering or helping the cause of women. But they did aim to break up the family in the conventional sense, even as they simultaneously preached traditional family values. This helped almost by accident to liberate women. From what we know of Hitler and his background, it cannot have been his intention to embolden women. *Mein Kampf,* written in 1924–25, sees the human ideal of the "racial state" in the combination of manly strength and in the strength of women who bring men into the world. "Education has to be based on this fundamental difference with boys brought up from the earliest age in an atmosphere of strict military discipline." Many pages were devoted to the education of boys. As to the education of girls, Hitler can only summon two sentences. Man-soldier, woman-mother was the working premise of the early Nazis.

When the Nazis failed in 1932 to reach their declared goal of providing the next *reichspräsident,* they started to look again at their strategic approach to women. The Nazis were not attracting women voters. Indeed, a Social Democratic Party election poster from 1930 declared: "Women and girls: do you want to be nothing but maids and servants as the Nazis want?"

In March 1932, Hitler developed his position on women: "Woman is the working comrade of the man. She has always been that and always will be that way. Even in present economic circumstances. The man is the organizer of life, the woman his assistant, his executive arm."

What does this mean? Even Goebbels was unsure. At first, in his diary, he praised Hitler's thoughts on women as being entirely "modern." A year later, Goebbels was saying—apparently entirely in line with the Führer—"[A]t the risk of appearing reactionary, I have to state clearly: the first, best, and most appropriate place for the woman is in the family, and the most wonderful task she can fulfill is to pre-sent children to the nation and the people."

This self-conscious tension between the reactionary and the modern was part of the fabric of Nazi rule. There was a recognition that some of the improvements in the standing of women in the Weimar republic could not be rolled back. At the same time, the Nazis were set squarely against the emancipation movement of the 1920s, the "unfettered individualism" proposed by the campaigners for women's rights. Emancipation put gender differences at the core of society; the Nazis insisted that race was the nub of it all, the solidarity of shared blood overrode sexual differentiation. Motherhood—on this there was no dispute and little fluctuation in policy—was the cornerstone of social and racial policy. From 1935, abortion was made legal, but only for the "racially inferior"—Roma, forced laborers, and from 1938, Jewish women. The sterilization of the mentally and physically handicapped, begun already in 1933, was also part of this philosophy—by 1945, half a million people had been sterilized. The Nazi plan was that only "racially valuable" women should give birth, but 20 to 30 percent of the German population did not meet the Nazi criteria of racial hygiene. The abortion trade boomed—600,000 a year according to some estimates. Racially "pure" Germans were forbidden to terminate their pregnancies at the risk of imprisonment. Newspapers were full of accounts of trials of gynecologists who had disposed of unwanted but racially acceptable pregnancies. The doctors faced the death sentence. Access to condoms was restricted to soldiers on the front; advertisements for contraceptives were banned. Sexual advice centers were shut down.

The Nazis used not only repressive means to boost the birth rates but also bribes. From October 1935, those wanting to marry had to secure a health certificate; no registry office could carry out a wedding without this document. But once certificates were signed, the couple qualified for shopping credit vouchers to the value of RM1,000 ($400)—the average annual salary in 1933 was around RM1,520 ($608). If the couple had four children, the debt was written off. The Mother's Day holiday was restored. Fertile mothers of Aryan children were awarded the Mother's Cross (bronze) for four to six children, silver for six to eight, and gold for nine or more. On Mother's Day 1939, three million women were awarded medals for their exceptional achievements in bringing forth children. The birth rate rose: 20.4 live births for every one thousand inhabitants in 1939, five points higher than in 1932 and almost at the peak level of 1924. In this way, motherhood became a political duty and responsibility. Hitler spoke of a "battle with existential importance for our people." Motherhood was no longer private but a contribution to the racial war against inferior peoples.

Sex also began to lose its private dimension. If sex is for reproduction, and reproduction serves the nation, then attitudes about marriage and extramarital relations also have to change. The incentive to many was financial, and in areas where the Catholic church still exercised some influence, traditional. But the stigma of illegitimacy, the prejudices against single motherhood, crumbled. The Lebensborn program—to breed a master race—made something of an honor out of illegitimacy. The single mothers were pampered, the children treated like infant heroes (see "The Lebensborn Project," opposite). "Not every woman can get a husband, but every woman can be a mother," was a slogan propagated by Nazi woman league chief Gertrud Scholtz-Klink. More than a thousand young members of the Bund Deutsche Mädel (the initials BDM were said, only half in jest, to stand for *bubi drück mich*—"boy squeeze me") returned pregnant from the 1936 Nuremberg party conference.

Martin Bormann, chief of Hitler's chancellery, received a letter from his wife in 1944: "My dearest best daddy, thank you for your dear letter. For some time, I had the feeling that there was something between you and M, and when you were with me last I knew it for certain. I like M. So much that I can't be angry, and all the children love her too. In any case, she is much more practical and domestic than I am....it is such a shame that such a fine girl does not have children. In the case of M, you can change that, but you must organize it that you give M a child in one year and me the next so that you always have a mobile woman."[4] Green light, in other words, from Frau Bormann for an extramarital affair, providing that it yielded more and more children.

The Lebensborn Project

Such was the Nazi mania for breeding a pure-blooded Aryan race that a network of special human stud farms were set up where suitably Germanic members of the BDM (Bund Deutsche Mädel, or League of German Girls) would be impregnated by SS officers. This was the Lebensborn program, organized by SS chief Heinrich Himmler, and one of the more bizarre and sinister footnotes in the annals of Nazi history. Twelve maternity centers were set up across the Reich to breed the new super-race of Nazi automatons, and their pregnant inmates were given the highest quality medical care. The children were then handed over to the SS, which took charge of their upbringing and education. Deprived of any parental love or affection, the children grew up emotionally stunted.

After 1939, the conquest of the eastern territories brought many more opportunities to replenish the German gene pool, thanks in part to the substantial *volkdeutsch* (ethnic German) communities in neighboring countries such as Poland and Czechoslovakia. There, Nazi eugenicists kidnapped children regarded as "racially pure," with the requisite blond hair and blue eyes, from their families. Thousands of these children were brought by force to the Lebensborn centers, where they were Germanized and Nazified and forced to reject and forget their biological parents. Those who refused the indoctrination were beaten and punished, and many were eventually killed. Those who accepted the reeducation would be adopted by SS families.

It is estimated that up to 250,000 children were brought back to Germany, and, after the war, just 25,000 were returned to their families. Some Germans refused to hand the child back. On other occasions, the children refused to

go home, believing that they were really Germans. The Nazi
propaganda had worked.

⊠ ⊠ ⊠

It could be said that women resisted the ethics of the Third Reich
insofar as they refused to meet the demanding reproductive norm of
four children. That, however, would make resistance heroines out of
SS wives—in 1939, the average number of SS family offspring was
only 1.1 children—and the case, though seriously argued by some
German historians, is a silly one. Far more significant were the various levels of conflict that arose over the question of working women.
Having persuaded women—by carrot and stick—to withdraw from
the labor market in the 1930s, the Nazis were confronted with serious shortages at the outbreak of war. To encourage motherhood,
women civil servants had been suspended from duty in 1933. Women
lawyers and doctors were discouraged. From 1935, it was forbidden
for a woman to run a dentist surgery. The December 1933 law on
overcrowded universities restricted the female student population
to 10 percent. Even when war was declared, Hitler was determined
that women should be protected from work. Families of civil servants
received the full civilian salary of men who joined the army. Hitler
and his *gauleiters*—the most responsive in the hierarchy to popular
discontent—wanted to avoid compulsory labor service for women.

Yet the labor shortage was becoming acute. A compromise
was worked out in February 1940 by Himmler and officials from
the labor and interior ministries: women should be encouraged to
return voluntarily to work. If they refused, their family allowances
would be cut. Married women would only be pressed in this way if
they had exceptional skills or if the empty post was of pivotal importance for a local community.

The arguments within the leadership continued, however. It
was Göring in the summer of 1940 who favored using prisoners

from the occupied countries to plug the manpower gap in Germany and spare German womenfolk. The generals were skeptical since they were still thinking in terms of blitzkrieg and understood how slow and how costly was the process of rounding up East European workers and transporting them back to the Reich. Underpinning these discussions was a wide-ranging argument about the nature of the war—whether it should be "total," including the whole population, or limited.

Women seemed to sense that the regime lacked confidence or direction on this issue. The result was a kind of passive resistance by all those whose commitment fell short of full Nazi fervor. Despite the extraordinary relationship that was developing between Hitler and the ordinary German woman, the regime itself lacked credibility when it came to demanding personal sacrifice. In July 1940, one region reported that it had issued appeals to eight thousand women to sign up for the war effort (the "Women Help to Bring Victory!" campaign) but only eight women had responded. The regime got tougher—and female resentment increased accordingly. Days before the invasion of the Soviet Union in 1941, Göring said that all women who had given up their jobs at the beginning of the war should return to employment. Exceptions would be made for pregnant and sick women as well as for those looking after elderly relatives. The result was a rush of pregnancies and women with medical exemption certificates, conjured up by friendly or bribable doctors. Long-lost elderly relatives were suddenly brought into the home.

There was across-the-board opposition. Working-class women were upset that they were being targeted rather than middle-class women who were still free to go to their tennis club or stock up with the latest fashions (see "Style Wars," p. 88). Their husbands shared the anger of their wives. A promise implicit in Nazi rule was that war would remain a men's business, that women would be shielded. This pledge was being breached. On top of that, the equal treatment of the classes, a key component of the *volksgemeinschaft* idea had also become a farce.

Among workers, there was no more unpopular Nazi group-
ing than the National Socialists' women's organization, The NS
Frauenschaft, which appeared to propagandize unjust policies.
Speakers from the Frauenschaft were whistled and shouted at in
some factories. Productivity slumped in industries, such as textiles,
run almost entirely by women. There was also strong protest from
the wives of farmers, who had received no financial support and
were having to run farms almost alone. To the working women in
the country and the city, it seemed clear that the Nazis were shelter-
ing the middle class.

Style Wars

From the carefully choreographed Nuremberg rallies to the
sharply-pressed black uniforms of the SS, the Nazis placed
great emphasis on presentation and a well-groomed appearance. (By the same token, concentration camp inmates were
ritually humiliated and dehumanized by having their heads
shaved and being forced to wear striped pajamas.) While not
every German wore a uniform, it was seen as a patriotic duty
to look well-presented; it was part of the country's national
rebirth. And not just in the Reich. For, in fashion, as well as
geopolitics, the Nazis had global plans.

The Frankfurt Fashion Agency (FFA) was set up in 1939
by the city's mayor, Dr. Friedrich Krebs, and its intention
was clear from the start: to challenge Paris. The strong Jewish
presence in the German fashion industry had already been
removed—80 percent of textile production in the early 1930s
was under Jewish ownership or management. These companies were among the first to be "Aryanized." The FFA would
bring German style to Europe. The wives and consorts of
high-ranking Nazis saw themselves as sartorial ambassadors
for the new European order.

"It is my duty to look as good as I can," said Magda Goebbels, wife of the propaganda minister. "I want to set an example to German women. The German woman of the future should be chic, beautiful, and clever."

The designers concentrated on narrow, straight dresses. Satin and silk were favored materials. A ball dress could be covered by a granite-colored, floor-length velvet coat. As cotton and wool fell in short supply, the young designers found inspiration in umbrella silk, fish-net, and fish-leather, which was used to make shoes. The agency's most famous invention was a shoe with a high Plexiglas heel, the so-called "glass slipper." But as the war ground on and supplies of fabrics dried up, manufacturers were forced to use some innovative materials to clothe Germans. As this Berlin gag about ersatz suits made from wood pulp illustrates: "If your suit sprouts in spring, please cut off the shoots and use them for patches."

❖ ❖ ❖

This message was picked up by Robert Ley at the DAF and by Goebbels. They tried to persuade Hitler to introduce a compulsory labor service for all women. This, they said, would put an end to the feeling of disadvantage felt by workers. The true lesson of November 1918 was not that women should be entirely removed from the war, but that women should be treated equally. Fritz Sauckel, plenipotentiary for the employment of labor, tried to make the same point in an audience with Hitler. He was shouted down in a rhetorical fit that lasted over three hours. Middle-class women, said Hitler, had to provide homes for heroes—maintaining the morale on the front—and concentrate on giving birth to racially pure children. The point was to free the women for motherhood.

One of Sauckel's priorities was thus to solve the "servant problem." Hitler's idea was that more domestic help would allow the women to focus on motherhood; the children would be needed to populate the captured Eastern territories. Sauckel ordered the deportation of 400,000 Ukrainian women to help in the kitchens and the parlors of the German bourgeoisie (after 1989, Ukrainians again became the servant class of wealthy Germans). Throughout the war, the servant population rose to an astonishing 1,360,000. It was only after July 1944, when Goebbels took over from Sauckel as labor plenipotentiary, that some 300,000 of these servants were taken away from their host households and assigned to the armaments industry.

Hitler opposed the common labor service to the last, despite the powerful arguments of virtually every member of the Nazi leadership. But more and more German women were pressed into working in factories—armaments work was particularly well paid—but they aggravated rather than solved the problems of industry, which far preferred East European slave laborers. German women had to be better paid, were given half days off if they had children, had to be treated like saints if they became pregnant (a pregnant slave laborer, by contrast, was forced to abort her child or, if she gave birth, to surrender the child to a factory nursery where, in the case of Volkswagen, it was frequently left to die). German women needed expensive, time-consuming training. The Sauckel girls, as they were known, were a disruptive force.

How successful, then, was Hitler's seductive appeal to German womanhood? Measured against his own declared ambitions, the seduction failed. There was never any chance that the birthrate would be sufficient to populate the East. Indeed, the birthrate was not even near enough to replace the number of men who fell in combat. For at least twenty-five years after the war, West Germany was dependent on male guest workers from the Mediterranean and Turkey. Hitler failed as well in the most straightforward task: to make German women happy, to build a lasting connection between them and the National Socialist ideology. Yet the discontent of women never became a critical factor in his war-fighting strategy.

Protest was splintered and led nowhere. The morale of the men on the front was sapped by defeat on the battlefield rather than rumblings of discontent on the homefront. Women grumbled but felt, at the outset of the One Thousand Years' Reich, relatively privileged. Many were seduced by an image, a dream; others by perks. The true transformation of women's status came in spite of Hitler, rather than because of him. But even so, that was enough to neutralize the female half of the Third Reich, because it allowed women to suspend their sense of injustice. Women should have been the strongest critics of the management of the German economy, yet their criticism was confined to the queues. They should have been among the most committed pacifists. Instead, for the most part, they accepted the goal of a greater Germany won through blood.

Chapter Four

The Führer and His Generals

"Dear Field Marshal,
 Gauleiter Greiser has informed me that you would like to acquire the Seestetten forest. It is my pleasure to tell you that the Führer is ready to give you a further cash gift to make this possible."
— *Letter from Hitler's administrative head Hans Heinrich Lammers to Field Marshal Ritter von Leeb, November 17, 1943*

"I would like to deeply congratulate the Führer on his wonderful escape from the despicable attempt on his life. Victory to the German army. Heil Hitler."
— *Letter from Ritter von Leeb to Hitler, July 26, 1944*

The blood of German soldiers, as well as their enemies, was on the battlefield. The rebirth of the German military can be traced back to 1923. Then General Hans von Seeckt set a task for the Troops Agency, the *Truppen Amt* (TA). The TA was a cover name for the general staff, banned by the Allies after World War I. The TA drew together fourteen young officers (six majors and eight captains) who were responsible for keeping alive, and developing, the planning mechanism that had once made the German army great.

It was a secret operation, and each officer carried a code name, such as "Milk Bottle," "Elephant," and "Arsenic." This was more than military paranoia. Germany was full of spies and the Inter-Allied Control Commission was watching very closely to ensure that Germany did not violate the Versailles treaty by reviving the *reichswehr* (army) or the arms industry. General von Seeckt's advice was straightforward: the TA should develop a plan for a war army with a strength of between 2.8 and 3 million men. There should be 102 divisions, broken up into thirty-nine border divisions, sixty-three mobile divisions, and five cavalry divisions. The project did not get off the ground, but the thick file of calculations ended up in a safe.

On September 1, 1939, Hitler began what was to become World War II. The troop's strength: 102 divisions. The TA planners had assumed there would be 252 generals. Exactly this number was at Hitler's disposal in 1939. Hitler's army was identical to that of the paper army created by a secret task force in 1923. Thus the argument that Hitler somehow forced war on an unwilling army is wrong. The German army wanted war, wanted a military that would allow them to win a European war, and it was more than ready to let Hitler create the political framework to make this happen. Long before Hitler came to power, the army was systematically building up its strength, violating the Versailles treaty and lying to the outside world.

Secret military funds were set up for weapons purchasing. After World War I, the navy in Kiel sold a great quantity of armaments abroad to save it from compulsory dismantling. The proceeds were used to fund ultranationalist groups like Consul and Viking. Secret arms depots were established, and the military treaties with the Soviet Union enabled heavy weapons to be built and soldiers to be trained. Von Seeckt saw the *reichswehr* as an organ of the Reich rather than of the Weimar republic. That much was clear in 1920, when the army demonstrated its reluctance to intervene on behalf of the republic during the abortive Kapp Putsch led by right-wingers and disgruntled army officers. The army under von Seeckt kept out of daily politics, but it was not apolitical.

The army was not a monolith, but on the whole, it regarded the rise of the National Socialists as a step in the right direction. Well before 1933, Generals von Reichenau and von Blomberg had regular contacts with Hitler. After the death of Hindenburg, the speed with which the generals accommodated Hitler was breathtaking. The personal oath of loyalty to the Führer, the murder of a few generals, the application of the "Aryan" paragraph to the Wehrmacht (excluding Jews from the ranks), all this was accepted. The quid pro quo was political support of rearmament, general national service, and the destruction of the SA brownshirts, regarded as a dangerous rabble and a threat to the army's power.

Many younger members of the officer corps were sympathetic to Nazi slogans. Others saw career opportunities shaping up. A few older officers were apprehensive about the policy toward the church and the intrusiveness of the Gestapo. But for the most part, even these officers were prisoners of the antidemocratic and national conservative philosophy of the *reichswehr*. The army believed, perhaps, that it was bringing Hitler under its control. That was a mistake that would cripple effective opposition.

Once in power, Hitler came quickly to understand the vanity and fickle nature of the eager generals. How long would they stay loyal? At what point would they resist political interference? Would they develop a separate political agenda? The combination of the generals' vulnerability and Hitler's political ambitions was not a marriage made in heaven. Hitler, Austrian, a former corporal with an unmilitary bearing, but with command of a deadly competitor—the SS—was taken only half-seriously by the conservative generals. His grasp of military science was regarded as deeply flawed. Yet the generals were often ready to swallow their prejudice. There were many stages, many subtle colorings between the initial enthusiasm for Hitler—military conformity, factual arguments about strategy, grumbling about wrong-headed political interference, and outright resistance. The officer corps was not divided between a majority of mindless yes-men and a small minority of heroes planning tyrannicide.

Sometimes the difference between conformity and rebellion was merely a mater of timing. Berthold von Stauffenberg was asked at the end of 1941 by Helmuth von Moltke, a resistance leader, whether he could win over his brother Claus to the secret anti-Hitler conspiracy. "I have spoken with Claus," reported Berthold, "he says first we have to win the war. You can't do such a thing during wartime, above all not during the war against the Bolsheviks.

But when we all come home then we will dispose of the brown plague." Two and a half years later, Claus von Stauffenberg laid a bomb in a briefcase next to Hitler, the closest anyone came to killing the dictator.

In May 1938, Hitler spoke of his plans to invade Czechoslovakia. Ludwig Beck, head of the general staff, was present, and although he had welcomed the Nazis and championed rearmament, he was shocked. Persuaded by Colonel Hans Oster of the *Abwehr* (counter intelligence), he started to openly criticize the Nazi war plans. He tried to mobilize other generals against war: "Your soldierly discipline has a limit, at the point where your knowledge, your conscience, and your responsibility precludes you carrying out an order."

Beck resigned. Different plans were hatched. As soon as France and Britain declared war, after the invasion of Czechoslovakia, a few generals would arrest Hitler and his inner circle, and occupy Gestapo headquarters, the broadcasting stations, and the propaganda ministry. SS troopers in southern Germany would be held in check by soldiers loyal to the conspirators. The Munich Agreement between Chamberlain and Hitler in the fall of 1938, however, took the wind out of the sails of the conspirators. Other plots met a similar fate either overtaken by events—a German victory on the battlefield made uncertain any popular support for a *putsch* (coup)—or were based on a misjudgment of the mood of the officer corps. Sometimes, key figures became ill—Beck underwent a stomach operation at a critical moment in March 1943—and at other times, plotters were thwarted by bad luck.

In the spring of 1943, a bomb disguised as a parcel with two bottles of cognac was planted on Hitler's plane. The aim was to pretend Hitler had died in a plane crash, avoiding an open confrontation with the SS. The English-made detonator failed to work. What would have happened if Hitler had been killed that spring? Would national conservative generals have tried to make their peace not only with the Western Allies but also with the National Socialists?

The failure of the generals to topple Hitler was more than incompetence or a lack of nerve. The National Socialists had been good to the army. Better than any ordinary German could imagine. Hitler made plain to his Adjutant Major Engel that he could buy loyalty even from his straight-backed Prussian generals. The Führer stressed that "he does not demand membership in the National Socialist party from a general but requires from generals and officers that they are politically subservient to the state and that they carry out orders without questions. It would be easier for the men concerned—even against their inner convictions—if they receive appropriate honors from the head of state and therefore feel obliged to the state."[1]

Hitler was explaining to Engel, at considerable length, his honors system. It was, he said, part of a long tradition for a ruler to reward the loyalty and achievements of his generals. This was certainly correct. Napoleon, the Austrian emperors, and the Prussian kings also handed out titles, cash, land, and pensions to their followers.

Hitler took a more systematic approach: he had to guard himself from his own generals, and no largesse was spared for the purpose. Even while German soldiers were resorting to cannibalism in Stalingrad, there was an active correspondence between Hitler's head of chancellery Hans Heinrich Lammers and generals anxious to increase their holdings. The list of beneficiaries is very long. Admiral-of-the-Fleet Erich Raeder, for example, was given RM220,000. By comparison, a worker was paid RM28 a month, a minister RM1,700. The rule-of-thumb exchange rate is that one reichsmark was equivalent to forty cents. Field Marshall Ritter von Leeb received RM118,000—the estate bought with part of the money is still in family hands. Field Marshall Gerd von Rundstedt received RM250,000; General Wilhelm von Keitel, later tried for war crimes, picked up RM250,000 in September 1942 and a further RM739,340 in July 1944—the month of the unsuccessful plot against Hitler. This was on top of the monthly income supplement of RM4,000 for field marshals and RM2,000 for generals. The supplement was tax-free.

Little wonder, then, that at a turning point for the army—the hours after the failure of the July 20 plot when the scales could have been tipped even against a living yet politically damaged Hitler—the generals stayed loyal to the Führer. Von Leeb had early contacts with general staff malcontents and clearly felt that his place was at Hitler's side. General Heinz Guderian, the most successful tank commander of his generation, called on his fellow generals to stay loyal to the Führer after July 20. He was appointed chief of general staff and a member of an honor tribunal that stripped all officers involved in the Stauffenberg conspiracy of their rank—a remarkable transformation for an officer who had been critical of Hitler's war-fighting strategy.

The change can be explained with reference to documents from Hitler's Reichskanzlei. On October 30, 1942, a section of the Reichskanzlei concerned with gifts and Hitler's personal subsidies received a letter from the *gauleiter* of the Wartheland (now western Poland). Gauleiter Arthur Greiser was worried: he had been told by General Guderian that Hitler had promised him an estate in the Wartheland and wanted to come to choose an appropriate bit of land. Greiser knew nothing of this and wanted chancellery confirmation. Hitler confirmed the offer. In December 1942, Greiser was instructed to find a suitable portfolio of possible estates. In February 1943, Guderian was given a new title—"inspector general of tank troops." The same month, he was approached by members of the anti-Hitler group in the army. They knew he had been critical of Hitler. Would he meet them? The presence of an acknowledged military hero could sway the balance.

Guderian showed no interest. He concentrated on tracking down a suitable country house. Greiser had narrowed the choice down to two estates, hundreds of acres of forest and farmland. Guderian's wife rejected both. "At the end of the viewing, he came to me with his wife and son and told me they had found somewhere else entirely....Frau Guderian liked it because the mansion house was in such architecturally good condition and situated in a particularly beautiful park."

Sadly, the estate was already reserved and so the search contin-ued. Stalingrad had fallen, the war in the East had turned against the Germans, the plotters were desperate to find a way of disposing Hitler—and Guderian was writing letter after letter demanding to know whether his new estate would be tax-free and who would pay for new furniture and farming machinery.[2] By January 27, 1944, Guderian had his 2,340-acre estate. The only remaining problem—which would take until July 1944 to solve—was how to house the German estate manager.

The remarkable fact is that in a few years of National Socialism, generals had abandoned a traditional Prussian code of behavior just as a child might set aside an unwanted toy in the nursery. Some ele-ments were later cited in self-defense—above all, unflinching obedi-ence to the commander-in-chief—but the etiquette of honor evapo-rated. Colonel Helmuth Groscurth, chief of the liaison between the general staff and the Abwehr was a committed Christian. When he heard about the killings in Poland, he spent most of December 1939 visiting commanders on the western front trying to persuade them to act against Hitler. They showed no interest. Groscurth was one of the few army officers who dared to stop a massacre by an opera-tional group (another was Colonel Dr. Albert Battel, who stopped or delayed the killing of Jews in Przemysl).

To slip out of the easy and increasingly corrupt pattern of cooperation with the Nazis, disgruntled officers needed a stronger moral corset than that provided by an aristocratic sense of decency. Noblesse oblige was not a helpful principle on the eastern front. Stauffenberg found his supporters at the side of the poet Stefan George who acted as a guru for a whole generation of aristocrats searching for a new kind of Germany, a "secret Germany" that would draw on the honorable tradition of the knights who had served the Hohenstaufen emperors.

General Fritz Halder said of Stauffenberg in his teens: "He was accustomed to making up his own mind and having his views accepted."[3] As a school boy, he acted in Schiller's *Wilhelm Tell* in which the key verse is: "Yes! There's a limit to the tyrant's power! When man oppressed has cried in vain for justice and knows his burden is too great to bear, with bold resolve he reaches up to heaven to seize those rights which are forever his."

The privileged separateness of much of the officer corps made resistance an option; yet most preferred to ignore the option and ignore facts that could prompt uncomfortable self-questioning. Even for members of the resistance—immune to Hitler's bribes and blandishments—certain premises of the Nazi regime were not seriously questioned. General Werner von Fritsch, dismissed from office after conflicts with the Nazi leadership, was a model for the younger members of the resistance. Yet Fritsch declared that to make Germany powerful again, it was necessary to win three battles: against the workers, against the Catholic Church, and against the Jews. In both military and civil resistance, there was a widespread acceptance that there was a "Jewish problem." In the case of the army, the dominant conviction was that bolshevism—the main enemy even for Claus von Stauffenberg—was intertwined with international Jewry. A resistance sympathizer such as General Carl-Heinrich von Stulpnagel cooperated without any scruples with Reinhard Heydrich after occupying Galicia, the area with Europe's most dense concentration of Jews and Jewish culture.

Carl Goerdeler—who could well have been chancellor if Hitler had been overthrown—wrote in 1941 about the necessity of a Jewish state in Canada or South America. Jews living in Germany should be treated as foreigners, he argued, and thus denied voting rights and access to public office. At the same time, he opposed the methods of the Nazis. Some resisters described the horrific scene of *Kristallnacht* as a psychological turning point, the moment when they realized how the Nazis had established a form of hateful mob rule. Yet, with very few exceptions—Helmut Groscurth and Hans Oster—nothing was undertaken to stop the progress of the Holocaust.

Von Moltke, as an officer in the *Abwehr*, was one of many who knew what was happening. In a letter to a friend in Stockholm on

March 25, 1943, he wrote: "At least nine-tenths of the population do not know that we have murdered hundreds of thousands of Jews. They still believe that the Jews have simply been segregated, that they are living in the East where they originate, perhaps somewhat poorer but without the worry of air raids."[4]

Von Moltke probably understated the level of awareness. Jews were being deported from Berlin almost every day from the railway station in fashionable Grunewald. They walked through the leafy streets and were beaten if they lagged behind. Germans watched through the windows of their villas; few doubted that something terrible was going to happen to them. But even if von Moltke's estimate is correct, at least 800,000 people must have been in the know. Among them were many upright members of Europe's proudest officer corps, bought off with money, rank, and military victories.

Chapter Five

The Triumph of Kitsch

Benign blue eye and iron sword-hand
Husky voice, thou and the children's most loyal father
Behold across the continents banded together
Stand man and wife in the flames of the soul
Sacredly joined, an endless chain
Wave-encircled before the morn
Which your shoulders alone
Have raised across the mountain-ridges out of the chasms
of distress.

           — *"Ode to the Führer," poem by Heinrich Zillich*

No evil priest can prevent us from feeling that we are the children of Hitler. We follow not Christ, but Horst Wessel [an S.A. brownshirt who was killed in 1930 and glorified as a martyr to the Nazi cause—his song became the official Nazi anthem]. Away with incense and holy water. The Church can go hang for all we care. The Swastika brings salvation on earth. I want to follow it step by step. Baldur von Schirach, [leader of the Hitler Youth] take me along!

           —*Song sung by the Hitler Youth at the 1934 Nuremberg Rally*

The cartoonist and writer Tomi Ungerer once made an interesting confession. Ungerer was a child during the Nazi years and has always been critical of anything that smacked of nostalgia for the Third Reich. Still, he told a radio interviewer: "Whenever I felt a bit down—not depressed, just down—I would automatically sing the Nazi songs we learned as kids...it was good medicine, a pick-me-up. These songs work like a drug. When you take heroin it stays in your blood system for a whole year. If you're brought up by the Nazis, then the songs stay twenty, thirty years in your brain." The interview was never broadcast—it was too close to the bone in a society that wanted to regard the Hitler years as a rotten tooth to be extracted from an otherwise healthy mouth.

One does not brood over a removed molar. But Tomi Ungerer had captured something important: the emotional intensity of the Third Reich, its ability to tap the national nerve. The success of Hitler, the abiding fascination of fascism, is bound up with this ability to identify and satisfy popular longings. The Nazis understood the German taste; they did not invent it. Hitler, so remote from everyday life and caught up in his own disturbed psyche, had nonetheless an instinctive feel for what appealed to Germans. In exploiting this talent—indeed, through Goebbels and Ley, marketing it—he managed to convince Germans that the regime was, despite all the evidence to the contrary, more democratic than its predecessors, more in tune with the people.

The postwar continuities are therefore important if one is to unravel Hitler's seductive powers. The psychologist Gudrun Brockhaus makes her own confession: "I did not realize that many things close to my heart had Nazi roots. That my favorite children's books were written by convinced Nazis, that the uncompromising nature of the 1968 movement had Nazi precedents, that the feminist slogan of the 1970s 'The Private is Political' stemmed from Nazi times, that current psychotherapeutic terms referring to authority and completeness were first defined in textbooks published in 1934."[1]

Even the ecological principles espoused by the present-day environmentalist parties were first put forth by the constructors of the autobahn. The German fitness cult deploys the same terms and methods as the Nazi body culture movement. The taste for natural medicine, the esoteric, the occult, and homeopathy; the fascination for extreme sports, for speed, for technological gimmickry—all this has strong echoes of the Third Reich. The millennium experience designed for Germany as the New Year's Eve 2000 event was an elaborate light show that directly copied the light "architecture" of Albert Speer, the leader of the Beauty of Work Campaign.

Yet there was more method, more calculation in Hitler's seduction techniques than the mere embracing of the leaden, unsurprising cultural prejudices of the lower-middle class. The fascination of fascism was rooted in its calculated contrast with Weimar. The chaos and terror of the 1920s (much of it, of course, initiated and stirred up by the SA), the stigma of defeat, the apparent cynicism, the decline in morals, the devastating effect of hyperinflation on savings and normal middle-class values: all this was laid at the door of weak parliamentary democracy. Weimar, and parliamentarianism, was deemed to be out of step with the true Germany. And most Germans agreed. Hitler's distaste for *entartete kunst*, or "degenerate art," was widely shared. Artists like Otto Dix and Georg Grosz were depicting a world in turmoil.

Germans, however, were tired of experiments. They were exhausted by the politicization of everyday life. The West had inflicted a massive reparations burden on Germany; the Soviet Union was a menace. It was time for Germany to count on Germans and define a culture of national solidarity, a celebratory, rather than a self-lamenting, culture. The National Socialists could provide precisely this with a lumpy package of pseudo-religious, classical, and Nordic traditions. Against all the odds, the Nazis could even conjure up a sense of safety and belonging at the very moment when they were practicing savage and exclusive policies.

Communist writer Ernst Bloch, writing in 1925, compared the effectiveness of Communist and National Socialist seduction. "Nazis lie, but in doing so, talk to and about people; the Communists speak the truth but only about things and issues." He quotes a young Nazi: "One does not die for a program that one can understand, one dies for a program that one loves."[2]

In fact, it is difficult to talk of a Nazi program at all, but the point was correct: the Nazis grasped the power of the irrational.

The genius of Hitler and his operators was to move a stage further: having made the Germans feel comfortable for the first time in two decades, he devised a way in which the mere act of being German could be translated into a significant event. It was Hitler who made the *spiesser*, the petit bourgeois philistine, feel like a world conqueror. All that was required, initially at least, was an act of belief and a German pedigree. No special talent was demanded, only a readiness to revere the Führer unconditionally and an open affirmation of the values and prejudices of the *volksgemeinschaft*. Daniel Goldhagen argues that this binding quality was a shared hatred of Jews. But anti-Semitism, even rabidly expressed and mantled in pseudoscience or mythology, was not sufficient social cement. The exclusion of the Jew (and the Slavs and the Roma) helped Germans to define their racial community. But Germans needed to be offered more than the opportunity to be non-Jews. Hitler sensed a spiritual thirst in Germans and found ways of slaking it.

The significance of this choreography of power cannot be understated. How could the ordinary German realize the availability of ethical choice if he operated in a world in which happiness was defined as the absence of choice? Germany wanted certainties, not choices. To consider alternatives was to step outside a stockade that not only protected the buffeted "true" German but which also gave his life meaning. No other system with totalitarian ambitions has managed to spin such a web of emotional commitment to a single leader. True, Russians cried in the streets when Stalin died in 1953. They had lost someone who had been built up by a crudely effective propaganda machine as the Father of the Nation.

The National Socialists, however, concocted a unique formula to seduce the Germans. They drew on legend and the occult, but the spearhead of the movement, and the Führer himself, was entirely modern. Goebbels was an innovator who understood quickly that every household had to have a radio—the voice of the Führer had to become part of a family ritual, and while this entailed some risk (that Germans could use the *volksempfänger*, or "people's receiver," to pick up foreign broadcasts), it was acceptable. Hitler was in love with speed—he took childish glee in his first Mercedes and was one of the first European politicians to make regular use of airplanes.

It was the era not only of the people's car, the Volkswagen (which in theory gave Germans a remarkable degree of personal physical freedom), and the autobahn, it was also a time of scientific breakthroughs and the first tentative moves toward the mass production of television sets. On March 22, 1935, the *Reichspost* in Berlin began regular television emissions. Only a few people were able to follow them on 25cm x 30cm screens, but the Germans could boast of being ahead of the United States and Britain in sending regular broadcasts. It was the 1936 Berlin Olympics that made television popular. Thousands of people gathered in television lounges set up by the *Reichspost* in Berlin to watch direct transmissions from sports contests. The war interrupted the development of television. Propaganda theorists were, in any case, divided over the virtues of television. Some argued that it would become "the electronic eye behind the Führer" (and therefore a good thing) while others objected that the television miniaturized the images of Nazi leaders.

The aesthetics of fascism are based on the elimination of imperfection; the moles and scars on the face of society. The propaganda purpose is clear: to suggest a utopian destination, a goal that can be obtained only through absolute loyalty and belief. Seducers offer a vision—of completeness, of perfect love, of unqualified happiness. And so it was that the Olympic games of 1936 became an attempt not only to seduce the German nation and the international community, but also, in a remarkably subtle way, to prepare the Germans for war. It did not take a great leap of imagination for foreign visitors and spectators to understand this. After all, only months after the elaborate Winter Games in Garmisch-Patenkirchen, Hitler broke the Locarno treaties and marched into the Rhineland. Ordinary Germans saw the Garmisch skiers and the Rhineland soldiers as if they were on the same spectrum, and Hitler's popularity was rarely higher. The international community ignored the Rhineland invasion, failed to make any connection between a sporting and a military event and, in the spirit of Avery Brundage ("the games must go on"), naïvely accepted the Berlin Olympics as a spectacle remote from politics, nice to look at, with no particular message to offer about Germany's future behavior.

Every effort was made to camouflage the reality of the Third Reich. The concentration camp in Oranienburg was only a few dozen miles from the Berlin stadium but far enough away to forget. No expense was spared in the building of the stadium. "If one has invited the whole world, then something great and beautiful has to be created," said Hitler, "a few million reichsmarks either way is of no consequence." The adjoining sports field was decked out with statues, the centerpiece of which was Josef Thorak's huge "Fistfighter." The so-called "Maifeld," the may meadow, was made into a parade ground (later, much later, it became a venue for the likes of the Rolling Stones); a bell tower, the so-called "Führerturm," was erected.

There was no avoiding the military component. The army supplied the floodlights, the signals unit provided the telephones for the correspondents, the air force set up a barrage balloon for film-maker Leni Riefenstahl. Hundreds of military carrier pigeons were co-opted to serve as "doves of peace." Army engineers put up the Olympic Village. Naturally, when the athletes were ready to parade through the stadium at the inauguration of the games, many chose to wear their army uniforms.

And still, international guests did not register alarm. Outside the stadium, Berlin did not seem to be so bad, not nearly as rabid as correspondents had led them to believe. The "Jews Keep Out" signs had been removed. Der Stürmer was suddenly unavailable in newspaper kiosks. Two "half-Jews" were on the German national squad. The point was, in part, to calm the nerves of the International Olympic Committee, which had come very close to a boycott following the Nuremberg race laws. But there was something more—a struggle for "perfection," defined in the narrow and racially menacing terms of the Nazis, even when that perfection had to be faked. Deception was at the heart of the fascist aesthetic, deception and self-deception.

Naturally, no open-air spectacle could hope to be perfect. German athletes were not all-conquering. Hitler behaved at times like a provincial buffoon rather than as a gracious international statesman. There were many diplomatic blunders, aside from Hitler's well-known dismay over the four gold medals of Jesse Owens, the black American sprinter.

The significance of documentary film dawned quickly on the Nazis. The artful director, the skillful use of scissors in the editing room, the soft focus, and the many new camera techniques that were opening up allowed the filmmaker to rub away the edges of real life and render perfect that which was not.

The true culpability of Leni Riefenstahl, who was edging toward rehabilitation at the end of her long life, is apparent in her two Olympic films. "Never neglect the background" was Riefenstahl's watchword whether she was filming tropical fish (as she did in her old age) or Olympic athletes. With cameras set in pits dug in the Olympic stadium, she could silhouette sportsmen against dramatic skyscapes and endow them with Greek God–like qualities. The overall effect—for all its astonishing photography—was to provide an advertisement for the master race. Riefenstahl's memoirs record countless arguments with Goebbels and subtle disagreements with Hitler, designed to show that she was concerned with her art rather than with the political message.

In the earlier *Triumph of the Will*, recording and idealizing the Nuremberg party congress, she clashed with General von Reichenau. For the first time, the Wehrmacht had taken part in a party rally. But the military exercises had been held in the rain, and the footage was bad. Riefenstahl told the general she wanted to cut out the army. Reichenau complained to Hitler who had earlier promised to allow Riefenstahl full independence. Hitler invited the filmmaker to Munich for Christmas and made a proposal: "I will ask the most important generals and members of the party to come to a film studio—I will be present too. Then we will line up, and the camera will move slowly down the line. This will make it possible to emphasise the contributions of each person with a few words. That could be the opening credits of your film. No one will be offended, and you will not annoy anyone."

Riefenstahl started to cry (a tactic which always worked with Hitler but never with Goebbels). She had a very clear idea of the opening sequence: Hitler's airplane would be shown flying to Nuremberg through a sea of clouds, over the spires and gables of the city. Riefenstahl recalled his response: "'For God's sake, what's wrong with you?' said Hitler. 'I'm only trying to help you.'...I forgot who was in front of me....My reaction was so vehement that I lost all fear. I leapt up and stamped my foot, shouting I can't do it."[3]

After she had calmed down, Riefenstahl proposed making a short film on the Wehrmacht the following year to appease the generals. That was how deals were struck in a dictatorship. Hitler wearily accepted and did not regret his decision. For the opening sequence of *Triumph of the Will* precisely stated the theme of his leadership: Hitler as Messiah coming from above to save, through an act of will, the German people.

Riefenstahl's memoirs are, naturally, self-serving. They make a Punch and Judy show out of her relations with Goebbels. (She recalls him fiddling underneath her dress at the opera while his pregnant wife sat at the other side.) And her purpose is plain: to demonstrate her integrity as a filmmaker and her distance from the bureaucracy of propaganda. In her account, Goebbels never abandoned his attempts to sleep with her. During one encounter, Goebbels "grabbed my breast and tried to force himself on me. I had to wrestle my way out of his arms and dashed to the door with Goebbels pursuing me. Beside himself with rage, he held me against the wall and tried to kiss me....I desperately resisted, and moving along the wall, I managed to push myself against the buzzer and press it....when I left his offices, I knew that the propaganda minister was my enemy for sure."

The truth is, though, that Riefenstahl deliberately fed a myth that was largely shaped by Goebbels: the separateness of Hitler, his transcendental qualities, his supposed charisma. She herself admits to Faustian bargains—agreeing, reluctantly, to Hitler's request to film Nuremberg in return for permission to make a cherished personal project, *Tiefland*, an allegorical film set in the Dolomites. Artists, according to her argument, cannot compromise their integrity, but they have to make some compromises in order to buy time and space to create; it was ever thus. But it is a fake argument that equates Hitler with Hollywood. Striking bargains with a dictatorship that had already forced her friends into emigration (and was doing far, far worse things), is not comparable to accepting the restraints of a commercial studio.

A comparison of Leni Riefenstahl and Marlene Dietrich is quite instructive. Both women were shunned by Germans after the war. Riefenstahl because she was so explicitly in love with Hitler: even if that emotion was shared by millions of postwar Germans, it was not something that could be publicly acknowledged. Riefenstahl was shamed and had to restore her reputation as a photographer of the Nubians and underwater seascapes.

Dietrich returned to Germany in an American uniform. She had left in 1930, following Joseph von Sternberg to Hollywood. She stayed in America, became an American citizen, and entertained American troops. That was enough for Berliners to spit on her and curse her as an "American whore" when she returned. She settled in Paris and returned to Germany only to be buried in Berlin where her grave is still frequently desecrated.

Dietrich was in love with Sternberg who admired Riefenstahl. The result was an uneasy relationship between the two women. Riefenstahl visited Sternberg on the set of *The Blue Angel*, and Dietrich was furious. "'You're so different from Marlene,' Sternberg said. 'But both of you are extraordinary creatures. I work my magic on Marlene, and I'll transform you too. Why, you haven't even been discovered yet.' He said a lot more, but those words stuck in my memory. After the war, I often regret that I had not gone to America with Sternberg."

The decision to stay and work in a dictatorship can be a more effective expression of resistance than to emigrate and criticize from abroad. The same choice has faced writers and artists for two centuries or more. In the Soviet Union, Alexander Solzhenitsyn left, Andrei Sakharov stayed. But Solzhenitsyn was more or less pushed out of his country since it had become impossible to work. Sakharov, meanwhile, was pushed to the margins of his own country by an intolerant regime.

The choices are thus never crisp, never precise. Dietrich left Germany in the first place because she had an exportable talent and a brilliant director who believed in her. Only later did the act of emigration become an act of resistance. Her chosen option was to reject the Nazis—who tried hard to lure her back. That option was also open to Riefenstahl. She decided instead to combine two goals: to serve her art and to serve Hitler, who seemed to her more a compelling actor than a monstrous dictator. The goals were irreconcilable. Riefenstahl ended up as a tool of Hitler, part of his grand seduction of the German people, and the art, though striking, was correspondingly flawed. Yet Dietrich ended her life no happier, nor could she seriously claim to have made a significant impact on the Hitler dictatorship. Emigration, especially when commercially motivated, is a distorted moral choice; it does not and cannot address the dilemmas of ordinary life in a dictatorship.

The cult of the Führer, the call for the Strong Man, was a feature of many European states in the inter-war years. It was not purely a fascist phenomenon—the Stalin cult raged for over two decades—nor was it confined to central Europe. In Spain, it was a Franco cult; in Italy, there was Il Duce. Yet Hitler's power, his manipulation of the symbols of power, was distinctive. Franco rose to power with the help of the army and before he was named *caudillo*, could not claim to be the head of a national movement. The result was a military dictatorship supplemented by a highly centralized government steered by the *caudillo*. In Germany, the cabinet did not meet after February 1938.

Hitler's style of rule conformed, in almost textbook fashion, with Max Weber's definition of charismatic leadership: decked out with a historic mission and a messianic claptrap, backed by a popular movement, the Führer created an essentially unstable system in which the only certainty was his word and presence. The bureaucracy, well developed in Germany, surrendered its grasp of the law and concentrated on interpretation and implementation of an ambiguously expressed Führer *erlass* (decree) or Führer *weisung* (directive), the guidelines dispatched from the chancellery. Within this chaotic improvisation, conflicts were waged between party factions, between party and state, and between different ministries. Hitler was able to present himself as being above the wrangling, knowing it was only a matter of time before the discontent, once voiced against parliamentary democracy, was directed at the National Socialist monopoly.

The conventional description of Hitler as charismatic has to be looked at in detail. The fact that he met Weber's definition of charismatic leadership does not in itself mean that Hitler was the hypnotic, radiant, irresistible controller of crowds normally described as charismatic. Historians cannot agree as to whether Hitler was a demon, a loser swept to the top by vested interests, a frustrated architect who decided to destroy rather than build, a colorless individual, or the crystallization point for many Germanic myths that still held sway over popular sentiment.

A majority of Germans questioned as recently as the 1960s, rated the prewar Hitler as one of the great German statesmen. Historian Joachim Fest speculated that if Hitler had been killed by Georg Elsner in 1938, the Nazi leader would still rank as "one of the greatest statesmen."[4] (Elsner, a carpenter apparently acting alone, placed a bomb in a podium behind Hitler—it exploded after Hitler had left the beer cellar.) German historian Hans Mommsen describes Hitler as an "indecisive, frequently insecure, in some respects weak dictator who was concerned exclusively with his prestige and his personal authority and who was always strongly influenced by his environment."[5] So, was Hitler the master of Germany or a weak dictator?

In the jargon of historical debate, Hans Mommsen counts as a functionalist or a structuralist, in which the Third Reich is radicalized by its warring factions carrying Hitler along like a fisherman's float bobbing on troubled waters. For many, this view comes too close to minimizing Hitler's role in the Holocaust. The opposing school of intentionalists sees Hitler as the master of his destiny and of his country. The intentionalists regard *Mein Kampf* as a blueprint that was systematically put in place by an evil ruler. The intentionalists are more likely to see Hitler as charismatic, the willful mesmeric seducer of a nation. The functionalists prefer to focus on the innate corruption of the system and the readiness to drift toward violence.

We can find merits in both arguments. Our Hitler is a man who had—until he buried himself in the concrete bunker of the Wolf's Lair—almost perfect pitch when listening to his audience. Those who testify in their memories to Hitler's magnetism—Leni Riefenstahl is only one of many—are projecting their own dreams, their awe onto this strangely insubstantial figure. His charisma, his ability to seduce the masses, seems to us to consist of two qualities: his ability as a public speaker and the vast, sophisticated apparatus that was dedicated to making a myth out of the man.

The NSDAP, little more than a splinter group in its early days, was dependent on speechmakers, highly mobile rabble rousers who could be counted on to fill a village hall or a beer cellar. But the standards of oratory were poor—so poor that from 1928, the party had to set up a speechmakers' school. By 1933, around six thousand activists had been trained in the art of rhetoric. From the beginning,

Hitler was an exception, outshining the other two NSDAP stars Hermann Esser and Gotfried Feder. Region after region, city after city started to ban Hitler's speeches. The calculation of the authorities was that the NSDAP, without the mobilizing force of Hitler's speeches, would shrink. The second *reichsparteitag* of the NSDAP was held in Weimar in July 1926, precisely because Thueringia was one of the few regions not to have banned Hitler's speeches. Already in 1926, Hitler was presenting himself as Führer, making the keynote speech and taking the raised arm salute from SA units as they marched past his open car. In the spring of 1927, Bavaria and Saxony lifted their ban, and by November 1928, Hitler was addressing a rally packed into the large Berlin Sportpalast.

Hitler's public rhetoric was part of the emotionalization of German politics. The texts of the speeches give no hint of their power: they meander, are riddled with bad grammar, present stereotyped circular arguments and, above all, go on for hours. Even filmed extracts of the performances do not give a clue: the mimicry and body language has all too obviously been learned in front of a mirror. The electricity of Hitler's speeches was generated by the setting and by the crowd. The words and the logical course of the argument were largely irrelevant.

For Albert Speer, "the power of suggestion and persuasion used by Hitler was so big that...it left an impression much deeper than the speech itself, about which I can actually remember very little."[6] A typical comment (quoted in Detlef Grieswelle's study of Hitler's rhetoric) acknowledged an almost mystical fusion of the speech and the person. "Man and word melted together, formed a union...there were speeches in which Hitler—gulping, screaming, almost inarticulate—spat out many incomprehensible words: this was not about verbal communication but a much more intense, elemental expression."[7] Another attendee of Hitler's party conference speeches recorded: "Hitler not only articulated the enthusiasm of his movement, the hatred of the 'system' and the Jews, he was himself full of enthusiasm and hate."[8]

Some observers with postwar hindsight have compared him to a satanical version of an evangelical preacher, driving the crowd forward but at the same time following its rhythms. The violence of his utterance attracted rather than repelled. "His passion was released like an explosion, he surprised with the direction of his hate and the violence of his anger. He would howl, then his voice would become a kind of crowing."⁹ The range was part of the seductiveness; Germans were used to sober monotones. They were accustomed to logical progression, the logic of parliamentary debate, and so the inconsistencies and contradictions of Hitler's rhetoric seemed to be a radical departure: it denoted a politician with passion, one who had more credibility than those with impeccably rational credentials.

Personalized politics was a remarkable phenomenon in Germany, a taste of the modern. It only began to make an impact, however, after Nazi propaganda managers devised what would now be known as a marketing strategy. Hitler became, in effect, a brand product. While Hitler was imprisoned, Alfred Rosenberg came up with the idea of producing and distributing millions of Hitler postcards which would raise his national profile. The party paper *Illustrierter Beobachter* was given the monopoly on distributing photographs of Hitler's rallies and other Hitler portraits. In present day terms, Hitler developed a form of fan club whereby word-of-mouth appeal was supported by picture marketing.

One of the most popular photo marketing campaigns was the picture reporting from Hitler's 1932 electioneering. Under the title, "Hitler Over Germany," the magazine reported on the Nazi leader's three flights over Germany—by using a private airplane, Hitler was able to speak in twenty-one towns on his first tour (the presidential elections), twenty-five in his second, and fifty in his third (the Reichstag elections). The aim was to sell Hitler as omnipresent, as a national figure, and as a political messiah (see "The Messiah from Braunau," opposite). Photo albums put together by Heinrich Hoffmann ("The Führer" and "Brown Army") served the same purpose.

The Messiah from Braunau

The coming of the "Führer" was predicted by many writers after World War I. The tone of the writing resembled that of prophets calling for messianic salvation. This pseudo-religious idiom was readily adapted by Hitler who at first presented himself as a "drummer boy" for the future Führer, rather than as a heroic leader himself. The national conservative Wilhelm Stapel said the new leader would be "simultaneously a ruler, a warrior, and a priest."[10] Ernst Bertram, writing in 1922, saw a leader emerging to renew the spirit of the country and fight off the threat from Asia.[11] Novelist and essayist Ernst Jünger, who had done more than any other writer to set out the attraction of battlefield violence, predicted the rise in the machine age of a "modern man of power" above the parties.[12]

None of these writers was referring to Hitler. They were expressing a deep fear of Bolshevism, contempt of parliamentary democracy, and the feeling that Germany had been robbed of its opportunity for heroic leadership by the premature and treacherous end of World War I. The passing of the monarchy left the Protestant churches especially with an unsatisfied need for a leader who could end the German crisis of faith.

Hitler took over the party leadership in July 1921, but he was little more than a conventional chairman with a rhetorical gift. Only the success of Mussolini and his "March on Rome" made Hitler understand that he could match the messianic expectations of the Germans with his own ambitions. The party press, by 1923, began to refer to Hitler as the Leader. He started to borrow consciously from biblical images: in Berlin, he said, he would throw out the money changers.

The looting of church ritual fed the Hitler cult. Kindergarten children recited:

Fold your hands, bow your head
and think of Adolf Hitler
who gives us work and gives us bread
and takes away all our troubles.

It was a short step from pseudo-Christianity to outright anti-Christianity. The German heathen myths and Nordic mysticism began to take hold. By 1934, teenagers were singing:

We are the happy Hitler Youth,
We do not need the virtues of the church
for it is our Führer Adolf Hitler
who stands at our side.

Hitler pictures were distributed like images of Jesus or Virgin Mary, to the seriously sick as an aid to healing. Propaganda stories told of people abandoning their wheelchairs at the mere suggestion that Hitler was going to visit their hometown.

"The nineteenth century was a century of reason, the twentieth is a century of cults," said Jünger in 1943. "Kniebolo (Hitler) lives and thrives on this. And that explains the complete inability of the liberal intelligentsia to begin to understand where he is at."[13]

* * *

Not much time was wasted trying to set out National Socialist policies. The Germans were being exposed to an emotional experience buttressed by rituals and legends which smacked of ancient certainties. The Hitler salute was a typical trapping of this political marketing operation. The so-called "German Greeting" was introduced—despite some opposition inside the party—as a ritual borrowed from the Germanic tribes. After 1933, the salute, used previously only among party members—became customary in normal public life. The regulations were very precise: straight right arm, with emphasis on the last word of *Heil Hitler!* When addressing Hitler himself, the stipulated greeting was, "Heil, mein Führer." At party rallies, the public cry was, "Sieg Heil" (salute victory), and the crowd was required to yell out *Heil!* The Hitler salute was regarded as compulsory when singing the national anthem, the anthems of allied armies, the Horst Wessel song, or the song "I Had a Comrade" when standing in front of Nazi, Wehrmacht, police, or Waffen SS banners. It was also required when visiting the graves and shrines of the National Socialist movement. Not saluting did not justify arrest, but the Gestapo was entitled to investigate anyone who did not salute at the required moment. The refusal to salute was therefore a small act of defiance.

Hitler's marketing men were divided into two groups—the mythmakers and the choreographers. The mythmakers reached back to the premodern world and tried to evoke tribal concepts— the Leader, the Community, the Empire. At the same time, they recruited modern ideas—the Nation, Technical Progress—and endowed them with emotional weight. The autobahn, for example, was firmly identified with the Führer and was regarded as an achievement on different symbolic levels, as a link between nature and civilization, rather than as a chunk of tar that could, one day, be put to use by car drivers. The mythmakers created a new calendar, new occasions of tribal celebration, and new cults. All, naturally, spun around the figure of the Führer. Mussolini had already understood the need for reinvention. "Every revolution creates new forms, new myths, and rites: one has to use old traditions and transform them....[W]e play the instrument on all chords—from violence to religion, from art to politics."[14]

Wilhelmine Germany had already mixed political and Protestant holidays and laid the foundation of merging Christian movements with a distinctly German populist element. The Nazis developed that calendar. The Nazis' celebratory year began on January 30 (Day of the Takeover of Power), through February 24 (Party Foundation Day), March (Hero Memorial Day), April 20 (Führer's Birthday), May Day (the traditional workers' holiday hijacked by the Nazis), Mothers' Day, the summer solstice, the November 9 harvest festival, and ended with the National Socialist People's Christmas.

The point was to erode and ultimately displace established religion and create instead a new set of values. The number of churchgoers had dropped steeply by the end of the 1930s, but Germans still felt the need to baptize babies, perform the marriage ceremony, and bury the dead under church auspices. The Nazis, however, gradually devalued the marriage ceremony and came up with their own death cult to compete with church funeral rites. Ten-year-olds were formally induced into Nazi youth organizations, fourteen-year-olds publicly "confirmed" their commitment to the Hitler Youth.

It was the SS that became the pioneer of the new ritualized Germany, and its leader, Heinrich Himmler, was the chief molder of myths in the Third Reich. Initially, the aim of dressing up the SS as a quasi-religious order was to distinguish itself from the plebeian SA—the black-uniformed elitists pitted against the brown-shirted street fighters. But it soon became more than a tactical device. Himmler introduced the Death's Head symbol, signet rings, and daggers of honor. "The masquerade of evil" was how the dissident priest Dietrich Bonhoeffer described the black-clad army. The cruelty of the SS was well known to Germans, yet its familiarity with death seemed to add to its attraction, a perverse style statement.

Aristocrats, dismissive of SA rabble-rousers, saw nothing wrong with taking a senior SS rank. By the end of the 1930s, between 10 and 20 percent of the SS officer corps were aristocrats. Some 30 percent of the SS leadership were university graduates (compared to 3 percent in the country as a whole). Lawyers and technocrats found a natural home in the ranks of the SS. Some were attracted to the practical career possibilities offered by the SS—Himmler had developed a shadow financial empire, picking up donations from big business, profiting from slave labor, looting the ghettos—but many also swallowed the idea of the SS as an anti-Christian religious order.

In Himmler's fantasy, the SS—or at least its leading officers—were a twentieth century variation of the German Teutonic knights. As in all ancient courts, there were tests of courage and of fighting prowess, rewards, and honors. Wewelsburg, the castle used by the Saxon kings, was a mystic gathering place for the SS. In the crypt, urns containing the ashes of SS generals (*obergruppenführer*) formed a "Reich of the Dead." The SS judged themselves according to a code of honor supervised by a special tribunal. After victory in the East and the West, the SS planned to set up fortified communities in the East and their own SS state in the West, in Burgundy. This constant process of reinvention was fueled by Himmler, who collected a ragbag of pagan and occult principles to persuade the SS men that they lived in an alternative world; they need feel no Christian guilt for their murdering since Christian values had been supplanted by an alternative spirituality.

History, too, had to be rewritten. Himmler became so obsessed with witchcraft that he looted 140,000 books on the subject from libraries across Europe and set up an SS unit to investigate and publicize the issue. When a Poznan librarian first stumbled on the witchcraft library in a baroque palace in Lower Silesia after the war, he noted that several books had been marked on pages where tortures were described. He assumed that Himmler had been studying torture techniques. But Himmler was in fact trying to prove that the persecution of witches in the seventeenth century represented a kind of holocaust of the German race carried out by the Catholic Church. "The witch-hunting cost the German people hundreds of thousands of mothers and women, cruelly tortured and executed," Himmler wrote. The SS teams were deployed to discover traces of an old Germanic culture that survived the witch-hunts.

The SS compiled a card index of 33,846 witch burnings in Germany and as far afield as India and Mexico in an attempt to prop up Himmler's thesis.

Himmler's interest in the occult may have begun with his marriage in 1928 to Margarethe Boden, a Prussian landowner's daughter who dabbled in homeopathy, mesmerism, and herbalism. At the time, he was a chicken farmer. Himmler believed that an ancestor named Passaquey had been burned as a witch. Reinhard Heydrich, head of the Reich Security Service, reported to his boss in 1939 that he had discovered the case of a witch called Margaret Himmbler burned in Germany in 1629. The similarity of names was enough to spur on Himmler and encourage a personal interest in rehabilitating German witches. The SS Amt [Agency] VII—concerned with churches, free masons, liberals, émigrés, and Marxists—was extended to include witches. The aim was to publish a series of short books highlighting individual German witches and glamorizing them.

In the meantime, however, the SS was obliged to work in secrecy, using university writing paper for its correspondence and pretending to be scholars. By April 1942, the witchcraft project had at least a dozen themes including "economic effects of witch trials" or "the intellectual foundation of the witch complex." Seminars sponsored by the SS earnestly discussed the biological implications for the German race of killing so many women.

Swinging Against Hitler

Fascist art, like fascist politics, deplores the imperfect, the irregular, and the improvised. Little wonder then that jazz was at the sharp end of opposition art in the Third Reich. Nazi propaganda attacked it as "Negro music," denounced its Americanisms and its lack of discipline, and waited for the population, suffering under Allied bombing, to turn against the "subversive" counterculture. But swing music flourished, though seemingly a revolt against fascist aesthetics, it was deeply political.

"Jewish and Negro" music was outlawed in Germany in 1933, but dance music remained popular even among the Nazi elite. At the 1937 foreign press ball in Berlin, both Göring and Goebbels danced with their wives to "The Organ-Grinders Song" played by the Jack Hylton band. German band leader Oskar Joost played at Goebbels' Olympics party at the Pfaueninsel on Berlin's Wannsee Lake.

The BBC transmission of dance music weakened Goebbels' use of the radio as a way of penetrating German households. And so the first priority was to Germanize swing. Karl "Charlie" Schwetler, who worked for the German foreign ministry, rewrote "You Are Driving Me Crazy" and other songs, setting them to anti-British lyrics. Charlie and his orchestra, having gained some popularity, were quickly countered by Allied propaganda: Glenn Miller and Johnny Desmond were soon singing anti-German versions of "Long Ago and Far Away."

Under Goebbels, the German entertainment business was allowed to make some concessions to popular taste, providing the culture dished out could be properly controlled by the authorities. He encouraged "German Jazz"—Peter Kreuter and Theo Mackeben—and opened up German radio. "We are not living in the Biedermeier epoch but in a century whose melody is determined by the hum of machines and the roar of motors...the radio must pay due attention to this fact....We feel bound to consider the justified demands of our fighting and working people." Louis Armstrong and Duke Ellington numbers were played, without giving their names.

But this was not enough for young Germans, many of whom were now on their way to the front. There was no stopping the rise of the "Swing Youth" (drawn, unlike the Edelweiss pirates, from the middle class). Some six hundred young people took part in the Swing Festival in Hamburg in February 1940. A report by Hitler Youth agents gave a critical account of the evening. "The dance music was all English and American. Only swing dancing and jitterbugging took place.

At the entrance to the halls stood a notice on which the words 'Swing Prohibited' had been altered to read 'Swing Requested.' The dances were an appalling sight. None of the couples danced normally. There was only swing of the worst sort. Sometimes, two boys danced with one girl; sometimes several couples formed a circle, linking arms and jumping, even rubbing the backs of their heads together. And then bent double, with the top of their body hanging loosely down, long hair flopping into the face, they dragged themselves around practically on their feet....Several boys could be observed dancing together, always with two cigarettes in their mouth, one in each corner."

The swing youth rejected the whole of the fascist aesthetic code. Anything that smacked of the orderly presence of the Hitler Youth or the Bund Deutsche Mädel was rejected. And this, in turn, became something of a political statement. The main form of dress consisted of long English sports jackets, shoes with light crepe soles, Anthony Eden hats, an umbrella on the arm, and a dress shirt, the button worn in the button-hole with a jewel stone. The girls had pencilled eyebrows, wore lipstick, and lacquered their nails. Nothing could be better calculated to upset the Nazis. Instead of shouting "Heil Hitler!" at each other, they said merely, "Good morning."

Goebbels lost the argument on jazz. There was no way that it could be tamed. In 1942, Himmler took charge. In a memorandum to his deputy Reinhard Heydrich, Himmler set out the appropriate punishments: "I am against half measures. All the ring leaders, and I mean ring leaders both male and female, and all teachers with enemy views who are encouraging swing in youth are to be assigned to a concentration camp. There, the youth should first be given thrashings and then put through severest punishment and set to work. I think that any sort of labor camp or youth camp would be inappropriate for these useless and worthless boys and girls.... The spell that these people should spend in a concentration camp must be a fairly long one, two to three years. It must be made clear that they will never be allowed to go back to their studies." The swing youth survived, however, as did Nazi propaganda against jazz. Even as late as the summer of 1944, several weeks after the D-day invasion, the party press was still attacking the "Jew Benny Goodman."

▦ ▦ ▦

The SS contributed to the mystification of German society, but it did not necessarily bring the SS closer to the person of Hitler. The Führer was at the center of many of the rituals—but that Führer could, it was implicitly recognized, have been someone other than Adolf Hitler. There is a distinction then to be made between the Führer cult and the Hitler cult.

For Goebbels—more of a choreographer than a mythmaker—there was never any doubt that only Hitler could be the Führer. It was Goebbels who professionalized the propaganda apparatus integrating all elements—building up the broadcasting medium, controlling and steering the press, sharpening the profile of Hitler, sometimes at the expense of the party. The party conferences illustrated how Hitler could be raised above the party and endowed with prophetic or quasi-divine status. The pseudo-religious symbolism, the torchlit marches, the fireworks, the Wagner, the military formations: Hitler actively cooperated in constructing the myth surrounding him. His love of fireworks was understood by Goebbels who integrated fire and pyromaniac displays into almost all major public performances.

Fire imagery, in turn, became a staple part of Hitler's rhetoric. Speer records how obsessed Hitler was with the element of fire. He became excited watching film footage of the firestorms in Warsaw or even the fire scenes in Richard Wagner's *Ring* cycle. Goebbels was a skeptic, a rationalist with an imaginative feel for the power of spectacle. His strength was to combine the technically experimental with the force of the irrational, to create a stage for Hitler. But at heart—if that is not too sensitive a word to apply to Goebbels—he believed in the persuasive image of technological progress. Spectacle could grab attention and focus it on one man; but spectacle was transitory in a way that engineering was not. That is why of all the Third Reich's seductive repertoire, the construction of the autobahn remained one of the most potent devices.

For years after the war, many Germans would admit that their love of Hitler was irrational, that they were held captive by black magic. In the midst of their self-defense, they would suddenly say: "and what about the autobahn?" The autobahn network built under Hitler was proof positive of a "good" National Socialism, of a forward-looking system that had non-evil goals. The autobahn created jobs and helped shape a motorized and, therefore, more modern and freer society.

The questioning generation that rose out of the 1968 student revolt refused to accept this line of argument. First, to praise the autobahn seemed, in some way, to diminish the horror of Auschwitz, as if there was a weighing scale with Hitler's achievements on the one side and Hitler's crimes on the other. National Socialism had to be judged as a whole. The autobahn was built with the army in mind. Fritz Todt, the Nazi engineer put in charge of road building, assumed that the autobahn would have to be capable of carrying 200,000 soldiers and their weaponry and 100,000 vehicles from the East to the western fronts in two nights. The autobahn thus had a sinister background.

Neither interpretation of the autobahn phenomenon—as a panacea for unemployment or a military asset—quite hit the mark. The autobahn was Hitler's pyramid. Third Reich propagandists compared the road network with gothic cathedrals, the Acropolis, or the Great Wall of China. It was part of the fascination of fascism that the state could—apparently responding to one man's will—embark on huge works of engineering. The scale may have been somewhat less than was claimed by the propaganda machine, but it was nonetheless gigantic. Six thousand engineers were employed, and at its peak, 250,000 people were engaged in the project, half of them building the bridges and digging the tunnels, the other half in the supply industries. The project began in 1933; by 1942, 3,800 kilometers were ready for traffic and another three thousand kilometers were under construction.

The chief point was not really to solve Germany's unemployment problem. Hitler never came near the goal of employing 600,000—10 percent of the unemployed in the early 1930s—and manpower shortages meant that labor camp prisoners, initially communists and socialists, were assigned to the quarries to dig out the necessary quantities of stone. The onset of the war diverted workers into the army and then into the building of the *Westwall*—the defensive line on the western frontier—and later still, the rebuilding of bombed bridges. Todt's initial brief, that it would be a road network that could speed thousands of troops across Germany, was never realized. The war against the Soviet Union saw a virtual end to autobahn construction. There were heavy losses of vehicles in the East and gasoline was tight. The railways became the military transport of choice.

The army naturally had an interest in the motorization of German society. The paramilitary National Social Military Vehicle Corps (NSKK) sponsored driving schools and car rallies. Graduates became the cadre of the motorized units of the Waffen SS. But the autobahn as such barely helped the military and did not transform Germans into a nation of car drivers. In 1938, every fifth American had a car. In Britain, one out of twenty-seven inhabitants owned a car, but in Germany the figure was one out of forty-four. Only after the postwar German economic recovery did the autobahn begin to make economic sense.

Hitler, however, was determined to make car drivers out of his people. The Volkswagen remained a dream for many, but the roads certainly became fuller. Hitler dropped the car tax and communicated some of his own love of fast cars to the Germans. Racing duels were staged on the autobahn between two top drivers, Rudolf Caracciola in a Mercedes-Benz and Bernd Rosenmeyer in an Autounion. "I am happy," said Hitler to his photographer Heinrich Hoffmann, "that I have managed to eliminate the German people's hostility to the car and their envy of car owners. That was only possible because I created the Volkswagen for the workers. Fortunately, the Bavarian state, by imprisoning me in Landsberg jail, gave me time to think about many problems and work out plans for the construction of the autobahn and the Volkswagen."[15]

In fact, detailed plans for the autobahn had already been drafted in the 1920s. They had not been realized, partly because of the financial burden of such a massive project, but also because of the complicated legal questions related to ownership of the land through which the autobahn had to pass. This was quickly resolved under Hitler: he issued a decree appropriating the land. Dictatorship allowed Germany to realize in a short time plans that would have taken many decades to implement under democracy.

This is precisely the seductiveness of a modernizing fascism: the sense of speed, of accelerated progress, the absence of long complaining debates about the allocation of resources. Soviet dictatorship demanded sacrifices from the present population in order to reward or benefit their children; this was known as the second generation compromise. Hitler was able to make things happen in months and years. This feeling of enablement affected all sections of society: the surgeons who could suddenly experiment directly on human beings made rapid progress in areas like cancer research. The motorization of German society was already a dream for designers like Ferdinand Porsche. National Socialism made it possible.

The practical aspects of the autobahn thus took second place to its aesthetic propaganda purpose. "The engineers, bridge builders, and architects involved in the construction of the autobahns, and the painters, photographers, and filmmakers who popularized it created together an extraordinary effective ideological message," says the British cultural historian Ian Boyd White. "It was a mythology for the new regime and the National Socialist revolution."[16]

The design of the autobahn was its message. A high-tech combination of steel and concrete and a minimalist design precession, were used. There was a preference for scenic routes with observation sites built at places with romantic views. Some of the aqueducts mimicked the Romans. Hitler admired the straight roads and ambitious civil engineering of Imperial Rome, a true model, he believed, for the look of his Thousand Years' Reich. Other modern design extended to the motorway gas stations with sloping flat roofs like the wings of an airplane. They were in the best tradition of the Neue Bauen of the 1920s.

The storage depots of the autobahn, meanwhile, were dressed up in German rustic style, easily mistaken, driving past in a fast car, for a medieval farmstead. This was the essence of reactionary modernism, sociologist Peter Reichel's term for Hitler's curious blend of the traditional German, an idealized reconstruction of the middle ages, and the truly new.[17] The autobahn could, had Hitler not embarked on war, have transformed the nature of National Socialism. Instead, they produced an image of change rather than a reality. Even the justification of the immense expense (not to mention the loss of life in the backbreaking work) was resolutely old-fashioned: that Germans were to be brought in touch again with the beauty of their landscape.

The real logic of the autobahn was that Hitler needed to demonstrate that technology could overcome nature, the physical world could be changed by an act of will. Germans began to understand the connection between political mastery and technological mastery. Nazi rule coincided with technical innovation and this became a key component of Hitler's seductive armory. Hitler brought science to the people, seemed to make it less elitist. And so, in a strange way, the consumer interest in the new refrigerators, vacuum cleaners, and washing machines added to Hitler's popularity. So, too, did modern advertising: the commercials for Coca-Cola were a source of excitement, and Coca-Cola sales were strong.

The popularity of the new media, including the radio and the huge number of moviegoers (never matched in the postwar years) gave a sense of impetus, a buzz to the Third Reich. The Hitler Youth constructed model airplanes; motorbike rallies were an important factor in attracting support for the SA brownshirts. The appeal of the autobahn, for young men at least, was in the technical challenge of moving so much earth. New machines had to be invented. Engineers, as in the Soviet system, were the new heroes. The Germans were being offered a perfectly planned environment, a world free of doubt and the incalculable.

The autobahn engineers had an equivalent in the form of social engineers who attempted "scientifically" to create a perfect race-based society. The struggle for technical perfection permeates the memoirs of Nazi grandees—Albert Speer's architectural plans, for example, to construct a conference hall in Berlin several times larger than St. Peter's cathedral in Rome. Had they been realized, these plans would have involved flattening hundreds of streets, thousands of apartment houses. Decades after the war, Speer still managed to talk with pride of his achievements in boosting arms production. He was given a technical problem and, in his own words, solved it.

It was in the same spirit that the Holocaust was planned. How to transport so many millions to the East? How to construct so many camps? How to kill them in the most cost-effective way? This was government by technocrats for technocrats. Insofar as the great technical feats succeeded, there was approval from the Germans. The chaos of Weimar had been replaced by a kind of order. That this order was illusory, that chaos lapped at the doorstep, became clear only gradually. It becomes difficult to sustain the picture of a technically complete world if one is confronted by the everyday reality of shortages and rumors of corruption and incompetence at the top. And so Germans allowed themselves to believe in a Führer separate and above his cronies, a Superman who could keep intact the early vision of a world safe and pure for Germans.

Chapter Six

From Boardroom to Birkenau

"The failure of most German firms to exploit handlungsspiel-raum—*freedom of action—to the betterment of their charges evinces an absence of humanitarianism that, if not sufficient to perpetrate mass murder, was exactly suited to allowing it to continue."*
— *Excerpt from* Extermination Through Work: Jewish Slave Labor Under the Third Reich, *published in 1999 by the Holocaust Education Trust*

"Behind the SS thugs who were beating us were the men who ran the companies, who wore smart double-breasted suits, looked like nice gentlemen, and went home to their families every evening. They were the ones making the decisions."
— *Rudy Kennedy, former slave laborer for IG Farben at Auschwitz*

Recent historical research into slave labor in concentration camps and factories—often by official German company historians—has thoroughly documented how the interests of the Nazi state, industry, and big business fused into an unprecedented synthesis of profit and institutionalized murder. Companies with household names, such as Volkswagen horrifically exploited Polish and Soviet slave laborers—many of them female—forcing them to toil in cruel and inhumane conditions. Nazi ideology regarded Slavs, as well as Jews, as *untermenschen*, or subhumans, who could be worked to death. The women's children, though, were too young to work and were regarded as a useless burden. Instead, they were incarcerated in a company home where they were allowed to die of neglect, illness, and starvation. Volkswagen was not unique. In 1944, at another such children's home, near Helmstedt, the death rate was 96 percent.

But the marriage of convenience between industry and Hitler, between the company balance sheet and Nazi racial imperatives, had not always progressed so smoothly. Before 1933, there was considerable apprehension among many German industrialists about the Nazis. Many of the Ruhr barons, the heads of Germany industry, were at first extremely unenthusiastic about the National Socialist German Workers' Party (NSDAP), the Nazi party's full name. After all, the party name included the word "Socialist." The industrialists' greatest nightmare was a takeover by the increasingly powerful German Communist Party, but there was also some trepidation about how big business would survive Hitler. Many Nazi leaders, especially among the brownshirts of the *Sturmabteilung* (SA), proclaimed their hostility to both capitalism and big business, whether Jewish-owned or not. In the economic chaos of the Weimar Republic, where inflation and unemployment reduced so many families to poverty, this emphasis on workers' welfare brought them many recruits, although not among the boardrooms. It was unclear exactly what the Nazi party's economic policies were. This Hitler had intended. He avoided concrete details to draw as much support as possible from across society.

By the early 1930s, Hitler began to smell power. He knew that he needed the active support of German industry both to run a successful economy and to finance the Nazi rearmament drive. Between launching the "Red-Brown" revolution of Socialist-Nationalism and bringing the Ruhr barons on board, the choice was straightforward. Left-wing ideology was dumped for practicality. Socialist-leaning Nazis were later dealt with by classic SS methods. (National) socialist rhetoric gave way to capitalist reality, and Hitler launched a drive to gain the support of Germany's industrialists.

He moved fast against his former leftist allies, such as the Strasser brothers, Otto and Gregor, who called for a socialist revolution to follow the national one. Expelled from the Nazi party, Otto Strasser formed his own splinter group, attacked Hitler as "the betrayer of the revolution," and moved to Prague, then Canada. His brother was less fortunate. Resigning his party leadership post in December 1932, Gregor Strasser never returned to politics, but politics returned to him. Arrested during the Blood Purge of June 1934, he was shot dead through the window of his prison cell.

It was the Blood Purge, also known as the Night of the Long Knives, that sent a signal to companies such as Thyssen and Krupp that the Nazi regime would do nothing to disturb their economic power. There would be no more demands for nationalizations from demonstrating brownshirts or troublesome trade unions calling strikes. In fact, there would be no more trade unions. Just as Stalin had his former revolutionary colleagues, such as Bukharin and Zinoviev, purged and shot to remove any threats to his authority, so Hitler disposed of his left-wing former allies, including his old friend and comrade Ernst Röhm. Like Gregor Strasser, Ernst Röhm was arrested by the SS and was shot dead in his prison cell. A revolver had been left in Röhm's cell to allow him to take the "honorable" way out and commit suicide, but he refused. At least seventy-seven leading SA officers were killed in the Blood Purge as well as others deemed inconvenient by the Nazi leadership, such as the retired General Kurt von Schleicher, the last chancellor of the Weimar Republic. Curiously, considering that homosexuality in the Third Reich was punished by a spell in a concentration camp, a strong homoerotic current ran through the SA leadership. Edmund Heines, an SA general and close associate of Röhm, was arrested in bed with his young chauffeur. Both were shot dead by the SS.

With the SA leadership killed, and the left wing of the Nazi party destroyed, the real symbiosis between business and industry and the Nazis could commence. The Ruhr barons soon realized that the question was less how to survive Hitler than how to extract maximum profits from the Nazi regime.

The groundwork had been laid when, in January 1932, the German steel magnate Fritz Thyssen invited Hitler to address the *Industrieklub* (Industry Club) in Dusseldorf. The audience, of industrialists and businessmen, was nervous of any radicalism of the right or left, fearing social unrest; confidence in the government had virtually collapsed as the economy approached meltdown. By then, unemployment reached six million, over 30 percent of the workforce. The stock market plummeted while state expenditures skyrocketed, as the bill for welfare grew ever higher, demanding ever higher taxes.

As a consummate orator, Hitler knew how to play to his audience. He adopted his customary didactic tone, but refrained from attacking the Jews, not even uttering the word "Jew" once. The anti-Semitism that roused the rabble on the streets did not play very well among the country's educated businessmen. Hitler called for a strong state and a mighty German nation, to be united through its national will. He defended private property, attacked communism, and proclaimed that, in a world where individuals' abilities varied, there could never be equal rewards for all. All welcome words for those assembled. The alliance between the German economic elite and the Nazis, that would reshape the country according to Hitler's plans, was being forged.

Middle and senior managers were well represented at Dusseldorf, but many of Germany's most senior industrial leaders, such as Gustav Krupp von Bohlen und Halbach and Carl Bosch of the chemical conglomerate IG Farben, were pointedly absent. A former diplomat, head of the leading armaments firm in Europe, Gustav Krupp was chairman of the Association of German Industry and was known as the "king of the munitions makers." He was also a "violent opponent" of the Nazis, according to his fellow industrialist Fritz Thyssen, and even warned President von Hindenburg against appointing Hitler as Chancellor. Thyssen was soon to alter his description of Krupp, less than a month later reporting that he had become a "super Nazi." The turnaround came at a meeting on February 20, 1933, at Hermann Göring's home, at a gathering hosted by Reichsbank President Hjalmar Schacht. There, a select audience of leading industrialists heard Hitler and Göring promise to eliminate not just Marxism, but also disarmament controls, and to delay any further elections, "probably even for the next hundred years." After years of economic and political chaos of the Weimar Republic, these were welcome pledges.

As Germany's leading arms manufacturer, Gustav Krupp was particularly pleased to hear Hitler's promise to restore the Wehrmacht. In May 1933, he was appointed chairman of the Adolf Hitler Spende in Berlin, an industrialists' fund administered by Martin Bormann. In exchange for generous contributions, industrialists received special consideration while government economic policies were drafted and implemented; it was generally regarded as money well spent. The Krupp family gave over ten million marks a year to Hitler and the Nazi party, as well as substantial amounts to the "Circle of Friends of Heinrich Himmler," which financed much of the SS. This sinister group of industrialists also helped finance the 1933 election campaign. In return, members were made privy to some of the Third Reich's darker secrets. Himmler took his supporters on a tour of the Dachau concentration camp; during the war, the SS intelligence chief Otto Ohlendorf lectured them on the operations of the *Einsatzgruppen*, the SS killing squads in eastern Europe.

So Krupp and Thyssen were on board, but Hitler still needed IG Farben, Germany's most powerful industrial cartel. Without IG Farben, Germany would have been unable to wage aggressive war. Fuel for tanks and airplanes, chemicals for explosives in shells and grenades, synthetic rubber for vehicle tires—the nuts and bolts of the German war machine—were all supplied by IG Farben. As a postwar U.S. report stated: "Without IG's immense productive facilities, its far-reaching research, varied technical experience, and overall concentration of economic power, Germany would not have been in a position to start its aggressive war in September 1939." IG Farben both regulated national chemical production

and controlled the international chemicals trade, squashing competition through a series of price-control agreements: a monopoly
by any other name. IG Farben controlled five hundred firms in
ninety-two countries, and its cartel agreement partners included
Britain's Imperial Chemical Industries and Standard Oil of New
Jersey. As the war progressed, IG's interests included poison gases
such as Tabun, Sarin, and Zyklon B, used in the gas chambers of
the camps.

IG was represented at the February 20 meeting by Baron
Georg von Schnitzler, a member of its managing board and known
as "IG's salesman" for his ability to present IG's terms in negotiations. Like their fellow industrial barons, IG Farben's leaders had
been shaken by the November 1932 Reichstag elections, when the
Nazis lost thirty-four seats, reducing their members to 196, while
the Communists gained eleven, bringing them up to one hundred.
The threat of a Marxist takeover seemed ever nearer. Following
the elections, several dozen powerful figures from German industry
and finance had come to Hitler's support, including Reichsbank
President Hjalmar Schacht and steel magnate Fritz Thyssen. IG
hedged its bets and then stayed silent. But at the February 20 gathering, Baron von Schnitzler pledged 400,000 marks, the largest
single contribution from German industry to the Nazi coffers.

IG Farben's head Carl Bosch was now an official supporter of
Hitler and the Nazi party. Or was he? Certainly, IG's donation was
well used. At the March 1933 elections, the Nazis won more than
17 million votes, enough to chase away the specter of communism.
The votes still did not give the Nazis an overall majority in the
Reichstag, but they were enough to maintain Hitler as chancellor
in a coalition government. It was time for IG Farben and the Nazis
to parley, but Carl Bosch had some demands of his own.

Born in 1874, Carl Bosch was the nephew of Robert Bosch, of
the Bosch electrical engineering and manufacturing concern. An
extremely gifted scientist, he was joint winner of the 1931 Nobel
Prize for chemistry and was chairman of the IG Farben board.

Under Bosch, IG Farben had set up a plant to synthesize gasoline from coal. He believed that it was vital for the future of IG that this project continue, so that Germany could be self-sufficient in fuel; the project needed support from the government, even if it was a Nazi one. Hitler also believed that it was vital for Germany, if it was to be able to wage war on its neighbors, to be self-sufficient in oil and gasoline. There could be no militarized Third Reich without IG Farben's cooperation and no future for IG unless its leadership came to an accommodation with the Nazis.

Caught between his feelings as a patriotic German and his distaste for the Nazis, Bosch made contradictory gestures. He authorized the massive donation to Hitler's party at the February 1933 Reichstag Palace meeting, but he was a vocal anti-Nazi, who was prepared to risk the wrath of the Gestapo for his principles. He compartmentalized his own feelings: as a good German, he supported his country's need for guaranteed fuel supplies. As a good human being, he did what he could against the Nazis. But as the Third Reich became more entrenched and his fellow executives became more and more pro-Nazi, his power in the boardroom steadily lessened. A decade after Hitler took power, IG Farben's directors had no qualms about running their own concentration camp using slave labor, but that mutual accommodation demanded enough time to travel down the dark but profitable path of compromise and moral corruption.

The concept of *autarkie*—self-sufficiency—wherever possible, was a bastion of Nazi economic policy. Hitler believed that Germany should strive for autarchy, both as a means of reducing dependence on foreign supplies and as an affirmation of national will. Autarchy was economic gibberish, but to strive for it made some strategic sense militarily. Hitler firmly believed that the British blockade in World War I had been a decisive factor in Germany's defeat. Hearing the reports back from his officials about Hitler's scientific knowledge and enthusiasm, Carl Bosch remarked, "The man is more sensible than I thought."

Bosch changed his mind after the March 1933 election when he met Hitler for the first time. The Führer and the chemist could agree that the Third Reich must be self-sufficient in gasoline. Carl Bosch then moved onto the question of Germany's Jewish scientists. If they were all forced to leave, then physics and chemistry would be set back a hundred years, he said. Hitler's reply was to shout that Germany would work for a hundred years without physics or chemistry. When Bosch tried to press the matter, Hitler left the room. So furious was he that he would never again occupy the same room as Carl Bosch.

Carl Bosch differed from many of his peers in the scientific world, who either supported the Nazis or buckled at the first sign of pressure. When he learned that his colleague, the eminent Jewish-born scientist Fritz Haber had been forced to resign from his position at Berlin University, even though he had converted to Christianity, Bosch attempted to rally support for Haber among Nobel prize winners. The physicist Max Planck asked Hitler to reverse his decision and received a stream of abuse. Another declined to help, saying: "We cannot draw our swords for the Jews." Haber left Germany and died in Basel, Switzerland, in January 1934. He was a broken man. Even as IG Farben cemented its role in the Nazi economy, Bosch carried on his defense of his Jewish colleagues. A year after Haber's death, Carl Bosch organized a memorial service for him. He invited government officials who had known Haber, IG officials, and other well-known scientists and teachers. The Nazis were furious. The minister of education forbade his officials to attend, describing the event as a "challenge to the National Socialist state." Nonetheless, more than five hundred people attended Bosch's service.

The Third Reich survived the challenge of Haber's memorial service, but the Nazi minister was more right than he knew. Bosch's subsequent support of Jewish scientists illustrates how there was room for maneuver against the Nazi hierarchy among Germany's top industrialists. The higher the rank, the more the rules could be broken. Friends and colleagues could be aided, sometimes even publicly, and the system was not a monolith of terror, especially in the early years before society became completely Nazified. Bosch's position as head of an industrial conglomerate, without which the German war machine—if not the German economy—simply could not function, protected him. Bosch had committed IG Farben to support the Nazis, even donating substantial amounts of money. But he himself walked a tightrope between realpolitik and morality. Like many of those who tried to say "no" to the Third Reich, such as the businessman Oskar Schindler, Bosch was full of contradictions. Believing that Hitler was the lesser of two evils, he donated IG's funds to the Nazis to prevent a Communist takeover that would have spelled the end of the chemicals giant. But when he realized that the Nazis were the greater evil, he still took a moral stand, at great personal cost.

Bosch was not the only German industrialist to view with growing horror the Frankenstein's monster they had helped create. Fritz Thyssen was one of Hitler's earliest backers, but by the mid-1930s was turning against the man he helped bring to power. Heir to the enormous Thyssen steel fortune, Thyssen donated over a million marks to Hitler, starting with a gift of a hundred thousand gold marks in 1923. Thyssen was an autocratic capitalist and fervent nationalist who saw Hitler as the savior of a reborn German nation. He joined the Nazi party in 1931, and he had invited Hitler to give the speech to the Düsseldorf industrialists that smoothed the way for big business to finance the Nazis. "I am firmly convinced that he [Hitler] is the only man who can and will rescue Germany from ruin and disgrace," he proclaimed. After the Nazis took power, Thyssen was picked to direct an economic institute that studied the corporate state, the planned-for fusion of the economy, and the German national will.

But the reality of life—and death—in the Third Reich shocked Thyssen. The Gestapo, the terror, and the concentration camps were not part of his vision of a stable, regulated society for which he had donated so much of his fortune. Even though Nazi Germany's rearmament drive was producing healthy balance sheets for the family steel empire, Fritz Thyssen was increasingly dismayed at the regime's increasing persecution of the Jews and its anti-Catholicism. In 1938, he resigned from the Prussian state council in protest against the Nazi persecution of the Jews. The following year, he denounced Dr. Robert Ley, head of the state-run German Labor Front that had replaced independent trade unions, as a "stammering drunkard." He protested in the Reichstag against the future war he saw was coming, and was horrified by the events of *Kristallnacht*, the anti-Jewish pogrom of November 9, 1938, that saw synagogues burned and Jewish businesses destroyed all over Germany. By December 1939, Fritz Thyssen was living in exile in Switzerland.

From there he wrote to Hitler, detailing the anguish of a patriot in pain over the fate of his country. With hindsight and our present-day knowledge of World War II and the Holocaust, it is easy to dismiss his testimony as the ramblings of someone who should have known better, but Thyssen's missive gives an insightful view of how the German business elite was seduced by Hitler, believing that he would be the best bulwark against the communism that seemed, before 1933, to threaten the interests of industry and finance:

> My conscience is clear. I feel free of any guilt. My sole error was that I believed in you, Adolf Hitler, the Führer, and the movement you led. Since 1923, I have made the heaviest sacrifices for the National Socialist movement. I solicited membership for the Party and fought for it, without ever wishing or asking anything for myself. I was always inspired by the hope that our endeavors would rescue our unfortunate German people....
>
> In the course of time, however, a disastrous change took place. At an early stage, I felt it necessary to voice my protest against the persecution of Christianity, against the brutalization of its priests, against the desecration of its churches.

When on November 9, 1938, the Jews were robbed and tortured in the most cowardly and most brutal manner, and their synagogues destroyed all over Germany, I protested once more. As an outward expression of my repugnance, I resigned my position of State Councilor. All my protests obtained no reply and no remedy.[1]

Nor did Hitler reply to this letter. Instead, Thyssen's property was confiscated and nationalized. He was stripped of his German citizenship. On a visit to France, he was arrested by the Vichy police and handed over to Germany, where he was imprisoned for the duration of the war.

Hjalmar Schacht — Hitler's Banker

As Reichsbank President and Nazi Economics Minister, Hjalmar Schacht used his grasp of finance and world trade to work an economic miracle. He stopped runaway inflation, stabilized the German economy, and so provided Hitler with the basis to wage war. One of the world's foremost international bankers, the tall, urbane, and patrician Schacht was ready to enter a Faustian pact with the Nazis as a means of rebuilding Germany and preventing a Communist takeover. "I desire a great and strong Germany, and to achieve it, I would enter an alliance with the devil," he once declared. And so he did.

Schacht was instrumental in bringing the titans of German industry into the Nazi orbit and recommended that firms such as IG Farben and Krupp support Hitler during the 1932 and 1933 elections to halt the march of the left. Schacht accepted the post of Head of the War Economy in May 1935, arranging the necessary finance for the reconstruction of the Wehrmacht. He was also the first commissioner of the Four Year Plan, the Nazi economic program.

But the autocratic Reichsbank president came into increasing conflict with the Nazi leaders over both economic policy and the increasing attacks on the Jews, attacks he regarded as financially unhelpful as well as morally unpleasant. Hitler had a curious affection for his economic wizard, even telling him so on occasion, and he allowed Schacht a freedom to speak his mind denied to others, which Schacht exploited as long as he could. Schacht was not personally particularly anti-Semitic and had several close Jewish friends, whom he helped, such as Bella Fromm, a society newspaper columnist. But like many in the German elite, Schacht had a disdain for the large number of Jews in the arts.

Nonetheless, Schacht launched a blistering public attack on the Third Reich's policies at the August 1935 trade fair in Königsberg in east Prussia (now Kaliningrad in Russia). Here Schacht reiterated the points of a memo he had sent to Hitler in May. In it, he had criticized Nazi attacks on the church and the Jews, and the excesses of the Gestapo. Schacht even berated those who "smear anti-Semitic slogans onto store windows by night and treat Germans who work for Jewish companies as traitors." A memo was a private matter, but a public speech attacking Nazi policy, broadcasted live on German state radio, was upping the stakes. Propaganda minister Jozef Goebbels was livid, but Schacht pressed home his points by having 250,000 copies of his speech printed by the Reichstag press. Hitler's response was mild, barely mentioning the incident at their next meeting.

At the 1938 Reichsbank Christmas party, one month after the *Kristallnacht* pogrom, Schacht went further, telling his audience: "The burning of Jewish synagogues, the destruction and looting of Jewish businesses, the ill treatment of Jewish citizens was so disgraceful that every decent German must blush with shame." As Schacht must have himself. Not enough to resign from the cabinet completely—although he stood down as Economics Minister in 1937, he remained as minister without portfolio until 1943—but enough to try, in January 1939, to negotiate the Schacht Plan to help save German Jewry. The plan died when Schacht was sacked in the same month from his post as Reichsbank president.

Like IG Farben's Carl Bosch, Schacht did not believe that by the summer of 1939, Germany was economically ready for a lengthy war. During the 1940s, he deepened his contacts with resistance circles, but remained ambiguous about any serious commitment to removing Hitler or replacing the government. Schacht's associations were enough to ensure his eventual arrest, and he was sent to Ravensbruck, Flossenburg, and Dachau concentration camps. Liberated by American troops in 1945, he was charged at Nuremberg the following year with preparing Germany for war. In court, he retained his arrogant disdain, continually proclaiming his innocence and protesting: "I do not understand at all why I have been accused." Once, when film of the concentration camps was shown in the courtroom, he turned his back. Found guilty at first, in November 1950, he was cleared of all charges connected with his involvement in Nazi Germany. In the summer of 1938, Schacht once said to a dining companion who wondered at his involvement with the Nazis: "Madam, how could I have known that we have fallen into the hands of criminals," but if anyone should have, it was the man who made possible the financing of the Third Reich's war machine.

※ ※ ※

Fritz Thyssen and Carl Bosch were the exceptions. Bosch's position as both a critic of the Nazis and head of IG became increasingly untenable. In 1935, he was replaced as chairman of the managing board by Hermann Schmitz, whom Bosch had recruited at the end of World War I. IG's new boss was such a keen supporter of Hitler that he was an honorary Nazi deputy in the Reichstag. Schmitz operated at the highest levels of the Nazi political and economic elite, but came from an impoverished background. Secretive and distrustful, possessed of an outstanding business brain, he was not popular among his more patrician colleagues, who regarded him as a working-class parvenu. He kept tight personal control over IG's business empire, running the company like his own personal fiefdom, placing his supporters at all levels in both Germany and its foreign outposts. "Most of his peers regarded Schmitz with distaste coupled with fear. But none questioned his skill at corporate legerdemain or his curious practice of keeping the most complicated financial transactions and involved financial details in his head without committing them to paper," records historian Joseph Borkin in *The Crime and Punishment of IG Farben*.[2]

It's a grim historical irony that, before 1933, IG was regularly attacked and pilloried in the Nazi press for both its global reach and power in the marketplace and its large number of Jewish officials. It was initially classified by the Nazis as a "non-Aryan" firm. For the Nazis, IG Farben was better depicted as "Isidore G. Farber," a sarcastic pun on supposedly Jewish names, "IG Moloch," the Canaanite god to whom children were sacrificed, or more directly "an instrument of international finance capital," working against the interests of Aryan Germany. But years of being pilloried in the Nazi press as a tool of Jewish capitalists ultimately did little to delay the mutual embrace between IG Farben and the Third Reich. In September 1936, Hitler announced the Four Year Plan at the annual Nazi party rally at Nuremberg. The Four Year Plan (one year shorter than Stalin's) called for Germany to become economically self-sufficient and the interests of the state and industry to be fused. Welcomed by Schmitz, the plan would bind IG even tighter to the Third Reich as the leading producer of chemicals. By 1937, IG Farben company was totally Nazified. All Jewish officials were removed.

But even then, Bosch was still prepared to speak his mind, a trait that had been noticed among leaders of the military as well as the economic elite. Hitler's secret directive to the Wehrmacht to prepare for an attack on Czechoslovakia by October 1, 1938, had not been universally welcomed by the army's leading officers who feared that the country was not ready for such a move, which could trigger intervention by Western powers and drag Germany into a continent-wide war. Generals Walther von Brauchitsch (commander-in-chief of the armed forces) and army chief General Ludwig von Beck asked Bosch if Germany was ready for war. No, he replied, industry was not running at a high enough capacity, and war was impractical at this stage.

The Generals asked Bosch to relay this message to the leaders of the Third Reich. Bosch decided to try to meet Hermann Göring, Hitler's number two, but Göring refused to see him. Bosch slid into a deep depression. With war spreading across Europe, he took to drink, believing that his achievements as a patriotic scientist had been perverted into instruments of death and destruction. In February 1940, he moved to Sicily, taking with him an ant colony for company. But a change of scene could not shift his deep malaise, and he worsened. In April, he returned to Germany, predicting that Hitler's policies would ultimately destroy both Germany and IG Farben. On April 26, 1940, Carl Bosch died.

By 1940, where the Wehrmacht went, IG followed. At the time of the March 1938 Anschluss, when Germany annexed Austria, the IG board presented a memo to the government entitled "New Order for the Greater Chemical Industry of Austria," outlining their takeover plans, arguing that IG's continued expansion would aid the Nazis' Four Year Plan for the economy. As Czechoslovakia was subsumed into the Reich, IG planned to take over Aussiger Verein, the country's largest chemical company. When, after the Munich Agreement, the Nazis occupied the Sudetenland, Hermann Schmitz, by then head of IG, offered the new rulers a donation of RM500,000 "for your disposal in Sudetenland." War, and the threat of it, was already proving a good business for IG. In 1933, IG donated RM3.5 million ($1.4 million) to the Nazi party, with annual net profits at RM74 million ($29.6 million). In 1939, IG donated RM7.5 million ($3 million). Net profits stood at RM240 million ($96 million).

When the Nazis invaded Poland in September 1939, IG's salesman, Baron Georg von Schnitzler, was right behind the troops, carrying IG's wish list, entitled "The Most Important Chemical Plants in Poland," with him. He telegraphed IG's office in Berlin that "The [Polish] factories contain considerable and valuable stocks of preliminary, intermediate, and final products...we consider it of primary importance that the above-mentioned stocks be used by experts in the interests of the German national economy. Only the IG is in a position to make experts available."[3] By the summer of 1940, IG Farben, like Hitler, had plans for world domination. Written plans spelled out how the chemical industries of France, Norway, Holland, Denmark, Luxembourg, Belgium, the Soviet Union, England, and even Switzerland and Italy would be taken over. IG would run a "Chemical Reich," as murderous and greedy as the Third Reich itself.

The capital of the chemical Reich was the vast complex of sites at Auschwitz. There, IG ran its Buna (synthetic rubber) and fuel plant at the satellite camp of Monowitz. IG Farben's officials wore shirts and ties instead of SS uniforms, but they were killers nonetheless. Monowitz was also known as Auschwitz III. The original site of Auschwitz, a Hapsburg military barracks, had opened in 1940. But as the Holocaust speeded up, the gas chambers and crematoria were unable to cope with the hundreds of thousands of Jews being killed.

A second camp, Auschwitz II, was constructed at nearby Birkenau. When IG's slave laborers could work no longer or were *verbraucht* (meaning spent, or used up), in the Nazis' chilling term, they were moved to Birkenau. There they were gassed by Zyklon B, the patent of which was owned by IG Farben. IG was also part owner of the Hamburg-based German Company for Pest Control, Degesch, that manufactured the gas.

Monowitz, known as "IG Auschwitz" in internal company documents, was so massive that it used as much electricity as a German city. Approximately 30,000 slave laborers were worked to death there. Monowitz belonged to IG, but it was fully equipped to Nazi specifications. Encircled by electrified barbed wire, it included refinements such as a special cell, constructed so that prisoners could neither stand properly upright, lie down, or kneel. The gallows usually had several bodies hanging from its beam.

How did it happen, that a company once full of Jewish scientists and directors, formerly headed by an anti-Nazi, could become an integral part of the Holocaust itself? For Hermann Schmitz and his colleagues were not fanatical eliminationist anti-Semites, determined to rid the world of its Jews. They were not SS officers supervising massacres on the eastern front, but businessmen, concerned with profits. They moved in the highest circles of Berlin's social and economic elite. Such men were pillars of German society, educated and cultured, little moved by Hitler's hysterical rantings.

We have already noted Hitler's approach, and careful vocabulary, at the Dusseldorf *Industrieklub* in 1932. There, in his key speech to the leaders of German business, he never once said the word "Jew." Indeed, IG's officials had Jewish friends themselves, Jewish colleagues. When twenty-four IG board members were tried at Nuremberg after the war, Jewish former employees and their relatives submitted detailed affidavits in their defense, detailing their attempts to help Jews. Carl von Weinburg recorded how Schmitz had bribed a Nazi official so that his brother, Arthur von Weinburg, would not have to wear a yellow star. When Arthur von Weinburg was sent to Theresienstadt, Schmitz intervened with Himmler himself to try and obtain his release, albeit without success. Carl von Weinburg fled to Italy where it was arranged that an IG subsidiary would pay him his pension all through the war.

In one sense, the Nazification of German industry followed a similar tactical pattern to postwar Communist takeovers. One step of corruption and compromise led to another. In Hungary, the party leader Matyas Rakosi perfected the notion of the stealth takeover. The Communists would never declare their ultimate aim of bringing the country within the Soviet orbit. Instead, Rakosi steadily removed slices of the government's power and autonomy, taking over a ministry one month, an important municipality in another. Within a few years, Budapest was a most loyal satellite of Moscow.

Hitler used similar tactics to bring German industry on board. Within a decade of the 1933 Nazi takeover, IG was not only profiting from the Holocaust, it was helping to organize it. Had Hitler in 1933 told the board of IG Farben that, within a few years, he would build a continent-wide economic empire based on plunder, murder, and slavery, with IG as a central pillar, Carl Bosch and his colleagues would have looked on aghast.

Yet industry and IG did not oppose the 1935 Nuremberg race laws. From that, they progressed to acquiescence over the *Kristallnacht* pogrom in 1938 and the Aryanization of Jewish business from which German business profited so handsomely. By 1940, IG was fully locked into the Nazi war machine, formulating its own demands to takeover national chemical industries in the newly occupied countries. By the mid-1940s, the establishment of Monowitz was merely the latest stage in a decade-long process of moral corruption, indeed, total moral collapse.

At the same time, IG and their fellow industrialists compartmentalized their own human feelings and IG's business interests. In Schmitz and his colleague's personal microcosms, there was room to take moral decisions to try and aid Jewish colleagues. We have already seen how Carl Bosch tried to aid and protect Jewish scientists, even as he supported Hitler's plans for German self-sufficiency in fuel. But within the framework of the interests of the company, of IG's profits and increasing economic dominance, such humanitarian considerations simply did not apply. As Nazi ideals and values became more entrenched within the Third Reich, and IG's interests more enmeshed in its policies, the interests of state and company fused. A moral deficit, a humanity deficiency, call it what you will, but the slave laborers at Monowitz were simply not seen as human beings, merely factors on a balance sheet. Indeed, they were referred to as "units."

This process of dehumanization was, of course, greatly fueled by anti-Semitism and the Third Reich's systematic degradation of Jews. But while anti-Semitism was a primary factor in the exploitation of slave labor, it was not the only one. Not all slave laborers at the camps and factories run by German industry were Jews. Many were Slavs, brought in from Nazi-occupied Poland and the Soviet Union. Others were drafted from western Europe. German industry systematically chose to profit from all of this human misery.

Nazism's racial policies offered industry, like other sectors of the *volksgemeinschaft*, the chance to realize its darkest ambitions, untrammeled by normal human constraints. Industry's concern was primarily profit. Nazi ideology dovetailed smoothly with its economic aims. The Nazis granted German industry and business a chance to maximize their profits without having to operate within the usual human constraints of reasonable work hours or to incur labor costs, such as salaries and paid holidays. Workers, whether Jewish or Slavs, could simply be worked to death—or near-death, when they would be killed, before being replaced from a seemingly endless supply of humanity. And German industry eagerly set its slaves to work. Until they died.

It remains difficult to bridge the comprehension gap preventing our full understanding of how something like Monowitz—run to benefit not SS officers, but businessmen—could exist. The 1999 Holocaust Education Trust report, *Extermination Through Work: Jewish Slave Labor Under the Third Reich*, notes that:

> Accounting fully for the overriding callousness of the industrial usage of slave and forced labor is extremely difficult. The evidence suggests that we should look to economic considerations, albeit in an environment of moral tunnel vision created over years of collusion with the Nazi regime. Profit, efficiency,

self-preservation, and long-term survival planning were con-
ceived in terms of instrumental rationality—that is, irrespective of the human cost.[4]

The report also notes that, at many factory sites, there were
far more civilian workers than SS officers, thus increasing the
opportunities to aid the slave laborers with extra food or medical help. But few employees of the companies using slave labor
helped when they could. Instead, the German civilian workers denounced the slave laborers for not working hard enough.
"Despite the influence of the SS *kommandoführer* (work leader),
it was not necessary for civilian workers and foremen to report
supposedly recalcitrant slaves to them for punishment—yet
many German employees did. The SS may have set the tone of
slave labor exploitation, but they found malleable accomplices
in German industry."[5] Ultimately, the road from boardroom to
Birkenau proved surprisingly easy to travel.

What all this horror actually meant in human terms is shown
in Rudy Kennedy's story. Kennedy, who was a slave laborer for IG
Farben, arrived at Auschwitz in March 1943 when he was fourteen.
Born into a family of patriotic German Jews, Kennedy had grown
up in the town of Rosenberg, now Olesno in Poland. His grandfa-
ther had been wounded in France in World War I, fighting in the
Kaiser's army. But like all German Jews, the Kennedys found their
patriotism counted for nothing after the Nazis came to power. The
family was expelled from Rosenberg, and the local newspaper published a story proclaiming that with their departure, the town was
now *"Judenrein,"* or free of Jews. The Kennedy family relocated to
the Jewish ghetto in the city of Breslau, now Wroclaw in Poland.
The numbers of Jews there were regularly reduced, as more and
more were sent east for "resettlement," as the Nazi euphemism
described the extermination camps. In the Breslau ghetto, Rudy
and his father worked at an underground workshop for electricians.
Practical skills were more use than intellectual knowledge, and the

young Rudy had an aptitude for electrical matters. It was a skill that would buy his father a few weeks more life at IG Farben's plant at Auschwitz, and save his.

Some in the ghetto tried, in their misery, to believe that a new life really did beckon for those deported, but rumors swirled through the dark and crowded streets and alleys. A few of those deported managed to send back coded messages, in a vain attempt to warn those left behind. "It was clear that something was wrong. People sent back postcards, telling their relatives to give their best regards to uncle Harry, for example, when uncle Harry had been dead for years. Of course, the censor did not understand that was a coded message," remembers Rudy Kennedy, now in his early seventies and living in London.[6] Kennedy recounts the horror of being packed off to Auschwitz:

Our turn came in March 1943, when I was fourteen. We were living in the ghetto, the whole family in one room, four of us, mother, father, and my little sister Katie. She was three years younger than me, and that was her last day alive. First, we were put in a holding place, at the "Freudenhalle," which had been a cultural hall. There were about a thousand people inside, for one night, with two toilets, so you can imagine how that was. They marched us through the town in the morning and we ended up on the cattle trucks. It was unimaginable what happened inside the wagon. We were taken to Auschwitz, but we didn't know what that was. We all had a little bag packed with the bare essentials. I kept my book on electricity with me. Before we left, we had to make lists of what we had, and they told us it would be sent on. Of course nothing was.

We were immediately relieved of our luggage at Auschwitz when we arrived, and there was a selection. We faced a figure dressed in black, and my father told me that I must say that I was eighteen. My father and I went to the right, my sister and my mother to the left. We were selected for work, my mother and sister were gassed. The guards kicked and beat us, and we went into a room with showers and basins at one end. My father was naked with hundreds of older men. Everyone was very agitated. They shaved our hair and told us to go into the shower. I was very disturbed by the shoes that I saw. All the shoes were piled up and jumbled up together in a big heap. I wondered how they would sort them out, if we were going to ever wear them again.

We went into the shower. Water came out. By then my mother and my sister were dead. The temperature was about minus ten and we were chased naked and barefoot down a frozen path to the blockhouse. There we were given a red blanket and a piece of bread and salami. In the morning, we were given clothes, completely at random, so nothing fit. Everything was too short or too long, and they gave us wooden clogs. They called out our names, and we had numbers tattooed on our arms. The tattoo needle was very thick, like a knitting needle and the blood of the previous prisoner was still running down it. I was in total fear. You could smell the fear in the wagons, and that smell will never leave me, the smell of fear. It's a special smell, very peculiar, like an animal smell.

They put me to work building a road outside the IG Farben factory by Monowitz. We were surrounded by a circle of guards. I was not athletic, and the work was beyond me. I had a wheelbarrow, and the earth was frozen. I had to hack away at the frozen ground with a pickaxe. The *kapo* [protected inmate] told me not to worry as I would soon meet my maker. I was far too weak, and I had no socks or underwear. My trousers were too long and I had a thin jacket, an enamel bowl, a spoon, and a cap. If you wanted to stop your feet from freezing you had to swap some bread for rags to bind your feet. This was the trade. People stripped rags from corpses, but if the guards saw you do that they would kill you on the spot.

IG's slave laborers worked in conditions of appalling brutality until they dropped. Violence, and violent death, was a daily occurrence. The only way out was to commit suicide by walking toward the perimeter fence. Shooting a prisoner, as he shambled off to his death, was considered a great sport by the camp guards Rudy Kennedy explains:

If you lost anything, you were beaten by a *kapo*. They beat you with electric cable in a rubber hose, between five and twenty-five times. If they broke a bone, you were dead because you couldn't work. One day, a guard threw my cap away, which meant a beating from the kapos. But the guards were distracted by a prisoner who just walked away. He committed suicide, because he got shot as soon as he reached the perimeter. There was a lot of competition among the guards to shoot prisoners like this, because each one counted as an attempted escape, and for that they got a weekend pass, a sausage, and a bottle of schnapps, so they could get away for a couple of days and make love to their girlfriends.

A young teenager, starving and undernourished in the freezing cold, Rudy knew that he could not last long at such hard labor. Thanks to his father, he was placed inside an IG Farben factory:

Soon afterwards, I was put into a special electrical kommando. My father was there, and he had managed to get me inside, although after a few days, he disappeared. My job was to install electric motors in the IG Farben factory. At least I was indoors. I was a natural with anything electrical, and one day, I saw that the current diagram would not work. I told the *kapo*, who was a criminal, previously in prison for twenty years, and I was marched off to the design office and explained the problem. I became a celebrity, and everything was upside down, like in *Alice in Wonderland*. I was appointed "official drawing checker," and a little desk appeared for me to sit at. I was fifteen. I became the *kapo*'s mascot, and so I had a chance to survive.

One of the managers, a man called Kurt Rodiger, had a soft spot for Rudy. Calling Rudy—a German-born Jew—into his office, he yelled loudly that his food was contaminated because it had been touched by a "dirty Jew." He called Rudy one as well for good measure (and the benefit of any passers-by). and threw his lunchtime sandwich on the floor. Rudy got the message, that the lunch was being discarded for him, and devoured the food in a few seconds. Rodiger later gave him a book about trains and electric motors on his birthday.

In fact, slave laborer is not really an adequate term to describe the life and death of IG's workers. Historically, slaves, whether in the Roman Empire or the Deep South of the United States, were part of their owner's capital, counted together with property and other assets. Their lives were miserable, but they were adequately fed and accommodated, just as farm animals would not be allowed to starve. But slave workers at Auschwitz were worked to death, often within weeks, their numbers immediately replenished from the continuous trainloads of Jews arriving at Auschwitz from all over Europe.

The diet of "Buna soup" meant weight loss of up to nine pounds a week for each prisoner. Few could live longer than three months before being sent to the gas chambers at Birkenau. By then, they were living skeletons. Prisoners slept on wooden bunks, built for one, that held three. There was no heat in winter, and in the summer, prisoners stifled. The IG foremen themselves asked the SS to implement punishments for any offenses committed by a prisoner. These offenses might include "eating bones from a garbage pail," "talking to a female inmate," "sitting down," or "possession of money." IG officials were not unwitting cogs in the Nazi genocide machine—they helped drive and direct it.

The conditions endured by Rudy Kennedy and his fellow prisoners did not bother visiting IG officials. He remembers, "We saw the civilian officials from IG all over the place. The site where we worked was very near where they were building a chemicals factory. We could see people dragging sacks of cement along, they would collapse and die. The IG officials had to walk past that on the way to the canteen. They knew absolutely what was going on, there is no question about that."

In addition to IG Farben, German firms such as Siemens and Krupp used slave labor at Auschwitz, setting up their own factories there and using company officials to oversee the work of the inmates. Germany industries' employees moved with ease between normally run factories in Germany and those attached to concentration camps. The latter were merely viewed as an unpleasant but necessary adjunct to the main plants. After the war, at the Nuremberg war crimes trials of the German industrialists, many defendants claimed that they had not known what was happening in the camps. This was a lie. The intertwined relationship between industry, business, and Nazi genocide meant that not just the industrialists, but much of Germany knew that was happening at Auschwitz and other concentration camps. Too many companies were involved in killing and profiting from the extermination of the Jews for the Holocaust to remain secret. As the Holocaust historian Raul Hilberg records in *The Destruction of the European Jews:* "The great extent of industrial activity in this camp [Auschwitz] resulted in a constant stream of incoming and outgoing corporation officials, engineers, construction men, and other temporary personnel, all excellent carriers of gossip to the farthest corners of the Reich."[7]

Henry Ford—Hitler's American Ally

Like his friend Adolf Hitler, Henry Ford, founder of the Ford Motor Company, believed in plain food, a puritanical lifestyle, and virulent anti-Semitism. Finding a kindred spirit, Henry Ford was one of the Nazi leader's earliest admirers. The feeling was mutual: during the 1920s, a large portrait of Henry Ford hung behind Hitler in his office at Nazi party headquarters in Munich, and the car maker was singled out for praise in Hitler's book *Mein Kampf*. The mass-produced Ford Model T was the inspiration for the Nazi plan to provide an affordable car for every German family. When Hitler was put on trial after the failed Munich putsch of 1923, a member of the Bavarian parliament testified that Henry Ford had given Hitler money. Ford's book, *The International Jew*, published in 1927, is full of anti-Jewish conspiracy theories, and he was the proud recipient of the Nazi Grand Cross of the German Eagle.

There is evidence that links between the Ford Motor Company and the Nazis continued after the United States entered the war, through Ford's German subsidiary, Ford Werke AG, set up in the 1920s. Ford Werke was an enthusiastic supporter of the "Aryanization" of the German economy, that is, the forced purchase at extremely low prices of Jewish-owned businesses. As early as 1935, Ford Werke used Nazi criteria for deciding who could be employed at the company. General Manager Erich Diestel carried out many of the dismissals, until he was sacked himself a year later for having a Jewish ancestor.

By September 1939, Ford Werke was the second largest producer of trucks in Nazi Germany. The company manufactured light trucks and spare parts throughout the war for the Nazi war machine. German troops drove into Poland on Ford trucks. The trucks were also used in the concentration camps. Declassified U.S. intelligence documents record that: "...Of the 350,000 trucks which the motorized German army possessed in 1942, 100,000 to 120,000 were Ford-built." The Ford truck plant at Cologne was supplied with forced labor from the concentration camp at Buchenwald, and Russian POWs were also used for war production work, in breach of the Geneva Convention.

In wartime Washington, D.C., there was anger that the German subsidiary of perhaps the most famous American company was churning out motor vehicles for the enemy. In spring 1943, the Treasury Department carried out an investigation into the files of the Ford company and its relationship with its subsidiaries in Nazi-occupied Europe, such as France, Germany, and the Netherlands. It discovered that the Ford factories in Nazi-occupied Europe were still producing vehicles for the Nazis.

There were strong ties of friendship and business between the Ford family and the Nazi economic elite, dating back to before 1939, with sinister implications for the American war effort. In 1925, Ford sold 40 percent of its German subsidiary's shares to IG Farben and other German companies. Henry Ford's son, Edsel, one of the directors of Ford Werke, was close friends with Hermann Schmitz, head of IG Farben. Hermann Schmitz and Edsel Ford were also among the founders of the American branch of IG Farben, known as American IG/Chemical Corporation. In turn, American IG owned the General Aniline and Film (GAF) company, which supplied khaki and blue dyes for army and navy uniforms. U.S. branches of German businesses were natural targets for espionage by pro-Nazi German expatriates and immigrants in the United States.

Ford subsidiaries in Nazi-occupied countries were not run directly from U.S. headquarters in Detroit during the war, records Christopher Simpson in his study of big business and genocide, *The Splendid Blond Beast*, nor did they repatriate profits or report directly to Ford headquarters. But, as with IG Farben, key individuals who had managed the firms during the Third Reich found their Nazi past no hindrance to a successful business career in postwar Germany. In fact, it positively helped. After 1945, Ford Werke director Heinrich Albert, leader of the company's effort to fire Jewish employees during the Third Reich, was appointed custodian of United States and British corporate properties in Berlin.

⊠ ⊠ ⊠

There was a contradiction between Nazi ideology and wartime economic reality. The former demanded the extermination of Jewry, the second that any able-bodied worker be exploited to the maximum to reach the necessary production quotas of the Four Year Plan. Working slave laborers to death made less economic sense than keeping them alive and productive, no matter how miserable their living conditions. And if Jewish slave laborers were alive, they could enrich the Nazi officials charged with running the ghettos in which they were incarcerated.

In the empire of competing interest groups that was the Third Reich, a struggle soon arose between two opposing schools of thought, which can be characterized here as exploiters versus exterminationists—or those who wished to use slave labor to increase Nazi profits and those who were determined to kill the Jews as fast as possible for ideological reasons, no matter what the economic cost. The ghetto at Lodz illustrates the first model, the extermination camp of Belzec, the second. The Lodz ghetto was sealed off from the rest of the city in April 1940, cramming 164,000 Jews into one-and-a-half square miles. Like all the ghettos in Poland, Lodz was established as a holding-point before the Jews' eventual extermination, but as long as they lived, ghetto governor Hans Biebow wanted to make as much money as possible from them. In 1940, he ordered that factories be set up, where workers were paid in soup and bread. The factories produced textiles and uniforms for the army and SS, as well as metal and wooden goods. The Jews' productivity kept them alive, for a while. Better a tailor at Lodz than a laborer at IG Farben's Auschwitz plant, but Hans Biebow kept the ghetto inhabitants starving and freezing. Still, the Lodz ghetto turned a profit of RM350 million ($140 million). Its factories made so much money that as late as 1943, there were still 80,000 Jews working in the textile industry. The ghetto-dwellers danced with joy in June 1944 when news came through of the Allied landings at Normandy, but the Allied troops got to France too late for the Jews of Lodz. The exterminationists won. By November 1944, the ghetto was virtually empty, its inhabitants taken away to be killed at Chelmno and Auschwitz.

While Hans Biebow ran a ghetto whose inhabitants had at least a chance of life, Hans Globocnik ruled a kingdom of death. Globocnik was in charge of Operation Reinhard (named after Reinhard Heydrich, the Nazi ruler of Bohemia and Moravia killed by partisans), the Nazi plan to exterminate Polish Jews. Unlike even Auschwitz, the four extermination camps established by Globocnik—Belzec, Majdanek, Sobibor, and Treblinka—were death factories. Jews sent here were not worked to death, but killed on arrival. Belzec, the first camp to begin operating under Operation Reinhard, was completed in March 1942. At its peak, up to 15,000 Jews a day could be gassed there. Whole communities of Jews would be taken off the train, stripped, shaved, and immediately killed en masse, at first by diesel fumes, later by Zyklon B.

"The majority knew everything, the smell betrayed it!" wrote Kurt Gerstein, an SS engineer who tried to alert the world about the Holocaust after witnessing a trainload of Jews arrive at Belzec from Lvov, in Ukraine. "They climbed a little wooden stairs and entered the death chambers, most of them silently, pushed by those behind them. A Jewess of about forty with eyes like fire cursed the murderers, she disappeared into the gas chambers."[8] The diesel engine would not start that day, recorded Gerstein, until almost three hours later. The Jews were dead thirty-two minutes after the engine finally fired. So tightly were they packed that most of the bodies were still standing once the door was finally opened.

These four camps, too, turned a tidy profit. In Globocnik's final accounting to SS Head Heinrich Himmler between April 1 and

December 15, 1943, when the camps were operating at their fullest capacity, the overall value of cash and valuables taken from those killed reached RM180 million ($72 million).

German industry, then, worked in tandem with the Nazi state, progressing from acquiescence in the anti-Jewish measures of 1933 to implementing the extermination of 1941 to 1945. Auschwitz and the slave labor factories were a separate (im)moral universe. Once past the gate proclaiming *Arbeit Macht Frei* ("Work Makes You Free"), normal constraints ceased to apply. But what of the multitude of smaller-sized German firms that financed and profited from the Holocaust? As the persecution of the Jews increased, intensifying to extermination as the war progressed, many companies such as Tesch & Stabenow found it easy to turn a blind eye to murder and carefully examine only their own, increasingly healthy, balance sheets.

It was in the Hamburg offices of Tesch & Stabenow, that evil was perhaps at its most banal, to paraphrase the philosopher Hannah Arendt. The firm's business was death, and death was good business in the Third Reich. Founded in 1927, Tesch & Stabenow was part of the German Corporation for Pest Control, and was known as Degesch for short. It held a monopoly on the manufacture of Zyklon B, was owned 42.5 percent by IG Farben, and 42.5 percent by Degussa, Germany's biggest firm dealing in precious metals. Five of the eleven members of Degesch's supervisory board worked for IG Farben. It was after the Wannsee conference that Degesch's production went into overdrive. Held on January 20, 1942, the Wannsee conference was a gathering of fifteen leading Nazi officials such as Reinhard Heydrich and Adolf Eichmann. There the decision was taken to adopt the "Final Solution," that is, the extermination of European Jewry. The Wannsee Protocol, adopted at the end of the conference, used the euphemistic language of bureaucrats, but its meaning was clear, as this extract shows:

The Jews should in the course of the Final Solution be taken in a suitable manner to the East for use as labor....The remnant that is finally able to survive all this—since this is undoubtedly the part with the strongest resistance—must be treated accordingly, since these people representing a natural selection, are to be regarded as the germ cell of a new Jewish development, in case they should succeed and go free [as history has proved]. In the course of the Final Solution, Europe will be combed from west to east.

The Wannsee Protocol was a tragedy foretold for European Jewry, but a portent of massive profits for Degesch. Before the mass killing could start in earnest, however, there was a technical point to clear up. Zyklon B had originally been invented as a pesticide to clear communal rooms, such as army barracks, of mice and insects, and early on in the war it had been used as such at Auschwitz. German law required that pesticides include a special smell, known as an indicator, to warn humans that it was being used so they could leave the area or take precautions. Of course, there was no need for an indicator to be included in the shipments of Zyklon B destined for the gas chambers as it was to be used on humans. An indicator might even trigger mass panic. The SS wanted Zyklon B without an indicator, but Degesch executives were unwilling to comply.

They refused, not on humanitarian grounds, but legal ones. Zyklon B was no longer under valid patent, as it had expired. But the company still owned the monopoly patent on the indicator. Manufacturing Zyklon B without the telltale warning odor would threaten Degesch's monopoly and was definitely bad for business. Others could take a slice of the profits of the Holocaust. But the demands of the SS, next to which stood the Gestapo, soon overcame the company's objections. The deliveries went ahead without the indicator, and it was clear for what purpose.

Following his arrest for war crimes at the war's end, Bruno Tesch, one of the founders of Degesch, tried to persuade the Allies that he had not known that his company's product was being used to kill humans. In his statement, given to the British army at Hamburg in October 1945, Tesch asserted: "I was never told in Berlin at a conference or by any other source that Zyklon B should be used against human beings. I mentioned this fact in none of my travel reports, and I have neither spread nor heard such a rumor in my office."[9]

Like many Germans, Tesch had joined the Nazi party in 1933, once he saw that Hitler was likely to come to power. Such comparative latecomers were contemptuously dubbed "March violets" by long-term party members. Tesch, however, also became a supporting member of the SS. He admitted having used Zyklon B in experiments on animals, but denied having any other connections with the Gestapo or the SS, except in the ominously-named "SS Hygiene Institute," where he gave courses in the use of Zyklon B for its original purpose as a pesticide and fumigator.

In his testimony, Auschwitz Commandant Rudolf Höss told a different story to Tesch's dissimulation. In 1942 and 1943, during the height of the killing at Auschwitz, Degesch was unable to ensure adequate supplies of Zyklon B by rail. Höss sent trucks from Auschwitz to the Degesch plant near Dessau where the gas was produced. The trucks were driven by SS officers, with SS number plates and signs in the shape of a triangle, in which the letter of each camp was written—in the case of Auschwitz, an *A*.

"I assume with certainty that this firm knew the purpose of the use of Zyklon B delivered by it. This they would have to conclude from the fact that the gas for Auschwitz had been ordered continually and in great quantities, while for the other departments of SS troops etc., orders were placed only once or in six-month intervals. I cannot recall the exact quantities of Zyklon B that we received from Tesch & Stabenow, however, I estimate that at least ten thousand cans, that is, ten thousand kilos had been supplied by them in the course of three years. This figure is arrived at by computing the number of 2.5 million gassed people and the consumption of an average of six cans for every 1,500 people."

Thus the mathematics of genocide. Bruno Tesch, and his colleague Karl Weinbacher were found guilty of knowingly supplying poison gas to kill allied nationals. Tesch and Weinbacher appealed against their death sentences to the British Army of the Rhine HQ. According to British Army declassified documents, their colleagues at Degesch, both former and current, submitted appeals for mercy, but to no avail. Both men were hanged. As was Rudolf Höss, the worst single mass killer in modern history, once commended in an SS report as "a true pioneer in this area because of his new ideas and educational methods."

IG's echoing of Nazi policies even included the peace feelers put out by sections of the Nazi leadership in 1944, as it became clear the war was lost and attempts were made to split the Western Allies from the Soviet Union. IG officials, such as Hermann Schmitz and Georg von Schnitzler, were among those German industrialists who sought contact with Washington and London through the offices of Allen Dulles, the Bern wartime station chief of the OSS, forerunner of the CIA. Schmitz, in particular, had good contacts among America's political and business elite, having traveled there often before the war on IG business. These German proposals would have left much of the Third Reich intact and usually included demands that there be no punishment for Nazi war crimes, that Germany be allowed to keep its plunder from occupied Europe, and that the Nazi war against the Soviet Union be allowed to continue. As the historian Christopher Simpson writes in his study of genocide and big business, *The Splendid Blond Beast:* "These were not 'peace' proposals in a fundamental sense, but rather efforts to rationalize the management of the war and to gain time to digest the billions of marks worth of personal and industrial property that had fallen into German hands."[10]

Such "peace" proposals did IG no good. After the war, its leaders were put on trial, but fared better than their colleagues at Degesch or Rudolf Höss. Twenty-four IG Farben executives were indicted for war crimes, including Hermann Schmitz, Georg von Schnitzler, and Carl Krauch, chairman of IG Farben's supervisory board. Krauch had once recommended to his officials at the IG plant at Heydebreck when they complained of a labor shortage that "...Heydebreck must establish a large concentration camp as quickly as possible following the example of Auschwitz."

The sixty-page indictment consisted of five separate counts detailing IG's role in the Third Reich, including "slavery and mass murder." This was the critical charge on which the defendants' fates would hinge. In their defense, IG's officials tried to show that they had helped their Jewish colleagues, either within Nazi Germany or to escape from it. At the IG trial, witnesses for the prosecution, such as Ernst Struss, secretary of the IG managing board, gave graphic testimony about IG's role in the Holocaust, and told the court that the company's directors were well aware of the genocide taking place there. Allied POWs, including captured British soldiers were also used as slave laborers, and held in concentration camps, including Auschwitz/Monowitz, in contravention of the Geneva Convention. Eric Doyle, a British former prisoner-of-war, appeared for the prosecution at the IG trial. His testimony was powerful:

The condition of the concentration camp inmates was deplorable. I used to see them being carried back at night, dead from exposure, hunger, or exhaustion....We would see the chaps hanging up in the gate of Lager IV [Monowitz], and the prisoners had to walk underneath them. I saw those bodies myself; working parties passed under the gate while walking to work.[11]

Charles Coward, another British former POW, told the court:

I was at Auschwitz nearly every day. The population at Auschwitz was fully aware that people were being gassed and burned. On one occasion, they complained about the stench of burning bodies. Of course, all the Farben people knew what was going on. Nobody could live in Auschwitz and work in the plant, or even come down to the plant, without knowing what was common knowledge to everybody.[12]

The evidence was compelling, but the political climate was changing. By 1947, when the IG Farben trial opened, the Cold War had begun in earnest. Although General Eisenhower had called for the industrial disarmament of Germany, the new realities of strategic politics demanded that German industry be rebuilt, not broken up. A strong Germany was needed as a bulwark against the Soviet Union's empire in central and eastern Europe. The Cold War, like World War II, was good news for IG's executives. Twelve of the defendants were found not guilty, and twelve sentenced to prison terms ranging from one-and-a-half years to a maximum of eight years. Hermann Schmitz was found guilty of plunder and sentenced to four years imprisonment. Carl Krauch was found guilty of slavery and mass murder and was sentenced to six years. Georg von Schnitzler, "IG's salesman," was sentenced to five years.

The prosecution and former slave laborers for IG were outraged. Once again, realpolitik triumphed over morality. Considering that the Nazi rocket scientist, Wernher von Braun, architect of the V-2 rocket, launched the U.S. space program and that Klaus Barbie, the "Butcher of Lyons," was recruited by U.S. counterintelligence, it is perhaps surprising that IG's executives were sent to prison at all.

IG Farben no longer exists as a trading entity. It was broken up and dissolved into three independent units, Hoechst, Bayer, and BASF, all three of which had been part of IG's original merger in 1925. The wheel of history turned once again. IG's executives were soon reemployed by the successor companies, even those convicted of war crimes. Friedrich Jaehne, convicted at Nuremberg of plunder and sentenced to a year-and-a-half in prison, was elected chairman of Hoechst's supervisory board in June 1955. A year later, Fritz ter Meer, sentenced to seven years at Nuremberg for convictions including slavery and mass murder, was elected chairman of Bayer's supervisory board. Curiously, Hermann Schmitz, the king of IG, died a relative pauper in 1960. The fate of his personal assets remains a mystery.

IG Farben still exists as a shell company. It has been in the process of liquidation for more than forty years, trying to reclaim its assets, mainly properties in East Germany. In 1957, IG Farben paid 30 million deutschmarks (DM) to the Jewish Claims Conference, which deals with compensation for Holocaust victims and their relatives. Over forty years later, even as Germany entered the new millennium, its businesses were still squabbling over paying adequate compensation for slave laborers. The German government agreed to set up a DM10 billion fund, half of which industry agreed to contribute. The government's policy is that all German firms contribute, even those that did not use slave labor. By May 2000, only DM2.9 billion had been raised.

As for Rudy Kennedy, in the late 1950s, he received his share of the monies paid by IG Farben to the Jewish Claims Conference. His time as a slave laborer at Auschwitz, where his mother, father, and sister had died, was judged to be worth the deutschmark equivalent of $446.

Propaganda poster: "Women Work for You." Despite the poster's message, Hitler's belief that World War I had been lost on the homefront meant that he strove to keep women out of the factories for much of the war. *(AKG photo)*

The reality: the homefront in Germany—German civilians loot a train carrying food supplies. *(The Trustees of the Imperial War Museum)*

This picture of a Nazi banquet was discovered in the Führer's desk in his bunker. *(Press Association)*

Munitions for the Nazi war effort produced by the inmates
of Dachau. *(Mary Evans Picture Library)*

"Arbeit Macht Frei" ("Work Makes You Free") greeted
arriving inmates to Auschwitz, which was transformed into an
extermination camp after the conquest of Poland.
(Mary Evans Picture Library)

Carl Bosch (left), head of
IG Farben in the 1930s.
Caught between his feelings
as a patriotic German and his
distaste for the Nazis, Bosch
made contradictory gestures.
(AKG photo)

Gustav Krupp (right), head of
the leading armaments firm in
Europe. Like many industrialists, Krupp was initially wary
of Hitler, but he soon became
a "super-Nazi" after hearing
Hitler's promise to restore the
Wehrmacht. *(Wiener Library)*

Adam Czerniakow (left), head
of the Warsaw *Judenrat*, a
tragic and controversial figure,
who tried to deal with the
devil but gradually became
more compromised and cor-
rupted. *(Wiener Library)*

Marlene Dietrich
(from *Marokko
Herzen in Flammen*,
1930). *(AKG photo)*

Leni Riefenstahl,
directing cameraman
Walter Frentz during
the filming of the Berlin
Olympics. *(Mary Evans
Picture Library)*

*Marlene was reviled in her
homeland for returning
to Berlin in an American
uniform after the war.
Riefenstahl spent the rest
of her days trying, almost
successfully, to rehabilitate
her reputation.*

Hermann Göring (second from right). *(AKG photo)*

Albert Göring, brother of Hermann. Albert's name helped him profit from the war, but it also helped him to rescue Jews. After the war, despite testimony from many he had helped, his infamous name meant his claims of innocence were greeted with immense skepticism.

Children in the Warsaw ghetto, 1941. *(AKG photo)*

Mordechai Chaim Rumkowski (middle row, second from right), Jewish head of the Lodz ghetto, who built a macabre empire where he ruled like a king with the power to decide who would live and who would die. *(Wiener Library)*

Jewish policeman in the ghetto: perhaps the grayest area of moral choice. *(AKG photo)*

The following photographs were taken from a collection of postcards pasted into a scrapbook and hidden in a Bavarian cave toward the end of World War II. A U.S. Army sergeant discovered the scrapbook in May 1945 and kept it as a war souvenir. The postcards of Hitler with Goebbels, Göring, Hitler Youth, and adoring crowds give chilling testimony to the effectiveness of Nazi propaganda and to Hitler's seductive power. (*photos courtesy of Thomas N. Tegge*)

Chapter Seven

Occupiers and Occupied

"Life in France is somber, every day is terribly like the next. There are only a few subjects of conversation: food, the black market, the Germans, and the Allied landing. If you make a mixture of all these subjects, you will have an idea of the atmosphere in France at present."

—Intercepted letter written in occupied
France in summer 1943, quoted in Report No. 13,
British Postal and Telegraph Censorship

"Wenig zu regieren." (Govern little.)

—maxim of Werner Best,
Reich Plenipotentiary in Denmark

Over five decades after the Allied victory, it demands a leap of the imagination to draw a mental map of wartime Europe. Travel back in time to June 1940, for example, less than one year into the war, and the Nazi blitzkrieg seemed unstoppable. British troops have fled home from Dunkirk, and German artillery is pointing toward Dover. France, Belgium, Holland, Luxembourg, Denmark, and Norway have all collapsed in the face of the Wehrmacht's onslaught. The Czech lands were incorporated into the Reich in March 1939, while Austria had subsumed itself into Germany by the Anschluss of March 1938. Further east, Slovakia was a pro-Nazi, clerico-fascist state, ruled by a Catholic priest, Father Jozef Tiso. Poland was approaching its first anniversary of Nazi and Russian occupation, sliced in two between Germany and the Soviet Union. A tense peace reigned between Berlin and Moscow.

The New Order was barely into its first decade, but to many, not just in Germany, Hitler's prediction that this German empire would last a thousand years seemed all too feasible. Nations and their governments began to plan how to survive Hitler, and whether by endurance, cooperation, or a mixture of both, reach a modus vivendi with the new Germany as the Wehrmacht marched in. The land itself might be occupied, but the nation and its spirit would live on, believed leaders such as King Christian X of Denmark and France's Marshal Pétain. The question was how, and at what moral cost?

The answer depended on two main factors: the nature and severity of the Nazi occupation, and the resilience and moral courage of the conquered nations. In all of these countries, Jews were sent to concentration camps, the blackest manifestation of Nazi occupation. But any picture of life for most non-Jews living under Nazi rule, at least in western Europe, must be drawn in differing shades of gray. While the Nazis brought the instruments of state terror—the Gestapo, arrest, torture, and the threat of deportation to the camps—everywhere in their wake, they were not deployed in a uniform manner in occupied countries. Life in wartime Denmark, under Reich Plenipotentiary Werner Best was, in many respects, more tolerable, more survivable than in the Czech lands. And better to be a Czech munitions worker under Reinhard Heydrich, head of the Reich Main Security Office, with his policy of the "whip and sugar," than a Russian peasant in a village on the road to Moscow.

The institutionalized criminality of the Nazi regime shaped Berlin's basic approach, but within that framework, there were varying policy options. Should the Nazis launch a battle for hearts and minds in an attempt to win over at least a portion of the elite and the general population, rally them around the swastika, and keep the newest subjects of the Reich as content and productive as possible? Perhaps even indulge their nationalist sentiments and midwife quasi-independent, pro-Nazi states such as in Vichy France or Slovakia? The warring groups among the Nazi leadership—often a consequence of Hitler's appointing more than one person to carry out the same job—and his lack of interest in the minutiae of many policy decisions, meant that senior Nazi officials could have considerable leeway in both deciding which policies to adopt and how to implement them as they constructed their mini empires. Political infighting reflected the differing aims of disparate interest groups in the faction-ridden leadership.

Like every nation seeking to build an empire, the Nazis also found that maintaining a vast international state also necessitated granting considerable autonomy to their local rulers and allies. Occupied territories did not all have the same status: western Poland and parts of eastern Belgium were immediately absorbed into the Reich proper, which was also the Nazi plan for Alsace-Lorraine, Luxembourg, Slovenia, and Poland's Bialystok. Huge swathes of occupied land, however, were neither technically part of the Reich, nor independent states: Bohemia and Moravia, the General Government of Poland, occupied Ukraine, the Baltics, and White Russia came under the rule of Nazi potentates such as Heydrich. Other occupied areas such as France, Slovakia, and Croatia retained varying degrees of independence. Holland and Norway, viewed from Berlin as fellow "Nordic" states, were placed under civilian rather than military administration.

The demands of geopolitics also necessitated some curious anomalies as allied—and conquered—nations refused to completely accede to all of Berlin's demands. All of these would eventually be remedied, believed Berlin, but in the meantime had to be grudgingly tolerated. The quasi-independence of countries such as Vichy France fostered—for the Germans—disturbing tendencies to actually implement autonomous policies. This was especially true of internal matters, such as an intermittent reluctance to facilitate the planned extermination of French-born Jews, although foreign Jewish refugees were readily sacrificed. Further north, Finland sent troops to invade the Soviet Union but maintained diplomatic relations with the United States and refused outright to deport its two thousand or so Jews. Bulgaria also refused to either deport its Jews or declare war on the Soviet Union.

For Nazi-allied Croatia, the Germans did not go far enough. Croatia's ruler, Ante Pavelic, leader of the fanatical anti-Serb Ustasha movement, devoted vast resources to carrying out a domestic policy of genocide against the country's Serbs, as well as Jews and Roma. They were killed in the tens of thousands, often by hand, to the disgust even of SS officers. Guards at the Jasenovac concentration camp held a throat-cutting competition, tossing their victims into the Sava River. The winner claimed more than two thousand kills. In one night. Not surprisingly, Pavelic's legions' quite astonishing brutality triggered widespread support for the rival Communist and royalist Yugoslav resistance movements. Much German manpower and matériel was deployed in the Balkans combating Tito's partisans, and the royalist Chetniks, which, from Berlin's view, could have been far more usefully used elsewhere.

In sophisticated Western capitals, different methods of corralling those now occupied were called for. There would be no throat-cutting competitions by the banks of the Seine or Amsterdam's Amstel. There too, the Nazis did not hesitate to torture and execute those whom they considered a threat to the Reich, but the extremes of mass brutality deployed in the East and the Balkans were generally avoided. It was simpler to use existing national institutions such as civil servants, courts, and police—the "desk murderers" of occupation bureaucracy—than impose the terror methods used in Poland.

In Holland, Reich Commissioner Artur Seyss-Inquart used Dutch bureaucrats to implement the Nazis' national identity card system. In October 1940, the occupation administration ordered the issue of personal identity cards for every Dutch citizen older than fourteen. The new system was to replace the previous chaotic system. Its aim, officially, was to regulate the issuing of ration coupons. Unofficially, it served several purposes. The information was needed for the Nazification of Holland. Tens of thousands of able-bodied men could be found for labor service and later deported to forced labor in Germany; the occupation administration would have a very extensive database for governing and, most important, all Jews would be registered as well. Many Dutch officials were enthusiastic advocates of the new system. The identity cards would not only have information about name, place and date of birth, profession, and a picture, but also two fingerprints, a procedure up until then only used for criminals. By the end of the following year, everyone had a new ID card. Dutch Jews, like their gentile compatriots, also registered for a place on the card-indexes that would eventually send them to the death camps. Their cards were stamped with a large, black letter *J*.

The Germans ordered the new system be implemented, but it was honed and directed by a Dutch civil servant, J.J. Lentz. Lentz was a hard-working archetypal bureaucrat who worked his way up the civil service ladder and reached the rank of head-of-the-state inspectorate for the Population Registers. As the man who before the war had been assigned to reorganize the old registration and a long-time advocate of ID cards, he was a natural choice for Seyss-Inquart. Lentz based his model on the German cards and improved them. Being a perfectionist, he put special stamps on them, using a specially made cardboard with a watermark. Lentz expended great effort in devising a unique way of attaching the picture to the card that made alterations immediately obvious. The resistance movement found it very difficult to fake the cards, known as *persoonsbewijzen*, or PBs. The Germans also ordered all the data from every PB to be copied into their Central Archive in The Hague. Any attempts at falsification could be checked rapidly in this way.

Instead of being appalled at the all-embracing reach of their Nazi overlords, Dutch civil servants such as Lentz were relieved to be working for an administration that would appreciate perfection, order, and organization. When Jewish local councilors in Amsterdam were removed from the council, the theater pass that came with the position was withdrawn immediately. Not by the

Germans, but by a Dutch civil servant. Or consider the example of the Dutch MPs' pay packets. The Dutch parliament had its last session on May 15, 1940. Since parliament was suspended by Seyss-Inquart, "until further notice," the MPs' pay was also cancelled, again by a Dutch civil servant. Dutch bureaucrats later granted them unemployment pay of 2,800 guilders a year, the amount set by the civil servants. It was Seyss-Inquart who later raised it to 4,800 guilders (in comparison, unemployment pay for a married man was fifteen guilders a month).

The years of German rule in the Netherlands, however, are full of contradictions, illustrating the extent of the choices that could be made. At the outbreak of war, Holland was home to 140,000 Jews, of whom 30,000 were refugees from Austria and Germany, including Anne Frank and her family. Of these, 110,000 were killed in the death camps, a total of 75 percent. With the aid of Dutch officials and police, the Nazi extermination machine operated extremely effectively in the Netherlands. Yet, those same Dutch skills of organization that helped doom Holland's Jews also saved the lives of thousands. A nationwide underground network sprang up to hide, shelter, and feed Jews. Many of the rescuers were Calvinists, who took strength from their faith that obedience is only given to God, and a government blessed by God. The Nazis clearly did not fall into this category. The Yad Vashem Holocaust Memorial in Jerusalem awards the Netherlands the second highest number of Righteous Among the Nations at 4,174. These were non-Jews who risked their own lives to save Jews. Only Poland has a higher count, at 5,264. And while Poland had 3.3 million Jews before World War II, and so many more opportunities to do good, Holland's total Jewish population was just 4.2 percent of Poland's, meaning the Netherlands had proportionately many more rescuers. Admittedly, the Yad Vashem statistics of saviors are not scientifically verifiable as a means of determining national rates of anti-Nazi resistance, but they are at least a guide to wartime attitudes.

Not every act of resistance, of a national determination to survive Hitler, was a matter of life and death. British and most American films disappeared from the screen after Holland's surrender, to be replaced with German musicals and comedies, accompanied by triumphalist Nazi propaganda newsreels. Some in the audience walked out, others booed. Seyss-Inquart responded with a decree that it was forbidden to leave a cinema while a German newsreel was playing. Seyss-Inquart had also forbidden public display of either the Dutch national flag or the Orange flag, symbol of the monarchy. On June 29, 1940, Prince Bernard's birthday, the streets were full of people wearing orange carnations. Small steps, but the first ones, and the most important.

The biggest step was taken in February 1941. After a skirmish in Amsterdam between Jews and Dutch Nazis in which a Nazi was killed, 450 Jewish males were sent to Mauthausen concentration camp in Austria. In response, the underground Dutch Communist Party called a general strike in Amsterdam, on Tuesday the 25th, the first of its kind in Nazi-occupied Europe. Initially, the strike was a success. Almost half of all municipal employees joined, as well as many white-collar workers and dockers. Many strikers took to the streets of Amsterdam instead of going to work. The streets were packed with defiant Dutch. Some lay down in front of the few trams that left their depots to stop them from running. One contemporary account quotes an elderly guard who lay across the tracks, shouting at the driver: "Ride if you dare, fascist! Traitor!" The Dutch police made no serious attempt to break the strike.

It could not last. Seyss-Inquart was in Vienna. One of his officials, Hans Rauter, took charge and demanded that the mayor of Amsterdam and the Dutch police stop the strike. A 7:30 P.M., curfew was enforced. The next day, although many municipal employees returned to work, private employees joined in the strike, many physically blocking the tramlines. Despite the Nazi control of the media, news of the strike spread to other cities. The Dutch news wire service ANP, also known as "Adolf's Newest Parrot," was ordered not to transmit any news on the strike. The editors put out a one-line story: "The strikes and riots in Amsterdam are not to be reported," probably as a means of getting the news out. Martial law was declared, and SS troops and German police took control of the streets. Many of the strike organizers were arrested and sent to concentration camps. By Thursday, two days after it began, the strike was over. The mayor was sacked, and Amsterdam was fined 15 million guilders. The strike both failed and succeeded. It failed to stop the deportation of the Jews. But it succeeded in destroying forever the fiction that Holland was not being Nazified; in showing the brutality and viciousness of the Nazi occupation and in showing that even under the swastika, national pride and solidarity lived on. Now there were no illusions about Holland's fate.

Different sectors of society cooperated with the Nazis to protect their own interests. Civil servants wanted a smooth and efficient bureaucracy. National leaders of allied or defeated countries wanted to preserve their nationhood and did not necessarily view Germany's policies and aims as synonymous with those of their nation. Hitler's allies, who are now reviled as traitors, such as Vichy's Marshal Petain, or Hungary's Admiral Horthy, first and foremost saw themselves as patriots, juggling national interests with the Germans' demands. In a sense, the Nazis could be caught in a policy trap of their own making. The more room for domestic maneuver they allowed countries such as Vichy France to retain, to try and win over local hearts and minds, the more the Nazis inadvertently fostered the spirit of national sovereignty. All of which meant that both the Axis nations and Nazi-occupied countries could, at times, retain differing degrees of autonomy. Certainly, they were compromised and corrupted by being in Berlin's orbit, but as this chapter illustrates, surviving Hitler did not mean having to slavishly follow the Nazis' every whim or obey all their demands. Even within the framework of national survival ethics, there were choices to be made.

In Denmark, the Nazis made considerable—and unique—concessions to preserve a semblance of national sovereignty in the hope of fostering sympathy for the Nazi cause, at least in the early years of occupation. The government and the parliament were allowed to continue operating, and the army was not disbanded. Relations between Copenhagen and Berlin were conducted by each country's diplomats and foreign ministries, behind the façade that Denmark remained a sovereign state. This more liberal policy (by Nazi standards), allowed the Danes to retain some autonomy. This was a trade-off for the decision by the government and the royal family not to offer military resistance to the German invasion of April 1940. And while the Dutch and Norwegian royal families had fled, the Danish King Christian X remained, providing a powerful national rallying point. Symbols of national sovereignty such as kings, anthems, and flags assume far more emotive significance under foreign rule, which is why occupying forces often take such thorough steps to eradicate and outlaw them.

But while Berlin was prepared to make some tactical concessions in the Danish occupation regime, Hitler's strategic imperatives remained uniform with the rest of the Reich. Danish economic assets and resources were hijacked for the Nazi cause, and pressure grew to deport its Jews. And, as the German pressure grew, so did the Danes' resistance. By autumn 1942, Berlin regarded the situation in its Nordic neighbor as becoming out of control. Danish SS volunteers were mocked by their compatriots, and the royal family had made clear its preference for England and Sweden over Germany. A memo by Werner von Grundherr of the Foreign Ministry, reported:

For the future it was impossible that in the New Europe established under German leadership, there should exist a form of state with a democratic government and under a royal house which up to now had displayed nothing but ill-will....

For the fact that things had gone as far as they had, the Danes themselves, with their king and government, were to blame. The king and the Royal House had never concealed their unfavorable attitude and their preference for Sweden and England. A Danish minister had been allowed to leave the country, and the volunteers of the *Freikorps Daenemark* [Danish SS troops] had been ridiculed and mistreated.

The Royal House and the present form of government were disturbing factors in developments as a whole, and there he [Hitler] had finally come to the conclusion that both should be put aside.[1]

In 1942, Hitler's new plan was to set up a puppet regime under the leadership of the Danish Nazis, recorded von Grundherr, noting that Britain had set up puppet regimes in Iran and Iraq. Nor did he have any illusions about the future narrow power base of the Führer in Denmark, adding laconically that: "The head of this government must always be aware that in the case of a possible withdrawal of German troops, he would be hanged on the nearest lamppost." The continuing diplomatic façade that Denmark remained a sovereign nation was destroyed. Denmark was to be absorbed into the Reich. Its rulers were the new military commander, General von Hannecken, who planned to dismantle the Danish army, and Werner Best.

Werner Best is one of those Nazi functionaries often classified as "desk murderers." An SS officer and chief legal adviser to the Gestapo, Best was the architect of the "legal" basis—such as it was—of the methods of the Nazi state. Working closely with both Heinrich Himmler and Reinhard Heydrich, his legal work on constitutional theory provided the supposed judicial justification for the Nazi terror, such as the Gestapo and concentration camps. The historian Robert Wistrich describes him as "a cool, amoral technician of power," and a "free-floating intellectual with a blurred sense of morality who devoted his legal talents to the service of a power-mad clique of criminals."[2]

Between 1940 and 1942, Best was chief of the civil administration in occupied France before being promoted and sent to

Copenhagen as Reich plenipotentiary. Yet the author of the 1941 book *Die Deutsche Polizei* (The German Police) was not a mere Nazi automaton. Some aspects of his role in Denmark remain ambiguous and illustrate how Nazi occupation was never monolithic. In accordance with his policy of letting occupied countries administer themselves as much as possible, he adopted the motto of *"wenig zu regieren"* (govern little). For Best this could mean, for example, using local police forces to carry out Nazi directives rather than the SS and Gestapo. Domestic institutions should be suborned for the Nazi cause, thus further merging indigenous and Nazi officialdom.

Yet this policy, of necessity, also allowed the authorities of occupied nations to retain some power. This the Danish government exploited to provide continued protection for the country's Jews. Until Denmark came under martial law with the arrival of Best and General von Hannecken, no anti-Jewish legislation was passed, and no property was sequestered. When the Nazis began to draw up their plans for the deportation of Danish Jewry, the Danish government organized one of the most remarkable acts of mass national resistance and rescue of the war. Almost all of the country's eight thousand Jews were hidden and then transported by sea to the safety of neutral Sweden. Interestingly, Wistrich credits Best with possible involvement in that episode. As he writes: "In spite of his record as a 'desk murderer' there is evidence that, in Denmark, Best sought to sabotage Himmler's orders concerning the implementation of the 'Final Solution.'"[3]

Either way, despite the efforts of the Danish government, some four hundred Danish Jews were eventually sent to Theresienstadt. The fate of these four hundred is also instructive, illustrating the degree of national autonomy that could be retained by a government determined enough, even under Nazi occupation. The Danish government was agitated by the fate of these four hundred and repeatedly requested permission to inspect the camp. In June 1944, delegates of the Danish Red Cross visited Theresienstadt. It was a successful strategy, and none of the four hundred was sent to Auschwitz.

What Would We Have Done?

A Britain under Nazi occupation is, thankfully, the stuff of fiction, detailed in novels such as Len Deighton's *SS GB*. We will never know if a German-ruled Britain would have produced a homegrown version of Marshal Pétain, leader of Vichy France, or Norway's Vidkun Quisling. But the widespread sympathy—even support—for Hitler among considerable sections of the upper classes and the political, financial, and industrial establishment, is a matter of record. Many titled British were pro-Nazis who viewed the Third Reich as a bulwark against the advance of Communism across Europe, which they feared would ultimately threaten their own privileges and riches. Britain's admirers of Hitler also appreciated, rather than were repelled by, the Nazis' anti-Semitism.

Nazi sympathies extended to the heart of the Royal Family, which, considering the Windsors' German ancestry, is perhaps not surprising. King Edward VIII was an enthusiastic advocate of racist and eugenicist theories about the inherent superiority of the white races, expounding them to leading politicians in his circle. His consort, Wallis Simpson, whom he later married, was also pro-Nazi and was put under surveillance by British intelligence.

In 1937, after his abdication the previous year, the Duke of Windsor (as he was then titled) visited Germany together with Mrs. Simpson, the Duchess of Windsor. They were snubbed by the British ambassador, but received a warm welcome from the Nazi leadership. On a visit to the SS Death's Head division in Pomerania, the Duke raised his arm in a "Heil Hitler" salute. The crowd went wild. As the *New York Times* reported at the time: "The Duke's decision to see for himself the Third Reich's industries and social institutions and his gestures and remarks during the last two weeks have demonstrated adequately that the abdication did indeed rob Germany of a firm friend, if not indeed a devoted admirer, on the British throne."

The Queen Mother was no friend of the Duchess of Windsor, viewing her as a dangerous interloper in the Royal Family, but shared her pro-appeasement views. When, in March 2000, Oxford University Bodleian Library released documents relating to the Royal Family, box no. 24 was kept back. This was, reported the *Independent on Sunday*, quoting "senior government sources," because its contents "spell out the true extent of the Queen Mother's pro-appeasement views on the brink of the Second World War." Hostile to Churchill, she wanted the pro-appeasement foreign secretary Lord Halifax to be appointed prime minister as a precursor to a possible peace deal that would guarantee the continuation of the monarchy, even under Nazi occupation, the paper said.

Thankfully, Britain's intelligence services were watching Nazi agents and their sympathizers. The leading Nazi official in prewar Britain, Dr. R.G. Rosel, who ran the Anglo-German Information Service—a pro-Nazi propaganda channel by any other name—was expelled in May 1939. At least nine British organizations were on the receiving end of Dr. Rosel's material, records the historian Nigel West in his book *MI5*. Some were extreme right-wing and openly fascist and racist political parties, such as the British Union of Fascists, the National Socialist League, and the Imperial Fascist League. More useful to the Nazis, and subsequently far more potentially dangerous, were organizations that kept Berlin in contact with leading members of the ruling classes, such as the Anglo-German Fellowship and The Link. Formed in 1937 as an "independent non-party organization to promote Anglo-German friendship," by May 1939, The Link had thirty-five active branches and more than 4,300 members. West describes its publication, the *Anglo-German Review*, as acting "as a mouthpiece for Dr. Goebbels."[5]

The Link boasted two Dukes, the eleventh Duke of Bedford, and the second Duke of Westminster. Members of the Anglo-German Fellowship included sixteen peers of the realm and the governor of the Bank of England, Frank C. Tiarks. Many members were also former MPs. Lord Stamp was a director of the Bank of England. Another fellowship member, Lord McGowan, was chairman of ICI, Britain's trading partner with IG Farben, the massive German chemical combine that would profit so handsomely from the Holocaust (see chapter 6). Lord Nuffield, chairman of Morris Motors Ltd., was a member of both The Link and the Anglo-German Fellowship. Perhaps the most disturbing name among the Fellowship's members was that of Sir William Strang, chief political adviser to the Foreign Office.

The wartime history of the only part of the British Isles to actually be occupied by the Nazis, the Channel Islands, is not particularly encouraging for those who would like to believe that Britain would have fought on forever against the Nazi invaders. The Channel Islands were occupied from the summer of 1940 until May 1945. There, hundreds of slave laborers, many of them Russian POWs, were worked to death in inhuman conditions building fortifications. Just as in nearby France, a homegrown resistance movement did spring up, and there were armed attacks on German soldiers, but many British officials, such as Victor Carey, bailiff of Guernsey, collaborated with the Nazis. On July 8, 1940, he offered a £25 reward for information leading to the arrest of anyone found guilty of painting a "V for Victory" sign. Anti-Semitic laws along the lines of the German model were introduced, and the teaching of German was made compulsory in all schools. Three Jewish women were deported to Auschwitz, where they died. After the war, British investigators began gathering material for expected trials of collaborators and evidence of war crimes. No trials took place, either of Germans or of islanders.

Instead, the bailiffs that had worked with the Germans, implementing the occupation, Victor Carey in Guernsey, and
Alexander Coutanche in Jersey, were knighted.

※ ※ ※

The case of France is more complicated and ambiguous. In May
1940, one month after the Nazi invasion of Denmark, France fell.
In Paris, the Wehrmacht marched in triumph down the Champs
d'Elysee. The country was divided into two zones under the terms of
the armistice of June 22: occupied, under German military occupation, and unoccupied, in the southeast. There, the National Assembly
moved to the spa town of Vichy, where in July 1940, it established a
quasi-independent authoritarian regime. Vichy was ruled by Marshal
Philippe Pétain, an eighty-four-year-old French military hero who
had served in World War I. The declaration of the rights of man
was abolished and the phrase "Liberty, Equality, and Fraternity"
was replaced with "Work, Family, Fatherland." On May 15, 1941,
Pétain made a radio broadcast to the French people, demanding that
they follow him without reservation, along what he called the "path
of honor and national interest," so that France could "surmount her
defeat and preserve in the world her rank as a European and colonial
power." For a conquered nation, these were truly the politics of delu-
sion. But for Pétain, an elderly, ultrareactionary, conservative military
officer, and his Vichy ministers, there was one, overriding consideration in France's wartime survival ethics: the preservation of that
same "honor and national interest." For this, almost anything would
be sacrificed, even to the point where the very notion of a quasi-
independent France, with any degree of autonomy, became virtually
meaningless—as, by the end of the war, it did.

Vichy's first target was its Jews. The tolerant policies of the
liberal Third Republic, which had taken in tens of thousands of
Jewish refugees (to the horror of the nationalists around Pétain)

were dismantled. In Vichy, anti-Jewish legislation was rapidly introduced, notably *without* any German pressure, argue Michael Marrus and Robert Paxton in *Vichy France and the Jews.*[6] Denmark showed its independence by saving its Jews; Vichy demonstrated its collusion by passing anti-Semitic laws and interning Jews before the Germans demanded it do so. Vichy passed its first anti-Jewish law in October 1940.

We can find no trace of German attempts to extend its own anti-Jewish policy to the Unoccupied Zone in the summer of 1940; at the beginning, Germany envisaged France as a dumping ground for its own refugees. Vichy's anti-Jewish policy was thus not only autonomous from German policy; it was rival to it. Vichy struggled with the occupying authority in an attempt to assert its own sovereignty in anti-Jewish matters and to keep the advantage of property confiscations and refugee control for itself.

Vichy's anti-Jewish policies were a disaster for the 350,000 Jews living in France. Less than half of these were native-born, the remainder were refugees from Germany and occupied lands, such as Austria, Czechoslovakia, and the Low Countries, as well as eastern Europe. Many had fled south to the Unoccupied Zone but found there only meager sanctuary. Also, in October 1940, the internment of foreign-born Jews was authorized, and about 25,000 Jewish refugees from Germany and Austria were interned in labor camps such as Gurs. Half-starved, sick, forced into labor brigades, many died. Alone among western nations occupied by or allied to the Nazis, Vichy France implemented its own autonomous anti-Semitic policies to incarcerate Jews in harsh-regime work camps with a high mortality rate. The first residents of France to die in the Holocaust died on French soil. They were killed not by Germans but by Frenchmen.

The precedent had been set in October 1939, when months before its surrender, France had begun rounding up refugees, many of them left-wing, Jewish, or both. Among these was Arthur Koestler, the Hungarian-born writer, who was interned in the camp of Le Verney, which he describes as the worst in France. There were chilling similarities with the Nazi camps, which he recorded in his autobiographical work, *Scum of the Earth*. There were roll calls four times a day, when inmates had to stand immobile in the frost, and camp guards had carte blanche to punch or whip them for the slightest offense. With regard to "food, accommodation, and hygiene," Le Verney was worse than the Nazi concentration camps. Koestler noted, "We had some thirty men in section C who had previously been interned in various German camps, including the worst reputed, Dachau, Oranienburg, and Wolfsbuettel, and they had an expert knowledge of these questions."[7] Koestler had himself been imprisoned by Franco's forces during the Spanish Civil War in Seville, where he claimed prisoners were better treated.

The following year, in June 1941, Vichy adopted new anti-Jewish regulations, based on those implemented in the Occupied Zone. Still, Vichy followed its own course when it could. Vichy even had, at one stage, a black cabinet minister for the colonies, which sat ill with Nazi notions of Nordic racial purity. But, then, French citizenship was based on patriotism, cultural assimilation, and loyalty, rather than Germanic notions of race. Unlike in Germany, there was no ban on intermarriage between Jews and non-Jews. Such anomalies aside, the French Holocaust, in both zones, followed the course dictated by the Nazis. Jewish businesses were registered, then sequestered, and then "Aryanized." Jews were banned from many professions. In occupied Paris, French police, supervised by Adolf Eichmann's aide Theodor Danncecker, began work on a citywide card index of Jews, listing their names, addresses, occupations, and nationalities. The French police went to work that summer, arresting thousands of Jews, many of them French-born. Most were sent to Drancy, the holding camp in a suburb of Paris, before eventually being deported to Auschwitz.

In one roundup on July 16 and 17, 1942, almost 13,000 Jews were taken. Almost four thousand were sent to Drancy, records historian Lucy Dawidowicz, while the remaining nine thousand were held in the Velodrome d'Hiver sports stadium, before being sent to Auschwitz.[8] Thirty adults returned after the war.

In the unoccupied zone, the Germans were putting increasing pressure on Vichy to hand over all Jews, whether French or foreign. Pétain and Vichy's answer that July was to agree to hand over foreign Jews, but not French ones, who would remain under Vichy's protection, such as it was. In August 1942, 15,000 foreign Jews were surrendered to the Nazis, part of a total of at least 75,000 Jews who were deported from France to their deaths, from both zones. Many thousands more were killed in reprisal shootings of hostages.

After the war, Vichy ministers such as Pierre Laval argued that Vichy policy had ensured the survival of most of French Jewry. Foreign-born Jews had been sacrificed, but the vast majority of French Jews had survived. But this was due more to Allied military victories and the turning tide of war than any humanitarian concern of Vichy. There is little reason to doubt that French Jewry would have suffered the same eventual fate as Polish or Greek Jewry. Laval himself admitted that he had some idea of what deportation meant:

> I tried to find out, by questioning them where the Germans were sending those convoys of Jews, and their reply inevitably was: "To Poland, where we want to create a Jewish state." I was well aware that this meant working there in terrible conditions, most often to suffer and die there.[9]

For Vichy, anti-Jewish legislation and the deportation of foreign and then some of their own Jews was a part of national survival ethics. These were regrettable, but necessary, sacrifices for the greater good of France, argued Laval and his colleagues. The Vichy regime wrongly assumed that Jews could be traded for political and strategic advantage, note Marrus and Paxton: "In what proved to be a colossal miscalculation, the Vichy leaders assumed that the German authorities would be grateful to the French for pursuing a parallel anti-Jewish policy and would respond by yielding greater authority to France over this and other spheres of national activity."[10] By the time the extermination camps were fully operational and the deportations began in 1942, Vichy had long before set up its own, autonomous, *French* infrastructure of registration, confiscation, and internment for Jews. Ethically, it was a short step from French Gurs to Nazi Auschwitz. Vichy authorities, on their own initiative, had already set the Holocaust in motion, and they kept it going.

Marshal Pétain's British Bank Account

While Marshal Philippe Pétain negotiated with the Germans, British officials deliberated over the vexing question of the 1941 annuity payment on his insurance policy. The reams of intra-government correspondence over this issue fill a substantial file at the British Public Records Office. Even Winston Churchill found time to consider the matter.

Marshal Pétain had a policy with a Canadian insurance company. Although Canada was independent, it was an Allied nation, and the Queen was still head of state. The company duly registered with Britain's Custodian of Enemy Property Department that it wished to pay out monies due to Marshal Pétain, but under the terms of the Trading with the Enemy Act, residents of enemy territory could not receive such payments. A tricky diplomatic dilemma. The British bureaucrats were divided between those who favored treating Marshal Pétain like any other French national, and those who thought that, as a head of state, even a Nazi-allied one, he deserved special treatment. The files flew back and forth, raising ever more complicated questions, both political and technical. Several officials raised the issue that if the monies were paid, they could open the Marshal to the accusation of being in the pay of Britain. A letter from the Treasury suggested that a British firm with a French subsidiary could make the payment from the subsidiary's account "probably in plain envelope," or in other words, under the counter.

By November 1941, Marshal Pétain's payments were even being discussed in the War Cabinet. The chancellor of the Exchequer and the foreign secretary were opposed to transferring any further funds, as it would be met with public disapproval, and because Britain had no diplomatic relations with Vichy. Prime Minister Churchill took a different view, arguing that, until recently, France had been Britain's ally, and stopping the payment would be "petty and vindictive."

Eventually, the War Cabinet agreed that, as Marshal Pétain was a head of state, the payments would continue, especially as the policy was with a Canadian company, and Canada—like the U.S.—then maintained diplomatic relations with Vichy. But that was not the end of the matter. Later that month, a question was asked in Parliament, igniting wider interest. And furthermore, Marshal Pétain let it be known that he wanted his payments in pounds sterling, not French francs, which was both unpatriotic and inconvenient. A blocked sterling account, to which the Marshal could have no access, had to be set up to receive the annuities. It was all getting increasingly messy and much too public. The monies, it was decided, would be paid into the blocked account, but there should be no more discussion of Marshal Pétain's sterling bank account. Government files noted that revealing this information would encourage "further embarrassing questions of a similar nature."

※ ※ ※

As late as August 25, 1944, the very day Paris was liberated, a train loaded with seven hundred prisoners crossed from France into Germany, en route to Dachau. Many of the passengers were captured *résistants* or Republican refugees from the Spanish Civil War, others were Jews. French *gendarmes* nailed the windows of the train shut before it departed from Toulouse station, and the driver and cattle trucks were provided by SNCF, the French railway company, which after the war was paid for the journey by the French government. The train wandered across France—in the chaos of war, air raids, and the Allied advance—for fifty-seven days, including a month stopover in Bordeaux. Even then, Vichy ensured some of its last victims made their way to Dachau. Among the passengers was Jean Nodon, arrested in 1943 at the age of twenty-three for shooting an informer. Members of the Milice, the Vichy pro-Nazi militia tortured him before handing him to the Nazis. He survived Dachau, and weighed seventy pounds when released. In an interview decades later, he said: "Vichy was worse than the Germans because the Germans were the enemy. But Vichy was Frenchmen. They tortured Frenchmen. It was Vichy who organized these trains. They knew exactly what the German camps were like. For them, the liberation was a catastrophe."[11]

Illuminating comparisons can be made between Vichy and Hungary and Italy. These nations, unlike France, were Axis allies rather than a defeated enemy, and so they would be expected to acquiesce more readily in the Final Solution. In fact, the opposite was true. For almost the whole course of the war, until the Nazi invasion of March 1944, Hungarian Jews enjoyed unique safety from deportation. Hungarian Jews were not forced into ghettos and did not have to wear yellow stars until April 1944. A series of increasingly repressive anti-Jewish laws were passed, yet communal life contin- ued for Hungary's 650,000 Jews, the largest remaining community on the continent. Several thousand Jewish refugees from Poland and Slovakia found sanctuary in Hungary, synagogues remained open, and Jewish welfare organizations continued their work. Under increasing pressure from Berlin, Hungary's ruler Admiral Horthy refused to hand over the country's native born Jews to the Nazis. In one incident in 1941, between 11,000 and 18,000 refugee Jews were expelled to Ukraine, but after reports reached Budapest that most were killed by the Nazis, the deportations were not repeated.

In the spring of 1941, Hungarian troops massacred Jews and Serbs in northern Serbia (see "One Who Said 'No,'" below), but the killings caused an outcry in Budapest, and the perpetrators were put on trial. Hungary, until the Nazis arrived, was a far safer place to be Jewish than Vichy France. Indeed, it was Horthy's refusal to hand over Hungary's Jews, combined with his secret contacts with the Allies (see "Our Man in Budapest," p. 188) that was a major factor in the Nazi invasion and the subsequent, unprecedented speed of the Hungarian Holocaust, when 450,000 Jews were deported to Auschwitz in the summer of 1944.

One Who Said "No"

When the soldiers in Gyula Dornbach's battalion of the Hungarian army marched into Voivodina, in northern Serbia, in the spring 1941 and reoccupied the former Hungarian territories, they kissed the ground in jubilation.

But that joy soon turned sour when the orders came through to carry out a mass execution as a means of instilling terror in the local Serb population. That shooting was a mere taste of the killings to come in the nearby town of Novi Sad and its environs.

Now ninety-one, Gyula Dornbach was then a military clerk, based in the city of Zenta, whose job was to type out the deluge of paperwork on which an army moves and operates. A week after the invasion, a colonel arrived from the southern Hungarian city of Szeged, remembers Dornbach. "He asked us for the list of all the people who had been executed. We told him that nobody had been executed, and he demanded that twenty-four people be shot immediately, just to show the power of the gendarmerie. There were three hundred people being held under arrest in the cellars of the army headquarters, people were denouncing each other all the time. They took two lots of twelve people and marched them to the bank of the Tisza River." [12]

The Colonel told Dornbach to pick up a weapon and join the firing squad. Dornbach refused. Normally, military discipline meant that anyone refusing an order would be shot himself, but Dornbach deftly turned the principle back on the officer. "He told to me to take a gun, but I told him I didn't have a weapon, I didn't even have a pistol. I told him that was not my job. I had my orders to do my work, and I said to him, 'Here are my orders, and my job is to follow them.'" It worked, and Dornbach was excused. Gyula Dornbach was also a member of Hungary's ethnic German minority. But Nazism held no attraction for him or his family.

Almost sixty years later, the former soldier still remembers the sound of the rifle shots as the bodies toppled into the Tisza's waters. "Of course, I heard the shooting. When the second group was taken to the river bank, one of them jumped in, and the soldiers started shooting at him. The Germans on the other side of the river began firing as well." Gyula Dornbach suffered no penalty for his act of defiance, although he admits it would have been a different story if he were not a company clerk, but a normal enlisted man. "I couldn't have said no, because I would have been executed. But I wouldn't have shot anyone. I would have shot above their heads. Nobody would have been able to tell."

※ ※ ※

Better still than Hungary was Italy. There was little anti-Semitism in Italy, and most Italians, even fascists, had little sympathy for Nazi concepts of racism, which they found ludicrous. Italian fascism was seen as a means of national, not racial, revival. In the 1930s, the distinction between nationalism and racialism was vital. Italian Jews were considered fully Italian. They were welcomed into the fascist party. In fact, several founding members were Jews.

Mussolini himself was indifferent to anti-Semitism, employing Jewish government officials when they were deemed useful and using anti-Jewish sentiment when it could bring advantage, such as dealing with Hitler.

By 1938, there were more than ten thousand Jewish refugees in Italy, mainly from Germany and Austria, as well as 47,000 Italian Jews. Under increasing pressure from Hitler, Mussolini introduced anti-Jewish laws in 1938 and 1939; yet, unlike in Hungary, there was little popular enthusiasm for such measures. Like Admiral Horthy, Mussolini refused outright to deport Italy's Jews. As Lucy Dawidowicz writes: "[W]hatever hardships the Italian Jews had to undergo from the end of 1938 on, their situation was enviable in contrast to those Jews who lived under direct German occupation."[13] Just as in Hungary, Italian Jews were not deported until the Nazis invaded, in autumn 1943.

Our Man In Budapest

Hungary willingly joined the Axis to regain territories lost after its defeat in 1918, but during the latter years of the war, Budapest put out feelers to the Allies, hinting it would desert Hitler. These overtures, and its ruler Admiral Horthy's refusal to deport Hungarian Jews, helped trigger the Nazi invasion of March 1944. Yet, even after the German occupation, and perhaps partly because of it, Admiral Horthy continued his secret contacts with the West, through an Allied officer living and working clandestinely in the Hungarian capital.

National survival ethics dictated that Admiral Horthy wanted Hungary to be liberated from the Nazis by the Western Allies, not the Soviets. He had choices, but the Admiral could not make up his mind, reported South African–born Colonel Charles T. Howie, charged with per-suading him to break with Berlin. Colonel Howie had made his way to Budapest after escaping from a German prisoner-of-war camp. On arrival, he was aided by the Hungarian anti-Nazi resistance, particularly the Reverend Alexander Szent-Ivanyi, of the Unitarian Church in Budapest, who ran a network aiding escaped Allied POWs. A secret radio transmitter was set up in the back room of Reverend Szent-Ivanyi's parsonage.

Through Szent-Ivanyi, Howie made contact with Admiral Horthy's son, Miklos Horthy Jr., a committed anti-Nazi. Miklos Horthy Jr. was one of the leaders of the "Extrication Group," which aimed to disentangle Hungary from the Axis and join the Allies. Through the summer of 1944, until the Gestapo got on his trail and he was forced to flee in September, Howie was quartered in the Royal Castle in Budapest, with the full knowledge of Admiral Horthy and many of his officials. He even transmitted messages from his radio set, installed, together with his Polish radio operator, in the room above.

Sometime in July 1944, Miklos Horthy Jr. first brought Howie to the Royal Castle in Buda to meet his father to try and persuade him to bring Hungary over to the Allies. As the records of Howie's debriefing in October 1944 detail:

This was the first of several meetings which H. had with the Regent. During these meetings, H. pressed Horthy to surrender immediately to the Russians, but Horthy could not make up his mind, partly, as H. put it, because his honor would not permit him to stab his country in the back, and partly because he still felt that he had everything to gain and nothing to lose by postponing the evil day as long as possible. H. said that Horthy always listened to the last people to see him, and as the Germans naturally saw him oftener than H., he allowed himself to be swayed by them.[14]

Howie also attempted to organize armed resistance to the Nazis. Unlike other occupied capitals, such as Warsaw, Prague, and Bratislava, there was no uprising in Budapest against the Nazis. Like Admiral Horthy, many Hungarians adopted a passive approach to the Germans, to Howie's disgust. According to the debriefing document, he was unable to even find half a dozen Hungarians willing to try to kill the head of the secret police:

> H. had no knowledge of any potential Hungarian resistance group. He frequently tried to organize such a group but failed, owing to the apathy and fear of the population. As an example of this, he wanted to get hold of six Hungarians to start an organization for shooting well-known collaborators, starting off with Peter Hain, chief of Hungarian secret police and SS formations. It took two months to find six Hungarians who were willing to do this, and by that time, the plan was not feasible and had to be dropped.

He had much more respect for the Polish underground, which also operated out of Budapest, and with whom he spent the most time, the same document notes. "When speaking of the Hungarians, of whom he has a very low opinion, he said, 'You see, I cannot stand cowardice in any form.' This remark is typical of him, and it is easy to imagine the mutual respect which he and the Poles must have had for each other." Colonel Howie's view of Hungarians was biased, the document noted: "Except for his contacts at the Castle, he lived an undercover life, almost entirely with the Poles, so that his picture of Hungarian conditions is, as he himself admits, somewhat one-sided."

In the end, Colonel Howie's efforts failed. By mid-October 1944, Admiral Horthy was ready to join the Allies, but it was too late. He was toppled in a German-backed coup by the Arrow Cross Hungarian Nazis. Miklos Horthy Jr. was arrested and sent to Mauthausen and then Dachau, where he was liberated by U.S. troops. Admiral Horthy was exiled to Germany, then Portugal, where he died. A case then, not of too few choices, but too many.

❖ ❖ ❖

When, in November 1942, Italy occupied eight departments of southern France around Nice, the Italian zone became a sanctuary of peace and safety for French Jews who could reach it. Italy had already demanded, and received, exemption for Italian Jews living in occupied France from wearing yellow stars. Italian officials in their zone prevented French officials from implementing the Vichy policy of expelling foreign and stateless Jews. The French prefect in the Italian zone was forbidden to apply the Vichy law that ID cards and ration books belonging to Jews should be stamped. The Italian consul general in Nice informed Vichy that he had sole power to deal with the Jewish question.

"Nice became a Jewish political and cultural center under the benevolent eye of the Italian army," note historians Marrus and Paxton.[15] Italian policemen stood guard over the synagogue; Jews were allowed to issue their own identity cards—of vital importance for stateless refugees—and the *carabinieri* commander, Captain Salvi, declared that any French policemen who interfered would be arrested. In Vichy, Laval was outraged at this assault on Vichy's powers and asked for German support in remedying the situation.

Ironically, the changing tide of the war in favor of the Allies meant that the Jews' Riviera idyll could not last. In September 1943, after the fall of Mussolini, the Allies announced an armistice with Italy. The Italians left their zone and the Nazis invaded. In one of the most severe roundups of the war, the Nazis, with the help of French collaborators, captured thousands of Jews in southern France who were rapidly sent to Drancy and then Auschwitz.

A twist of history meant that fascist Mussolini, Hitler's ally, had proved to be their best protection.

All of which begs the question: Could Vichy have saved more of its Jews? The answer is, almost certainly yes, had it chosen to. Vichy France was more than a puppet government—it enjoyed diplomatic relations with the U.S. until 1942, for example—although perpetually in the shadow of the swastika and less than a true independent state (especially after the German invasion of November 1942, when all of France, apart from the Italian zone, came under German rule).

Even so, Vichy's local officials still retained considerable autonomy. When, in 1943, Vichy officials began to drag their feet over the deportations, their pace slowed. Had Vichy officials not compiled indexes of Jews and interned them in French camps, the Germans would have had to proceed at a much slower pace. And, if Vichy was not overly concerned over the fate of French Jewry, where matters of French *national* interest were concerned, its leaders were vociferous and determined.

As early as December 1940, Pétain had dismissed Laval, arch-exponent of the policy of collaborating with the Nazis, and replaced him with Admiral François Darlan, who was less pro-German. Pétain opened channels to the Allies, sending an emissary to London. Mindful of French possessions in North Africa under threat from the German advance, he urged neutral Spain's leader, General Franco, not to grant the Nazis passage through Spain to North Africa. When the Allies landed in North Africa in November 1942, Pétain ordered Admiral Darlan to bring French forces in North Africa under their command. The French fleet at Toulon was scuttled by its crews. Pétain refused to allow the German navy to attack British forces in the Mediterranean from French ports in North Africa.

Like the Third Reich itself, the Vichy government was also riven by ideological factionalism, with some ministers and officials leaning toward the Allies. Perhaps not surprisingly, the leaders of the pro-British faction were based in the Vichy foreign ministry, as foreign ministry officials usually possess a more acute sense of real-politik than their domestic counterparts. A 1942 telegram from the British embassy in Portugal, forwarding information received from Hugo Bachet, the former press attaché at the Romanian embassy in Paris, records: "The officials of the Vichy Ministry of Foreign Affairs, beginning with the Secretary-General, M. Rochat, who was his [i.e., Bachet's] personal friend, are almost unanimously pro-British, so too are the General Staff whose influence was constantly exerted to counter Darlan and the collaborationist elements at Vichy."[16] The telegram also notes the refusal of the Vichy authorities to deliver 50,000 horses, forcing Germans to buy them on the black market and the effect of German censorship on newspaper sales. *Le Matin's* circulation had plunged from 600,000 to 60,000, while *Petit Parisien* and *Paris Soir* had also dropped to less than 10 percent of their previous figures.

Concerned with its continent-wide diplomatic reach, Vichy even intervened on behalf of the French Jews living in Salonika, after the Nazis invaded Greece. But distorted through the prism of France's fading imperial glory, Vichy's moral lapse ensured its survival ethics focused on preserving the remnants of empire, on maintaining international prestige, rather than on saving the lives of French citizens who were Jews. But *la gloire* became ever more tarnished as the war progressed. By the end, Pétain and Laval (who the Germans reimposed in April 1942) were little more than ciphers, utterly corrupted by their compromises with the Nazis. Pétain even called on the French not to aid the Allies after the D-day landings. In July 1945, Vichy's leader was tried for treason and sentenced to death, commuted to life imprisonment, and he died in prison in July 1951. Pierre Laval was also found guilty of treason, but received no commutation, and he was executed on October 15, 1945.

Pétain and Laval found a receptive channel to Berlin in Otto Abetz, Germany's ambassador to Vichy France. Abetz enthusiastically advocated using a policy of anti-Semitism to cement Franco-German ties, which was well received by many Vichy officials. Under Berlin's direction, Abetz had launched his public relations drive several years before France surrendered. Sophisticated, even charming, Abetz had made considerable social headway with sections of Paris' prewar cultural and literary elite, according to a wartime British declassified document. It credits him with both a French wife, "sometimes described as beautiful and wealthy," and a film star mistress.

Otto Abetz was expelled from France in 1939, but his work of political seduction was not without results, helped by the growing sentiment that the country was slipping out of control. The domestic chaos of the Third Republic, its weak and wobbling governments, riots on the streets, brawls inside the National Assembly, and the mass influx of refugees all helped boost the French far right. Among some of the country's governing elite, the desire grew for a strong hand to take charge, even a foreign one.

Just as in prewar Britain, some key French political and economic figures supported cooperation with Nazi Germany (see "What Would We Have Done?" p. 176). In Britain, members of The Link aimed to foster good relations between London and Berlin, while in Paris, the Comité Franco-Allemagne did similar work. Abetz was a key figure in the committee, "which seems to have succeeded in reaching somewhat wider circles than did the 'Link,' its counterpart in England." Abetz employed classic Nazi propaganda tactics in cultivating support for the Third Reich— outright bribery and lush hospitality on free trips to Germany, the British document records:

By means of the first, "corruption par l'editeur," French authors were directly or indirectly invited by German publishers to have their works translated into German in exchange for the payment of large sums of money: the books, however, frequently remained untranslated. The second method employed by Abetz was to lure visitors to Germany. Prominent Frenchmen, frequently quite unaware of the real object of the invitations, were asked to Germany. Not only was valuable information extracted from them, but above all they returned home dazzled and charmed by German hospitality.[17]

After the fall of France and his return to Paris, Abetz declared that there was an ideological continuity between Napoleon and Nazism, proclaiming that, "It is with Napoleon that the great popular movements began, which are being recreated in fascist Italy and National-Socialist Germany, and even in France, in spite of certain reactionary tendencies." A few days later, he was received by Marshal Pétain at Vichy. According to the document, just as in his prewar work, Abetz expended much energy on wooing the city's elite: "Abetz'[s] actual role in Paris would appear to be connected with 'social' rather than diplomatic matters and thus forms a continuation of his earlier mission: flattery and corruption to achieve collaboration."

For the vast majority of French people, of course, there were no invitations to Abetz's champagne receptions. Life under Nazi occupation was a dreary grind. They lived—were trapped—in a web of daily, petty corruptions, of fear, curfews, and blackouts. As the opening epigram records, their main concerns were food, the Germans, and the eventual, long-awaited arrival of the Allies. As in other occupied countries, men were deported to Germany for forced labor in harsh conditions. Survival ethics meant getting enough to eat and keeping warm and out of the Germans' way. There were no guarantees. The Nazis plucked people from the street at random and held them as hostages. After acts of resistance, especially armed attacks on Germans, the hostages, usually Communists and Jews, would then be shot en masse for each German death, unless the perpetrators were found. Not surprisingly, this brutal tactic restricted the number of attacks on Nazis. The executions would be dutifully recorded in the local press, which was closely monitored by the Allies' intelligence services.

Sometimes, a whole city would be punished for acts of resistance. The *Pariser Zeitung* of April 22, 1942, recorded that, as a

German soldier had been shot dead from behind at Molitor Metro station, ten Communists, Jews, and "other instigators" were to be "shot immediately." If the culprit was not arrested within a week, another twenty Communists and Jews would be shot, and a further five hundred Communists, Jews, and others would be deported to labor camps in the East. In addition, all cinemas, theaters, and other amusement places would be closed from April 21 to 24. Two days later, the newspaper reported that the closure order was to be lifted and the twenty hostages would be reprieved, as French civilians had handed over those responsible for another attack on German soldiers. Minor offenses, such as showing humanity to Slavs, brought lighter penalties. The *Strassburger Neueste Nachrichten* reported in April 1942 that an innkeeper at Keffenach was sentenced to two months imprisonment for the offense of giving a drink to Polish prisoners the previous New Year's Eve.

Even in daily life, there were opportunities for ethical choices, sometimes in the most unexpected quarters, such as the famed French fashion industry. A 1943 British record of intercepted letters is full of fascinating day-to-day details about life in France under Nazi occupation and the differing ways in which the French responded to their German overlords. According to one letter, Paris herself became a symbol of resistance:

> Alongside the grim endurance and prayers for victory and revenge, there exists yet another spirit. Some French people and the people of Paris in particular, are determined to deprive the Germans of the pleasure of destroying their long-enjoyed reputation for elegance and lightheartedness. In spite of the curfew and the blackout, of scarcities and appalling prices, and of the shaming presence of the occupiers, a defiant gaiety is everywhere.[18]

One letter recorded: "The Parisienne does not give in and is still pretty, smiling and elegant. All the shows, theaters and cinemas are packed," while another noted: "...the fashions are fantastic, and because the Germans have said that as little material as possible should be used, all leading houses show skirts yards wide, and the hats are so enormous that women cannot get through doorways."

Not everyone remained defiant. In the capital, surrounded by defiant compatriots, it was perhaps easier than in the countryside. There, some admitted that their spirit and their bodies were fading, and they could see no end in sight, such as the writer of this letter, sent from France to England, via Portugal:

Just lately I have become much thinner, I have dropped from 66 kilos to 56 kilos. It is a torture which becomes ever harder to endure....Our only hope is to see the end of this accursed war which is doing so much harm to the whole world. We must hope that it finishes soon. Whatever happens, I shall always be glad to know that you are at length secure. Here, there is always one death a day. Our curé [priest] is drinking...when returning from the annual feast at Benoit, he had to be carried in a cart harnessed to an ass and held on both sides lest he fall. Poor curé, he is dying of hunger too....The other day when saying his mass, he fell down twice.[19]

Surviving Hitler could also mean taking a German soldier as a lover and protector, usually to the disgust of other French women. In May 1943, a woman in Toulon wrote to a friend in the French navy: "I am not like certain ones who do not know how to respect their husbands. French women who walk out on the arm of *messieurs les Allemands!* There are many of them in Toulon, and it revolts me to see it. How many broken homes there will be after the war."[20] Such women were subjected to dreadful humiliation and punishment after the war, not just in France but across occupied Europe. Their heads were shaved, they were tarred and feathered, and they had swastikas painted, sometimes carved, on their bodies. Some were driven around in open lorries wearing placards around their neck that announced "German Whore," or in Denmark, "Army Mattress." A famous photograph by Robert Capa shows the former lover of a German soldier, her head as smooth as a billiard ball, clutching the illegitimate child of her doomed relationship, as she strides through mocking crowds in Chartres. Within a few months of liberation, ten thousand women had their heads shaved. Deprived of male protection, weak, and alone, they were easy targets on which to vent the impotent rage and hatred their compatriots had felt for the Germans. And, often those who howled loudest for their punishment had themselves collaborated and hoped their calls for vengeance would distract their compatriots from their own murky wartime record.

However unpatriotic it was to sleep with the enemy, taking a German lover was the collaboration of comfort, meeting a human need for companionship. On a scale of moral corruption, the black marketeers and war profiteers score far higher. They not only survived Hitler, but profited greatly from Nazi rule and the commercial opportunities it engendered. The 1943 British intercepted-post report noted that:

> Even though they may not collaborate with the occupiers, many Frenchmen are increasing the distress of their compatriots by their graspingness. The peasants particularly are reproached for persistently holding back produce and forcing prices up. In Finistere, they are said to be "still obstinate, it never enters their heads that we have lost the war, they have no consciences and do not think of the afflicted who need their supplies."[21]

The peasants of Finistere aside, the all-encompassing nature of the Nazi occupation, which reached into every facet of existence, meant that, just to survive, even reasonably upright and moral individuals were inextricably drawn into daily small corruptions. French society's morals withered and decayed. Trading on the black market became a necessity to live and eat. Yet when did survival become profiteering?

Consider the case of Antoine Pereire, a twenty-year-old Frenchman who escaped from Paris to Portugal in August 1943. In Lisbon, British embassy officials interviewed him at length about conditions in wartime Paris. Pereire had worked as a waiter on the terrace of a café near the Gare St. Lazare and, thus, was in a good position to encounter a wide cross section of both French and Germans. By 1943, after Stalingrad, there was little enthusiasm among the Nazi rank-and-file for the war, he said in a 1943 interview. Most German soldiers wanted to go home: "[W]hen alone, they expressed the hope that the British would hurry up and land, so that the war would be over and they could go, many of them not having had leave for three years. They frequently offer drinks to the French and seek by every means to cultivate friendly relations."[22]

Pereire, who also dealt in cloth on the side, gave a detailed rundown to embassy officials of how the black market worked. Most of the black market economy ran on barter, with paper money "a very small feature in average dealing." The major black marketeers converted paper fortunes into tangible assets as soon as possible, especially land (buildings were less popular because of air raids), furniture, diamonds and jewels, gold, tapestries, furs, and so on. The main currency was not the franc, but cigarettes. Black market merchants bought a packet of twenty Gauloises for eighty francs, and resold it for 140 francs. "Informant stated that tobacco was an article which opened all doors and that, with sufficient cigarettes, one may obtain any article. Cigarettes are so scarce that they are sold separately at ten francs each." A tailor had even made him a suit, for which he paid in tobacco. By way of comparison, Pereire was paid a salary of one thousand francs a month, plus meals.

Municipal officials, who had access to stocks of ration cards, without which the only food available was that sold on the black market, could profit handsomely. They sold blank ration cards, but with the vital municipal stamp, to the black marketeers for one hundred francs. These would then fetch between three hundred and five hundred francs. So lucrative was this trade that several municipal offices were raided by armed robbers. A massive parallel black economy ran alongside the legitimate one. It could not be avoided, according to Pereire:

> Informant himself was amazed at the extent of the black market traffic.
>
> It is quite impossible to obtain even the necessaries of life without having recourse to it: the huge turnover quite eclipses the turnover of legitimate purchases with tickets.
>
> It is necessary to have a "bon" [i.e., ticket] for the purchase of almost any article in the legitimate market; he stated that one could not even buy a screwdriver, a saucepan, or a yard of cloth, in fact any article without a "bon" from the Marie [municipality], and that when one presented a "bon" at a shop, it usually took three months to get the article which it called for, whereas exactly the same article would be found on the black market immediately and of better quality.

There could also be handsome legal profits in legally trading with the enemy, and not just in France. Young men in northern Norway were paid one thousand crowns a week to work on German building projects, while they had previously earned four thousand crowns a year as small farmers. Before the Nazi occupation, many farmers in northern Norway were deeply in debt. By the end, many were rich. Roads and airstrips had to be built, uniforms laundered.

The gap between surviving Hitler and reaching a comfortable, if not profitable, accommodation could be narrow, at least for those whom the Germans—still in awe, perhaps, of French culture and sophistication—courted at their salons. Yet an ethical line could be drawn. There were no penalties for refusing Abetz's champagne.

The many shades of gray between compromise and collaboration are well illustrated in the realistic novel by Alan Furst, *Red Gold*, set in occupied Paris.[23] Marie-Claire is married to Bruno, who is trading very profitably with the Nazi occupiers. She enjoys the material comforts and security this brings, but her moral and patriotic doubts are steadily gnawing at her. She declares: "I don't like the Germans. I never did like them, and I like them even less since they took the country. There was a time when Bruno was bringing them here, for cocktails and dinner parties. Well, I put a stop to that. Maybe it doesn't get me a statue in the park when the war ends, but it's better than nothing."

From that, Marie-Claire progresses to providing illegal accommodation for associates of General de Gaulle, just as Germans hosted Jewish "U-boats" for a few days. The character is fictitious, yet she realistically encapsulates the essential dilemmas of life under occupation, of surviving rule by Hitler. It was here, in the cracks and crevices of daily life, that ethical choices could be, and were, made.

In the East, the situation was radically different. There, Nazi occupation was implemented not on grounds of logic or military sense, but was shaped by a manic adherence to racial doctrine and policies based on terror and plunder. Viewing the Slavic lands through the blinkers of Aryan ideology, the Nazi leadership was blind to wider strategic opportunities that could have altered the direction of the war.

When, in 1941, the Nazis occupied much of the Ukraine, for example, there was a considerable groundswell of support for the Germans, who were regarded by many there as liberators from the Stalinist regime. This was because the Ukraine had withered under Soviet rule. The country's independence movement had been crushed, and millions had died of starvation in the famine of 1932–1933. Cannibalism had been widespread as the harvests and the Soviet collective farms failed. Among the peasants, there was widespread hatred for both the Communist commissars and their Russian overlords who had confiscated crops, wrecked the country's agriculture, and ruled by terror and *diktat*. There was widespread hope that the short-lived independent Ukrainian Republic, which sprang out of the chaos of the end of World War I, would be revived. Many Ukrainians also identified communism with Jewry and, as in neighboring Poland, anti-Semitism was widespread. Throughout the war, there was a steady supply of Ukrainians serving as guards in the concentration and extermination camps such as Treblinka and Belzec.

Not suprisingly, as the Nazi tanks rolled across the fertile plains, German troops were at first greeted with bread and salt. Early in the war, many thousands of Ukrainians also joined the Nazi armed forces to fight against the Communist Red Army. As late as 1944, 50,000 former Soviet troops were fighting under the turncoat Russian officer Andrey Andreyevich Vlasov in the Nazi-sponsored "Russian Liberation Army." But Nazi racial doctrine, which regarded Slavs and Jews, especially Eastern ones, as *untermenschen,* or "subhumans," meant that the occupying forces acted with utmost brutality. Houses were burned down, their inhabitants killed, their contents plundered. Nazi actions in the Ukraine were truly a triumph of racial ideology over military sense. Had the Nazis fostered even a quasi-independent Ukrainian state, such as in neighboring Slovakia, they could have built a strategically vital bridgehead of support for the war against neighboring Russia with millions of supporters who hated Communism and everything it stood for.

In Berlin, Nazi officials such as Dr. Otto Braeutingen, head of the Main Political Department in the Ministry of the Eastern Territories, saw how counterproductive the mass executions of hostages and the burning of villages was. On October 25, 1942, he wrote a memo that was severely critical of Nazi policy in the Soviet Union:

A form of administration that was not intent simply on plunder and exploitation and that abolished Bolshevist methods would have kindled the greatest enthusiasm and would have put at our disposal a mass consisting of millions. And the enthusiasm in the occupied territories in the East would have had its impact on the powers of resistance of the Red Army. It would have been easy to persuade the Red Army man to say to himself: "I am fighting for a system that is far worse than that which I can expect in the event of a defeat. Under the Germans, things will be much better than they have been up to now." If this view had become general among the members of the Red Army, the war would soon have been over.[24]

Dr. Braeutingen went on to criticize the Nazi failure to restore the individual property rights that the Communists had abolished and condemn the failure to give a clear, preferably positive, message about the eastern territories' future under the Nazis. This policy, he argued, was throwing away the opportunity to bring over many anti-Communist Slavs to the Nazi side: "Many would like to desert, but they don't know to whom they are going. Under the banner of a recognized counter-revolutionary leader, they would fight gladly and bravely against the Bolshevist regime." Laborers were being shipped back to Germany from the eastern territories to fill the man-power gap with the utmost brutality, he recorded: "With the usual unlimited abuse of Slav people, 'recruiting' methods were used that can only be compared to the blackest periods of the slave trade.... It needs no elaboration to appreciate that these methods, which of course are being applied in this form not to nationals of enemy countries like Holland or Norway, but only to the Soviet Union, have their repercussions on the resistance of the Red Army."

Hitler was unable to see the benefits of a more conciliatory approach. His plan instead was that the Ukraine would be colonized by human waves of German settlers in a *Drang nach Osten* ("Drive to the East") who would till the soil, bringing forth the crops that would feed the master race. As he wrote in *Mein Kampf*: "The New Reich must set itself on the march along the road of the Teutonic knights to obtain by the German sword the sod for the German plough and the daily bread for the nation." Instead, the rich earth of the Ukraine once known as "Europe's bread-basket," was soon blackened and scorched by advancing SS troops, as dead as its people's aspirations for independence.

204 \ SEDUCED BY HITLER

But the war in the East was always fought under different rules to the war in the West. The military orders for Nazi commanders fighting the Red Army decreed that Jewish leaders, Communist officials, and partisans should be executed immediately. Unlike western POWs, Red Army soldiers taken prisoner were often sent to concentration or extermination camps or worked to death as slave laborers. There was to be no mercy, and no Geneva Convention rules would be applied. Of 5.7 million Russians captured by the Nazis, 3.3 million, almost 60 percent, died or were killed in captivity. For many eastern Slavs under Nazi occupation, there was no opportunity to survive Hitler. If there was a choice, it was not how to live, but how to die.

Chapter Eight

Rescuers and Rescued

"For instance, when the Archduke Joseph Ferdinand of Austria was moved to Dachau, or Schussnigg was incarcerated, then I used to go to Berlin and bang my fist on the table, and I would say: 'Listen, Hermann [Göring]—Himmler, or Kaltenbrunner, has put these people in prison, and that is wrong'...In the beginning he would help me, but later on, he did not have enough interest."
— Testimony of Albert Göring, brother of Hermann,
while in Allied custody at Nuremberg, September 1945

"Our wretchedness contains as much talent and expertise as Paris could summon in the days of her prime, and none of it is visible, only hunted, terribly tired men at the limit of their resources.... If it had not been for Varian Fry's Relief Committee, a goodly number of refugees would have had no reasonable course open to them, but to jump into the sea."
— Russian revolutionary Victor Serge on the American rescuer
Varian Fry in wartime Marseilles, dubbed "the Artists' Schindler"

As the details of the Holocaust are documented with ever more rigor, and an increasing number of survivors come forth to record accounts of their lives, the argument that the Nazis fought not one, but two wars, gains currency. The first was launched against the Allies, the second against the Jews, whom the Nazis planned not just to conquer and plunder, but to exterminate. Certainly in military terms, the logistics of the Holocaust diverted a massive amount of transport, manpower, and matériel from the Germans' conventional armed struggle. Nazism's racial imperative often overrode all other considerations. In the summer of 1944, over a year after the defeat at Stalingrad, as Allied troops fought through France, Nazi leaders such as Himmler began to put out tentative peace feelers to the West through intermediaries. Yet that same summer, 450,000 Hungarian Jews were killed at Auschwitz.

Ranged against this determined genocide, Jews rapidly learned that surviving Hitler demanded not just their own bravery and resolve but the help of others. At the Yad Vashem Holocaust Memorial in Jerusalem, the Department for the Righteous Among the Nations lists those rescuers it is satisfied saved Jews from the Nazis, usually at risk to their own life. Extensive research is required before that status of Righteous Among the Nations is bestowed, at a commemoration ceremony. The statistics make for interesting reading.

As the previous chapter notes, Poland, often accused of an endemic anti-Semitism, tops the list with 5,264, and second on the list is the Netherlands, at 4,174. France has 1,786, while countries such as Hungary, Czechoslovakia, Lithuania, Russia, and Belarus— whose combined populations once included many millions of Jews—have less than five hundred each. Germany itself boasts just 327. That figure does not reflect the strength of anti-Nazi feeling, for many more individuals than 327 were needed just to operate the "U-boat" network across Berlin. The Yad Vashem statistics are a guide, but they do not tell the whole story. Denmark and Bulgaria, both of whose governments refused to hand over their Jews to the Nazis, score fourteen and thirteen, respectively.

German officialdom trumpets the failed attempt on Hitler's life on July 20, 1944, by the army plotters led by Claus von Stauffenberg, as the proudest hour of those opposed to the Nazis, but many more acts of more mundane bravery took place every day. In Berlin alone, for example, as many as two thousand Jews secretly hid out the war and only emerged in the spring of 1945, with the arrival of the Red Army. Known as "U-boats" because they lived underground, they were passed along a citywide network of hundreds of safehouses, where they received both food and shelter (see "Berlin's Human U-Boats," below). The penalty for those thousands of stubborn Berliners helping the hidden Jews—had they been caught by the Gestapo—was death. Other Germans took smaller risks to help Jews, but the gestures were no less welcome. A Jewish woman from Stuttgart recounted how in September 1939, at the outbreak of war, neighbors supplied her and her mother with food, often anonymously:

> When the foodstuffs allocated to us begin to get scarce, a woman who is a complete stranger gives my mother a quarter of a pound of butter as she passes her in the street. Now and then we find a basket of vegetables, fruit, and eggs in front of our door. These are in short supply, particularly for us. Sometimes, such things are brought to us in our flat by loyal people, to a flat which non-Jews should not have entered. But these are the only glimpses of light in this gloomy hopelessness.[1]

These were small acts, certainly dangerous and risky, but something that was within both the moral and logistical reach of many. That some Germans persisted in showing human solidarity with their Jewish friends was noticed by the Gestapo. On October 24, 1941, Gestapo Chief Heinrich Müller issued a nationwide instruction to Gestapo branches. It noted that "persons of German blood continue to maintain friendly relations with Jews and appear in public with them in a blatant fashion." Such behavior showed "a lack of understanding of the most elementary and basic principles of National Socialism." Perpetrators would be arrested and, in serious cases, sent to a concentration camp. The Jews would, as a matter of course, also be incarcerated in a camp.

Berlin's Human U-Boats

The several thousand Jews living underground in wartime Germany were known as "U-boats" because of their clandestine existence. The largest number of U-boats lived in Berlin, where about two thousand lived out the war until the final liberation of the city by the Red Army in April 1945. Berlin was the very epicenter of the Nazi dictatorship, site of the headquarters of the police, SS, and Gestapo. For the U-boats, every minute of existence was fraught with danger, but through courage, luck, and the help of thousands of Berliners, the U-boats were able to survive. The city's own character helped. Until the Nazis took power in 1933, much of the city, especially its workers' suburbs, were a stronghold of the German Communist Party. Even non-political Berliners often regarded Nazism as an alien import, from its birthplace in Catholic, conservative Bavaria. Jews had been part of the city's life for centuries, especially well integrated into Berlin's artistic and cultural community, whose Bohemian members were less likely to be ardent Nazis.

Like their waterborne namesakes, the U-boats kept moving in a dangerous and hazardous environment. They stayed in an Aryan house for one night, or a few nights, passed along an underground railway of safehouses where they found temporary sanctuary. The two thousand or so hidden Jews were only a tiny percentage of the Jewish citizens of Berlin who were expelled or killed, but each U-boat needed several helpers. The German writer Peter Schneider quotes Wolfgang Benz, of the Center for Anti-Semitism in Berlin, who says that for every Jew who survived in Berlin, at least seven people must have intervened to help.

The hidden Jews show that not only were there choices, but also degrees of choices. The myriad of actions taken by the U-Boats' saviors shows that on a daily, mundane basis, there were also opportunities for what Schneider calls "quiet heroes" who refused to follow orders. "When you consider how frequently they [the underground Jews] changed hiding places and how many people helped them to do so, the demographics of resistance change," writes Schneider.

"These few rescuers threaten the conformists' self-portrait more than the resistance fighters and would-be assassins who knowingly bet their lives against Hitler and lost. We know too well that heroism can't be mandated. But it isn't necessarily life-threatening to give bread or a bed or an address for the following night to a man on the run, an outcast; it may only take decency, some cunning, and courage."[2]

They were quiet heroes such as Ursula Meissner. Now seventy-seven, living in Geneva, Meissner's wartime Berlin home was a way-station on the underground railway that saved the life of the conductor Konrad Latte, who still lives in Berlin, where he hid out the whole war. When Meissner saw Latte and two relatives turn up at her door, she let them into her apartment. "What else could I do? I didn't think of the risk. You wanted to be able to look yourself in the mirror in the following morning."[3]

Berlin's U-boats were saved by the fact that they were natives of the city and knew well its streets and native slang. But that same familiarity could also bring the greatest danger. As the war ground on and the Nazis' determination to make the capital *Judenrein*, or Jew-free, increased in ferocity, the Gestapo invented a new and macabre weapon in its hunt for underground Jews—other Jews. Once arrested, they would be offered a choice: go out on the streets and find their fellow Jews or be sent to a concentration camp. A few even agreed to work for the Gestapo. One of the most dreaded, and most successful, was Stella Kuebler, known as the "Blond Ghost." Accompanied by Gestapo officers, she would roam her old haunts of Berlin's parks and cafés where she knew Jews might venture out—for such was the U-boats desperation that many could not bear to stay inside day after day—and, if she saw a face that she knew, she would point the poor victim out to the Gestapo. After the war, she was denounced by Jewish survivors and arrested by the Russians, who sentenced her to ten years in prison.

At the other end of the moral scale is Ursula Meissner, who even stayed with her fugitive guests during bombing raids, as they could not be taken into the shelter. Meissner, like many rescuers—such as the Bulgarians Dimiter Peshev and Dimo Kazasov—has been awarded the title of Righteous Among the Nations at Yad Vashem. These are just three out of the millions who lived under Nazi rule who said "No."

※ ※ ※

There is no record at Yad Vashem of Albert Göring, one of the war's most extraordinary rescuers. Although he was the brother of Reichsmarschall Hermann Göring, Hitler's deputy, and an arms dealer for the Nazis, Albert Göring saved dozens of Jews and anti-Nazis. And each time he came up against the Gestapo, he turned to his brother Hermann, its founder, who gave him aid and support in his rescue work. Albert Göring's story shows how, not only was there room for maneuver at all levels of the Third Reich, but that the higher an individual's connections, and the greater his determination to exploit them, the more good could be done.

Like his fellow rescuer Oskar Schindler, Albert Göring was a successful businessman. Schindler ran a factory in Krakow, Poland, producing enamel goods and munitions. Albert Göring was export director for Skoda, the arms manufacturer based in Pilsen, Czechoslovakia. Like Schindler, Albert Göring made a good living from the war. Both men were bon vivants, who enjoyed fine food and plenty of drink, the company of women, restaurants, and café society. And like Schindler, Albert Göring also had a list. His was compiled after the war, detailing those he had helped or rescued, such as Kurt von Schuschnigg, Chancellor of Austria, and the composer Franz Lehar, who had a Jewish wife. Hermann Göring's daughter Edda, now in her seventies and living in Munich, well remembers her uncle Albert:

Of course, there were a lot of differences between the two of them. In their professions: Albert did his diploma in engineering. I don't think he was at all interested in politics. My father's background was in aviation, then he became very active in politics. There was a fundamental difference between them. Albert always said that he felt most comfortable in the triangle between Vienna, Prague, and Budapest, the very hub of Europe, and that was where he had most of his friends. He fitted in very well, he was elegant, charming, bright.[4]

Born in March 1895, Albert was the youngest son of Dr. Heinrich Ernst Göring, a former German diplomat, and his wife Franziska, twenty years his junior. Albert shared with Hermann a half-Jewish godfather, Dr. Hermann von Epenstein. The Göring children spent much of their childhood at Veldenstein castle in Bavaria, owned by von Epenstein, who was openly having an affair with the boys' mother. While Hermann had a glamorous career as a fighter pilot in World War I, Albert passed his time in the trenches, where he was wounded in the stomach. After the war's end, Albert trained as an engineer. During the early 1930s, while his brother raced up the Nazi hierarchy, Albert worked as a commercial agent with Junkers and Co., before joining the Austrian Tobis-Sascha film company as studio manager.

When the Nazis invaded Austria in March 1938 and arrested Oskar Pilzer, the Jewish owner of Tobis-Sascha, Albert went into action immediately, remembers Oskar Pilzer's son Georges. "My father and Albert Göring did not meet socially, but they had a very correct business relationship. The Nazis broke into our house and took away my father, and Albert Göring immediately located him and had him freed that same afternoon. I want to emphasize here that Albert Göring was absolutely instrumental in freeing my father and also assisting other members of my family."[5]

Albert was simply disgusted with the Nazis' racialism, remembers Jacques Benbassat, whose father, a businessman, was among those helped by Albert after the Nazi takeover of Vienna. "To him, a human being was a human being, it didn't matter what race or color he was. He had absolutely nothing good to say about the Nazis, or Hitler, or his brother's activities in Germany. He told my father, 'I have a brother in Germany who is getting involved with that bastard Hitler and he will come to a bad end if he continues that way.'"[6]

In June 1939, Albert Göring joined Skoda as head of export, lured by a generous salary and a sales brief encompassing most of southern Europe. Skoda was a center of anti-Nazi sabotage and resistance, activities that Albert Göring must have been aware of.

"[Albert] Göring often warned us about certain Germans who had been planted into Skoda, some of them criminals many times over," said Hans Modry, a Skoda director, in his postwar testimony held at the Skoda archives in Pilsen. "Albert Göring in my presence never presented himself as a Nazi, he did not greet Nazi salutes with a Nazi salute, he replied by lifting his hat, or else saying 'Gruss Gott' [Good day]....He often criticized the dealings of the Nazis and even Hitler openly and without being careful about it."[7]

At Skoda, Albert rescued Jan Moravek, a fellow employee who was involved with the resistance. During the search of the Moravek family house, the Gestapo discovered a folder of bonds held in a bank in Buenos Aires, a serious misdemeanor. Luckily, Moravek was out of the country at the time, in Yugoslavia. The two men were old friends. Jan Moravek first met Albert Göring in 1930 in Buenos Aires, while Göring was working for Junkers. "Albert Göring was a very close friend of my father. He advised him to come back to Prague, but behind the scenes he was helping him," says Jan Moravek's daughter, Elsa Moravek de Wagner, now living in Miami.[8] "Luckily, at the same time, one of the Skoda directors in Bucharest escaped through Turkey, so Albert Göring sent my father to take his job. He told the Nazis he needed my father, and my father also paid a bribe of one million crowns. Albert Göring gave him a good salary so he could pay it."

Göring also helped send on Moravek's family from Prague to Romania, where Jan Moravek continued working for Skoda. They stayed in Romania from the summer of 1940 until the Russians arrived in 1944. Those were happy days, remembers Elsa, and Albert Göring came often to visit. The Moraveks and Albert Göring would walk in the woods and, in the evening, sit drinking and talking. "In the winter, we went skiing, in summer, we went mushroom-picking. He knew how to cook very well, and he even taught my mother. He made a very good mushroom omelette, he would know which mushrooms to pick, cook some, and pickle the rest in jars to keep during the winter. He was a bon viveur and wanted to have a good time, enjoy good company and good food. My mother always had a good cigar, some coffee, and a glass of Fernet Branca ready when she knew he was coming to visit us."

Nonetheless, despite his anti-Nazi activities, Albert played his role in keeping the Nazi war machine running. Like Carl Bosch at IG Farben, he compartmentalized his own personal feelings from his company's interests. Albert Göring's humanitarian work ran alongside the demands of business and the German war effort. He maintained a profitable business relationship with Hermann, supplying weapons from Skoda to the Wehrmacht. Records survive of the agenda of a meeting between the two brothers in March 1943. Items include: two hundred tanks for Bulgaria; arms for Hungary; development of new arms and antiaircraft weapons; and whether the whole capacity of Skoda was being successfully utilized.

Albert Göring was not motivated purely by altruism, but was also planning for his personal future, says Vladislav Kratky, archivist at the Skoda works in Pilsen. "He wasn't a Nazi, he didn't believe that the Germans would win the war, so he tried to establish some channels for the postwar period, through peaceful production. He wanted to carry on working for Skoda after the war."[9]

Albert also had plenty of opportunities to contribute to Hermann's massive and growing collection of looted art. Paintings were exchanged for lives between the two Göring brothers, speculates Elsa Moravek de Wagner. "One of the families that he helped told my mother that when he heard a family was to be taken to the camp, he would show up without announcing himself and offer to help. Of course, the family would be incredibly grateful, then he would point out a painting, saying it was very nice. The family would give it to him immediately. Those pictures probably ended up in his brother's collection. Perhaps that's how he was able to continue helping people, by taking those gifts and passing them on to Hermann Göring."

In the autumn of 1941, five senior officials of Omnipol, the foreign trade subsidiary of Skoda, were arrested by the Gestapo. Skoda director Hans Modry asked Albert Göring for help. Albert persuaded Hermann to order that the five be released, but they remained in custody. By then, the real power in Nazi-occupied Czechoslovakia was Reinhard Heydrich. After the Battle of Britain, Hermann Göring's star was beginning to wane. Nonetheless, Albert again turned to Hermann for help in trying to free the Omnipol directors via his aide, General Bodenschatz, in January 1942. Albert Göring and Bodenschatz visited Heydrich, records Hans Modry. Albert Göring openly threatened Heydrich. "[Albert Göring] requested that he pay attention to Hermann Göring's order that the imprisoned be set free or else the reports would be passed on to Berlin and decided there," Modry noted in his testimony. The five directors were released later in January 1942.

Eventually, of course, his luck ran out. In 1944, Albert Göring was finally arrested after he had caused a scandal at a German diplomatic dinner in Bucharest. He refused to sit down with ambassador Manfred Killinger, a Nazi who had killed the Socialist politician Walter Rathenau. He told his American interrogators at Nuremberg:

> I wouldn't have anything to do with the German Envoy and members of the Party there. I used to keep company with some of my engineers and Yugoslavs. That was the same in Prague, Sofia, Bucharest, wherever I went. Now Killinger, as it was his

duty, invited me several times to come to a dinner or come to
a lecture, or something of that sort, but I refused the invitation
all the time. Then one day, one of the counselors of the lega-
tion met me and he asked why I refused these invitations all the
time, and I told him I would rather sit with the chauffeur of a
taxi than sit down with a murderer, because Killinger was the
murderer of Rathenau.

The Göring name could not protect him from such public out-
bursts. As the end of the war approached, even Hermann's loyalty
was wearing thin because of his brother's antics, although he once
again came to Albert's rescue.

In May 1945, Albert Göring surrendered to U.S. troops. Perhaps
naïvely, he believed that once he had given an honest account of his
rescue work to U.S. intelligence officers, he would be allowed to
go free. But now that same name that had, all through the war,
been Albert Göring's shield against the Gestapo, condemned him
to rot in prison, a few yards away from the cell where his brother
was also incarcerated. "It has been the tendency all my life to help
whenever I could, without looking at their nationality, their country, their age, or whether they were Jews or Christians," Albert
Göring told his interrogators. "I have helped people from Romania,
Bulgaria, Hungary, Czechoslovakia, and Germany, whenever I
could, whether they were poor or whether they wanted to emigrate,
or what, I never expected or received compensation for it, because
I did this for religious reasons." But the Americans did not believe
him. As Albert Göring's interrogation report, written by Major Paul
Kubala, of the U.S. Seventh Army Interrogation Center, in June
1945 stated harshly:

Albert Göring claims his life was nothing but one long battle
with the Gestapo. It seems the Reichsmarschall had nothing to
do but extricate his brother from scrapes where Albert Göring
protected old Jewish women, refused to give the "Heil Hitler"

salute, and made politely disparaging remarks about the Party. In 1938, he even struck two SA men who were forcing a sixty-year-old Jewish woman to mop the streets with hydrochloric acid!

The records of Albert's interrogation at Nuremberg in September 1945 shed an interesting light on the relationship between the two brothers:

Q: Now, will you tell us about your relations with your brother, Hermann?

A: You must differentiate here between two things when you speak of "relations." The first thing is my relations to him as a private person, as my brother, and the second point is my relations to him as a statesman. In his capacity as a brother, he was good to me and also helpful, as you already know from previous interrogations. As brothers, we were very close together, and we had the usual relationships as brothers would have inside a family. I have had no relations with him as a statesman. I want to say here, that from 1923 on, that is, from the day the [Nazi] Party was founded, I was one of the strongest opponents and an active opponent against this Party, and I had no contact with him in this capacity.[10]

Hermann also warned his brother to stay out of what he called "affairs of state," the extermination of European Jewry, Albert said. In 1941, or 1942, he had met a Dr. Max Winkler, who had just returned from Poland. Dr. Winkler told Albert Göring of the terrible massacres taking place there. "He said that people said that whole trainloads of Jews—men, women and children, old and young—had been taken up into the mountains there and shot by machine guns. I was very excited at this report, and I did not have any reason to doubt his veracity." Albert wrote a report to alert his brother about these events to try to stop them. The report was written and filed with Hermann Göring's Air Ministry. Ironically, his report was then passed to Himmler, Albert Göring believed. "[T]hus the vicious circle was completed. In other words, the thing ended where the murder had started."

If the U.S. officers did not believe Albert's account of his rescue work, it would be easy to check, he told them, as his brother was just a few yards away in a different cell. "He said for me not to mix into affairs of state, and affairs of history, because I had no political knowledge, or whatever. His very words were: 'You are a political idiot.' I made many difficulties for him, because I always did mix into these things, well you know, he is over there in cell no. 5, and he can tell you about it. I also know, with another interrogation report, he called me 'Black sheep of the family.' He called me an 'outsider.'"

Albert was extradited to Czechoslovakia where he was put on trial in 1947, accused of collaborating with the Third Reich. Found not guilty after the testimony of his colleagues at Skoda, who testified in detail about how he stood up to Heydrich to demand the freedom of the Omnipol executives, he was finally freed.

Albert Göring was haunted to his end by his family name, and spent his last years working for a construction company in Munich, where he lived in an unpretentious apartment. The glory prewar days of café society never returned. Shortly before he died in December 1966, he took a fourth wife, Brunhilde. He is buried in a Munich graveyard. Mystery still surrounds much of Albert Göring's life. How could a man who saved Jews and anti-Nazis keep in close personal contact with Hermann Göring, Hitler's heir apparent, even if he was his brother? How could he supply weapons to the Nazi war machine, even as he repeatedly professed his disgust with Nazism? Such moral gymnastics demanded considerable compromises. When we examine the minutiae of life within the Third Reich, the many shades of gray in the Nazis' dark universe, we find such contradictions are often the rule rather than the exception, part of the human price of helping others survive Hitler.

And who was Albert Göring really working for? Among the paper trail that records his wartime life are several intriguing documents that hint at contacts with the western Allies. Was this avowed anti-Nazi, with contacts at the highest level of the Nazi leadership, in touch with the Allies? He certainly facilitated the work of the Czech resistance movement. Skoda official Josef Voracek testified at Albert Göring's Prague trial how company chairman Hromadko had, on business trips to Belgrade, sent monies to the Czech resistance movement abroad. Skoda's German management was suspicious of Hromadko, and Albert Göring was delegated to accompany him and keep him under surveillance. He did not. Instead, he left Hromadko alone to carry out his business. "[H]e waited for the chairman at the train station, or else the airport, and after a time, gave him unlimited freedom of movement. In that way, he allowed him to pursue his resistance activities,"[11] recorded Voracek.

There was a British connection, too. Before the war, Albert Göring was also chairman of a British firm called Bickford and Co., he informed his interrogators at Nuremberg. The company was run by an ex-army officer, and Albert Göring was appointed trustee of its interests during the war. Bickford and Co. was based in Vienna, and was later incorporated into ICI, a prewar trading partner of IG Farben. "This was headed by a Major Frank Short, who left Vienna for Cairo when all this Nazi trouble came up, and he asked me to take over the company for him and take care of his interests until after the war."

Most intriguing are a set of several telegrams in the British archives, documenting how, on January 29, 1940, Albert Göring had called on the British Consul in Trieste, Italy. Representing himself as a businessman, he asked for safe conduct for himself and his Hungarian secretary on a ship leaving from Naples to Piraeus, Greece. This triggered a flurry of diplomatic cables between London, Rome, and Athens. Should Hermann Göring's brother be taken prisoner? Opinions were divided. The Admiralty, wrote one official, "would be delighted to catch Herr Göring if there is no political objection. I suppose he could be called an 'agent.'"[12] A dramatic snatch at sea of such a VIP would also greatly boost the British Navy's image. Other officials thought this a bad idea, as there was no evidence that Albert Göring was engaged in espionage for the Nazis. "Göring should not be touched unless there was very strong evidence against him being a spy," wrote another official. The matter was eventually referred to the secretary of state for a personal decision, "as a matter of extreme urgency." The order went out from the Admiralty on February 24 to the British commander-in-chief, Mediterranean: "No, repeat, no action should be taken to remove Herr Göring."

And little action has been taken to commemorate him. No plaque has been erected in his memory, and even now, his story remains largely unknown. If he had been in contact with the Allies, whether directly or indirectly, it brought him no benefit. However morally questionable Albert Göring's ambivalent relationship with his brother Hermann and his work as a Nazi arms dealer was, he is vindicated by the numbers of lives he saved. Oskar Schindler also made a handsome living from the war. Other cases, such as that of Wilhelm Kube, mass murderer of the Jews of Minsk, are far darker, yet can still be tinged with an element of ambiguity.

An avowed German nationalist since his Berlin student days, Wilhelm Kube, the son of a professional soldier, joined the Nazi Party in 1928, sitting as a deputy in the Reichstag. But he failed to conform to the Nazis' public moral code, and his personal life was scandalous. In 1936, Kube's career appeared finished after he was found guilty of embezzlement, blackmail, and seducing the wives of his Nazi colleagues. Nonetheless, he volunteered for the Waffen SS at the age of fifty-three, and in July 1941, he was appointed *gauleiter* of White Russia. There he was, by his own admission, an efficient mass murderer. He worked enthusiastically with the SS *Einsatzgruppen*. In July 1942, he reported to his superior that in the previous ten weeks, 55,000 Jews had been killed in White Russia and its capital, Minsk.

Yet Kube had doubts about some aspects of the Final Solution. As the Nazi ruler of White Russia, he welcomed the murder of its eastern Jews. But the mass killings of the German and Austrian Jews deported to Minsk disturbed him. Kube took some late and limited steps to save or, more precisely, gain a temporary reprieve for several dozen German and Austrian Jews deported to his fiefdom. His hesitancy was framed by the warped racial "logic" of the Nazi mindset, which caused him to view German Jews quite differently from Russian ones. As those who shared the same mother tongue as Goethe and Kant, German Jews deserved a better fate, he believed.

In December 1941, Kube wrote to his boss Hinrich Lohse, Reich commissioner for the Baltic States, expressing his doubts: "I am certainly tough and prepared to do my bit towards the solution of the Jewish question, but people from our own cultural sphere are rather different from the brutalized hordes living here."[13] Such arguments were, not surprisingly, dismissed out of hand by his Nazi superiors. They were in complete contradiction of Nazi doctrine, which viewed Jews strictly on a racial—not cultural—basis, thus rendering the language they spoke irrelevant.

Nevertheless, while most German and Austrian Jews deported to Minsk were killed in July 1942 and May 1943, Kube managed to gain a temporary reprieve for seventy. He informed his Jewish barber, who shaved him every day, that all Jews who worked for him in his office were under his personal protection. Just as the path of compromise with Nazism began with the first small step, so did the journey away from it. Kube progressed from comforting his barber to publicly defending the honor of German Jews against the Nazi security forces. On one occasion, Kube came to the defense of a German-Jewish man who had won the Iron Cross in World War I. When a German policeman struck the Jewish man, Kube demanded to know if he, too, had won such a medal. (He had.)

Such incidents quickly brought him into open conflict with other Nazi leaders, both in Berlin and in Minsk, particularly Dr. Eduard Strauch, an SS officer and commander of the Security Police in Minsk. On July 20, 1943, Strauch arrested Kube's seventy privileged Jews. They were executed, but before being killed, their gold teeth were removed. On learning of these killings, Kube complained vociferously to Strauch. The latter's report to his superiors, written on the same day, provides a macabre insight into the mentality of a senior Nazi officer, carrying out the Reich's bloodiest work:

> I emphasized that I could not understand how Germans could quarrel over a few Jews. I said that people kept accusing me and my men of barbarism and sadism, while I was only doing my duty. Even the fact that those Jews who were to be specially treated [i.e., killed] had had their gold teeth removed by qualified doctors in accordance with instructions was being talked about. Kube replied that this way of carrying on was unworthy of a German or the Germany of Kant and Goethe. The fact that Germany's reputation was declining all over the world was our fault. Moreover, he said, it was quite true that my men would really enjoy these executions. I protested vigorously against these comments and said it was regrettable that in addition to having to carry out this unpleasant work, we were also subjected to mudslinging.[14]

Kube's belated attempts at limited humanitarianism merit a footnote in the annals of the Holocaust, but they personally profited him nothing. A Russian partisan, working as a chambermaid at his headquarters, shot him dead on September 22, 1943.

A world away from the killing fields of Minsk, an American named Varian Fry was based in the southern French port of Marseilles. He ran an underground network there, smuggling refugees across the border into neutral Spain in one of the most audacious rescue operations of the war. Fry saved the lives of at least fifteen hundred members of Europe's refugee intellectual elite, including the painters Marc Chagall, Max Ernst, and Andre Masson; the sculptor Jacques Lipchitz; the writer Lion Feuchtwanger, and the philosopher Hannah Arendt, who coined the phrase "the banality of evil."

Fry was an unlikely hero. Born in New York in 1908, he was the son of a rich stockbroker. An ailing, arrogant child, who held himself in high esteem, he made no friends at Harvard University, where he studied. Perhaps as a defense mechanism, he cultivated an Oscar Wildean foppish image, wearing a fresh flower in his buttonhole and a silk handkerchief in his jacket pocket. This fussy, bespectacled Ivy League scholar, arrived in Marseilles in August 1940 as the emissary of the U.S.–based Emergency Rescue Committee (ERC), armed with a U.S. passport (difficult to obtain then, as the State Department did not encourage American citizens to travel to Europe), a list of intellectuals he wished to save, and three thousand dollars strapped to his leg. Often obstructed by the State Department, many of whose officials were overtly anti-Semitic and keen to keep Jewish refugees out of the U.S., his rescue work is testimony to the power of one supremely determined individual to work for good in the face of evil.

Fry first saw for himself the reality of life in Nazi Germany when, as editor of *The Living Age* magazine, he went to Berlin in 1935 to report on the persecution of the Jews. His account of an anti-Jewish riot, when he witnessed SA thugs beat Jews senseless on Berlin's Kurfurstendamm made the front page of the *New York Times* and changed his life forever, setting him on the path that would, five years later, bring him to Marseilles. As graphic as his reporting was, Fry's story was just another ominous straw floating in the winds of coming war. It was the German attack on France, and the prospect of hundreds of writers, artists, and journalists falling into Nazi hands that prompted action. The day after France capitulated, a fundraising lunch for refugees was held at the Commodore Hotel in New York, and the Emergency Rescue Committee (ERC) was formed. Among those at the lunch was Erika Mann, daughter of Thomas Mann. "We mustn't forget that money alone is not going to rescue these people. Most of them are trapped...without passports, without visas. Somebody has to be there who can get them out."[15]

That was Fry. A multilingual student of classical civilization, Fry decided that he would save the European culture that he admired so much. He wrote in his memoir, *Surrender on Demand*: "Among the refugees who were caught in France were many writers and artists whose work I had enjoyed: novelists like Franz Werfel and Lion Feuchtwanger, painters like Marc Chagall and Max Ernst; sculptors like Jacques Lipchitz. Now that they were in danger, I felt obliged to help them if I could; just as they, without knowing it, had often in the past helped me."[16]

Fry's greatest ally was Eleanor Roosevelt, the first lady and a friend of the writer Lion Feuchtwanger. It was a photograph of Feuchtwanger in a French detention camp that first sparked the concern of Mrs. Roosevelt. The ERC asked the president's wife to persuade her husband to issue emergency visas to Feuchtwanger and everyone else on the committee's list. Eleanor, a feisty woman not bound by political considerations, rapidly agreed. She even threatened her husband that if he refused, she would fill a ship with refugees that would then cruise up and down the East Coast, shaming his administration.

Once in Marseilles, Fry set up shop in room 307 of the Hotel Splendide, not far from the railway station. Eager to prove its pro-Nazi and anti-Jewish credentials, Vichy France was passing law after law against Jews, especially foreign ones who wrongly thought that unoccupied France could provide a refuge of sorts. The police were given new powers to intern foreign Jews without cause, a precursor of the law permitting the arrest and holding of all foreigners between the ages of eighteen and fifty-five. But in the same bureaucratic catch-22 that condemned Jews to death all over the Third Reich itself, Jews were not allowed to leave. All applications to depart Vichy needed an exit visa, and these were issued by the Gestapo. So a Jewish refugee wishing to flee had to bring him or herself to the attention of the Nazi authorities, which in turn guaranteed a trip to a concentration camp and "resettlement" in Germany.

Word soon spread among the exiled Jews and anti-Nazis that a young American, supposedly with magic powers granted by the State Department, was in town. The Czech writer Hans Natonek recalled: "Like the first bird note of a gloomy morning, a rumor ran around the cafés. It was said that an American had arrived with the funds and the will to help. It was another distraction in a city in which black market operators sold hysterical men berths on ships that did not exist to ports that, in any case, would have denied them entry. But the rumor persisted. It was said that this American had a list..."[17] As well as his list, Fry also had three helpers who would prove invaluable: Albert Hirschmann, a twenty-five-year-old German economist nicknamed "Beamish," Mirian Davenport, an American who had been studying art history at the Sorbonne, and an American adventurer named Charlie Fawcett. Fawcett's specialty was bigamy: he married six Jewish women in three months, often in a concentration camp, from which he would walk out with his new "wife" on his arm.

After the rescue operation was set in motion, some kind of cover had to be established and as much official permission obtained as possible for it to work. Fry explained to the Vichy officials that he wanted to set up an American Relief Center to help displaced people. Armed with his State Department passport, Fry appeared innocent enough to the French bureaucrats. The Centre Americain de Secours opened soon after in an abandoned handbag factory. The center was open to all: genuine refugees were given food aid, while those on the magic list were told to wait and be ready to depart. Although his background was academic, Fry took easily to the secret life. Important documents were secreted in furniture in case of an overnight raid, and the index cards that detailed those who came for help were left in a particular pattern on Fry's desk so that he could see if they had been touched or examined in his absence. Fry's messages to New York were typed out on airmail paper, which he then cut into long strips that were glued into a single line. The message was rolled up and put into a condom, which was then hidden in a tube of toothpaste.

The way into Spain demanded documents and "proof" of identity—principally a passport and an identity card. These were forged by an Austrian cartoonist named Bill Frier who had left Vienna after the Anschluss in 1938. First out on one of Frier's passports was Konrad Heiden. Heiden was a writer, author of a coruscating biography of Hitler, *Der Führer*, who was in extreme peril. Reborn as a businessman named Silbermann, he eventually reached Lisbon.

But not everybody wanted to leave. Marc Chagall claimed that he could never depart his beloved Europe for a philistine wasteland like America. But as Vichy's relentless anti-Jewish drive continued, he began to waver. He asked Fry if there were any cows in America. Informed that there were, Chagall prepared to leave. Others worried that the risks of the journey were too high. The Czech novelist Franz Werfel and his wife Alma Mahler Gropius Werfel, like Heinrich Mann, were worried that they would not be able to climb to the Spanish border. So Fry offered to go with them.

Considering the risks involved and the need to be inconspicuous, the escapees did not behave very sensibly. Great talent, it seems, brought great ego in its wake, as Fry was to find repeatedly. For example, there was the problem of the twelve suitcases that Alma Werfel brought with her. Eventually, Fry had to take them through the border himself on the train to Port-Bou in Spain. Traveling with the Werfels were Heinrich Mann, his wife Nelly, and their nephew Golo, the son of Thomas Mann, Heinrich's brother. Heinrich Mann was the first person to be stripped of his citizenship by Hitler after the Nazis took power. His "crime" had been to be proposed as a presidential candidate by the Social Democratic press. There was a nerve-wracking interlude at the Spanish border where a guard asked Golo: "So you are the son of Thomas Mann?" "Does it displease you?" replied Golo. Luckily for the group, it did not. "On the contrary. I am honored to make the acquaintance of the

son of so great a man," replied the border guard. Others, not connected to Fry's operation, were not so lucky. The German-Jewish
writer Walter Benjamin committed suicide after being turned away
by Spanish border guards.

These were dangerous but exciting times, bringing risks,
rewards, and satisfaction of which Fry had never dreamt. Originally,
he had planned to stay in France only a month, but four months
later, he wrote to his wife Eileen: "This job is like death—irre-
versible. We have started something here we can't stop. We have
allowed hundreds of people to become dependent on us. We
can't say we're bored and we're going home." Fry's underground
railway was running smoothly enough, considering the myriad of
potential pitfalls. Although it was Eleanor Roosevelt's concern
about Lion Feuchtwanger that helped start Fry's operation, once
out of Vichy France, safe in the U.S., Feuchtwanger stupidly gave
an interview to the *New York Times*, describing how he escaped,
thus alerting the German and Vichy authorities to one of the
escape routes.

The rescue center was also devouring funds. Three thousand
dollars did not last long. Bringing in further funds was proving difficult. Moving funds across the world in 1940 was a slow and complicated business, even without the war. Exchange controls demanded
a mountain of paperwork and permissions.

Fry could not run his operation legally, but he was in the right
place to run a black market operation. Like Istanbul and Casablanca,
Marseilles was a nest of smugglers and black marketeers, all looking
for the main chance and a quick, profitable deal. Some even kept
their promises, such as the prominent Corsican gangster whom Fry
approached. This man also had difficulties moving his money, the
classic obstacle that every successful mobster eventually faces—
how to shift and launder cash funds. Here was a pleasing symbiosis
of needs: Fry needed cash in hand, the gangster wanted his cash
out of his hands. The answer was simple. When the gangster
wanted to move funds out, Fry's friends in New York would pay

the same sum into a bank account there, and the gangster would give Fry the cash.

Fry was not helped by American officials at the U.S. consulate in Marseilles. They viewed him as a maverick, which he was, because his humanitarian activities disrupted the normal course of diplomatic contact between the U.S. and Vichy France. The Consulate was coming under increasing pressure from the Pétain regime to stop Fry. Consular officials refused to renew his passport unless he returned to the United States. He asked his old ally, Eleanor Roosevelt, for help. She wrote back to Fry's wife, Eileen: "I think he will have to come home because he has done things which the government does not feel it can stand behind."

On August 28, 1941, Fry was arrested, held overnight, and expelled into Spain. For a rank amateur, he had had a good run. Under the very noses of Vichy France, one of the most enthusiastic collaborators with the Third Reich, he and his helpers had rescued the cream of Europe's intelligentsia.

"When I left New York on August 4, 1940," he wrote to Eileen, "I had no idea at all what lay ahead of me. Today I think I understand as well as anyone else what is happening to France. And yet I still don't quite know what happened to me. What I do know is that I have lived far more intensely in this last year than I have ever managed before....For the experiences of ten, fifteen, and even twenty years have been pressed into one."

For rescuers such as Albert Göring and Varian Fry, their time saving lives was the highlight of their lives. A humdrum peacetime routine could never offer the kind of adrenaline buzz of outwitting the Gestapo. Both found it difficult to settle down once back at home. Back in New York, Fry, like Albert Göring in postwar Munich, faced repeated disappointment. He was refused entrance into the army. Fry's skills and experience of the clandestine world and espionage—and his detailed knowledge of conditions in Vichy France—should have made him a natural for at least a desk job with the Office of Strategic Services (OSS), the forerunner of the CIA.

Instead, such was American government suspicion of Fry that the FBI opened a file on him and kept him under surveillance, thus ruling out any job with the U.S. government.

Most of the refugees whose lives Fry had saved showed no interest in helping him or recognizing his work, despite the glittering prizes that many collected in their new homeland. Franz Werfel, the overweight Czech who had balked at the climb up the mountains to the Spanish border, wrote a book, *Song of Bernadette*, that became a bestseller. The German poet Walter Mehring moved to Hollywood to write film scripts and spent his time driving up and down Hollywood Boulevard in a fancy car. Such ostentatious behavior was not appreciated by the ERC, to whose members he owed 31,000 francs.

After the war, Fry returned to teaching, disillusioned with his encounters with Europe's cultural great and good. The creative ego, it seemed, had no time for the needs of others, or even human contact with the man who risked his own life for theirs. France, at least, recognized his achievements, grateful perhaps that its Vichy officials had been prevented from sending hundreds of great writers and artists to their deaths. Andre Malraux, the French minister of culture, had been amazed when, in the 1960s, he met Fry and discovered that he had never been honored. Malraux ensured that he was given the Legion d'Honneur.

Shortly after he received his award, Fry died in 1967 at the age of sixty. He was comforted at the end of his life by very belated support from the artists he had saved. Before he died, the International Rescue Committee (formerly the ERC) asked Fry to commission a series of twelve lithographs on the theme of "Flight," in which he was supported by the sculptor Jacques Lipchitz. The series was completed after Fry's death and included works by Masson and Chagall. In 1996, Varian Fry was recognized as the first American Righteous Among the Nations by the Yad Vashem Holocaust Memorial and Museum. Secretary of State Warren Christopher attended the commemoration ceremony, representing the U.S.

government that had, during the war, done so little to aid Fry's rescue organization.

The words of his assistant Charlie Fawcett, who rescued Jewish women by marrying them, aptly sum up the motivation of those who made the progression from survival ethics to rescue. "We were taught that the strong should protect the weak. I saw that if there was anything I could do, I could do it only in France," he said decades later in an interview, when he was asked why he stayed on in France after the Nazis came, when, as the holder of a U.S. passport, he could easily have left. "I wouldn't say it was courage because I wouldn't have dared not to do what Fry asked me to. I would have felt disloyal to him. We all felt that way about him. You look back and wonder why, how did I do it? But suddenly it's there and you do it. And I just think that if you're in a position to do things, you have to do them...everybody, everybody can do something."[18]

Bulgaria: A Most Righteous Nation

About 50,000 Jews lived within Bulgaria's prewar borders, over half in the capital of Sofia. Ottoman traditions of multi-ethnic tolerance, and the civic and political equality guaranteed under the 1878 Congress of Berlin, gave the Bulgarian Jewish community peace and security. Increasing German influence in the Balkans and White Russian émigrés heightened anti-Jewish sentiment, but as late as 1937, a Jewish journalist gathered the signatures of sixty notables, including sixteen former prime ministers and cabinet ministers, against anti-Semitism.

Bulgaria joined the Axis in March 1941, annexing Yugoslav Macedonia and substantial areas of Greece, and was itself occupied by the Germans. Like Hungary, its main interest in allying with the Nazis was irredentist—the recovery of lost territories. Romania had already ceded territory to

Bulgaria in September 1940. Although Bulgaria declared war on the United States, it never declared war on the neighboring Soviet Union and refused increasing German pressure to do so. Still, a raft of anti-Jewish legislation was passed, based largely on the German model, which restricted Jewish rights and institutionalized discrimination. Jews were subject to curfew and forbidden to use telephones and radios at home or at work. Many Bulgarians were strongly opposed to the persecution of the Jews. In 1940, when the first anti-Jewish laws were being drafted, Dimo Kazasov, a former editor of Bulgaria's largest newspaper, wrote a strongly worded open letter to King Boris and the parliament condemning anti-Jewish measures.

Kazasov's attack sent shock waves through Bulgaria's political establishment. He was arrested by the political police, but his popularity and moral authority ensured his release. He was warned that if he intervened again on behalf of the Jews, he too would be sent to a concentration camp. But, as the Yad Vashem website records: "His letter, however, had caused a chain reaction. Now other individuals and organizations no longer hesitated to publicize their opposition. Kazasov himself remained undeterred and did not give in to threats. He took advantage of every opportunity and every medium to protest the persecution of the Jews." He personally hid three community leaders, and by late 1943, was himself living underground, from where he continued to publish attacks against the persecution of the Jews.

In August 1942, Bulgaria established a Commissariat for Jewish Affairs, the first stage in the planned "final solution" for Bulgarian Jews. Plans were drawn up to deport Jews from Bulgaria proper. But local opposition to the German plans was growing. In March 1943, the Jewish community informed its ally, Dimiter Peshev, a vice president of the Bulgarian parliament, that a transit camp was to be built for Jews about to be "resettled" in the East. Peshev confronted the interior minister, Peter Gabrovski, in his office, demanding that the deportation order be rescinded. Gabrovski backed down, and Peshev personally called the local prefect to ensure that the new counter-order would be implemented. Not content with this, Peshev stood on the podium in parliament and publicly denounced all deportations and drafted a letter of protest. Signed by more than forty members of parliament, the letter was addressed to the king and the government and pleaded with them not to disgrace the name of Bulgaria by deporting its own Jewish citizens to Nazi camps.

As one of the country's most famous and influential politicians, Peshev's voice carried great weight. His actions triggered a wave of public protest that, together with the support of the Bulgarian Orthodox Church and King Boris himself, was enough to stand against the Germans' demands to deport Bulgaria's Jews. Orthodox priests thunderously denounced the government's plans from their pulpits. Yet Bulgarian protection did not extend to the thousands of Jews living in the newly annexed territories of Macedonia and Thrace. More than 11,000 were deported to the camps and killed.

In August 1943, King Boris had died in mysterious circumstances after returning from a meeting with Hitler, possibly poisoned for his refusal to follow Berlin's wishes and deport Bulgaria's Jews. Stalingrad, the invasion of Italy, D day, and the impending Allied victory helped ensure the survival of Bulgarian Jewry. By the summer of 1944, the Bulgarian minister in Istanbul was negotiating with the U.S. War Refugee Board over evacuating the country's Jews to Palestine. In August, he wrote to the board that the government regretted its anti-Jewish measures and would abolish them at an "opportune moment." The following month, the Soviet army entered Bulgaria. The 50,000 Bulgarian Jews had survived the war, testimony to the power of not just individuals, but public opinion—even in a country occupied by the Nazis—to simply refuse to implement Germany's plans for the Holocaust.

※ ※ ※

Varian Fry and Albert Göring worked as individuals, with help from their aides. The Jugutis, a small central Asian Jewish community in Paris, rescued themselves from the Holocaust. They redefined themselves as "Muslims of Jewish extraction," paid substantial bribes to the SS and Gestapo, and cut themselves off from the mainstream French Jewish community. The strategy of self-containment worked, and only a handful were deported. Almost all of the community, 150 or so strong, survived the war. "The Affair of the Jugutis," as recounted here, is based on a decades-old account written by community leader Dr. Asaf Atchildi, deposited at Yad Vashem in Jerusalem.

Dr. Atchildi was born in Samarkand, central Asia. His family described themselves as "Jadirs," that is, Jews who were forced to convert to Islam for appearances sake, but carried on living as Jews, an experience that would later prove useful in Nazi-occupied Paris. After practicing in Moscow, Dr. Atchildi left Russia as a political exile and ended up, like so many fleeing the Stalinist terror, in Paris. As a French citizen, he was drafted into the army as a medical officer, returning to Paris in 1940. In October of that year, the Germans passed a law obliging every Jew to register at the police station. Most French Jews, keen to stay on the right side of the authorities who were already making so much of their lives a misery, complied and registered with the police. Dr. Atchildi was about to register when his wife, Alexandra, stopped him. Her words proved prophetic: "No! You are not going to hand yourself over. It would be foolish to put the rope on our necks. If the Germans are looking for Jews, we don't have to help them. Let them find us and prove we are Jews."[19]

Alexandra Atchildi had seen the likely fate of French Jews under the Germans and had already taken preventative steps to save her family. A friendly diplomat at the Afghan embassy, unnamed in the documents, had already promised to take the Atchildis under his protection. The diplomat warned her not to show the authorities their birth certificates, which had the word "Yahud," Arabic for Jew, written on them. With that meager bureaucratic a shield, Dr. Asaf Atchildi set about saving the rest of his small community.

And bribes could also help obtain the right paperwork. Nazi officials were often extremely venal. That greed often opened the door of salvation as the Zionist official Hubert Pollack had demonstrated in prewar Berlin. There, Pollack worked both for a Jewish welfare organization and Frank Foley, an MI6 agent in Nazi Germany, who helped many thousands of Jews escape. Foley's cover was officially head of Passport Control at the British embassy in Berlin, but he also ran a network of local agents, both Jewish and Nazi, who fed him intelligence. Very often the best way of ensuring Nazi connivance in the departure of a Jew was through bribery, records Michael Smith in his book *Foley: The Man Who Saved 10,000 Jews.* Pollack said:

I alone paid out more than eight thousand reichsmarks in bribes to Nazi officials. They were Reichsbank exchange control inspectors, Gestapo, and SS of all ranks. Individual sums ranged from twenty to 350 marks. The normal amount was around twenty-five marks.

Passports, tax clearance certificates, foreign exchange approval, visas for stateless persons and foreigners, and release from prisons, although not from concentration camps, were all produced as if by magic. I would meet two or three men in civilian clothes or black or blue uniform in a certain wine restaurant on Potsdamer or Franzosischen Strasse and handed over the right sum. It always worked.[20]

Although Dr. Atchildi had no sympathetic British MI6 agents to help him, or even mainstream Jewish welfare officials, he did have contacts as well as funds. He met with two Georgian émigrés in Paris, one a former prime minister of the short-lived Georgian Democratic before its absorption into the Soviet Union. The Georgians were optimistic, as they had successfully helped arrange protection for Jews of Georgian extraction and the small community of Karaites originally from Crimea, a Jewish sect who had broken with mainstream Judaism centuries before. Dr. Atchildi was directed by them to a man called Misha Kedia, who, they promised, could arrange everything. The meeting with Misha Kedia was successful, and he promised to act for the Jugutis. A few days later, the two men met again. Kedia told Dr. Atchildi to call a certain telephone number on October 5 at 6:00 P.M. and ask for a Dr. Weber, promising, "He will see you at once and will see that the matter is arranged without delay."

This unlikely promise did not fill Dr. Atchildi with confidence: "I left Kedia full of doubts. How could I believe that in two-and-a-half months time, at 6:00 P.M., a man with whom I was unacquainted would expect me to ring him up?"

Meanwhile, the situation of the Jugutis was rapidly deteriorating (as was that of all the Jews in Nazi-occupied France), as the Germans and their allies pumped out edict after edict terrorizing and persecuting French Jews. By the autumn of 1941, few Jugutis slept at home for fear of being rounded up—six had already been arrested and imprisoned in Drancy, Paris' staging post for Auschwitz.

But when Dr. Atchildi telephoned Dr. Weber at 6:00 P.M. on October 5, he was told to report to 19 Avenue Foch, the following morning at 9:00 A.M. Dr. Atchildi took one of his compatriots with him, instructing him to tell his wife if he had not emerged by 11:00 A.M. In any event, Dr. Atchildi was in and out in ten minutes. Dr. Weber told him: "Doctor, your problem has been solved in a positive way. I have decided to grant the Jugutis the same privileges enjoyed by the Karaites and the Georgian Jews. Draw up a list of your friends, which you will sign and for which you will be responsible. When the list is ready it will be passed to the prefecture of Police. All the restrictions affecting you will be canceled. Come back tomorrow with the list. Everything has been arranged."

At this, Dr. Atchildi was overjoyed. As he recorded: "I left with the feelings of a man from whose shoulders a weight had been removed." But it was too easy. The Germans did not give up their prey—or an easy source of income—that easily. Now began a bureaucratic dance—with death the result of a single wrong step—that would last for four years, until the Allied liberation of Paris. Dr. Atchildi drew up the list and was told to present it to a Lieutenant Bandorf at the Chamber of Deputies. The list still exists, and many of the Jews' names on it could indeed be Muslim, as they were spelled in an Arabicized version: Ibrahim Acheroff; Soltan and Djahanguir Morady, or Mousa Yehya, for example. But others were obviously Jewish and hard to disguise, such as Emmanuel Sassoon, Aron Abramoff, or Natan Davidoff.

Lieutenant Bandorf, all six feet of him, with blond hair and blue eyes, as Dr. Atchildi noted, was not impressed. "Look at this beggar who says these people aren't Jews. Ha! Ha! Ha! They're all Jews—Aaron, Abraham, Isaac, Miriam, Rebecca, and the rest. But orders are orders...I will give this list to Dr. Schultze to pass the order to the Prefecture of Police to erase the names of your friends from the [German] lists. Now get out, in case I lose my temper."

From the ravings of Lt. Bandorf, Dr. Atchildi was passed on to a Dr. Schultze, who was polite and helpful. This wartime version of the "Good cop/bad cop" routine was to continue, leaving, as undoubtedly was its intention, Dr. Atchildi perpetually dazed and confused. Dr. Schultze then passed Dr. Atchildi to a Mr. Tular, a French official at the Commissary of Police. Mr. Tular was not helpful, telling Dr. Atchildi: "What's this new story? After the Karaites and the Georgian Jews, a new affair—the Jugutis. And do you, Dr. Atchildi, really think that we shall let this be done without protest? The Germans want to ban, prosecute, imprison, and expel the French Jews. At the same time, are we to exempt from all trouble the oriental Jews who've come from heaven knows where?" Tular did agree to grant temporary dispensation, as he described it, "for the time being."

Two days later, Dr. Atchildi was called to the office of Xavier Vallat, at the General Commissar for Jewish Affairs. "He made no attempt to conceal his intentions; he informed me that he would energetically oppose the German decision and would appeal to Pierre Laval, Vichy prime minister, himself." Soon after a letter arrived from the Commissariat for Jewish Affairs, bringing mixed news. On the plus side, it had been decided that the Jugutis would not be regarded as belonging to the Jewish race, the temporary trustees that had been appointed to run their businesses would be removed, and their property restored. On the minus side, the word "Jew" still appeared on their identity documents, making them liable for arrest at any moment. Several Jugutis were under arrest, held in Drancy, and in prison.

More bureaucratic salvation came in January 1942, when the commissariat wrote that the occupation authorities recognized that the Jugutis did not belong to the Jewish race, and the anti-Jewish measures did not apply to them. The next step was to amend their identity cards marked with *J*. The following month, Dr. Atchildi was called to the prefecture, to meet again with Mr. Tular, the truculent French official. Mr. Tular and his colleagues were far more opposed to exempting the Jugutis than their German overlords, records Dr. Atchildi. "Doctor, the matter of the Jugutis is arranged for the time being. That doesn't mean that we like it, but we are obliged to grant you the status of people who need not be kept under surveillance. But tell your protegés that they must report in order to exchange their identity cards, for we might change our minds."

Armed with the necessary paper, Dr. Atchildi then went to Drancy to try and obtain the release of the four Jugutis held there. For a Jew—even with bureaucratic protection—to enter Drancy voluntarily demanded courage of the highest order. Presenting his papers to the commandant, Dr. Atchildi explained that the Jugutis were Afghans and Iranians, and did not belong to the Jewish race. Three were indeed released, but the fourth, David A., was held under other charges as well, and could only be transferred to a holding prison. When David A.'s father was called to the commandant's office and told he would be released, but without his son, he became hysterical, in what Dr. Atchildi describes as a "shocking spectacle":

> Arcadie fell on his knees screaming that his dear son was lost and would be hanged and so forth. For the first time throughout the Juguti affair, I lost my temper and gave him a slap in order to bring him back to reality. I explained to him in Iranian in the presence of the commandant and the surprised soldiers that he must keep quiet and use the unexpected opportunity vouchsafed him and his two brothers to get out of this loathsome camp safe and sound.

That outburst aside, Dr. Atchildi understandably described that day as a "Sabbath of miracles." Dr. Atchildi eventually gained the release of David A., by arguing at 86 Avenue Foch, the headquarters of the Gestapo, that the young man was detained because of a policeman's malicious report. There, a Gestapo official told him that the case would be investigated. If it were true, the young man would be released. If not, Dr. Atchildi would join him. At noon the next day, David A. was home.

Word of these miracles—and it was unheard of for a Jew to enter Gestapo headquarters, and walk out a free man having arranged the release of a fellow Jew—was rapidly spreading through occupied Paris' Jewish community. Certainly, the release of the three Jugutis brothers from Drancy had been observed with amazement.

Dr. Atchildi does not record the reaction of the mainstream Ashkenazi (western) and Sephardi (eastern and North African) Jewish communities to his rescue work. It appears that there was little, if any contact between the Jugutis and their less fortunate coreligionists. Indeed the Jugutis, to maintain the fiction that they were not "racially" Jewish, would have avoided interaction with most other Jews. "The affair of the Jugutis, Afghans, and Bukharans caused a sensation, and numerous people came to beg of me the impossible—inclusion in the list of Jugutis. It was a very grave problem for me because I would have liked to include all of them in the list, but a certain credibility had to be maintained where membership of the Jugutis was concerned," recorded Dr. Atchildi.

Iranian Jews, bound by ties of language and culture to Afghan Jews—could be included. Iranian diplomats drew up a list of Iranian Jews in Paris, and their names were successfully added. Iran, like Afghanistan, was neutral and of strategic importance. Over the next few months, other Afghan and Iranian Jews were added to the list, not always to the joy of the Jugutis. "[S]ome of our society did not like these doings, because they feared that the society would become too large," noted Dr. Atchildi.

As the war continued and the prospect of an Allied victory advanced, the Jugutis faced increasing hazards and dangers. Often less from the Germans and the Gestapo than their fearful and vicious French collaborators, who realized that they had picked the wrong side and would soon face their countrymens' justice. At the end of July 1944, Dr. Atchildi was summoned by an officer of the pro-German Darnand militia to see his German superior. "So you are Dr. Atchildi, president of the Jugutis?" asked the Nazi official. "However did you and your gang obtain acknowledgment of not being Jews? Tell me openly, whom did you buy and how much did you pay? There's no point in telling lies, we know you're a Bukharan Jew, and so are all the rest."

The verbal onslaught shook Dr. Atchildi, for it was the truth. Avoiding the central accusation, he nimbly turned the accusation back on the German officer, accusing him, in effect, of accusing his fellow German officials of taking bribes. "Monsieur, if you really know everything, you will know that our file was signed by the Germans. That being so, how can you ask whom we bought? And you, a German, say that to me. In your place, I would take those words back." The brave words hit home. Demanding confirmation of the Juguti's papers, the Nazi official let Dr. Atchildi go, albeit promising him that, "You and your people will yet go where the other Jews have gone."

The German was wrong. The Jugutis survived Hitler. But moral questions still remain over this curious wartime episode, admittedly ones that are hard for us to answer. Few would doubt the need to bribe the Nazis in the cause of salvation. But could the Jugutis have further aided more of their fellow Jews, instead of cutting themselves off from the mainstream community and disowning their faith? Probably not, for it was the very uniqueness of this tiny, ethnically homogeneous group that facilitated its escape from the Holocaust. Had they admitted their Jewish ethnicity, as well as religion, there is little doubt that the French would have deported them as well to Drancy. Yet decades later, when one of the authors attempted to interview survivors, including those named on Dr. Atchildi's fateful list, there was a widespread reluctance to discuss the Juguti affair. Perhaps it was survivors' guilt, or the memories were too painful. Either way, the Jugutis' self-rescue was not without a moral cost.

Chapter Nine

Neutral Collaboration

Last night, ah, yesternight
when Papen came to dine
the shadow of the big three
seemed to spread
athwart the feast between the sauerkraut and the wine
but though he wooed me with Teutonic passion
through Cairo nights I kept my head
I have been faithful to the Allies in my fashion.
— "Chanson Inönü" ["Song of Inönü," named for Turkey's wartime
president], published in March 1944, New Statesman

The visitors, however, were not the least interested in our welfare.
It was a curiosity trip, nothing else....Nobody listened or paid any
attention.
— Charlotte Opfermann, former inmate of Theresienstadt
concentration camp, on the visit by the Red Cross in June 1944

Few of the part-Jews who survived Hitler went to the lengths
of Ludwig Moyzisch, Berlin's spymaster in wartime Turkey.
Moyzisch was born in Austria, where he was baptized and raised
as a Catholic, although his maternal grandmother was Jewish. As a
mischlinge of the second degree according to Nazi racial doctrine,
Moyzisch was relatively safe from the Holocaust, at least in comparison with full-blooded Jews. But that was not safe enough, so
he joined the Nazi foreign intelligence service (SD), as a means
of getting his family out of Germany, British intelligence records
suggest.

His wife and son duly joined him in Ankara. But his bosses refused permission for his mother and sister to leave. Moyzisch remained aware of his somewhat precarious position: "at once a Jew and a member of a Nazi organization."[1] When an anonymous letter had been sent to Nazi officials denouncing him for his Jewish ancestry, a senior SS officer had been "helpful to him in this matter," he said. Moyzisch's claim that he worked for the SD to escape the Reich can be doubted, and it may have been a means of persuading the British that he was never an ardent Nazi.

Both the British records and SD chief Walter Schellenberg himself noted that Moyzisch was very proficient at his work. He ran Nazi agents throughout the Middle East with such efficiency that he was even "well thought of" by Himmler. Schellenberg recorded in his memoirs that after his own arrest by the Allies, a British officer told him that Moyzisch claimed he was Jewish and had been forced to work for the Nazis at gunpoint. Schellenberg found this idea amusing: "For the first time since I was interned I laughed. Moyzisch and I had always worked on the very friendliest of terms."[2]

Perhaps Moyzisch had been a British double agent all along: after the war, he took a Swedish freighter to Liverpool. Whatever his real motivation, Moyzisch's greatest triumph was recruiting an Albanian former juvenile delinquent known as "Cicero." Cicero, whose real name was Elyesa Bazna, was probably the most successful spy the Nazis ever had, providing Berlin with a steady stream of photographs of top secret British documents until March 1944. In intelligence terms, he was a "walk-in," someone who just turns up and offers his services. Bazna had held a succession of jobs, working as a locksmith, fireman, and a driver. From there, he progressed to driving diplomats, working in turn for the Yugoslav ambassador, a German diplomat—who fired him for reading his mail—and a British diplomat, before landing the plum post of valet for Britain's ambassador Sir Hughe Knatchbull-Hugessen. His dubious past seems to have not been noticed by the embassy's personnel vetters.

Lulled perhaps by Turkish neutrality during most of World War II, the British ambassador's security procedures were shockingly lax. Strike one against Sir Hughe was that he took the highest security documents home so he could read them in his bedroom late at night. Admittedly, the papers were transported in a locked dispatch box, but the very fact of moving them out of embassy premises constituted a major security risk. Strike two was that one night, Sir Hughe left the keys on his bedside table while he took a bath. Bazna moved fast then. He quickly made wax impressions of the keys. He had just put them back on the table when he noticed a sliver of wax sticking to one, and cleaned it off with one of the ambassador's handkerchiefs. At that moment, Sir Hughe came back in, dropped the keys in the pocket of his bathrobe, and returned to his bath. If only Sir Hughe had returned a few minutes earlier, one of the war's greatest spies would have been caught in the act.

A friend of Bazna's copied the keys, and Cicero was ready to go to work. He bought a camera and visited his old boss at the German embassy who introduced him to Ludwig Moyzisch. Bazna demanded £20,000; Moyzisch prevaricated, saying that he must contact Berlin. When Bazna brought over the first roll of film of fifty-six photographs, Moyzisch realized he had struck intelligence gold. The money was handed over, but there was no need to haggle anyway: the British currency was counterfeit, forged by a special unit of engravers in the Sachsenhausen concentration camp. Just one more of the myriad double-crosses in wartime Turkey.

The Turkish capital of Ankara, like Istanbul, was a nest of intrigue, spying, and trading in information—some genuine, much fake—during World War II. Single, double, and triple agents, and others who no longer knew where their loyalties lay, all lurked in the cities' streets, cafés, and hotels. Operatives of every Allied and Axis intelligence service, from the U.S.'s Office of Strategic Services (OSS, forerunner of the CIA), the Soviet NKVD (People's Commissariat of Internal Affairs), and the *Abwehr* to the Jewish underground of the Hagana and, of course, Turkey's own intelligence agencies, followed each other's agents, intercepted telegrams, and tapped each other's telephones. So many secret agents of differing nationalities would congregate in the bar of Istanbul's luxurious Park Hotel, just across the street from the German consulate, that an American agent walked inside and greeted his multinational colleagues by shouting "Hallo spies!" The chorus of a song favored by the pianist went "Boo, boo, baby, I'm a spy." One Allied agent competed with a Nazi rival for the affections of a Hungarian nightclub chanteuse—and who knew for whom she was really working? Beneath the Casablanca-style intrigue, there was vital war work to be done in a region of major strategic importance. Allied and Axis espionage networks aimed to nudge Turkey, the bridge between Europe and the Middle East, further into their orbit.

In response, Ankara flirted graciously with both her suitors, favoring first one, then its rival. Allowing the spies to operate was a key component of Turkey's strategy for surviving Hitler. There could be no better method of keeping Ankara informed about the progress of the war, so that it might adjust its policies accordingly, as indeed it did. For example: like Switzerland, Turkey turned away Jewish refugees in 1941, but gave them sanctuary in 1944, when the Allies' victory was inevitable. Turkey's prewar and wartime strategy of neutrality must be seen as a means of surviving both Hitler and the Allies.

Born in 1922, modern Turkey was a young and somewhat nervous state. It was midwifed in the wreckage of the Ottoman empire, its disastrous defeat and subsequent occupation by the western allies. These were national humiliations, still fresh in the memories of many politicians and national leaders. It had been a tragic mistake to enter World War I, which had delivered the *coup de grace* to the tottering Ottoman empire. Such events must never be repeated, and modern Turkey's boundaries must shrink no more, believed both President Kemel Ataturk and Ismet Inönü, Ataturk's successor after his death in 1938. A policy of neutrality and isolation was the answer, Ankara believed. But if these were the justifiable demands of geopolitics, there was none for the campaign Turkey later launched against its ethnic minorities, including Jews, using them as a scapegoat for its wartime economic woes.

Nations, like individuals, made choices during the war, whether to cooperate with the Allies or the Axis. Neutral countries such as Turkey and Switzerland opted for both. But this was a tainted neutrality, adopted by governments that saw a moral equivalence between the two sides, as though World War II was on a par with its predecessor, with armies and regimes that, more or less, respected the codes of civilization even as they fought, instead of a struggle between democracy and a criminal genocidal regime.

And neutrality was extremely profitable. Turkey supplied both sides with the vital war material of chrome, Sweden shipped the iron ore that was turned into Panzer tanks, and Switzerland exchanged looted Nazi gold for vital hard currency. Turkey, unlike Switzerland and Sweden, swung between one side and the other, forging and breaking alliances at its convenience. Seeking some form of security guarantees for the fledgling state, President Inönü entered into an alliance with Britain and France in October 1939. But Germany's lightning victories in Poland, and its rapid occupation of the Low Countries and France made Inönü think again. Perhaps he had hitched Turkey's destiny to the wrong wagon, or rather tank, and the alliance was not implemented. In June 1941, Turkey signed a nonaggression pact with Germany.

Among some Turks there was sympathy for the dynamic Axis powers as they swept through Europe and Africa. Hitler and Mussolini's programs of massive modernization and infrastructure struck a chord among the successors of Kemel Ataturk. He had shaped the modern Turkish state, dragging the backward remnants of the Ottoman empire into the twentieth century, abolishing *Sharia* (Islamic) law, replacing the lunar calendar with the Gregorian one, and instituting a modern legal system, based on the European model. Women were given the vote, and polygamy and the veil were outlawed. The fez was no longer to be worn; it was replaced by brimmed hats. The old Ottoman government was destroyed and in its place was a secular nation-state that drew on 1920s ideas of nationalism and some aspects of the corporate state that also inspired Benito Mussolini and the Soviet Communists.

Even so, before the outbreak of war, Turkey had given sanctuary to many German and European Jewish refugees, especially scientists and academics to revitalize the modern state's universities. This was in keeping with Ottoman traditions of tolerance that stretched back centuries to when Istanbul had accepted en masse the Jews expelled from Spain in 1492. Yet during the war, Turkey shamefully turned on its Jews and members of the Greek and Armenian Christian minorities. The Ottoman cosmopolitanism that had made Turkey such a vibrant, multiethnic, and relatively tolerant land, was shunted aside in favor of modern European, exclusivist nationalism. This was, in part, nationalist Ankara's victory over cosmopolitan, multinational, Ottoman Istanbul.

Like Nazi Germany, Ankara decided the country needed a scapegoat for the economic crisis in which Turkey found itself. So popular discontent with the precarious state of the economy in the early war years was directed against Jewish and Christian businessmen, in a dreary rerun of Nazi anti-Semitic propaganda. The Turkish press launched an anti-Semitic campaign, blaming Jewish and Christian speculators for the country's financial woes. This was followed by an extremely punitive capital tax, known as the *Varlik Vergisi*. The Turkish authorities levied massive payment demands on Jewish and Christian businesses that usually, in effect, amounted to de facto confiscation as they could not be satisfied.

Worse followed. Jewish, Greek, and Armenian males were rounded up and exiled to the Anatolian plains. There they were put to work in special camps, where they labored building roads or on other construction projects. Conditions were harsh, work hours long, and diet poor, although they were not as hellish as the Nazi concentration camps. Still, persecuting minorities was a signal well understood in Berlin. Certainly, this was not a genocide on the Nazi scale, but it was a planned and sustained attack on vulnerable communities. A series of articles on the persecution of Turkey's minorities by the *New York Times* correspondent C.L. Sulzberger triggered anger in the United States, enough to worry Ankara that aid to Turkey might be cut off. *Varlik Vergisi* was cancelled.

In December 1943, at the second Cairo conference, Churchill and Roosevelt tried unsuccessfully to persuade President Inönü to enter the war on the side of the Allies. But as the inevitable defeat of the Axis powers became clear, Inönü changed his mind, and Turkey began to reorientate its policy, unwilling to face a victorious Soviet Union alone after the inevitable Allied victory. The pro-German chief of staff was sacked and replaced by a pro-British officer. Chrome deliveries to Germany were halted and, in August 1944, diplomatic relations broken off. In February 1945, Turkey declared war on Germany. Doubtless better late than never, but this was not Turkey's finest hour.

As Ankara's policymakers swung between the Allies and Axis, in Istanbul, Cicero settled into a steady routine, handing over his films to Moyzisch who paid him in crisp, newly forged British pounds. Amazingly, Bazna hid the money under the carpet in his room at the embassy, although he spent some buying a house for himself to entertain his mistress. His material was regarded in Berlin as of the highest importance. Britain and the Allies exerted much diplomatic effort to bring Turkey onto their side. Knowledge of Allied strategies and offers could give the Germans vital leverage to prevent this. The documents Cicero copied gave the Germans access to high-level, British policymaking on Turkey.

Cicero's films were first passed to the German ambassador in Turkey, Franz von Papen, a former chancellor of Nazi Germany. His task was to keep Turkey neutral, and as pro-German as possible within the confines of neutrality—a diplomatic state that offered considerable room to maneuver in favor of one side or another. Cicero's material helped greatly. It provided details of the Cairo conference and Churchill and Roosevelt's attempts to bring Turkey over to the Allied side; it alerted the Germans to British requests for pursuit planes to be based on Turkish airfields and for radio stations to be placed in European Turkey to aid British bombing raids on Romanian oilfields.

Von Papen threatened a reprisal raid on Istanbul if this was allowed, and the stations were not built. The British Military Mission to Ankara, charged with trying to bring Turkey onto the Allied cause, left empty-handed in February 1944. Von Papen was in no doubt of the importance of Cicero's material. "The first round in the battle over Turkey's entry into the war has doubtlessly been won by us."[3]

Cicero's documents also had regional strategic implications. Even Hitler walked into a situation conference in 1943 with a sheaf of Cicero's documents in his hands, exclaiming: "I have mostly studied through these documents. There is absolutely no doubt that the attack in the west is coming in the spring."[4] At the same time, Hungary, was wobbling, and there were growing fears in Berlin that its ruler, Admiral Horthy, was about to sign a deal with the Allies. The Nazi foreign minister von Ribbentrop used Cicero's material to show Budapest that the Turks were resisting British demands, and so the country was not about to join the Allies, soothing Hungarian fears. Thus was the Axis bolstered, although in March 1944, the Germans invaded Hungary anyway, while Admiral Horthy was in Germany.

Cicero continued working for the Nazis until March 1944. He was a star, shining brightly in espionage's firmament. He even predicted an air raid on Sofia, which duly occurred. His control, Moyzisch, promised him a gift of a villa from Hitler after the war. But his work was becoming increasingly difficult: an alarm system had been installed in the ambassador's safe which had to be disconnected each time he broke in. He was chased one night by a young man. And Moyzisch had a new secretary, named Nele Kapp. One day Cicero saw her in the company of the man who, months before, had chased him. He destroyed his camera and moved into a hotel room, although, for a while, he continued working at the British embassy, so as not to alarm his employers with a sudden disappearance. But there would be no more stolen photographs of secret British documents for Hitler to brandish in the war room.[5]

In Berlin, the Nazi intelligence services exerted great efforts in intercepting both Turkish cryptograms and Allied diplomatic communications from Istanbul. The German naval attaché was responsible for running spies against Turkey itself, while the *Auslandorganisation* (AO), that ran the foreign branches of the Nazi party, also had its own networks. These were regarded as pretty amateur operations by the professionals. AO operatives were "dilettantes lacking completely in know-how or experience," said one Luftwaffe intelligence officer. Much of the work of the German Foreign Office department, known as "Pers Z" (Section Z of Personnel and Administration), was devoted to intercepting Turkish diplomatic cables, many sent from Moscow. They provided a rich harvest of information. As historian David Kahn writes in his book *Hitler's Spies*:

> After German invasion of Russia in 1941, these intercepts formed the great bulk of Pers Z material that Foreign Office submitted to Hitler. The need for the Turks to know as much as possible about their powerful and dangerous neighbor, and the excellence of their diplomatic and attaché representation in Moscow, obtained for them detailed and accurate reports about events in the Soviet Union. The solution of these [Turkish] dispatches gave the Germans access to an acute and comparatively unbiased observation post in the enemy capital.[6]

This was top grade material, including information such as:

▸ Reports on war matériel seen at October 1941 anniversary parade
▸ Stalin's pleasure with the situation on the front line after the stopping of Moscow offensive in December 1941
▸ Results of Stalin-Eden talks

‣ Plans for Soviet attack around Smolensk

‣ Arrival of U.S. lend-lease matériel

Not only did Turkey allow Axis intelligence networks to operate, it even financed them by its acceptance of looted Nazi gold, which German banks sold for Swiss francs through their branches in Istanbul. Turkey had no qualms about accepting stolen gold, a murky wartime episode tainting its neutrality that was highlighted in the late 1990s, when the scandal over Switzerland's role in laundering looted Nazi gold inevitably threw an unwelcome spotlight on the wartime record of her fellow neutrals.

The U.S. Government's "Holocaust Assets Supplement," published in June 1998, details how Turkey, like Switzerland, profited from Nazi genocide. U.S. officials estimated that Turkey received as much as $10 to $15 million in gold, most of it to pay for exports of chromite, the ore from which chrome is refined. After the war, $3.4 million worth of looted Belgian gold was traced to Turkey. According to the report, the Istanbul branches of two major German banks, Deutsche Bank and Dresdner Bank, "took advantage of the high prices on the Turkish free gold market to sell looted gold provided by the Reichsbank in return for foreign currency, particularly Swiss francs."[7] Some of this gold was as tainted as that metal could be: it came from the infamous "Melmer" account at the Reichsbank, where the SS deposited jewelry, gold coins, and dental gold yanked from the teeth of concentration camp victims.

Turkey's readiness to accept looted Nazi gold provided a steady income: the gold sales financed German diplomatic missions, anti-Allies propaganda, and espionage activities. These monies also subsidized other Axis missions and legations considered friendly to the Axis, the U.S. Government report records, adding: "Other German gold acquired by Turkey during and after the war included coins and ingots from the account of German foreign minister Joachim Ribbentrop at the Reichsbank, which had been stocked with gold looted from occupied Europe." The Cold War came to the rescue of the Turkish treasury. By 1946, as the Soviet Union appeared to be threatening the Dardenelles, the U.S. needed Turkey to bolster its policy of containment. Allied efforts for the restitution of the looted gold in the Turkish treasury were never pressed.

The "Pure" Swedish Aryans

Like its fellow neutral nations of Switzerland and Turkey, Sweden also found it profitable to maintain healthy economic links with Nazi Germany. Its neutrality was also corrupted and compromised, but arguably more within its business community than by its government, which took one of the most moral decisions taken by any nation during the Holocaust.

Sweden accepted almost the entire Danish Jewish community as refugees after an extraordinary mass evacuation by a fleet of ships and boats. By the end of October 1943, more than seven thousand people had been ferried across the sea to the safety of the Swedish shore. The mass evacuation followed an offer by the Swedish government to accept all of Denmark's Jews. On the debit side, it was Swedish iron ore that was refined into the steel that built Panzer tanks and German artillery. German troops were allowed to cross Swedish territory en route to invading Norway, and Sweden accepted German gold as payment for the iron ore until March 1944. Like those bars accepted by the Swiss, much of that gold was looted, and after the war's end, Sweden returned gold to both Holland and Belgium.

While Jewish refugees from Denmark were given sanctuary and a new home in Sweden, they were unlikely to find work at many major Swedish firms, who boasted of their staffs' Aryan credentials to boost trade with Nazi Germany. Companies with household names, such as Ericsson, AGA, and Hasselblad cameras, and much of the country's wood and paper industry organized or supported purges of Jewish staff and board members, according to documents published in the *Dagens Nyheter* newspaper.

One report also reveals how one company, SCA, secured massive orders from Germany by refusing to export cellulose to make paper to both Britain and the United States.

Secret police records and transcripts show that many leading firms sacked Jewish employees to keep their German trading partners happy. Swedish companies trading with the Nazis also drew up a *warnungskarten*, or blacklist, of non-Aryan or anti-German firms.

A furrier in Stockholm wrote on February 21, 1941: "Our firm is pure Aryan, and there is, thank God, not a single drop of Jewish blood in it. Heil Hitler." The managing director of one small company in western Sweden assured his German client in May 1941, that, if anything, the Swedes were the true and pure Aryans: "We feel it is our duty to inform you that we very probably have purer Germanic blood in our veins than you, especially since you come form the Rhineland." Jewish refugees and immigrants living in Sweden were well aware that firms were campaigning and discriminating against them. One man in Stockholm wrote to a friend in Italy: "Here, only native-born employees are hired. Firms that have connection with Germany refuse to hire us."

Not just Sweden's Jews, but also the bastions of the country's financial establishment, such as Jacob Wallenberg, knew about the *warnungskarten*. Jacob Wallenberg, together with his brother Marcus controlled the Stockholm-based Enskilda Bank, through which ran much of the trade with Nazi Germany. The brothers played a clever double act: Marcus portrayed himself as pro-Allied, while Jacob was more pro-German, but both were always in favor of profit, whatever its source. The Wallenberg brothers were cousins of the father of Raoul Wallenberg, the Swedish diplomat based in wartime Budapest who saved many thousands of Jewish lives. The brothers' wartime record was less illustrious. Their profitable trading with the Nazis was closely monitored by Allied intelligence services.

Once the war ended, Allied economic intelligence began to pick over the records of the massive German industrial conglomerates such as Bosch. The role of the Wallenberg brothers and Enskilda Bank in propping up the Nazi economy became clearer. Declassified documents at the Public Records Office show how Enskilda acted to cloak Bosch's interests in Allied countries, so as to prevent the German companies assets from being seized as enemy property.

In September 1945, Marcus Wallenberg attempted to disentangle the issue of Enskilda's holding of Bosch shares, which had been seized in the United States by the Alien Property Custodian. He received a frosty reception. U.S. Treasury Department officials had long been suspicious of the Wallenberg brothers and Enskilda Bank. A memo signed by Treasury Secretary Henry Morgenthau, dated February 7, 1945, listed eight points of concern about the brothers, accusing them of acting for German economic interests and claiming that "Enskilda Bank has been repeatedly connected with large black-market operations in foreign currencies, including dollars reported to have been dumped by the Germans."

Little wonder, then, that British officials in Washington, D.C., reported to their colleagues at the Economic Warfare department that: "In conversation with the head of Foreign Funds Control of U.S. Treasury, the latter told me that if Wallenberg sought discussion on the topic of the Enskilda holding of the Bosch shares, he would be kept waiting, to 'cool' for a reply, and then told that there was nothing to discuss since the shares were the property of the Alien Property Custodian....I was left with the impression that a particularly chilly reception was reserved for Wallenberg if he succeeded in getting inside the building."[8]

⊠ ⊠ ⊠

If Turkey's wartime record is ambivalent, in its favor, like Switzerland, it can point to its tolerance of both Allied and Jewish/Zionist underground intelligence operations. Many of the Allied underground networks in the Balkans were organized from Istanbul. Turkey's land borders with Greece and Bulgaria and shared Black Sea coast with Romania made the country a natural launching point for both exfiltration and infiltration. While Cicero was copying documents from the dispatch box at the British embassy, the Jewish underground, the Haganah, was running rescue operations from Nazi-occupied Europe and the Balkans into Palestine. These were directed by Teddy Kollek, later mayor of Jerusalem. The Haganah's activities were closely monitored by several enemy and Allied intelligence agents. "We were very suspicious. We always thought of what to say and what not to say. You had to be careful about the housekeeper, about everything," Kollek later said.[9]

The Agency's attempts to save Jewish refugees who somehow made it out of Nazi-occupied Europe and into Turkey, or Turkish waters, and then send them on to British-ruled Palestine were not always successful. Britain exerted much effort in limiting Jewish immigration to its mandate-administered territory. In May 1939, Parliament passed a law limiting all further Jewish immigration to Palestine to 75,000, with a limit of ten thousand a year. But laws passed in Westminster had little deterrent effect on those fleeing the Holocaust, and illegal immigration continued. Ships that successfully ran the British naval blockade would deposit the immigrants on the beach from where they would be spirited over the sand dunes into nearby Jewish settlements.

Others were less fortunate: the *Salvador* sank in the Sea of Marmara, off Turkey, in December 1940; more than two hundred refugees drowned. This was not unwelcome news to the British Foreign Office officials who were charged with stopping illegal Jewish immigration. Sir Martin Gilbert, in his book *Auschwitz and the Allies*, records, "T.M. Snow, the head of the Refugee Section of the British Foreign Office, noted: 'There could have been no more opportune disaster from the point of view of stopping this traffic.'"[10]

But it was the tragic voyage of the doomed *Struma*, in December 1941, that highlighted Turkey's inhumane refugee policy. Just as Swiss border guards turned back thousands of Jewish refugees fleeing Vichy France or Nazi Germany into the arms of the Gestapo, Turkey refused entry to the miserable and terrified souls floating on this rusty ship as it meandered across the Black Sea, trying to get to Palestine. It was Britain that first refused permission for the *Struma* to pass through the Dardenelles to Palestine, triggering a storm of protest by Jewish organizations. The ship held more than 750 refugees, mainly Romanian Jews, but they could not obtain Palestine immigration certificates as they were considered enemy nationals, despite Romania's viciously anti-Semitic government. When the *Struma* arrived in Istanbul after leaving the Romanian port of Constanta, the Turkish authorities only allowed one passenger, a pregnant woman, to leave the ship. They then asked Sir Hughe Knatchbull-Hugessen, the British ambassador, if the boat could continue onto Palestine. If not, the *Struma* would be sent back out into the Black Sea. Turkey would not allow the refugees to land.

Sir Hughe's reply reminded the Turks that Britain did not want the refugees to land in Palestine, as they had "no permission to go there." But he did add that he objected on humanitarian grounds to Turkey's proposal to send the *Struma* back out into the Black Sea. Surprisingly, for a man steeped in the traditions of Foreign Office pusillanimity, he even took a moral stand of sorts, sending a telegram to the Foreign Office that suggested the *Struma* and its passengers proceed on to Palestine. "If the Turkish government must interfere with the ship, on the ground that they could not keep the distressed Jews in Turkey, let her go rather towards the Dardanelles. It might be that if they reached Palestine, they might despite their illegality receive humane treatment."[11]

Sir Hughe's moral qualms over this human tragedy in the making left the Whitehall mandarins distinctly unmoved. The bureaucrats refused to alter their position, and if anything, his humanitarian plea backfired. As one Colonial Office official, S.E.V. Luke, recorded: "This is the first occasion on which, in spite of numerous efforts, the Turkish government has shown signs of being ready to help in frustrating these illegal immigrant ships, and then the Ambassador goes and spoils the whole effect on absurdly misjudged humanitarian grounds."[12] Lord Moyne, the Colonial Secretary, went even further, writing on Christmas Eve 1941 that Sir Hughe's proposal must be refused:

I find it difficult to write with moderation about this occurrence which is flat contradiction of established government policy, and I should be glad if you could perhaps even now do something to retrieve this position, and to urge that Turkish authorities should be asked to send the ship back to the Black Sea, as they originally proposed.

Conditions deteriorated rapidly on board the *Struma* over the next few weeks of early 1942, as Jewish leaders tried to persuade Whitehall to allow the passengers into Palestine. Food began to run out, and sanitary conditions worsened. The ship had originally been built in Newcastle in 1867 and was now barely seaworthy. The Turks took Britain's hesitation over the ship as a sign to take matters into their own hands. Turkish officials boarded the *Struma*, overpowered any passengers who resisted, and towed the doomed vessel back into the Black Sea. The next morning it exploded and sank, possibly having hit a German mine. Of more than 750 passengers, one survived. The two survivors of the *Struma*—the other the pregnant woman who had been allowed to go to a hospital in Istanbul, where her baby had died—were later among a group of twenty Jewish refugees trying to reach Palestine. British officials refused them permission to enter Palestine. Later on in the war, as the full horrors of the Holocaust became better known, these rules were relaxed. In November and December 1943, for example, over two hundred Greek Jews were smuggled out of German-occupied Greece by boat and taken to Turkey, from where they were sent to Palestine, with the permission of British authorities.

By March 1944, Istanbul even meant, more or less, sanctuary for any Jewish refugee en route to Palestine who managed to cross the German lines into Turkish territory. As the prospect of Allied victory drew closer, Turkish attitudes toward Jewish refugees, as well as the Allies themselves, changed. The key turning point was Anthony Eden's statement on March 30 in the House of Commons, which was even stronger than a similar declaration by President Roosevelt condemning Nazi war crimes:

> Evidence continues to reach His Majesty's government and Allied governments that the Nazi policy of extermination has not been halted. The persecution of the Jews has in particular been of unexampled horror and intensity. On this His Majesty's government, in common with their Allies, now that the hour of Germany's defeat grows ever nearer and more certain, can only repeat their detestation of Germany's crimes and their determination that all those guilty of them shall be brought to justice.
>
> But apart from direct guilt there is still indirect participation in crime.
>
> Satellite governments who expel citizens to destinations named by Berlin must know that such actions are tantamount to assisting in inhuman persecution or slaughter. This will not be forgotten when the inevitable defeat of the arch enemy of Europe comes about.

Eden's powerful warning had a resounding impact through British officialdom and helped change attitudes to Jewish refugees among neutral countries such as Turkey, who wished to maintain good relations with the Allies. British officials also instituted a new liberal policy for admitting Jewish refugees to Palestine, once they reached Istanbul. Colonial Secretary Oliver Stanley agreed in a meeting with Moshe Shertok, then head of the Political Department of the Jewish Agency in Jerusalem and a future prime minister of Israel, to "keep matters elastic, reviewing policy in light of actual escape from Nazi lands" and to request in Britain's name an approach of "liberal transit" for Jewish refugees from Turkish authorities.[13] The results were rapid. Just over a week after Eden's statement in the House of Commons, on April 8, the steamship *Maritza*, carrying 244 Romanian Jewish refugees, arrived in Istanbul. The *Maritza's* passengers fared better than those on the *Struma*, but then by spring 1944, it was clear that the Allies would eventually win the war. It took just a couple of days for permission to be granted for their onward journey to Palestine.

Franco, the Jews' Fascist Friend

While Switzerland and Turkey turned back Jews into the arms of the Gestapo or the waters of the Black Sea, some who headed for Europe's westernmost outpost found an unlikely savior in the shape of Spain's fascist dictator Generalissimo Francisco Franco.

Spain too was neutral, trading profitably with both the Allies and the Axis, supplying Germany with vast quantities of vital war materials such as wolfram, from which tungsten is extracted. Spanish businessmen also sold diamonds and platinum to Germany, goods often smuggled in from South America. Unlike in Switzerland, however, this profitable traffic did not affect Franco's humane Jewish refugee policy.

Estimates vary of the numbers of Jewish refugees given sanctuary in wartime Spain—from which Jews were expelled en
masse in 1492. Chaim Lipschitz, author of *Franco, Spain,
the Jews, and the Holocaust,* claims as many as 45,000 were
saved.[14]

A Spanish passport, or protection papers, could prove a
lifesaver for Sephardi (Jews from eastern Europe and Germany
were generally known as Ashkenazi) Jews who could trace
their lineage back to Spain, even if they lived within the borders of the Third Reich. A 1924 Spanish citizenship law gave
citizenship to many Sephardi Jews of Spanish descent living
in France and the Balkans. Following the wholesale expulsion
of the Spanish Jewish community in 1492, many Jews had
found sanctuary in the Ottoman Empire, which then stretched
through Bulgaria up to Bosnia. Sephardi Jews who held
Spanish passports were not considered refugees, but Spanish
citizens. Repeated Spanish diplomatic communications to the
governments of Vichy France, Italy, and Romania emphasize
that Spain did not recognize differences based on religion
among its citizens. If necessary, Jews with Spanish citizenship
would be evacuated to Spain together with Spanish diplomatic personnel.

General Franco also refused Nazi requests to return
German Jewish refugees. Madrid's position was that Spain
would be happy to return German citizens back to Germany,
but as the German government did not consider German Jews
to be German citizens, Spain could not return them without
their consent.

Why was Franco pro-Jewish? Franco was a fascist, not a
Nazi. Like Mussolini, he stood for a fusion of nation and state,
but race and anti-Semitism was never a major component of
the fascist creed in Spain. Nor was it, initially, in Italy, at least
until the introduction of the 1938 racial laws. Many Italian
Jews joined the Italian fascist party. Franco agreed with Hitler

on the need for a crusade against Bolshevism and even dispatched Spanish soldiers to fight on the eastern front against the Russians, the Blue Legion. But Franco had no sympathy for Hitler's notions of a pure Aryan race and the need to exterminate the Jews.

Many Jews also found refuge in Spanish Morocco, specifically Tangier. Among them was the Reichmann family, who would later find fame as property developers in Canada and London. The Reichmann family left their home in Hungary and traveled through France and Spain before arriving in Tangier. One reason that Franco was pro-Jewish was that he had many friends in the Tangier Jewish community, according to Edward Reichmann. "All Franco's friends there were Jews, prominent Jewish businessmen," he said in an interview.[15] The Reichmanns' Hungarian roots proved a lifesaver for several hundred Hungarian Jews in wartime Budapest.

Renee Reichmann, mother of Edward, persuaded J. Rives Childs, a U.S. diplomat in Tangier to appeal to General Orgaz, the Spanish high commissioner, to issue visas for twelve hundred Hungarian Jews. He agreed, and once the visas to enter Morocco were issued, the Spanish Embassy in Budapest provided provisional passports, stating that the holder had the right to enter Spain and that the Spanish authorities asked for all assistance to be given to the bearer of the passport. Under the auspices of the Red Cross, the twelve hundred Jews were placed into apartment buildings under the protection of the Spanish Embassy. Thanks to the close ties between Spain and Nazi Germany, the Hungarians respected these protected houses' diplomatic status.

Spain also protested to Admiral Horthy in the spring of 1944, when the deportations to Auschwitz of Hungarian Jews began. Spanish protection papers became highly sought-after. As Chaim Lipschitz writes: "In some instances...Spain's protection was actually the most effective of all, due to the diligent efforts of Charge d'Affaires Sanz Briz."[16]

⬚ ⬚ ⬚

Istanbul was also a key site of the bizarre and doomed mission undertaken in the summer of 1944 by Joel Brand, a Hungarian Jew who had been offered a deal in Budapest by Adolf Eichmann. The deal was to swap a million Jewish lives for ten thousand trucks and large amounts of consumer staples such as cocoa, coffee, and soap. These would be supplied by the western Allies and used only on the eastern front against the Soviet Union. In exchange, the Jews would be transported through Nazi-occupied Europe to neutral Spain and Portugal. Unlikely as it sounded, the Brand mission was one of several proposed deals between the Nazis and Jewish/Zionist leadership in wartime Hungary and Slovakia, both as a means of making money and establishing some humanitarian credentials as the Allied armies, and the prospect of war crimes trials, drew nearer. It was also part of an intermittent strategy by Himmler and other Nazi leaders to divide the Allies by splitting off Britain and the United States from the Soviet Union.

Brand was allowed to leave Budapest, but his wife and two children were held behind as hostages. This was a Faustian choice: to try and save Hungarian Jewry by supplying goods and war matériel to the Third Reich, thus inevitably boosting its military prowess, or to refuse to cooperate. Refusal would have been suicidal. A brave man who had spent much of the war running rescue operations of Jews from Poland and Slovakia into Hungary, Brand felt he had no choice and left for Istanbul, arriving on May 19. Flown in from Vienna on a German plane, he was accompanied by the shady figure of Andor Grosz, a Hungarian Jew, smuggler, and black marketeer, who was working for the *Abwehr* (German Military Intelligence), the Hungarian Secret Service, and probably the Zionists as well.

From Istanbul, the unlikely duo planned to travel to Palestine, to negotiate with the British and the top officials of the Jewish Agency in Jerusalem to swap Jews for trucks and cocoa, or "blood for goods" as the mission was now dubbed.

The arrival of Brand and Grosz in Istanbul sent tremendous ripples through the Allied diplomatic community. The U.S. ambassador to Turkey forwarded Brand's proposal to Washington while, in Istanbul, officials of the Jewish Agency briefed British diplomats. Many diplomats regarded the proposal as a macabre joke. While there was interest in saving Jewish lives, the practicalities of suspending hostilities while one million Jews were transported through Europe were seen as insurmountable. Still, for the West, there were choices to be made in responding to Eichmann's offer. It could be refused outright, used as a stalling tactic to try and delay the last stage of the Holocaust, or even taken seriously as a start of negotiations.

But wartime realpolitik—the Allies' demands for an absolute German surrender—meant that Brand and Grosz's mission never stood a chance. They were arrested by the British authorities as soon as they left Turkey. Brand was held in Aleppo, Syria, and then Cairo until October 1944, when he was moved to Jerusalem and finally released. Brand lived in Israel with his wife and children until he died in 1964. He took revenge of sorts on the man who had sent him to Istanbul when he testified at Eichmann's trial in Jerusalem in 1961. Andor Grosz was imprisoned in Turkey for espionage from 1946 to 1953 and then moved to Israel. He died in Munich in the 1970s, the same city where Elyesa Bazna (Cicero) ended his days. Like his embassy contact, Ludwig Moyzisch, Bazna later wrote a book about his exploits in the pay of Nazi intelligence, *Ich War Cicero*, ("I Was Cicero"), but his dreams of great wealth never materialized, and he spent his last days working as a night watchman.

In his memoirs, Walter Schellenberg hints that the flow of Cicero's material was, in fact, directed by the Turks, with the aim of alerting Germany to the range of forces massed against the Nazis. By showing the impossibility of Germany winning the war, it was hoped that Cicero's documents would encourage the Nazi leadership to sue for peace before the total collapse of the Third Reich. In other words, to help Germany itself survive Hitler. This may be Schellenberg's own wishful thinking, as he was, by 1944, actively seeking negotiations with the West and pushed Himmler to contact the Swedish Red Cross official Count Folke Bernadotte over a possible German surrender in the West. As he notes: "Again and again, I wondered whether perhaps there lay behind 'Cicero' the shadow of the Turkish Secret Service. The more I thought about this, the more likely it seemed to me that through his material, Turkey had tried to warn Germany and prevent her from continuing on her path to total destruction."[17]

Of all the neutral countries and organizations, none was so compromised and corrupted by its relations with Nazi Germany during World War II as the International Committee of the Red Cross (ICRC), as its officials themselves now admit. The Red Cross's wartime policies were shaped not by the aim of surviving Hitler—the Nazis also needed the humanitarian organization—but of preserving its unique privileges and power. To that end, throughout the war, the Red Cross remained silent about the Holocaust.

One of the earliest documented reports of the Nazi genocide of the Jews was a cable sent by Gerhard Reigner, the World Jewish Congress's representative in Geneva, the Swiss city that was also home to the headquarters of the Red Cross. The Reigner cable was sent on August 8, 1942, to Sidney Silverman, the Labour MP whose intervention provoked Eden's declaration in the House of Commons two years later condemning Nazi genocide, and to Rabbi Stephen Wise in New York. Based on information supplied by Eduard Scholte, a businessman from Leipzig who wanted to get the news of the Holocaust to the Allies. The Reigner cable was chillingly accurate. It detailed a Nazi plan to deport and kill between three-and-a-half and four million Jews in occupied Europe, starting in autumn 1942, with the killing method of prussic acid (Zyklon B) to be used. After some months of debate about the likely veracity of the cable's contents, Rabbi Wise broke the story to the press in New York in November 1942. After that, the Red Cross could no longer claim ignorance of the Holocaust. But it failed to issue a single protest over the mass killings of the Jews, fearful that such a move would jeopardize its privileged access across the front lines to prisoners of war.

Perhaps, like most of the world, the Red Cross was simply unperturbed that European Jewry was being slaughtered en masse. "Today you cannot justify this silence. The Red Cross could have done something else. It could have informed the world, or cried out, but it was not the same organization as today," said Doris Pfister, a spokeswoman for the organization.[18]

The Red Cross did make one attempt via the German Red Cross, in December 1939, to arrange for delegates to visit Jews from Vienna who had been deported to Poland. The request was refused, and the organization basically gave up trying to prevent, halt, or ameliorate the greatest human catastrophe that had taken place since its inception in 1863. As news spread about the Holocaust and the massacres of Soviet and Polish civilians by the Nazis, in 1942 the organization again considered whether or not it should launch a general appeal against the continuing violations of international law. A draft was even prepared, but in the end, the organization kept silent, preferring bilateral approaches to specific governments.

Historian Arieh Ben-Tov records these events in his book, *Facing the Holocaust in Budapest*, a detailed study of the role of the Red Cross in wartime Hungary:

In 1942, the representatives of the WJC [World Jewish Congress] already knew about the murder of Polish Jews and the "Final Solution" plan for the Jews of Europe. Carl Burckhardt, too, possessed this information, received through his own channels. He passed it on to the president of the ICRC, and they debated possible ways of reacting.

On October 14, 1942, a proposal for an appeal, prepared by Huber and Pictet, secretary of the president, was presented to the meeting of the ICRC as follows: "Appeal in favor of the application of the essential principle of jus gentium [international law], relating to the conduct of hostilities."

After reviewing the numerous categories of civilian victims and types of persecution, the appeal dealt with the plight of the Jews as follows: "...Besides the interned civilians, properly so named, certain categories of various nationalities are, for reasons depending on the war situation, deprived of their liberty, deported, or taken as hostages, and they may even for this reason suffer attacks on their lives for acts they did not commit."

This text did not condemn anybody in particular and was not addressed directly to Germany. The Jews were not mentioned by name. The plenary session of the ICRC voted against the resolution.[19]

One of those present at the fateful Red Cross meeting was Philip Etter, a former Swiss foreign minister, representing the Swiss government. He argued so strongly that even this draft appeal for humane conduct of war could be seen as a violation of neutrality that he helped swing the vote in favor of silence. After that, the matter was viewed as closed. As the ICRC's own website—only two pages of which are devoted to the Holocaust—records: "From then on, the ICRC opted for a strategy of no longer addressing the question of Jews directly—it did so only in general approaches concerning the victims of mass arrests or deportation, and then it made no reference to their religious affiliation or racial origins, although it was clear that the people in question were, for the most part, Jews."[20]

The Red Cross did manage to send some parcels to inmates in concentration camps, after the Nazi Foreign Ministry granted authorization. It started with fifty, and numbers rose rapidly once the precedent had been sent. By May 1945, it sent more than 122,000 relief packages to the camps. The ICRC website notes that, while welcome, the deliveries had no impact on the Holocaust itself: "But this operation did not succeed in reaching those deportees who were subjected to the harshest regime, nor did it give captives any protection from torture or massacres."

The passive approach taken by headquarters filtered through to the national committees. The German Red Cross even felt embold-ened enough to inform Geneva in April 1942 that it would not communicate any information on what it described as "non-Aryan" detainees and asked that headquarters refrain from asking questions about them. The full extent of the humanitarian organization's cra-ven attitude to the Third Reich was revealed in 1997, when 60,000 pages of documents were released by the Geneva headquarters to the Yad Vashem Holocaust Memorial in Jerusalem. Red Cross officials themselves, such as archivist Fabrizio Bensi, admit that the papers highlight the organization's utter moral failure in neglecting to come to the aid of Jews during the Holocaust. "When you know that people are being murdered all around you and that you did nothing, it is a failure of your moral principles. Both the Red Cross and the West knew about the extermination of the Jews, but they couldn't understand it."[21]

The most embarrassing of these records is probably the report by delegate Maurice Rossel, on June 23, 1944, to the Theresienstadt concentration camp in Czechoslovakia. Theresienstadt, thirty-five miles from Prague, was originally the site of a Hapsburg fortress, set in picturesque rolling countryside. It was initially designated a model ghetto, for "privileged" Jews, such as Jews married to Aryans, war veterans, and community leaders, with marginally more humane conditions than those at similar concentration camps such as Belsen or Dachau, let alone the extermination camps of Auschwitz or Belzec. The camp was constructed by Reinhard Heydrich in 1941. Eminent visitors, professing concern about the fate of the Jews, would be brought to Theresienstadt and shown that they lived in comparative comfort, at least in comparison to their fellow Jews in Poland or the Soviet Union. Propaganda films were made, showing Jews strolling among the barracks, wearing their own clothes, drink-ing coffee, and chatting. The reality was different. About 33,000

Jews died in Theresienstadt, while a further 88,000 were sent to the extermination camps, mainly Auschwitz, to be gassed.

All of this escaped Maurice Rossel, who fell for the Nazi propaganda line that Theresienstadt was a model ghetto, run humanely. Reading his impressions, more than fifty years later, it's hard to imagine that a representative of the ICRC could be so comprehensively deceived.

Rossel's report is divided into a series of subheadings, covering subjects such as living conditions, food, clothing, work, culture, and study. His visit was a grotesque charade organized by the Nazi camp officials, who deceived Rossel completely. "The barracks are of a large type and well lit," he found. The childrens' homes were "particularly well furnished" with murals of an educational nature. There was enough for the prisoners to eat, as well. He claimed: "As soon as we entered the ghetto, we could convince ourselves that the population is not suffering from undernourishment." There were communal canteens, run like restaurants: "very spacious and pleasant. The people who come to eat are promptly served by a young girl in an apron, just as in any restaurant."[22]

Perhaps most bizarre are Rossel's observations on the sartorial standards of the inmates of Theresienstadt, which did at least conform to his ideas of the proper relationship between someone's clothes and their station in society. "The people who we meet in the streets are correctly dressed, with the differences that one would normally meet in a small town between the rich and less rich. Some elegant ones have all the hats, scarves and modern handbags." He does note that with limited opportunities for study, some of the Jews incarcerated in the camp were finding it difficult to adapt to the demands of manual work. There is no mention of beatings, torture, or onward deportation to Auschwitz and the gas chambers. His sprightly conclusion about living conditions in Theresienstadt is testimony to both the obtuseness of the Red Cross and the efficiency of the Nazi pantomime organized for his visit, during which he was not allowed to meet alone with any Jewish leaders.

Surviving inmates of Theresienstadt, such as Charlotte Opfermann, have different memories. Together with her family, she was deported from Wiesbaden, Germany, and arrived at Theresienstadt in June 1943. Her father and brother were sent on to Auschwitz, she and her mother survived, barely. Here, in her own words, are extracts from her description of camp life, and death:

A typical day: I'd wake up (then living with six thousand other women in the unfinished, unheatable, vermin-infested attic of one of the large barracks for women, not counting additional thousands in the rooms downstairs) from the noise and commotion of all the women around me trying to get ready for work.

I would go downstairs and stand in line at the latrine or in front of one of the six or eight toilet fixtures (two or three such set-ups for many, many thousands of women). There usually was no water for flushing or for washing. No separating, privacy-affording stalls. No toilet paper. Everybody cussing and telling us to hurry up. Then, if there was time, I would rush to the food distribution center to fetch our assigned cup of imitation coffee (made from grain and chestnuts) for my mother and me. No other food was provided. If I had any bread left (usually I didn't) I'd soak a dry slice of bread in this brew. Then I'd rush to report for work and march off to wherever our "Hundertschaft" was assigned to that day. In the evening, we would again line up for food. Three times a week, this evening meal consisted of the same "coffee" with nothing else to accompany it. Other times it was a ladle of barley. Or some indefinable, tasteless, unflavored soup in which swam (if I was fortunate) a chunk of unpeeled, dirty potato or a bit of carrot or a slice of turnip. If I was extremely lucky (and/or if I knew the kitchen personnel, could persuade them to scoop my ladle from the bottom of the container) even two or all three of the above. That was heaven for an evening.[23]

In correspondence with the authors, Ms. Opfermann detailed her recollections of the Rossel visit, which she describes as a "charade":

We knew the IRC Rossel visit would be something special because we were ordered to scrub the streets, paint the fronts of houses, barricades came down, walls were pulled down, flowers were planted and everyone who was not previously trained and instructed to take part in the charade was under house arrest.

The central square had been off limits to inmates, heretofore, except for workers at the Kistenproduction carpentry shop. It was now converted into a pleasant little park with fountain, grass, flower beds, etc. Many children were trained like circus animals to curtsy, to play-act, to use playground equipment, and such. A few weeks later, they were all killed.

The visitors, however, were not the least interested in our welfare. It was a curiosity trip, nothing else. Ellen Oppenheym, daughter of the leader of the Danish inmates, managed to speak briefly with the Danish [Red Cross] visitors and tried to convey information. Nobody listened or paid any attention.

As for the wretched Rossel himself, he concluded: "We would add that our surprise was immense to find a lively town, with an almost normal life, although we were waiting for the worst."

The worst took place at the extermination camps such as Belzec, in southeast Poland, and Auschwitz. Belzec was a pure death factory, where Jews were taken straight from the trains to the gas chambers before being cremated. By 1944, Belzec, the site of the death of 600,000 Jews, no longer existed, demolished by the SS as it retreated from the advancing Russians. But Auschwitz still stood, and it was at the Nazis' most notorious extermination camp that Maurice Rossel arrived on September 27, 1944. Rossel's report on his visit to Auschwitz shows that by September, he is somewhat better acquainted with the realities of the Holocaust. Rossel was denied access to the main camp area, as this was one place where it would be impossible for the Nazis to organize a Theresienstadt-style deception. His visit was ostensibly to check on the distribution of food aid parcels to camp inmates, although as most arrivals had an average life expectancy of seventy-two hours, the packages had little impact. On the road to the camp, he saw a procession of inmates passing by and gives a chilling description of these human beings reduced to automatons:

> These people, even if they work in open air, have the complexion of ashes. They walk four together, and the guards, with pistols under their arms, are of the SS Death's Head division. We do not seek to describe the atmosphere, everybody can imagine that without difficulties, that there are no individuals any more, only numbers. Every prisoner in the camp, men and women, is dressed in blue and gray material with stripes, their number is written on their left side...the men wear jackets and hats like a beret. When a group passes in front of the black flag of the SS, an officer, or guard, the prisoners take off their hats like a machine, very quickly, and brush their hair into place in synchronization.
>
> All their shaved skulls look similar from a distance. When you look at them closer, at their naked head with their berets, you can see the faces are drawn and tired, with some intelligence. Without moving their heads, their eyes show curiosity.[24]

Inside Auschwitz, Rossel saw "six or eight barracks, buildings that look like new, every window has bars, and the camp is surrounded by high walls and barbed wire." He noted that a British POW working at one of the camp satellite sites, asked if he was aware of the "shower rooms": "There is a rumor that there is a shower room in the camp which is very modern, and the prisoners are killed by gas continuously. This British trustee prisoner had tried, through his Auschwitz *kommando* [work group] to obtain confirmation of this. This proved impossible to prove. Even the prisoners did not talk at all." Finally, at the end of his report, Rossel stopped prevaricating and came to a conclusion, of sorts: "Once again, leaving Auschwitz we have the impression that the mystery is still very well kept. However, we are certain that people are being sent [to the gas chambers] there, and of the biggest quantity, as fast as possible. One more time, we believe that the prisoners are among those who are sent."

Thankfully for the Jews of Budapest, Rossels' colleague, Friedrich Born, the Red Cross delegate in the Hungarian capital from May 1944, took a more vigorous approach to saving lives. His predecessor Jean de Bavier had already raised the alarm over the certain fate of Hungarian Jewry under the Germans but had run into a wall of bureaucratic indifference. In early 1944, Hungary was the site of eastern Europe's largest remaining Jewish community, about 650,000. By July 1944, 450,000 Hungarian Jews from the provinces had been sent to Auschwitz. Under diplomatic pressure from the Allies and neutral countries, the country's ruler, Admiral Horthy, stopped the deportations. Born went into action to save the remnants of Hungarian Jewry, about 200,000 strong and concentrated in Budapest.

Hungary was in a different situation to other Nazi-occupied countries, such as Poland or Czechoslovakia. Even after the invasion in 1944, it remained a sovereign, independent state, with its own army, government, and internal security forces. These parallel and sometimes competing systems of authority gave greater scope to maneuver than in Warsaw or Prague, which were fully absorbed into the Third Reich. Born's courageous work shows how much a determined individual, ready to exploit any avenue, could achieve, and how much room there was to take a moral stand in the chaos as the war drew to a close.

In July, Born obtained authorization from the Hungarian government to provide Jews in Budapest with certificates showing that they possessed immigration certificates issued by countries in Latin

America. The logistical difficulties of getting from Nazi-occupied Hungary, surrounded by Germany's allies, across the Atlantic Ocean, were almost insurmountable, but the papers afforded a certain amount of protection from German and Hungarian authorities anxious to keep good diplomatic relations with neutral countries. As the news of the Hungarian Holocaust spread, Born's lifesaving work was finally supported by his bosses at Red Cross headquarters in Geneva, where they were also coming under increasing pressure from the Swiss public to do something to stop the Holocaust.

In fact, it was a Swiss diplomat, Carl Lutz, who had initiated the technique of issuing protection papers earlier that year. Like Born, Lutz had not been supported by his bosses—in his case, at the Swiss Foreign Ministry—but had carried on nonetheless. Lutz represented the interests of Allied countries in Hungary, including Britain. With the agreement of Britan, he issued entry certificates for Palestine, which was then under British rule, stating that the bearer would eventually receive Palestinian citizenship. By including the holder's family, about 50,000 Jews were so protected as potential British subjects. Even though Hungary was at war with Britain, Hungarian officials were unlikely to arrange for their deaths, especially as hopes were high that Britain and the United States, rather than the Soviets, would liberate Hungary. The same technique was used by the Swedish diplomat Raoul Wallenberg to save many thousands of Jews, and later, other neutral diplomats, such as Spanish officials, followed suit.

From pieces of paper, franked with official seals, the principle was extended to actual buildings. Born declared houses where Jews lived to be under the protection of the Red Cross and gave them extra-territorial diplomatic status. Working in tandem with Lutz and Wallenberg, he persuaded the Ministry of the Interior to issue a decree outlawing looting; provided asylum for members of the Jewish Council; protested against the treatment of Budapest's Jews; organized food supplies for the ghetto; and issued about three thousand letters of protection. Born's lifesaving work continued after the Arrow Cross coup of October 15, 1944, which replaced Horthy's government with that of Ferenc Szalasi, leader of the Hungarian Nazis.

From that date, anarchy descended onto the streets of Budapest. It was a time of terror for Budapest's Jews—when the Blue Danube ran red with blood—until the liberation of the city by the Red Army in January 1945. Tens of thousands of Jews were sent to Austria on foot, a trek known as the "Death March" that claimed thousands of lives. Many more were killed by roving gangs of Arrow Cross youths who roamed the ghetto, taking Jews to the banks of the Danube, tying them together, and shooting them into the water.

Even in these extremely dangerous conditions, Born, Lutz, and Wallenberg daily risked their lives, pushing the limits of their diplomatic status ever further. That the murderous Arrow Cross regime, desperate for international recognition, would hesitate before simply killing three neutral diplomats does not diminish their bravery—especially considering the ambivalent support all three received from their superiors (who were often unenthusiastic about their humanitarian missions, and who preferred the safety of a dry and legalistic interpretation of their envoys' work).

As the war drew to a close, other Red Cross envoys helped save lives and salvage something of the organization's tarnished honor. In the concentration camps of Dachau, Mauthausen, and Turckheim, officials helped prevent a final slaughter of inmates and negotiate the Germans' surrender to the advancing Allies. But most of the credit must go to Friedrich Born, who refused completely to be corrupted or compromised by his privileged position as a Red Cross envoy. As Arieh Ben-Tov, a historian of the Red Cross and its role in the Hungarian Holocaust, writes:

> Born adopted an extensive interpretation of his humanitarian mission which went beyond the instructions from Geneva.... Born was on the spot, and his view of what should be done was dictated by the tragic reality and not, as was the case for the Geneva headquarters, by the formal provisions of a convention....

When it [the ICRC] abandoned its narrow interpretation of its principles and accepted the fact that its delegate in Hungary, Friedrich Born, has taken the practical steps...then the institution's achievement in Hungary was truly great.[25]

Or as the ICRC's own website records:

Apart from the work of Friedrich Born in Hungary and a few sporadic instances elsewhere, the ICRC's efforts to assist Jews and other groups of civilians persecuted during World War II were a failure.

Friedrich Born, together with Carl Lutz and Raoul Wallenberg, is commemorated at the Yad Vashem Holocaust Memorial in Jerusalem as a Righteous Gentile. We can but speculate on how the course of history, and the Holocaust, would have turned, had Rossel and his wartime superiors in the Red Cross been men of a similar moral caliber.

Chapter Ten

Impossible Choices

I, Gens, lead you to death, and I, Gens, want to save Jews from death. I, Gens, order hideouts to be blown up, and I, Gens, try to get certificates, work, and benefits for the ghetto. I render the account of Jewish blood and not the account of Jewish honor. When they ask me for a thousand Jews, I hand them over; for if we Jews will not give on our own, the Germans will come and take them by force. Then they will not take one thousand, but thousands....I had to befoul myself and act without conscience.

—Jacob Gens, chief of the Vilna ghetto,
justifying his cooperation with the Nazis

The Central Council is the only authorized and responsible organ of all Jewry and is the competent organ to maintain contact with German authorities....We emphasize the need for strict and conscientious adherence to all these regulations. Only by following the rules can it be possible for everyone to pursue his civilian life within the permitted framework.

— "Appeal to Hungarian Jewry" published in the official newspaper,
the Journal of Hungarian Jews, *March 23, 1944,*
shortly after the Nazi occupation of Hungary

This is a book about survival ethics and the choices they demanded. The hardest choices of all in the Third Reich were faced by the members and leaders of the Jewish Councils (*Judenräte*). These ran the communal affairs of the ghettos where Jews were incarcerated before being transported to the death camps. Members of the Jewish Councils were forced to implement the Nazis' orders, sometimes including the selection of who would be deported. Their role remains deeply controversial, with some Holocaust survivors—and many victims—accusing them of complicity, whether active or passive, in the extermination.

On occasion, the *Judenräte* officials used the ghettos' own Jewish police officers to help round up their fellow Jews and deliver them to the cattle trains. This was the Third Reich's ultimate moral corruption: Jews sending other Jews to die that others might yet survive Hitler. The ghastly inner turmoil and self-loathing of those policemen is recorded in the testament of Calel Perochodnik, a ghetto policeman in Otwock, near Warsaw, who witnessed the Nazis deport his own wife and child. The ghetto police, he wrote, "lead their own father and mothers to the cattle cars; themselves close the door with the bolt—just as if they were nailing the coffins with their own hands."[1]

In the epigram at the beginning of this chapter, Jacob Gens, initially police chief and then head of the Vilna ghetto, gives the classic defense of *Judenrat* members: that by cooperating with the SS and Gestapo, some Jews at least would live. Many would die anyway, so better to deal with—to negotiate with—the Nazis, to save as many as possible. But as the Nazis' intent to eliminate European Jewry became clearer, that argument lost both its moral force and logic. Others saw in the dark universe of the ghettos a chance for Gens' fellow potentates, such as Mordechai Chaim Rumkowski, head of the Lodz ghetto, to build macabre empires based on their power. Rumkowski, a former insurance agent and orphanage director in his early sixties, ruled like a king, deciding who would live and who would die. In the end, the privileged status of Rumkowski and his counterparts across Poland counted for nothing. They too were killed.

Hans Frank, governor general of occupied Poland, issued the order for the establishment of the *Judenräte* on November 28, 1939. Communities of up to ten thousand inhabitants would have a twelve-member *Judenrat*. Those of more than ten thousand would be served by a twenty-four–member council. Each council elected a chairman and a deputy chairman, who presented the membership list to the local Nazi commander. Point five of Frank's decree was the Nazis' masterstroke:

> It is the duty of the *Judenrat* through its chairman or his deputy to receive the orders of the German administration. It is responsible for the conscientious carrying out of orders to their full extent. The directives it issues to carry out these German decrees must be obeyed by all Jews and Jewesses.

Thus were the Jews of wartime Europe terrorized into helping organize their own destruction, through the offices of their own community leaders, who were sometimes the same officials of the prewar community—which was the Nazis' intent. In both villages and cosmopolitan cities such as Warsaw, many Jews had limited social interaction with the gentile population. The *Judenräte* leaders' orders were sweetened by familiarity and reassurance and so, initially at least, were generally obeyed. Their own people were more palatable bringers of bad news than SS officers. To resist the Germans meant resisting the Jews' own leaders.

The *Judenrat* members, middle-aged or older, were of another, prewar era, when Jewry's leaders believed that negotiation with and/or bribery of officialdom was the best way to ensure their community's survival. Until Hitler, they were correct. Tsars, kings, emperors, even empires, came and went, but the Jews of eastern Europe endured, survived, and sometimes flourished. The *Judenräte* had—initially at least—thought the Nazis merely the worst incarnation so far of state persecution. That the Nazis planned not merely to confine, control, exploit, and persecute Jews, but exterminate them, was a slow and awful revelation.

To take a place on the council was complicity of a sort, even under duress, and certainly a kind of compromise. *Judenräte* members themselves were fed a poisoned brew of threats and promises as they implemented the SS orders. They and their families were given protective papers to ensure their compliance and interest in cooperating, although these sometimes proved of little worth. To refuse to serve was also an abnegation of communal responsibility. It would leave the Jews open to direct rule by the Nazis and their local auxiliaries and remove the mediating, sometimes ameliorating, layer of Jewish officialdom.

Membership could also be extremely dangerous. In many places early in the war, the *Judenräte* were a convenient way for the Nazis to gather up respected communal leaders, teachers, rabbis, and former officials—in short, the community elite—and then kill them, thereby removing those around whom resistance to the Nazis might gel. Hundreds of *Judenräte* members were killed or sent to camps.

In Lodz, in October 1939, Rumkowski invited thirty leading Jews to form a council. On November 7, nearly all of them were arrested by the Gestapo. In Vilna, in July 1941, two *Judenräte* members were shot after the community failed to raise two million rubles overnight. In September, another sixteen were arrested and disappeared. In Lvov, members were hanged in public. Once enrolled on the council, the choices became harder and sharper. A choice of life or death itself, in fact. Refusal to implement orders meant execution or deportation to the camps.

Jewish leaders who refused to flee the Nazis and stayed with their people saw serving on the *Judenrat* as a continuation of their communal responsibility. The leader of Berlin Jewry, Rabbi Leo Baeck, declined repeated offers of sanctuary from abroad and announced he would stay in Berlin until the last *minyan* (prayer quota of ten Jews). Sent to Theresienstadt in Czechoslovakia, the Nazis' "showcase" camp (see chapter 9), he assumed the same leadership role, lecturing on philosophy and religion. In the camps, as well, there could be choices in dealing with Nazi officials, and not just for Jews. In Buchenwald, where the German Communist leader Ernst Thaelmann was held for eleven years (he was shot in August 1944), the Communists set up a resistance movement, following the rules of strict party discipline and providing aid, food, and news from the outside world. It was so well organized that, after the war, controversy erupted over whether its members had aided the Nazis in the running of the camp. Similar structures were organized in Sachsenhausen and Mauthausen. In his book, *Communist Resistance in Nazi Germany*, Allen Merson notes of these three concentration camps: "…the camp administration at prisoner level became virtually identical with the Communist Party leadership in the camp."[2]

In Theresienstadt, from where inmates were transported to their deaths at Auschwitz, Rabbi Baeck's choice was starker than the Communist cadres'. Baeck arrived in Theresienstadt in January 1943. In August, a fellow inmate informed him of the reality of Auschwitz, that Jews were not sent there to work, but to be gassed. "So it was not just a rumor or, as I had hoped, the illusion of a diseased imagination," he commented. Should he inform his fellow Jews of what he had learned, or should he keep silent? Like the leaders of Hungarian Jewry a year later, Baeck kept silent. He rationalized his decision by arguing that disseminating the news would merely induce useless terror among the Jews. And perhaps it was not true, anyway:

> I finally decided that no one should know it. If the Council of Elders were informed, the whole camp would know within a few hours. Living in the expectation of death by gassing would only be the harder, and this death was not certain at all: there was selection for slave labor; perhaps not all transports went to Auschwitz. So I came to the grave decision to tell no one.[3]

Charlotte Opfermann, former inmate of Theresienstadt, informed the authors that in fact all members of the camp's Jewish Council knew about Auschwitz. Such places could not be kept secret. But for the philosopher Hannah Arendt, the learned Rabbi Baeck and the power-mad Rumkowski were one and the same. In her work, *Eichmann In Jerusalem*, a report on Eichmann's 1961 trial, she is scathing about the role of the *Judenräte*, describing their role in the Holocaust as "undoubtedly the darkest chapter of the whole dark story":

> We know the physiognomy of the Jewish leaders during the Nazi period very well; they ranged all the way from Chaim Rumkowski, eldest of the Jews in Lodz, who issued currency notes bearing his signature and postage stamps engraved with his portrait, and who rode around in a broken-down, horse-drawn carriage; through Leo Baeck, scholarly, mild-mannered, highly educated, who believed Jewish policemen would be "more gentle and helpful" (whereas in fact they were, of course, more brutal and less corruptible, since so much more was at stake for them).[4]

Arendt's rage is perhaps misdirected. However morally ambiguous were some aspects of their roles, it is a fact that even in the midst of death, the *Judenräte* tried to continue their public service and ensure that life continued. Larger ghettos such as Lodz and Warsaw were complete microcosms. The *Judenräte* set up social and welfare services such as hospitals, soup kitchens, clinics, pharmacies, public health inspectors, and homes for the elderly and children. There were ghetto factories, schools, newspapers, rival political parties, a postal service, and even entertainment, such as nightclubs and theaters. Lodz had its own currency and mini-economy. More than 160,000 Jews lived in an area of 1.5 square miles. Tens of thousands slaved in more than a hundred factories in the Lodz ghetto, many making uniforms for the Nazis. In 1941, its industrial production was worth RM16 million ($6.4 million). Rumkowski's strategy was to keep the ghetto, a necessary part of the Nazi war effort, as productive as possible, as a means of keeping his people alive.

Among those workers was Holocaust survivor Jack Weisblack. "The Germans took everything from us and concentrated us in a ghetto," he recalls. "We were mechanics, and we had to work. We had tailors, machinists making German uniforms and shoes. Life in the ghetto was murder. There was no food. We were freezing in the winter, stifling in the summer. We didn't have any contact with the Germans, and none of them showed us any humanity."⁵ Unlike Warsaw, the Lodz ghetto was sealed off from the outside world, which some inhabitants welcomed as a macabre kind of safety against attack. The Jews incarcerated inside were not fully aware of the fate of fellow Jews, says Weisblack. "We knew there were death camps, but we didn't know it was that bad until we found out in 1944. We were closed in the ghetto, no mail and no newspapers." In the summer of that year, the Jews of Lodz were transported to the camps. Jack Weisblack was taken to Auschwitz in August. "There was no food, and they put us in cattle cars. It took a day-and-a-half. I was there for a month, but the Germans wanted mechanics, so I was taken to Chemnitz, to make vehicle parts."

In such conditions, criminality also flourished. There was often little solidarity between the different nationalities and classes of Jews. Many Lodz natives were of the working class. When thousands of bourgeois Jews arrived in Lodz from Austria and Czechoslovakia, many with personal possessions that could be sold or traded, they took over the black market in bread. Even potato peelings fetched a high price. The grim conditions inspired the ghetto's mordant poets:

> *When we had nothing to eat,*
> *They gave us a turnip, they gave us a beet,*
> *Here, have some grub, have some fleas,*
> *Have some typhus, die of disease.*

Not surprisingly, thievery and pilfering of the ghettos' limited food stocks were widespread. Some workers took food for themselves and their families, others stole supplies for the black market. The illustrated book, *The Warsaw Ghetto in Photographs*, shows what it describes as the "Ghetto Elite," dressed in their best clothes, playing cards, drinking and smoking at a nightclub, dancing on the edge of disaster. Jewish black marketeers made a handsome living smuggling food into the ghetto from contacts on the Aryan side and could afford such diversions. Other photographs in the same work show a more common reality: stick-thin corpses, victims of typhus and starvation that littered the streets, and child beggars, skin stretched tightly over their skeletal faces. Stanislaw Rozycki's ghetto diary recorded what he saw on the ghetto's streets:

> The streets resound with the futile screams of children dying of hunger. They whine, beg, sing, lament, and tremble in the cold, without underwear, without clothes, without shoes, covered only by rags and bags which are tied by string to the meager skeleton. Children swollen from hunger, deformed, semiconscious; children who are perfectly adult, somber, and tired of living at age five. They are like hoary old men and know only one thing: "I am freezing, I am hungry," so quickly have they grasped the fundamentals of life.[6]

Smuggling food was one of the ghetto's main industries. Many children, driven mad by hunger, daily risked their lives to sneak onto the Aryan side and find some scraps to eat. Those caught were shot by the Germans, recorded Emmanuel Ringelblum, the Warsaw ghetto's archivist:

> Among the Jewish victims of the smuggling, there were tens of Jewish children between five and six years old, whom the German killers shot in great numbers near the passages and at the walls....And despite that, without paying attention to the victims, the smuggling never stopped for a moment. When the street was still slippery with the blood that had been spilled, other smugglers already set out, as soon as the "candles" [lookouts] had signaled that the way was clear, to carry on with the work.[7]

In Warsaw, and other major ghettos, such as Lodz, Vilna, and Bialystok, Ringelblum and his fellow archivists gathered and commissioned material on life and death in the ghetto. Theirs was the age-old instinct of the people of the book, as Jews are known, to record events for posterity and future generations. They might die, but their work at least and a record of their lives, and deaths, would live on. Ringelblum's secret archives, code-named *Oneg Shabbat* ("Sabbath pleasures") employed a substantial staff, gathering and cataloguing materials, everything from mordant jokes to official German pronouncements. Ringelblum's *Oneg Shabbat* was buried in crates in Warsaw and unearthed after the war.

In December 1940, the *Gazeta Zydowska*, the official Polish Jewish newspaper, had announced that the *Judenräte* had "become the central place where all the various Jewish affairs are organized. This gives it certain rights, but also imposes duties. The maintenance of balance between these rights and duties is a difficult task, but an important one, and the satisfactory relationship between the Council and the [Jewish] public depends on its achievements."[8] But as the trains kept rolling to the death camps, the *Judenräte's* authority slipped away. In the end, there were no "achievements." The *Judenräte's* orders began to be ignored and disobeyed. Their members believed they operated in a world of shades of gray, but it steadily became clear that the choices were black or white. In the eyes of many ghetto dwellers, the *Judenräte's* initial compromises with the Nazis became collaboration. The *Judenrat* became known as the *Judenverrat*, the "betrayal of the Jews." In Warsaw, the writer Chaim Kaplan wrote in his diary on April 23, 1941:

> The Community Council—the *Judenrat* in the language of the Occupying Power—is an abomination in the eyes of the Warsaw Community. When the Council is so much as mentioned, everyone's blood begins to boil. If it were not for fear of the authorities, there would be bloodshed. I am certain that at the first opportunity, if only we were freed a little from the Nazi

tutelage, we will fall on Grzybowska 26 [the *Judenrat* office]
and not leave one stone standing on another....According to
rumor, the president [Adam Czerniakow] is a decent man. But
the people around him are the dregs of humanity.[9]

Despite being despised, the *Judenräte* also provided employment for thousands of Jews: almost 13,000 in Lodz and six thousand in Warsaw at their peaks. A job at the *Judenrat* was hotly
contested: employees were not usually drafted for forced labor
and received bigger food rations. Family connections, business
relationships, friendships, all were exploited to try and gain a place
in the *Judenrat* office. Those considered valuable for the future, if
there might be one, such as writers, teachers, and rabbis were often
given work there as a means of keeping the core of the community
alive as long as possible. "Agents of the oppressors, the *Judenräte*
nevertheless regarded themselves as comforters of the oppressed.
In their brief, wretched existence, they tried to reconcile their
irreconcilable tasks," writes Lucy Davidowicz in *The War Against
the Jews 1933–45*.[10] They tried to bribe and flatter the Germans
with presents of money and valuables. The *Judenräte* leaders
exploited every avenue to reduce the Nazis' demands, but the beast
was insatiable, as Adam Czerniakow, leader of the Warsaw *Judenrat*
eventually understood.

In the annals of the Holocaust, Czerniakow is a tragic and
controversial figure, who tried to deal with the devil but became
gradually more compromised and corrupted. Before the war, he
was a teacher and a member of Warsaw City Council and the Polish
Senate. He was also a member of the Jewish Community's executive
council. Soon after Warsaw fell to the Nazis, he was ordered to serve
as *Judenrat* head. Other political leaders left Warsaw soon after the
occupation, but Czerniakow stayed and was critical of his colleagues
who, he said, had deserted their fellow Jews in their hour of need.
Czerniakow was not motivated by personal self-aggrandizement.
In his contacts with the Nazi authorities, Czerniakow attempted

to gain as much room to maneuver as possible through negotiations and building a relationship with the Nazi ghetto commissar, Heinz Auerswald, but Auerswald deceived him about the true fate of those Jews deported. The stress and psychic cost of attempting to ameliorate the ever-present panorama of human misery can only be imagined. "In the town, the rumors about deportations continue. People speak of tens of thousands," wrote Czerniakow in his diary on May 15, 1942. "To work according to plan under such conditions is remarkable. Nevertheless, we do the job day by day. I always go back to what Dickens wrote: 'A watch is not wound with tears.'"[11]

But for his detractors on the streets and in the tenements, Czerniakow and his family were little more than collaborators, profiting on the back of the ghetto's misery. Mocking rhymes circulated through the ghetto about him and his wife:

> *Prexy Czerniakow, the fat pot*
> *Gets his chicken soup hot,*
> *How so? Just dough!*
> *Money is a dandy thing.*

> *Madam Czerniakow is sure to get her hair done*
> *She takes her tea with sugar and bun*
> *How so? Just dough!*
> *Money is a dandy thing.*

By May 23, 1942, the ghetto diarist Chaim Kaplan was pouring vitriol on the *Judenrat* and all its works. "After the Nazi leech comes the *Judenrat* leech....There is no end to the tales of its mischief and abominations."[12]

For Adam Czerniakow, the end came two months later. On July 21, forty *Judenrat* officials were arrested and held hostage. The next day, the *Judenrat* was informed that all Warsaw Jews were to be "resettled" in the East, except those employed by German factories, most employees of the *Judenrat*, other ghetto staff and officials, and their families. The *Judenrat* was to deliver six thousand Jews a day, using the Jewish police force. Anyone evading the transports or any Jew who did not belong to the exempt categories who was still in the ghetto would be shot. On the morning of July 23, Czerniakow again attempted to negotiate with the Nazis, winning exemption for vocational school students and the husbands of working women, but the Germans refused to exclude the many Jewish orphans from the transports.

Czerniakow broke. Perhaps he remembered the rabbinical saying: "Let them kill you, but don't cross the line." At 4:00 P.M., the *Judenrat* head took a cyanide tablet. He wrote in his suicide note to his colleagues: "I am powerless. My heart trembles in sorrow and compassion. I can no longer bear all this. My act will prove to everyone what is the right thing to do."

Czerniakow's suicide was a signal that only one course of action was left for the ghetto's remaining Jews. Five days later, on July 28, 1942, representatives of the ghetto's Zionist and other organizations, both left and right, met to set up the Jewish Fighting Organization (ZOB). As plans for military resistance were drawn up, power in the ghetto gradually seeped away from the *Judenrat* to ZOB. In part, this was a generational transition. ZOB's members were young, militant, and committed to building a Jewish homeland in Palestine, by force if necessary. By then, they knew they were unlikely to get there, but they planned to kill as many Nazis as possible before they died, not negotiate with them.

How Much Would Have Been Enough?

ZOB's fighters received but little aid from their counterparts in the main Polish resistance organization, the Home Army (AK). The AK, which operated outside the ghetto walls and across Poland, had a nationwide organization and cell network and comparatively large stocks of arms and ammunition. ZOB's

valiant last stand was hailed in AK publications, but only a
trickle of munitions was supplied. One AK unit attempted to
blow up the ghetto wall early on in the uprising, but otherwise most Poles on the other side of the wall merely watched
and continued with their daily lives as the ghetto was elimi-
nated. There was no systematic or organized attempt by the
AK leadership to support the ghetto fighters or simultaneously
attack the Nazis on the Aryan side of the ghetto wall.

Many Jews blamed endemic Polish anti-Semitism for the
failure to properly aid them, despite ZOB's appeals in 1942
for weapons. In mid-November of that year, the AK high
command had finally agreed to supply some guns, but only
if ZOB's fighters would take an oath that, in the event of war
between Poland and the Soviet Union, the Jews would not
fight on the side of the Red Army. ZOB's officers agreed. In
December, the long-awaited consignment arrived: ten guns.
That ZOB was dominated by left-wing and pro-Communist
Jewish youth groups, such as the Marxist Hashomer Hatzair,
admittedly did not help its case with the fiercely patriotic
and anti-Russian AK. (In one of the traditional splits that
perennially bedevil Jewish organizations, even military
ones in the middle of the Holocaust, the right-wing Zionists
formed their own corps: the Jewish Military Union, which
had links with similarly nationalistic Polish groups outside
the ghetto.)

The AK's attitude was best summed up by its commander-
in-chief, General Stefan Rowecki, who radioed to the Polish
high command in London on January 4, 1943:

Too late Jews of various groupings, also Communists,
appeal to us for arms, just as if we had full arsenals.
As a trial, I gave them a few pistols. I am not sure that
they will use the weapons altogether. More weapons I
will not give because as you know we don't have them

ourselves. We are awaiting a delivery. Inform us what
connections our Jews have with London.[13]

After the January 1943 fighting in the ghetto, the AK leadership eventually handed over forty-nine revolvers, fifty grenades and some explosives, about 10 percent of ZOB's total
arsenal. The AK also provided some military instruction and a
formula for producing gasoline bombs. Other weapons were
bought or smuggled in from the Aryan side or were supplied
by sympathetic AK units. Polish resistance units also warned
Poles who betrayed Jews to the Nazis that they would be
sentenced to death. It was not until the following autumn, in
September 1944, that the AK and the rest of Warsaw finally
rose up against the Nazis. By then it was too late for Warsaw's
Jews, although many who had been living on the Aryan side
under false papers also fought alongside the AK.

Even now, decades later, the paltry response of the AK to
the Jewish ghetto uprising is a touchy subject with AK veterans
who fought in September 1944, such as Zbigniew Wolak. "The
Jews are very unfair to accuse us of not doing enough. I lived
ten meters from the wall of the ghetto and it's not true to say
that nobody helped. They should say that Poles did not help
enough. There was even a special unit in the AK to help Jews
and help mobilize western opinion," argues Wolak, who still
lives in Warsaw.[14]

The special nature of Nazi terror in Poland, where the
Nazis treated the indigenous population as subhumans, as
opposed to, for example, occupied France or Holland, where
many local officials remained in place under Nazi rule and
some efforts were made to win over the local population,
prevented further solidarity, he claims. "We helped the last
hundred fighters escape through the sewer system, and my
colleagues broke through the walls of the ghetto to help Jews
escape. People were terrorized here under the Nazis. But if

you ask if they could have done more, I would say yes. But if you say it was too little, then tell me how much would have been enough to say that we had behaved properly."

⊠ ⊠ ⊠

Building a combat organization could not be done overnight. ZOB's total initial arsenal was one pistol. ZOB's command sent out a delegation to the Aryan side, to contact the Polish underground and try to obtain weapons. Meanwhile, the deportations continued. By the end of September 1942, perhaps 50,000 Jews remained in the Warsaw ghetto. That month, a Jewish *bundist* (socialist) underground newspaper called for mass resistance to the final roundups. No one should go meekly to the trains, it exhorted: "Today every Jew should know the fate of the resettled. The same fate awaits the remaining few left in Warsaw. The conclusion then is: Don't let yourself be caught! Hide, don't let yourself be taken away, run away, don't be fooled by registrations, selections, numbers, and roll calls. Jews help one another!"

ZOB's aim was not just the defense of the ghetto, but also, its leadership declared in October, to "teach a lesson to the Jewish police, the *werkschutz* [factory guards], the managers of the 'shops' [factories] and all kinds of informers." On October 20, ZOB carried out its first execution—not of a Nazi, but a Jew: Jacob Leikin, head of the Ghetto Police. ZOB's first sustained armed resistance took place on January 18, 1943, when Jewish fighters held off the Nazis for four days and beat back the SS. That was a brief dress rehearsal for the ultimate conflagration to come. That winter, ZOB's fighters built a network of bunkers throughout the ghetto, many linked through the sewers. Others began manufacturing petrol bombs and trained with ZOB's meager arsenal.

At 6:00 A.M. on Monday, April 19, 1943, the first day of Passover, two thousand heavily armed SS troops poured through the gates of the Warsaw Ghetto in the Germans' final sweep. Or so the SS ghetto commander Jurgen Stroop mistakenly believed. For the tens of thousands of Jews huddled in its cramped and disease-ridden streets and tenements, it was the final hour of reckoning. On that April morning, all in the ghetto knew the fate of those who had been deported for "resettlement" in the East, as the Nazis attempted to disguise the one-way trip to Treblinka.

Most of those left were young, under forty, and comparatively fit, kept alive by the Germans to work in the ghetto factories. Like the last of their fellow Jews still alive elsewhere in Poland, few had parents or relatives left to worry about, a macabre liberation from familial responsibility. "They were free. Their last links with everyday life were broken," wrote Gusta Dawidsohn, a young Jewess in Krakow, when just five thousand Jews were left of the city's 65,000. They "suddenly felt free to plunge into the maelstrom of underground work; it was a feeling of freedom which sprouted out of the rubble of shattered family life."[15]

The Young Women Couriers

The unsung heroes of the Jewish underground were the young women couriers. Often blond-haired or blue-eyed, not fitting the Nazi stereotype of how Jews looked, they traveled across Nazi-occupied Poland under false papers, posing as Aryans. Some even wore crosses as part of their disguise. They brought messages, instructions, news, and money from one ghetto to another, risking arrest and torture by the Gestapo at any moment. Emmanuel Ringelblum, the Warsaw Ghetto archivist, paid tribute to their bravery:

The heroic girls Chaika (Grosman), Frumke (Plotnicka), and others—theirs is a story that calls for the pen of a great writer. They are venturesome, courageous girls who travel here and there across Poland to cities and towns, carrying Aryan papers which describe them as Polish or Ukrainian. One of them even wears a cross, which she never leaves off and misses when she is in the ghetto. Day by day, they face the greatest dangers, relying completely on their Aryan appearance and the kerchiefs they tie around their heads. They accept the most dangerous missions and carry them out without a murmur, without a moment's hesitation. If there is need for someone to travel to Vilna, Bialystok, Lvov, Kowel, Lublin, Czestochowa, or Radom to smuggle in such forbidden things as illegal publications, goods, money, they do it all as though it were the most natural thing. If there are comrades to be rescued from Vilna, Lublin, or other cities, they take on the job themselves. Nothing deters them, nothing stops them. If it is necessary to make friends with the German responsible for a train so to travel beyond the borders of the Government-General [occupied Poland], which is allowed only for people with special permits—they do it quite simply, as though it were their profession....How many times did they look death in the eye? How many times were they arrested and searched? But their luck held. "Those who go on an errand of mercy will meet no evil."

⊞ ⊞ ⊞

For the last Jews of Warsaw, in the crucible of death that April 1943, the only choice left was how to die: in the gas chamber or in combat. The Jews fought. Once past the gates, the SS troops advanced into the maze of cramped streets and alleys until the command was given. Then, from their underground bunkers, from the rooftops, from the windows of apartment blocks, the young fighters rained down molotov cocktails on the tanks and the soldiers. Others opened up with the weapons they had bought, stolen, or smuggled inside the ghetto from the "Aryan" side of the city. Against the Germans' tanks and heavy armaments, ZOB's fighters had homemade bombs and grenades, "do-it-yourself" mines fired from drainage pipes, pistols, rifles, and a few machine guns. As the tanks floundered on the narrow streets, they burst into flame when the gasoline bombs landed. When the soldiers inside clambered out, their uniforms on fire, ZOB's snipers and machine gunners picked them off. The Nazis were no longer supermen, but flesh and blood. They bled and then died, like their Jewish victims. "We were happy and laughing," said one Jewish fighter. "When we threw our grenades and saw German blood on the streets of Warsaw, which had been flooded with so much Jewish blood and tears, a great joy possessed us." At 5:00 p.m., the Germans retreated, with losses of two hundred dead and wounded.

The Herbert Baum Group

In Warsaw, many of those who fought in the ghetto uprising were left-wing Zionists. For them, the genocide of the Jews was confirmation that a socialist Jewish homeland in Palestine was the only guarantee of a future for Jewry. A minority were communists, who looked to the Soviet Union as humanity's salvation. Under such conditions, absolutist ideologies of salvation, whether nationalist or internationalist, had a powerful appeal. In Berlin, the main Jewish underground organization was the pro-Communist Herbert Baum Group, named after its charismatic leader, born in 1912. Like the ghetto fighters, the Baum Group had its roots in left-wing Jewish youth organizations, but its political orientation was Marxist. Many of its members were associated with, or were members of, the Communist Party's Youth League.

The group began in 1938–39 at the Siemens plant in Berlin. Initially, its members' main activities were studying Marxism and disseminating anti-Nazi propaganda. The Baum Group also made contact with other resistance cells around the Rote Kapelle (Red Orchestra), the Soviet spy ring that broadcast intelligence from Berlin to Moscow. Its thirty-odd members were aged between twenty and thirty, and it was in contact with another forty sympathizers, notes the historian Allen Merson in *Communist Resistance in Nazi Germany*.[16] The group published fourteen issues of a monthly news-sheet, entitled *Der Ausweg* ("The Way Out"), which announced itself as "A Paper of Anti-Fascist Struggle," published by "German Anti-Fascist Action." The group's belief in class, rather than national politics, meant its members refrained from emphasizing their Jewish ancestry. The December 1941 issue survives, with its label "Frontline Edition." It was targeted at German soldiers, instructing them that the news-sheet was to be "passed on to all your comrades who are ready to fight with us for the overthrow of the Hitler regime."

The Herbert Baum Group's most successful act of public defiance was also its last. On May 16, 1942, Goebbels' anti-Soviet propaganda exhibition, sarcastically entitled "Soviet Paradise" opened in the center of Berlin. The exhibition purported to give a picture of a Soviet population that was terrorized by "Jewish Bolshevik" commissars and lived in poverty and starvation. Ironically, much of the exhibition's descriptions of the Soviet secret police's modus operandi could have applied verbatim to the Gestapo. Members of the Red Orchestra plastered the walls of the exhibition with anti-Nazi posters, but the Baum Group wanted to go further. In an audacious, but suicidal act of bravery, group members set fire to the displays. Within a few days, most of the members were arrested. Baum died in prison after being tortured. His comrades were tried for treason and later executed or imprisoned.

The authorities were shaken by this public display of Jewish defiance and exacted a high price. Soon afterwards, the Gestapo arrested another five hundred Jews and killed them in reprisal for the action.

※ ※ ※

That night in the ghetto, they celebrated, even as ZOB's fighters mourned their fallen comrades. The following morning, the Germans, through the *Judenrat*, issued an ultimatum to ZOB, to surrender by 10:00 A.M. But the *Judenrat* had no more authority, as its leaders admitted. ZOB now ruled the ghetto. Latvian SS members attacked, together with German SS troops. A hundred Germans were killed by an electric mine. German reinforcements arrived with more tanks and heavy artillery, and SS officers appealed to the Jews in hiding to come forward for evacuation. No one did. The Germans began to burn the ghetto, and cut off the water, gas, and electricity supplies. Banners flew on the roofs, mounted by the jubilant ZOB fighters, proclaiming, "We shall fight to the last." The Polish flag flew alongside the blue-and-white Jewish banner. As the flames spread, the ghetto was a vision of hell: black plumes of smoke spread out across Warsaw. "The ghetto was a roaring sea of fire," records Davidowicz. "People were seen silhouetted in the window frames of blazing buildings, sheathed in flame, like living torches." ZOB fought on. Its commander, Mordechai Anielewicz, sent his last letter to a friend living illegally on the "Aryan" side of the city:

It is impossible to put into words what we have been through. One thing is clear, what happened exceeded our boldest dreams. The Germans ran twice from the ghetto. One of our companies held out for forty minutes and another for more than six hours...

It is impossible to describe the conditions under which the Jews of the ghetto are now living. Only a few will be able to hold out. The remainder will die sooner or later. Their fate is decided. In almost all the hiding places in which thousands are concealing themselves, it is not possible to light a candle for lack of air...

Peace go with you, my friend! Perhaps we may still meet again! The dream of my life has risen to become fact. Self-defense in the ghetto will have been a reality. Jewish armed resistance and revenge are facts. I have been a witness to the magnificent, heroic fighting of Jewish men in battle.[17]

Incredibly, the one thousand or so fighters of ZOB—including many women—held off the Nazis for four weeks. From April 23, they switched from set battles to partisan tactics, flitting from bunker to bunker in hit-and-run raids. Outnumbered and outgunned, knowing they would soon die, and fueled by hatred, revenge, and desperation, the fighters turned the ghetto into a deathtrap for the Nazis, using the sewers to move under the battlefield. SS reports record the details of one day's fighting, on April 19, 1943, when sixteen officers and 850 soldiers attacked at 6:00 A.M.:

As soon as the units had entered, strong concerted fire was directed at them by the Jews and bandits. The tank employed in this operation and the two SPW [armored cars] were attacked with Molotov cocktails. The tank was twice set on fire. This attack with fire by the enemy caused the units to withdraw in the first stage. Losses in the first attack were twelve men.... About 5:30 P.M., very strong resistance was met with from one block of buildings, including machine gun fire. A special battle unit overcame the enemy and penetrated into the buildings, but without capturing the enemy himself. The Jews and criminals resisted from base to base and escaped at the last moment through garrets or subterranean passages...[18]

Armed Jews forcing back SS troops did not fit in with the Nazi worldview. News of the uprising soon reached Berlin, where the Nazi leadership was incredulous at the resistance. "The only thing noteworthy is exceptionally sharp fighting in Warsaw between our police, and in part even the Wehrmacht, and the Jewish rebels," wrote Goebbels in his dairy on May 1, 1943. "The Jews have actually succeeded in putting the ghetto in a condition to defend itself. Some very hard battles are taking place there, which have gone so far that the Jewish top leadership publishes daily military reports. Of course, this jest will probably not last long. But it shows what one can expect of the Jews if they have arms. Unfortunately, they also have some good German weapons in part, particularly machine guns. Heaven only knows how they got hold of them."[19]

For all its sheer heroism, the ghetto uprising could not last. The Germans destroyed the ghetto, block by block, with explosives and flamethrowers. The sewers were flooded. There was nowhere left to hide. Smoke and debris clogged the air. Captured fighters were shot on the spot. On May 8, the ZOB bunker was surrounded. The entrances were blocked and gas pumped in. The one hundred fighters inside, including Mordechai Anielewicz, committed mass suicide in a scene that resembled the fabled last stand at Masada in first century Palestine, when the last Jewish fighters against the Romans killed themselves rather than surrender. Perhaps seventy-five ZOB fighters escaped through the sewers, under the wall, onto the Aryan side of the city. Hidden under the charred and smoking rubble, Ringelblum's archives survived.

The Warsaw ghetto was leveled, but the aftershocks of the uprising reverberated across Nazi-occupied Europe. Eleven months later, on the morning of March 19, 1944, German tanks rolled into Hungary. Europe's last great Jewish community, 650,000 strong, was now in reach of the Nazis. The failed Warsaw ghetto revolt would influence the course of the Hungarian Holocaust, shaping the Nazis' initially reassuring approach to Hungarian Jewry's leadership. That, in turn, would help mold the Hungarian Jewish Council's passive response to the genocide.

Among the Nazi officers was Adolf Eichmann, the man charged with ensuring the transports to the death camps went smoothly. At all costs—even if several hundred specially chosen Jews would have to be spared in negotiations with the Jewish Council—there could not be any repetition of the events in Warsaw, recalled Eichmann, in an interview published in *Life* magazine in November 1960. With the Russians advancing across the Carpathian Basin in the east and the fall of Mussolini in the west, an uprising in Budapest would be strategically disastrous, even threatening the neighboring Romanian oil fields at Ploiesti. Eichmann's orders were to "ship all Jews out of the country in as short a time as possible," he noted, recalling that there was no resistance to the Nazis when they invaded, and that he was greeted with bread and wine by the peasants. Eichmann described the significance of the Warsaw revolt to the Nazis' plans for Hungary:

> The Warsaw ghetto uprising had an equally strong effect with authorities in the other occupied countries. Every national leadership was anxious to remove factors of unrest. My advisers now had a perfect entrée in the countries where they were assigned. We could and did use the Warsaw example like a travelling salesman who sells an article all the more easily by showing a special advertising attraction.
>
> With Hungary we were particularly concerned. The Hungarian Jews had lived through the war relatively untouched by severe restrictions. Now Himmler made it clear that he wanted Hungary combed with a tremendous thoroughness before the Jews there could really wake up to our plans and organize partisan resistance. For this reason he chose me to lead the march into Hungary in person.[20]

Eichmann's fears of an armed revolt were unfounded, at least in terms of one led by the official Jewish leadership. Living in an island of comparative security, Hungarian Jewry's officials put their faith in the changing military situation, believing that as the tide of war had turned against the Nazis, the Germans would have neither the time nor the logistical ability to deport hundreds of thousands of Jews to their deaths. They would, they believed, survive Hitler. There was also a natural human inclination to disbelieve the reports of genocide in Poland that were circulating in Budapest. Time, and the impending German defeat, was, they believed, their best weapon. Those at the very top, such as Samu Stern, also put their faith in their extensive contacts with government circles, up to and including Admiral Horthy, and anti-Nazi circles. Stern, a counselor of the Royal Hungarian Court, was president of the Pest Jewish Community and became chairman of the *Judenrat*, known in Hungary as the Central Jewish Council. Stern was an assimilated, patriotic Jew, who considered himself a true Hungarian, much as the leaders of Germany's prewar Jews had thought of themselves as German. He was also a successful businessman, with good relations with the aristocratic-conservative circles of Hungary's elite. Throughout the Nazi occupation, he maintained a highly legalistic, formalistic approach in his dealings with both the Hungarians and their Nazi overlords, mistakenly believing that the prewar methods of petitions, appeals, and personal approaches could mitigate the anti-Jewish drive. In June 1944, at the height of the deportations, he even forbade the distribution of a planned clandestine appeal to Hungarian Christians to aid their Jewish compatriots.

Stern's leadership of the Central Jewish Council and his passive approach were ultimately disastrous for Hungarian Jewry. Many of his high-ranking contacts and sympathizers in Hungary's ruling class were arrested immediately after the Nazis' arrival. The expected political opposition among Hungarians to the anti-Jewish drive did not materialize. Quite the contrary, in fact. A prisoner of his time and outdated in his approach, Stern was no match for Eichmann and the SS, who wooed him and the rest of the Jewish Council with the usual promises that no harm would come to Hungary's Jews.

And more. The Nazis issued 250 immunity certificates to the Jewish Council, signed by both German security and the Hungarian police. The certificates allowed the holders to move freely about without hindrance and were priceless. Council members were exempted from having to wear a yellow star, although ultimately the Nazis planned the same death for their holders. Their critics accused the Budapest Jewish Council of being bought off and abandoning their fellow Jews. After the deportations ceased on July 7, Stern, together with two fellow members, became preoccupied with protecting his property rights. The trio even filed petitions and appeared before government officials to argue their case.

What were their options to defend their people? Eichmann's nightmare of a partisan uprising was never feasible, even if the Jewish Council had wanted to organize it. Guerrilla armies need an outside supplier of arms and ammunition, effective military training, and the support of a sympathetic population to provide food and shelter. None of these were available in Hungary. The first real choice was whether or not to serve on the Council and implement the Nazi decrees. Stern could have refused, risking arrest and possible execution.

But Eichmann needed Stern and his colleagues to put their imprimatur on the anti-Jewish regulations, as their names acted as a kind of reassurance to Hungarian Jewry that one day, this too would pass. The historian of the Hungarian Holocaust, Randolph Braham, argues that had Stern been arrested, "the Jewish masses might have learned about the realities of the German occupation early and possibly would not have followed the orders of nonentities and Jewish quislings as subserviently as they followed those of the traditional leaders they trusted."[21]

As it was, the Nazis' had little to worry about. On April 13, Stern issued an appeal entitled "Work and Do Not Despair." It informed Hungarian Jews that "all the instructions, orders, decisions, and decrees of the authorities will have to be carried out exactly and without any complaint or grumbling." So hidebound by legality was the Hungarian Jewish leadership that a year earlier, in 1943, it had refused an appeal by the Slovak Jewish underground organization, the "Working Group," for money to be sent illegally to bribe the Nazis and help Slovak Jews in labor camps. Monies could only be transferred through a bank, they responded, which was, of course, impossible.

There was room to maneuver in negotiating with the Nazis, at least for Council members. When the brother of Baron Fulop Freudiger, leader of the Orthodox Jews, was arrested by the Gestapo on March 21, the Baron went to see Eichmann's assistant, Dieter Wisliceny, who gave him assurances that his brother would be released. Over the following months, Freudiger bribed Wisliceny with cash and jewels to bring eighty mainly Orthodox Jews to Budapest from the provinces. In August 1944, Wisliceny helped Freudiger and his family escape to Romania. Other members enjoyed similar favors. In his memoirs, Freudiger recorded that Eichmann ordered close relatives of Council members to be brought to Budapest.

So keen was Wisliceny to maintain good relations with Freudiger that he even brought him a letter from Rabbi Michael Dov Weissmandel, of the "Working Group" resistance committee in Bratislava. Written in Hebrew, thus incomprehensible to Wisliceny, it was a warning that Hungarian Jewry would now share the fate of other Jews across the Third Reich. Nevertheless, Wisliceny could be trusted, it wrongly advised. In Slovakia, Wisliceny had been involved in an abortive rescue attempt by the Working Group, called the "Europa Plan," under which deportations from all of Nazi-occupied Europe to Poland would cease, in exchange for a massive bribe. Shortly after Wisliceny opened initial negotiations, deportations from Slovakia did indeed cease, although for other reasons, thus giving the SS officer credibility. Little good it did him in the end. After serving as a prosecution witness at the Nuremberg trials, Wisliceny was hanged in Bratislava on May 4, 1948.

Rabbi Weissmandel's letter was one of many warnings to the Hungarian Jewish leaders. In 1943, his colleague Gisi Fleischmann had written reports detailing how "We know today that Sobibor, Malkyne-Treblinki [Treblinka], Belzec, and Auschwitz are annihilation camps. In the camps, small work parties are being maintained to create the impression that they are ordinary camps." The *Judenrat* was also in contact with a former partisan and refugee living in Hungary named Bruce Teicholz. In April 1943, eleven months before the Nazi occupation, Teicholz met with leaders including Freudiger and Rezso Kasztner of the Budapest Vaada, records Braham:

> He identified the specific steps employed and reviewed the techniques utilized to lull the Jews into submission and cooperation in their own destruction. He warned the Hungarian Jewish leaders to take all necessary precautionary measures and be aware of the Nazis' techniques of extermination. These leaders, however, "assured" Teicholz that what happened in Poland could not possibly happen in Hungary.[22]

Except it could happen in Hungary, and it did. And further details of the impending catastrophe were provided to the Hungarian Jewish leadership in the form of a minutely detailed, thirty-two-page report known as the "Auschwitz Protocols." In April 1944, five Auschwitz inmates had escaped, with the aid of the camp resistance movement, with the specific intention of warning Jewry, particularly Hungarian Jewry, about the planned extermination. Two of these, Rudolf Vrba and Alfred Wetzler, compiled the Auschwitz Protocols after they reached Zilina, in Slovakia. The Protocols stretch over many pages. Both men had worked as clerks and gave a comprehensive picture of the killing machine, even listing the groups of serial numbers tattooed on inmates on their arrival. The numbers 45,000 to 47,000, for example, were given to French prisoners, communists, and political prisoners, including the younger brother of Leon Blum, the former Jewish French prime minister, who was tortured and killed. The Protocols included details of the camp's geography, organization, administration, architectural drawings of the buildings, and a harrowing description of the workings of the gas chambers.

Controversy continues over who received a copy of the Protocols, and exactly when. The precise dates are important as on them hinges the crucial point of whether or not the Budapest Jewish Council and/ or the Vaada (which operated independently) could have warned their fellow Jews in the provinces of their dreadful fate, before the deportations began on May 15, 1944. Braham notes that Vrba claimed that he was assured that the Protocols had been sent to Budapest on April 26, the same day they were typed up. Martin Gilbert, in *Auschwitz and the Allies*,[23] records that Kasztner traveled to Bratislava on April 28, when he was given a copy of the Protocols by Oskar Krazsnyansky, of the Slovak *Judenrat*, who compiled the report in Zilina and translated it into Hungarian. Stern, in his memoirs, does not mention them specifically, while other members of the Jewish Council only allude to them. Freudiger admitted that he received a copy from Rabbi Weissmandel between June 5 and 10, 1944.

Either way, unlike their counterparts in Warsaw, Vilna, or Lodz, Stern and his colleagues had been briefed in detail about the reality of Auschwitz long before the deportations began. So the second choice the Council had was whether or not to warn the Hungarian Jews of their planned fate. Here the record is bleak indeed. Like Rabbi Baeck in Theresienstadt, the Budapest Jewish Council kept silent. Panic, they believed, had to be avoided at all costs. But panic would have been better than docilely boarding the deportation trains. Neither the Protocols, nor a summarized version, or indeed any warning, was distributed to Hungary's provincial Jewry.

Ultimately, the reasons why remain a mystery. Perhaps they simply did not believe the reports they had received. Undoubtedly, a major factor was that the Council leaders were prisoners of their time, a prewar age of community grandees who put their faith in official channels. They erroneously believed that the honors that they had received showed that there was an eternal place in Hungary for loyal, patriotic Jews. Such Jews were mocked by the more radical as "court Jews," or establishment lackeys. The idea of acting illegally, encouraging resistance or opposition to the authorities was simply not part of their mind-set. Certainly, had Samu Stern told the provincial Jews to flee, many would have been caught, but some would have evaded the roundups. The smooth running of the Holocaust depended, to some extent, on its victims' cooperation, their belief that they were "merely" being relocated for labor. Soothed by the reassurances of their national leaders, the Jews of the countryside boarded the trains that took them to their dreadful deaths.

In fact, there was some armed resistance among young activists in Zionist, left-wing, and other youth movements, just as in Warsaw. They were aided by sympathetic Hungarians, often anti-Nazi army officers, and the Communist underground. In Budapest, resistance fighters stockpiled arms, built bunkers, and engaged in hit-and-run raids with the SS and their Hungarian Nazi Arrow Cross allies. In a daring masquerade, some even donned Arrow Cross uniforms in rescue operations. Claiming higher orders from Arrow Cross headquarters, they would march into Arrow Cross prisons and take out Jews in custody. Once outside, they would tell their fellow Jews to flee for their lives.

Other resistance fighters tried to persuade the Council to take a more active stance. "We took pictures that the Germans were taking away political people, putting them in trucks and killing them," recalls Ernest Stein,[24] now living in the United States. "We went to the Jewish Committee and told them people should be informed what is happening, so they could run in every direction and couldn't be found. Freudiger, who was president of the synagogue that I used to go to, said no. I was only twenty-one, but I really told him off."

After the war, Samu Stern also admitted that he knew of the extermination of Jewry in Nazi-occupied Europe. He wrote: "I—nor others I suppose—was not taken in by the faked good will, hypocrisy, and treachery of the Gestapo's debut. I knew what they had done in all German-occupied states of Europe. I knew their activities to be a long, long, sequence of murders and robberies...I knew the Nazis' habits, deeds, and terrifying reputation, and yet I accepted the chairmanship of the Council. And the others knew as much as I did when they joined the Council as members."[25]

Not just Jews, but many anti-Nazi Hungarians were also angered at the Jewish Council's supine following of the SS orders. There is evidence that the underground warned Stern and his colleagues that they would be held accountable after the war as collaborators and would be charged with war crimes. After the war, the Hungarian State Police collected statements and other evidence toward this end. Stern, and several others were held in protective custody for some time after the liberation. Stern justified himself as follows:

In my eyes, it would have been a cowardly, unmanly, and unjustifiably selfish flight on my part to let down my brethren in the faith during the very instant they were in dire need of being led, when men having both experience and connections and ready to make sacrifices might prove useful to a certain extent. What would Jewry abroad have thought of me had I looked for some excuse to escape doing my duty?[26]

For Holocaust survivors such as Katalin Csillag, Stern did not do his duty. "He had a lot of power, but he just kept telling people to relax, to be calm because nothing would happen to them, but he should have warned us," says Csillag, who was deported to Auschwitz and still lives in Budapest. "He knew a lot more than we did, and a lot of people would have left if he hadn't always been telling them to calm down, especially the Jews in the countryside. I have a copy of his memoirs, and he is trying to whitewash himself. I tried to read them, but I got too upset."[27]

Stern died in 1947, but in Israel in 1961, Freudiger, no longer an ennobled baron, but simply "Pinchas" (his name, Fulop, in Hebrew), gave evidence at Eichmann's trial. He was the only prominent Jewish Council member to do so. The trial of Eichmann soon turned into the trial of Hungary's wartime Jewish leadership. During his testimony, Hungarian survivors screamed abuse at Freudiger in Hungarian and Yiddish, accusing him of not telling them and their families to flee. The court had to interrupt the session, recorded Hannah Arendt:

> Freudiger, an Orthodox Jew of considerable dignity, was shaken: "There are people here who say they were not told to escape. But 50 percent of the people who escaped were captured and killed"—as compared with 99 percent for those who did not escape. "Where could they have gone to? Where could they have fled?"—but he himself fled, to Romania, because he was rich and because Wisliceny helped him.[28]

As for Vrba, he survived the war and eventually moved to Canada. He remains convinced that had his information been disseminated to Hungary's Jews, it would have triggered some kind of resistance to the deportations. He wrote to Sir Martin Gilbert: "Passive *and* active resistance by a million people would create panic and havoc in Hungary. Panic in Hungary would have been better than panic which came to the victims in front of burning pits in Birkenau. Eichmann knew it; that is why he smoked cigars with the Kasztners, 'negotiated,' exempted the 'real great rabbis,' and meanwhile, without panic among the deportees, planned to resettle hundreds of thousands in orderly fashion."[29]

Who was this Kasztner with whom, Vrba alleges, Eichmann "smoked cigars"?

Rezso Kasztner was born in 1906, the same year as Eichmann, in the Hapsburg-era city of Kolozsvar, then in Hungary, now Cluj in Romania. A journalist, lawyer, and ardent Zionist, he was the de facto leader of the Budapest Vaada, the Zionist rescue organization. Working independently from the Jewish Council, Vaada operatives, particularly Joel Brand, ran a rescue network smuggling

Jewish refugees from Poland to Budapest, via Slovakia. The Vaada also ran a network of couriers bringing news and information from Nazi-occupied countries. Those reports were then passed to Jewish officials in Istanbul. It was difficult and extremely dangerous work. As the Auschwitz Protocols were being typed in Zilina, Joel Brand was summoned to meet Eichmann in Budapest to discuss the terms of the "Blood for Goods" deal. Eichmann proposed the exchange of one million Jewish lives for ten thousand trucks, to be used only on the eastern front (see chapter 9). That deal, like the Europa Plan, fell through. But Kasztner's own arrangement with Eichmann would prove successful.

While the Jewish Council was essentially passive, the Vaada was active. According to Hansi Brand, wife of Joel, it originated in a chance meeting between Samu Springmann, a watchmaker who operated the courier line between Budapest and Istanbul, and a former schoolmate of his who was an agent for the Hungarian Secret Service. The secret service agent agreed to help Springmann. "In the beginning, the Jewish Council did not want to hear about the Vaada. When things started to turn ugly, they started to be interested in the Vaada. It took them a while," said Mrs. Brand in an interview with one of the authors.[30]

Zionist-Nazi Relations

Surviving Hitler could produce some strange bedfellows. In the early years of the Third Reich, some saw a crude community of interest between Nazism and Zionism. At that stage, before the implementation of the Final Solution, the Nazis wanted the Jews out of Germany and Austria, and the Zionists wanted the Jews in Palestine. Most German Jews—most European Jews in fact—did not support the attempt to build a Jewish homeland before the Holocaust. They considered themselves citizens of the nation in which they lived. From the perspective of some Jewish leaders in Palestine, anxious to bring in new immigrants, there seemed to be room to cooperate, to exploit the Nazis' anti-Semitism, even as they condemned their anti-Jewish outrages.

On the extreme right, the "Revisionist" wing of the Zionist movement, there was some initial sympathy for fascism's trappings. The German youth section of the Revisionists, known as "Betar," advised its members to treat any Nazis they encountered with politeness and reserve. Betar members were allowed to wear their uniforms, which included brown shirts, and to publish mimeographed pamphlets, notes the Israeli historian Tom Segev, "in a nationalistic, para-Fascist tone, in the spirit of the times."[31] In Austria, after the March 1938 Anschluss, Betar delivered a memo to the Gestapo offering to organize mass emigration of the remaining Jews. Betar and other Jewish leaders met with Adolf Eichmann and were allowed to maintain an emigration office. On occasion, the Nazis protected Betar. When some SS soldiers attacked a German Betar summer camp, its head complained to the Gestapo, who later informed him that the SS soldiers had been disciplined. Left-wing Jews, and many others, dismissed Betar as "Jewish fascists."

In Palestine, the situation was reversed. Ze'ev Jabotinsky, the Revisionist leader, was appalled at the Hitlerist influence on his young German protégés and supported calls for a boycott of Germany. Betar members pulled down the swastika flag flying over the German diplomatic mission. But the Jewish Agency, the Israeli government-in-waiting, attempted to maintain correct relations with the Third Reich. A condolence telegram was sent to Adolf Hitler on the death of President Hindenberg in 1934. Arthur Ruppin, a Prussian-born senior Zionist official, was sent to Berlin to negotiate with the Nazis over plans to allow German Jews to emigrate and bring their property to Palestine. Among others, he met with Hans F.K. Gunther, a Nazi race theorist, at Jena University (see chapter 5).

Perhaps the most macabre event—as it appears with hindsight—was the visit of Baron Leopold Itz von Mildenstein. Von Mildenstein, head of the Nazi Office for Jewish Affairs, was invited to Palestine in 1933 to write a series of articles for *Angriff* (Offensive), Goebbels' newspaper. Accompanied by Kurt Tuchler, a Zionist activist from Berlin, together with the mens' wives, von Mildenstein toured the country. Back in Germany, his sympathetic articles were published under the headline "A Nazi Visits Palestine." A special medallion was struck by *Angriff* to commemorate von Mildenstein's trip, records historian Tom Segev—with a swastika on one side and a Star of David on the other. He was eventually succeeded by Adolf Eichmann.

※ ※ ※

Those were the dog days of World War II, when the Nazi leadership, always marred by perpetual infighting, began to fracture as the Allies advanced on two fronts. The idea for the "Goods for Blood" deal had originated with Himmler. Unlikely as it seems now, Himmler saw the proposal both as a means of splitting the western Allies from the Soviet Union as a precursor to some kind of peace treaty that would leave as much of the Reich intact as possible, and as a humanitarian alibi. When Joel Brand was arrested by the British in Syria, Kasztner took over the negotiations with Eichmann. Duped by years of Nazi propaganda, Himmler and Eichmann apparently believed in the power of an international Zionism that had channels to the Allied leadership and could influence the grand course of events in the war. For the Vaada, here indeed was room to maneuver. In Kasztner, Eichmann found what he later described in *Life* magazine as an "equal" negotiating partner:

This Dr. Kasztner was a young man about my age, an ice-cold lawyer and a fanatical Zionist. He agreed to help keep the Jews from resisting deportation—and even keep order in the collection camps—if I would close my eyes and let a few hundred or a few thousand young Jews emigrate to Palestine. It was a good bargain....Except perhaps for the first two sessions, he never came to me fearful of the Gestapo strong man.

We negotiated entirely as equals. People forget that. We were political opponents trying to arrive at a settlement, and we trusted each other perfectly. When he was with me, Kasztner smoked cigarettes as though he was in a coffeehouse. While we talked, he would smoke one aromatic cigarette after another, taking them from a silver case and lighting them with a cigarette lighter. With his great polish and reserve, he would have been an ideal Gestapo officer himself.[32]

Eichmann is, at best, being disingenuous here. Joel Brand's wife, Hansi Brand, who attended both the "Goods for Blood" meetings and the negotiations with Kasztner, with whom she later worked very closely, remembered things differently. Of the first negotiations, she recalled: "He [Eichmann] asked me whether I knew what it was all about and said that I had to stay there with the two children as hostages. And that Joel's mission was the Reich's secret, which must not be revealed to anyone. So that's how I met Eichmann." Hansi Brand found the Nazi leader edgy. "He wasn't too loud, he sometimes said something to me, I said something to him, and I received an answer for that. But he was very nervous, his weapon was always there on his desk, and his helmet. I had to report to him all the time. If there was any news [of Joel Brand's mission], I had to report it to them."

Hansi Brand was not impressed by the performances of two other Zionist officials she took to meet Eichmann. Understandably, these men, whom she did not name, were scared and showed it. "When we left, I was ashamed because they had seen them trembling in there. That was an uncomfortable feeling for me, because all we had was our dignity. When I took Rezso up there and introduced him to Eichmann, Rezso acted the same way, so I felt really bad. When we came out, I told him we had nothing left but to show that we're not afraid of them. He said yes, took out a cigarette and lit up. I stood there watching him, and I asked him, 'You didn't expect the SS to offer you a cigarette, did you?'"

Kasztner's negotiations with Eichmann were partially successful. He failed to save the bulk of Hungarian Jewry, but on the night of June 30, 1944, Eichmann allowed 1,685 specially selected Jews to leave Budapest on a train to Switzerland. After being held for many weeks at a special "VIP" annex to the Bergen-Belsen concentration camp, where they were not forced to work and were fed, they eventually reached Switzerland. Each passenger paid a thousand dollars or the equivalent in gold and valuables for a place on the train. Some rich Jews, desperate to leave, subsidized places for those who could not raise such a substantial sum.

As news of the Kasztner train spread across Budapest, anger spread among those who could not afford a place. Many claimed after the war that Kasztner had made a dreadful deal with the devil, sacrificing the many so that a chosen few could survive Hitler. Kasztner was accused of agreeing with Eichmann to keep silent about the Auschwitz Protocols in exchange for safe passage out on the train. Holocaust survivor Ernest Stein says: "I was trying to get in with my mother. I could not get in: they only had people who were paying money and their friends, major functionaries in the Zionist movement. Kasztner wasn't paying Eichmann off, he followed Eichmann's orders. The Jewish Committee followed Eichmann's orders, because they were chicken."[33]

Kasztner's defenders, such as Hansi Brand, dismissed this allegation as a lie. They also point to the fact that, compared to the Council, the Vaada was a small, illegal organization, whose members could have easily fitted into one room. In addition, Kasztner

310 \ SEDUCED BY HITLER

was a relatively unknown figure in the wider Jewish community, whose words would anyway have carried little weight.

Paradoxically, they also claim that the Vaada also sent some emissaries out to the provinces, whose warnings were ignored. Hungarian Jews simply did not believe the reports of mass killings by gas at Auschwitz, says Laszlo Devecseri, a childhood friend of Kasztner's and a passenger on the train. Now in his nineties and living in Israel, Devecseri recalls: "A Polish refugee came to my home and told me the story of Auschwitz, he had escaped from the deportations. I told him that he didn't need to tell me such stories, I would help him without saying such things. Now we know these things, but then they could not be believed, and nobody believed it. The Zionists knew, because they were politically prepared."[34]

After the train was delayed at the Austrian border because of Allied air raids, Laszlo Devecseri returned to Budapest to try and get it moving again. The passengers were terrified that the SS would change their minds and send them to Auschwitz instead. Devecseri found Kasztner. "He couldn't believe that I was back in Budapest. He went to Eichmann and settled it, and we were sent to Bergen-Belsen, we were put in a special camp there. We didn't have to work and had better conditions. But at each moment, if the discussions with Eichmann went wrong, he would have sent us to Auschwitz."

Devecseri says the idea of a deal between the Zionist leader and Eichmann over the Auschwitz Protocols was absurd. "Eichmann never spoke at this level to Kasztner. He [Kasztner] was a nothing to him, but he [Eichmann] was obliged because of Himmler. He never did a deal. Eichmann was a god in Hungary, the highest dictator who could do with the Jews whatever he wanted, as he had done in other places. He did not need any permission from Kasztner to send the other Jews to Auschwitz. This is an absolute fantasy."

Kasztner lived in fear of Eichmann, says Devecseri. "He was afraid every day that Eichmann would send him to Auschwitz. Eichmann had said, several times, 'Kasztner, if you want, I will send you to Auschwitz, it would be better for you.' He sent [Gisi]

Fleischmann, the Slovak Kasztner, directly to the gas, and he wanted to do the same with Kasztner."

Kasztner's main ally in the negotiations was an SS officer called Kurt Becher, who dealt with economic affairs. Before arriving in Budapest, Becher had served on the eastern front, in the SS Death's Head Equestrian Unit I, which had executed Jews in Warsaw and in occupied Russia. In Budapest, his role was to channel Nazi loot to neutral countries for his ultimate boss, Heinrich Himmler. "Becher was bartering Jews for foreign exchange and goods on direct orders from Himmler," said Eichmann, in *Life* magazine. The payment for the train, over $1.5 million, became known as the "Becher deposit." After the war, some of the Becher deposit was returned, but much of it disappeared, almost certainly into Becher's own pocket. Kasztner and Becher built up a relationship, if not based on friendship, then certainly founded in a community of interest. In early 1945, as Himmler increasingly favored a separate peace with the western Allies, Becher, under his instructions, traveled across Germany to try to prevent the destruction of the camps and the surviving inmates. Kasztner went with him.

The mission was successful, but here the story turns darker. After the Allied victory, Becher was arrested as a suspected war criminal, which, with his record on the eastern front, he almost certainly was. Kasztner came to the rescue, testifying that he had helped save Jews. "There can be no doubt that Becher was one of the few SS leaders to take a stand against the extermination program and who made an attempt to save lives," wrote Kasztner. This unprecedented gesture worked. Becher was eventually released and became a rich and successful businessman, developing agricultural trade between Hungary and West Germany.

"Becher got rich because he was a very good merchant and he had great connections. During the war, before the war, after the war," recalled Hansi Brand, who personally took two cases of the Becher deposit to the Eichmann's office at the Hotel Majestic. Becher did testify at the trial of his former boss, Adolf Eichmann, in a written deposition. After the war, there were rumors and reports in the Israeli press, denied by the government, that Becher had been involved in supplying agricultural equipment to the nascent Jewish state. Either way, had he come to Israel, he too would have been arrested.

Controversy also continues over Kasztner's role in what is known as the "Parachutists' Affair." In spring 1944, three Hungarian-born Jews living in Palestine were trained by the SOE and parachuted into Yugoslavia before being infiltrated into Hungary. There they planned to organize armed resistance to the Germans. One, a woman poet named Hannah Szenes, was arrested after crossing the border. The two others, Peretz Goldstein and Joel Nussbecher, arrived in Budapest in late June. Both were from Kasztner's hometown, Kolozsvar, and contacted him. He was not happy to see them. They were being shadowed by Hungarian and Nazi counterintelligence. Their appearance threatened the deal over the train, due to leave in a few days. Nussbecher was arrested. The Vaada took Goldstein into hiding, to a special holding camp on Columbus Street, where the train passengers—including his parents—were held under SS guard.

There he met Hansi Brand, who wanted to know the details of the planned armed resistance against the Nazis. As Mrs. Brand recalls, she laughed bitterly at the encounter. "I asked him whether he had some kind of program, some idea what should be done. He reached into his pocket and pulled out a stocking with something sewn inside. When I saw that, in the big *tsures* [sorrow] there was, I could only laugh."

Soon after, Kasztner and Hansi Brand were arrested, interrogated, and pressured to reveal Goldstein's hiding place. Goldstein then decided to give himself up to the Nazis, possibly under pressure from Kasztner. Hannah Szenes was executed in Budapest on November 7, three weeks after the coup by the Hungarian Nazi Arrow Cross. Goldstein and Nussbecher were deported to the camps. Nussbecher escaped and survived the war, but Goldstein died.

After the war, Kasztner wrote a long and self-serving report about his work before moving to Israel. Like Jacob Gens in Vilna, and Mordechai Rumkowski in Lodz, he too had wielded the power to help decide who would live or die. But he could never escape his past. As Laszlo Devecseri says: "I told him when I saw him that 'this action which you did will only bring difficulties in the future.' Because so many Jews died, and other Jews who stayed alive would accuse him of collaborating."

In 1953, a Hungarian Jew named Malchiel Gruenwald living in Jerusalem did just that. He published a newsletter accusing Kasztner of collaborating with the Nazis and stealing Hungarian Jews' wealth via the Becher deposit. Kasztner sued for libel. In June 1955, the judge, Benjamin Halevi, delivering his judgment, ruled in favor of Gruenwald, except for the claim that Kasztner had stolen part of the Becher deposit. He accused Kasztner of having "sold his soul to the devil," by allowing himself to be used by the Nazis to prevent resistance to the deportations in exchange for the safe passage of the 1,685 train passengers. Kasztner appealed. In January 1958, the Supreme Court upheld his appeal, rejecting Halevi's ruling, except the charge that he had testified in favor of Kurt Becher. But the ruling came too late for Kasztner. In March 1957, he was shot outside his home in Tel Aviv. His killer, a former agent of Shin Bet, the Israeli internal security service, was caught and imprisoned. Perhaps Kasztner had known too much about the murkiest example of Jewish compromise with the Nazis.

Whatever the terms, known or secret, of the deal between Kasztner and Eichmann, the 1,685 passengers on the Kasztner train survived. The Jewish Council leaders mainly saved themselves and their families. "They cannot come to terms with the fact that these simple people did something, so they keep silent about it because it hurts their dignity," said Hansi Brand, who died in April 2000. "With their great connections and ideals and everything, they could do nothing. Meanwhile, there were four or five people who tried to do things, and they succeeded."

Afterword

In May 2000, fifty-five years after the collapse of the Third Reich, the following letter was published by the newspaper *Die Welt*. It was addressed to the editor:

Dear Sir,

I would be interested to know how many books were burnt by the Nazis in 1933 and how many by democrats in 1945? I would also like to know how many robberies there were per thousand inhabitants under the Nazis and how many today. How great was the danger under the Nazis of a girl being raped after going dancing, and how great is the danger today? How many songs and poems were learnt by schoolchildren under the Nazis and how many now? What were the chances of an elderly person being offered a seat in a bus during the Nazi period and what are the chances now? How many presents were made by children for their parents, grandparents— and how many today? How many women married in white, how many marriages stayed intact, and how many today? How many drug addicts were there under Hitler—and how many now? How many work-shy, subsidized by the gainfully employed, existed in those days and how many now? How long should this list continue? Germany has reached a cultural nadir and the situation will not improve as long as we leave it up to neo-Nazis to point out the good aspects of the past...[1]

The correspondent was not a notorious historical revisionist, nor a front man for the likes of David Irving. He was not even speaking for an embittered older generation trying to explain how, as a young German back in the 1920s or '30s, he came to support Hitler. No, the letter writer was giving voice to a new mood, a sense that the Nazis did address some of the needs of the (German) people—whether personal, through the provision of work and leisure, or national, through the revival of Germany's pride. And that Hitler's policies presented an alternative and sometimes preferable approach to the world.

The letter writer's voice is not alone. As the survivors of the Third Reich years die, as the concentration camps crumble and the physical evidence of the Holocaust fades away, so it will be easier to steer the discussion in this direction. It is still easy enough to answer the letter writer.

No books were burnt in 1945. Even the banned *Mein Kampf* can be bought in second-hand bookshops in Germany and is read in libraries, imported from abroad. The crime rate, in Berlin at least, was substantially the same in the 1920s, 1930s, and late 1940s. If anything, crime increased in the chaotic last years of the Reich; rapes and burglaries were common in the blackout as general lawlessness spread. As for drug abuse, cocaine was snorted in the 1920s and 1930s as frequently as it is today. One of the leading members of the Reich, Hermann Göring, was a morphine addict.

The Nazis' supposed "morality" was utterly hypocritical. Members of the leadership, such as Joseph Goebbels, professed their attachment to Aryan family values, but led totally immoral personal lives rooted in serial adultery and promiscuity. Martin Bormann's wife wrote to him detailing her approval of his choice of mistress. As the Reich's borders spread, plunder and looting of artworks and valuables, both state-owned and personal, were rapidly institutionalized, pure theft by any other name. And, of course, the letter writer's idyllic world was bought at terrible cost—to Jews, to non-Germans, and Germans who opposed the Nazis. Whatever order and discipline existed under Hitler was built on a comprehensive system of slave labor and concentration camps.

Will it be so simple to slap down such a letter writer in ten or fifteen years time? We fear not. New generations will be offered simplistic, heroic myths in which the Nazi era is seen as a Manichaean contest between black and white, good and evil. The number of resistance heroes will grow out of all proportion to those actually involved in actively opposing Hitler and the Nazis. The villains will defy analysis, presented as something incomprehensible, a macabre quirk of history about whose possible reappearance we need not worry. History, an account of actual events, will be increasingly rewritten, manipulated, or reduced to a near fictional minimum.

Talking to school children—in Britain, Germany, Hungary, and Poland—we have been faced with very similar questions. If Hitler was the epitome of evil, why did so many millions of Germans follow him? Either the German people were evil themselves or fatally flawed—impossibly gullible or morally weak? A child born in 2010 will be even less capable of assessing the circumstances that kept Hitler in power; it will be one of the many riddles of the twentieth century seen as having little contemporary relevance. In *Seduced by Hitler*, we present a different picture, one that is nuanced and complex, by setting out in detail the range and depth of moral conflicts that characterized life and death in the Third Reich.

We have tried to demonstrate that there is no straightforward explanation for ethical—or unethical—conduct in a police state. The army officers who tried to assassinate Hitler with a bomb conspired in the spring and summer of 1944 after the defeat of Stalingrad and the Allies' D-day landing, when the Third Reich began to crumble. There was rather less opposition to Hitler four years earlier when Europe's states collapsed one after another in the face of the Wehrmacht's advance. The bomb plotters are now fêted as heroes sacrificing themselves in the fight against tyranny, but it was the prospect of military defeat and the hope of salvaging something of Germany from the wreckage of the Third Reich, rather than any moral horror over the Holocaust that prompted their attempt to kill Hitler. Perhaps the Nazis' darkest achievement was to also morally debase their victims as they struggled to survive. Even in the Warsaw Ghetto, there were Jewish black marketeers who profited handsomely from the misery of their fellows, before they too met the same deaths.

For many Aryans, of course, it was not difficult to grow rich under Hitler or turn a comfortable profit from the misery of the Third Reich. The Nazis offered a form of social mobility for "true" Germans. Even those left behind were given the opportunity to feel superior and comfortable compared to the Jews who were being loaded into cattle trucks. Hitler accelerated the pace of German politics, gave his citizens a feeling that if they did not act quickly and, of course, loyally, they would end up as losers. It was trickery—like speed chess played in Manhattan parks, tempo replacing reason—but it was effective. Choices became blurred.

What are the limits of tolerance of any given regime? How far can individuals influence the regime? Part of the mechanics of dictatorship was to make these frontiers fluid. Goebbels declared that he was not interested in a uniform press; he knew that a degree of criticism and a variety of opinion was needed as a safety valve and as a way of retaining interest in the printed word. Independently minded newspapers such as the *Deutsche Allgemeine Zeitung*, the *Berliner Tageblatt*, and the *Frankfurter Zeitung* were allowed to continue, in part because of the favorable impression they made abroad in the early 1930s.

Such tactics are still favored by dictators today. In Yugoslavia, Slobodan Milosevic permits the radical, anti-government news magazine *Vreme* to publish, as proof of his government's supposed commitment to a free media, even as his security forces close down independent television stations. Skilled journalists in Nazi Germany found ways of writing between the lines. The economic specialist Fritz Werkmann described, for example, the construction of the autobahn but subtly shared doubts on Nazi claims that it was solving Germany's unemployment problems.

The room for maneuvering, even in such a closely monitored area as the printed press, raises intriguing questions. The licensed freedom could be exploited for the general good; that is, some support could, in a camouflaged way, be passed on to those unhappy with the Nazis or as a way of mobilizing against specific Nazi policies. To what degree was this a form of collaboration (for collaboration, we have shown, has to be measured in degrees, each compromise carrying different weight)? Journalists, unlike say novelists or philosophers, were forced into quick ethical decisions; theirs was a daily or weekly business, and each edition brought moral dilemmas. Many ended up tying themselves in knots, censoring their own writings, smuggling messages into articles that were barely understood even by sophisticated readers. The need to survive—more precisely, the fear of government displeasure—competed with the need to demonstrate that they still exercised independent judgment.

Oskar Stark, who worked for both *Berliner Tageblatt* and *Frankfurter Zeitung* during the Nazi years, reflected in 1965: "Everyone, including me, who lived, breathed, ate, and in one form or another participated in the events between 1933 and 1945, belongs to a generation whose backbone has been damaged."[2] Stark confessed that journalists who thought they could continue to function under a dictatorship were fooling themselves, their logic "based on the false premise that you can experiment freely in a despotic regime and freely decide when you want to abandon that experiment."

His judgment touched us, partly as we are ourselves journalists, but also because we knew in communist Europe that many reporters faced similar dilemmas. There is never an easy answer. In Poland under martial law, which began in 1981, there was a massive withdrawal of journalists from the profession even though censorship was gradually eased and provided loopholes. Some became taxi drivers, some wrote books that were destined not to be published for a decade, some emigrated, some switched from political to nonpolitical subjects, some moved to specialized publications for the blind or for anglers. Others tried to stretch the limits of tolerance within the system. Most accepted censorship, as one accepts an editor's judgment—grudgingly, but as an integral part of the daily professional routine.

The response of journalists under the Third Reich was rather less principled. Perhaps some believed in National Socialism as a modernizing force. Certainly, Goebbels was not universally unpopular with newspaper editors and journalists—for them, his personal weaknesses and public rantings were outweighed by the conviction that he was an intelligent man who understood the media and the compelling need to modernize Germany.

We have dealt with many variations of a choice in *Seduced by Hitler*. The compromises made by intellectuals seem to bear little resemblance to the life-or-death choices in the camps and the ghettos. The leaders of the Jewish Councils had to face the most ghastly choices of all. First, whether to serve or risk execution for refusal. Second, whether or not to implement the Nazis' orders as a means of softening their impact and hopefully delay the deaths of Jews that council members did not initially realize were certain, anyway.

Yet they were all part of the spectrum of survival ethics. Hitler, like all dictators (but more efficiently than most) blurred choice. For ordinary Germans—for the professors, the housewives, the shipyard workers, the generals, the bankers, and industrialists who are featured in our book—these choices often remained cloudy. They deluded themselves, allowed themselves to be bought or bullied, chose comfort over risk. For them, surviving Hitler had a very specific meaning: they became increasingly aware after Stalingrad that Germany could lose the war and its Führer. Choices were framed accordingly: career advancement within Nazi-managed organizations came to have only a limited value while self-enrichment survival tactics for the post-Hitler era took on a greater, even central importance. Fear of losing everything created a moral jungle out of Germany from 1933. Even the Aryan lawyer comfortably ensconced in his villa in Berlin's luxury suburb of Grünewald lived in a haze of self-deception.

Much of the appeal of Nazism was that it removed many of the constraints, both legal and moral, that govern behavior across every sector of society. For many individuals, this often had little to do with furthering the triumph of Nazi ideology itself. Rather, Nazi principles could be invoked as a means of, and justification for, settling personal grievances and satisfying personal greed. In one sense, the Third Reich was a kind of macabre wish-fulfillment factory where an individual's basest desires could be met, for everyone from an uneducated peasant tilling his fields to a sophisticated international banker. Even if by any normal standard these wishes were deeply immoral, as long as they fell into the parameters of the Third Reich's aims, they might be realized. For loyal citizens of the Third Reich, it was open season on everyone from business competitors to unwanted rivals in love, as the case of the Königsberg shopgirl, in love with her boss, who denounced his wife for passing food to a Jewish friend. Such wishes could be grandiose, involving the construction of massive economic empires based on plunder and slave labor, or more mundane, such as killing local Jews by hand for personal satisfaction as the following incident in the Holocaust illustrates: When the Germans invaded Lithuania, as in other occupied countries, deep-seated resentments against the Jews and murderous anti-Semitic hatreds were let loose. In Lithuania's second city of Kaunas, locals, encouraged by watching Germans, killed several dozen Jews they claimed were Communists. The Jews were beaten to death with crowbars in a courtyard of an apartment block. Once the massacre was over, a local man picked up an accordion, stood on the bodies and began to play the Lithuanian national anthem. For him, the Jews' death was an occasion not just for satisfaction, but celebration. A hatred that can inspire such personalized, bloody murder is impossible to comprehend, yet the accounts of atrocities committed just a few years ago by Bosnian Serbs against their Muslim neighbors, the massacre at Srebrenica, remind us that it endures today.

To some extent, the Germans terrorized themselves. A large part of the Gestapo's work, as we have seen, was not involved in combating threats to the stability of the Nazi state, but rather of processing the denunciations pouring in from "good, law-abiding Germans," who used the system to try and resolve old personal scores, grudges, and even disputes with neighbors. So prevalent was this at one stage that the Gestapo had to threaten the denouncers themselves with arrest for wasting their time on irrelevant matters. This was not confined to Germany.

As the Nazis occupied neighboring nations, there too the denunciations poured in. Locals informed the authorities, for example, about the Jewish background of unwanted rivals in business and asked to take possession of Jewish-owned shops, often outstripping the Germans and their local allies in their enthusiasm. We have noted that in Budapest in May 1944, the government felt obliged to publish a declaration that members of the public should stop deluging the authorities with "dozens of applications for the assignment of Jewish shops and stocks," after they were sequestered.

But at the same time, the Nazi state provided a strict, even if deeply warped, legal framework and a belief system so that the individual could feel that he was not acting alone and atomized out of greed, but rather as part of a great project that was remodeling the very nature of humanity. The great spectacles of party rallies and Albert Speer's "Cathedrals of Light," which encouraged individuals to subsume their own desires into those of the *volksgemeinschaft*, increased this feeling.

The process of moral compromise with the Third Reich did not take place overnight. Rather it was a stepped accommodation, but one where the first steps were the hardest. Each subsequent one became progressively easier, as we have examined in the case of the chemical conglomerate IG Farben, which moved from being demonized in the Nazi press before 1933 as a "Jewish" firm, to a decade later, running its own dedicated concentration camp at Auschwitz III. There its slave laborers were accounted as "units," and they were worked to death on a planned starvation diet before being sent to nearby Birkenau, to be gassed by Zyklon B, also part of the IG chemical empire. Auschwitz III was merely the latest stage in a decade-long process of moral corruption—indeed, total moral collapse.

At the same time, IG and its fellow industrialists compartmentalized their own human feelings and IG's business interests. IG's officials themselves had Jewish friends, Jewish colleagues. When twenty-four IG board members were tried at Nuremberg after the war, Jewish former employees and their relatives submitted detailed affidavits in their defense, detailing their attempts to help Jews.

Compartmentalization was a key component of survival ethics, even among those who stepped outside the safe limits and actively tried to rescue some of Hitler's victims. The paradoxes of human behavior are well exemplified in the case of Albert Göring, brother of Hermann, who was both an arms dealer, supplying weapons to the Nazi war machine, but who repeatedly took risks to save Jews and other Nazis from the Gestapo.

If that was a moral compartmentalization, the case of Wilhelm Kube, the *gauleiter* of White Russia was a warped ideological one. While most German and Austrian Jews deported to his fiefdom were killed in July 1942 and May 1943, Kube managed to gain a temporary reprieve for seventy. His rationale—perverse to us, but logical to him—was that cultured, German-speaking Jews should not die the same deaths as eastern European ones, whom he regarded as subhumans. Kube informed his Jewish barber, who shaved him every day, that all Jews who worked for him in his office were under his personal protection.

Just as the path of compromise with Nazism began with the first small step, so did the journey away from it. The first act of defiance was a foundation for further resistance. Kube progressed from comforting his barber to publicly defending the honor of German Jews against the Nazi security forces. He also complained to his Nazi superiors that removing gold fillings from Jews scheduled for execution was "conduct unworthy of the Germany of Kant and

Goethe." Kube's protests were brushed aside, but when German women demonstrated in Berlin's Rosenstrasse, demanding the return of their arrested Jewish husbands, the regime took notice. A massive arrest of protesting Aryan housewives, unlike Jews, could not be carried out without cost to morale. It could inspire further demonstrations by the relatives of the wives, with unforeseeable consequences. The Nazi leadership buckled under pressure: the men were released.

Choice in a closed society exists because of ambiguity, uncertainty. But, as Oskar Stark wrote, ambiguous resistance to the ambiguities of the establishment is also destined to fail. Hence, the failure of the organized churches in the Third Reich. Their desperate attempts to survive as an established expression of religious faith and at the same time pay tribute to biblical principles left the churches deeply compromised.

This book has tried to shift the focus away from the collapse of organized opposition in the Third Reich, a well-trodden if still controversial area, toward the crisis of the individual. How should I behave? Under what circumstances do I change my behavior? That, for us, has been the motivation to write *Seduced by Hitler*: to provoke self-questioning, above all, among the young. One does not have to live in a police state to face dilemmas demanding civic courage or sound ethical judgment—as every university professor, newspaper reporter, office worker, or hospital nurse can testify, there are occasions in the course of a normal working week when difficult choices have to be made.

Dictatorship naturally politicizes these choices and obliges individuals to ask, What do I believe in? How much am I willing to risk for those beliefs? My life? *Seduced by Hitler* is about ordinary lives lived under extraordinary pressure, the changing value attached to those lives, the moral options exercised or neglected to preserve life. The Third Reich, the ugly, formidably evil face of the twentieth century, still has a great deal to teach those growing up in the twenty-first century.

Seduced by Hitler examines whether or not there are general principles governing the way people behave in a dictatorship. Why do they abandon core moral and ethical values even when they are under little threat? The Third Reich was exceptional in its brutality to people it defined as outsiders, almost protective of those considered insiders. "True" Germans were offered opportunities—sometimes crudely bribed—to such an extent that they accepted their rulers long after the regime had lost the gloss of success. It is this contract, rather than any ethnocentric generalizations about German servility, that is at the heart of *Seduced by Hitler*.

National Socialism developed a sophisticated combination of the traditional and the modern, a remarkable governing system that made itself attractive to its citizens even as it was deploying vicious mass murder. We have explored this magnetic quality and seen how it narrowed ethical choice. Our aim throughout, however, has been to demonstrate that Germans were not uniquely susceptible to the siren call.

National Socialism was a cynical precursor to many aspects of contemporary politics—an autocratic regime that was nonetheless sensitive to public opinion. The key to understanding the fascination of this brand of fascism is to look, microscopically, at the relationship between the leader and the led. This, rather than a unique weakness in the German national character, is the most useful approach to grasping the seemingly incomprehensible Holocaust.

But this was a dynamic process, and the popular mood fluctuated, enthusiasm ebbed and flowed. The fanatical core of National Socialism was rather small. Instead, the regime was increasingly judged by its citizens in pragmatic terms—on its ability to satisfy consumer needs, to protect them against crime and competition. National Socialism was a machine-age ideology, a mobilizing force that pretended to bridge class divisions. Many workers suspended their disbelief, blocked out the knowledge that the regime had crushed Social Democracy and communism, and accepted the benefits of a new leisure culture. Unemployment was banished or concealed; it was possible to persuade oneself that the regime was not all bad. It was a system open enough to allow some form of social modernization. Even at their most traditional, the Nazis left space for the modern: women, for example, were sometimes given extraordinary managerial authority within party organizations. Men were provided with nonpolitical role models. The engineer, the builder of bridges and roads, was the hero of the Nazi epoch.

There were moments of doubt. The Night of Broken Glass (*Kristallnacht*) on November 9–10, 1938; the outbreak of war; the defeat at Stalingrad. Such moments crystallized choices and reminded at least a section of German society that it had been tolerating an unjust or an incompetent leadership. The self-delusion of German citizens and the fraudulent nature of the regime was suddenly spotlighted, like a trapeze artist in the big top. The Nazis, and in particular Goebbels, were sophisticated enough to identify pockets of dissent—and found ways of muzzling or diverting it. The Nazi ideology may have been crude, the regime enforcers were certainly savage, the governing temperament amoral, but they were remarkably adept at calibrating domestic policy with domestic mood. The distaste for *Kristallnacht*, the notorious night of rage when synagogues were set ablaze and Jewish shops looted, raised a crisis of conscience for many middle-class Germans.

For five years, Germans had been able to tell themselves that the systematic discrimination against Jews was a halfway "legitimate" move designed to Germanize the economy. If jobs were to be created by Germans for Germans, then Germans had to take command of their own economy and finances. They turned a blind eye to the measures that restricted Jewish rations, that forbade them to shave, that made of them not only second-class citizens, but also desperate, marginalized figures scrambling to survive. The Night of Broken Glass, however, showed that the Nazis would be satisfied only with the total uprooting of Jewish culture from Germany, with their elimination, with the rewriting of history. And, in allowing mob rule, even for a night, the Nazi regime showed that the whole force of the judicial and police system would be turned against Jews. The more thoughtful of the German bourgeoisie understood on that night that this was no longer "just" about Jews but about a regime demonstrating its capacity for evil and violence that could be turned equally against the liberal professors, non-conformist writers, or outspoken churchmen. The most powerful stories of Germans shielding Jews stem from the months following *Kristallnacht*, small triumphs of conscience and of individual responsibility. Yet, the vast majority of Germans—including metropolitan middle-class Germans whose neighbors and friends were always Jews, who would sing the praise of their Jewish dentist, or who gushed approval of Jewish actresses—did nothing. They were aware of an ethical choice and did nothing.

It was not the intention of our book to set out the case against Daniel Goldhagen's *Hitler's Willing Executioners* and his thesis that Germans were programmed for extermination or anti-Semitism. We do not doubt that anti-Semitism was a strong political emotion and that it blurred choices, that Germans were too ready to accept the slow suffocation of the Jewish people and their ultimate destruction. Certainly, Goldhagen has no problem explaining German silence after *Kristallnacht*. We, however, question whether anti-Semitism was such a smothering blanket to human reason and conscience. Indeed, in our research, we found cases of anti-Semites who saved Jews, Germans who differentiated between German Jews (who they protected or helped abroad) and eastern Jews. There were Germans, too, who strove to prevent Jews denouncing other Jews. The picture is complex, individual, and beyond—like most issues of conscience—the broad sweep generalization. There were choices; there were always choices. In the case of *Kristallnacht*, the repugnance of seeing a place of worship set on fire translated only years later into an act of resistance. For some, *Kristallnacht* was the moment when Germans started to lose their sense of Hitler infallibility. Others merely concluded that Hitler had nothing in common with the thugs acting in his name.

We have considered all the variants in the maze. The outbreak of war in September 1939 marked another level at which
moral choices could be identified and exercised. Germans did not
want war, in contrast to August 1914, when war came as a kind
of national relief. Germans were overjoyed by the annexation of
Austria in 1938 and seemed to support Hitler's defense of German
minorities abroad. The text of "Deutschland über Alles," the
German national anthem written by Fallersleben, talks of Germans
being united from the Maas River in the west to the Melee in the
east (now Lithuania), from the Etsch River in the South Tirol (now
Italy) to the Belt in Denmark; these were the emotional outpour-
ings of a nineteenth-century national liberal, not a fanatic Nazi.
The sense of Germanness, defined by literature and the spread
of German language throughout central Europe, stretched well
beyond conventional and politically agreed frontiers. The use of the
army to change these frontiers in the German interest was not in
itself repulsive to most Germans, who saw territorial expansion into
German-speaking areas as a just return of former Germanic lands.

We have seen then how, domestically, Nazism met many of
the personal needs of the Reich's citizens, supplying work, paid
holidays, food, shelter, and resurgent national pride in exchange for
its citizens' support and their turning a blind eye to terror initially,
and then mass murder. Similar principles, of forging an immoral
pact, worked on the international, diplomatic stage with regard to
the states allied to Berlin. At first, a shared nationalist ideology, vis-
ceral anti-Communism, and fear of the Red Army helped unite the
Axis and its satellite states. It brought together such comparatively
disparate national leaders as Hungary's authoritarian, reactionary
Admiral Horthy and Fascist Italy's modernist—in comparison—
Benito Mussolini. Italy and Hungary, like many of Germany's allies,
joined the Axis for geopolitical reasons as much as ideological ones.
In fact, they were seduced not so much by Hitler himself, but by
what Nazism could offer their national interests. And when, after
Stalingrad and the D-day landings, it became clear that the Allies

were winning, those same policies of expediency saw these nations turn increasingly away from Hitler.

This pursuit of national interest meant that early on in the Reich, irredentism—seizure or return of lost territories—was a key factor in driving several nations into Berlin's orbit. This is true for countries such as Hungary and Bulgaria. Hungary's defeat in World War I and the loss of about 60 percent of its territories to its neighbors, such as Romania and Czechoslovakia, was a burning scar in the national psyche. Hitler, and a Wehrmacht allied with the Hungarian army, could heal that patriotic wound, Hungary's leaders believed. Similarly, for Bulgaria, alliance with the Third Reich was an opportunity to regain swathes of land in Thrace and Macedonia, which the country believed were rightfully its own. Yet irredentism was not always the answer: Germany's ally Romania actually lost territory when sections of Transylvania were returned to Hungary after the outbreak of war. There, a tradition of virulent, medieval anti-Semitism, more vicious and more ingrained than in Italy or Hungary helped keep Bucharest allied to Berlin.

Other protonations, such as Slovakia and Croatia, which previously had never truly existed as independent states, saw the Nazis as a guarantee of fulfilling their national aspiration for independence. Immediate, pressing concerns of geopolitics and nationhood often overrode ideological and cultural differences between Berlin and its allies. Slovakia and Croatia, for example, based their national identity and culture firmly on Catholicism, a religion whose priests could be persecuted under Nazism within the Third Reich proper. This "national-cultural" Catholicism was far more than a rite of worship. The very essence of the nation and religion fused together, especially in the case of Croatia, where Catholic priests were accomplices to the genocide of Orthodox Christian Serbs and Jews. In the wartime NDH, the Independent State of Croatia, it was not possible to consider yourself an Orthodox Christian or a Jewish Croatian. The nation and its faith were synonymous. To a lesser extent, this was also true in Slovakia, although Slovaks avoided the extremes of genocide carried out by Pavelic's Ustasha Black Legions. Yet, both Croatia's Ante Pavelic and Slovak leader Father Josef Tiso were prepared to overlook the Nazis' persecution of Catholic priests. Their alliance with Berlin served what they saw as a greater national need: independent statehood and the chance to kill or deport unwelcome minorities, such as Serbs and Jews.

Anti-Semitism, at least of the genocidal kind, was not always a necessary factor in turning a country into a Nazi ally. Although Hungary's prewar and wartime government willingly passed a raft of increasingly strident anti-Jewish laws, its government refused to deport its Jews or incarcerate them in ghettos. Mussolini, like Spain's General Franco, had little sympathy for, or interest in, Hitler's maniacal anti-Semitism, and both leaders gave sanctuary to Jewish refugees. Mediterranean fascism was based on nation, not mystical notions of race and blood, an important distinction, especially for Jews. The Nazis could also be flexible on race when it suited: witness how the Japanese, hardly a Nordic nation, were reclassified as "honorary Aryans." Until German troops actually marched in and occupied Nazi allies, there was room to maneuver, there were moral choices to be made. Hitler and the Nazi leaders were enraged by Hungary and Italy's reluctance to kill their Jews. Eventually, the Germans invaded both Italy and Hungary, after which many of those nations' Jews were rapidly deported en masse to the death camps.

Meanwhile, the leaders of Vichy France, including the aging reactionary Marshal Pétain, saw an alliance with Nazi Germany as a means of preserving some national sovereignty and patriotic *gloire*, no matter how warped and tarnished by Vichy's subservience to Berlin. The need to keep sovereign nations as allies, willingly working with the Nazis, rather than as subservient client states, meant that compromises had to be made. As we have noted, while Bulgaria chose to demonstrate its sovereignty and national autonomy by refusing to deport its native-born Jews (those in the annexed territories of Macedonia and Thrace were quickly sent to the camps), Vichy France chose the opposite approach and set up its own autonomous French structure of registration, confiscation, and internment for Jews. Vichy France set the French Holocaust in motion before the Germans even demanded that its officials do so. Marrus and Paxton, authors of *Vichy France and the Jews*, note: "In what proved to be a colossal miscalculation, the Vichy leaders assumed that the German authorities would be grateful to the French for pursuing a parallel anti-Jewish policy and would respond by yielding greater authority to France over this and other spheres of national activity."

And while Vichy outstripped even the Germans in its eagerness to rid France of its Jews, its officials could be surprisingly recalcitrant when it suited them. Vichy authorities refused to deliver 50,000 horses requested by the Germans. The Germans were forced instead to buy them on the black market. If that was an example of outright obstructionism, there were other, passive ways to demonstrate dissent or opposition to the regime. The sale of French newspapers plummeted in occupied France (to around 10 percent of their prewar sales figures) once these dailies lost their independence and became pro-German mouthpieces. So 90 percent of French newspaper readers demonstrated their dissatisfaction with their news sources under Nazi occupation. Even in a dictatorship based on terror, nobody can force its citizens to read propaganda. Still, it is clearly nonsensical to compare a refusal to buy a pro-Nazi newspaper with actual acts of resistance or opposition that could bring terrible penalties of incarceration or death in their wake. There is no single answer why the citizens of some nations, such as Denmark and Bulgaria, showed considerable moral courage in refusing to implement the Holocaust, while officials of others, such as Vichy France, surpassed even the Nazis in their eagerness to round up their Jews. But it is clear that, especially in war, a nation is led from the top, and it was the policies of the national leaderships that helped shape the responses and inspire the moral courage—or lack of it—among their countrymen.

Notes

The following abbreviations refer to these archives: PRO—British Public Records Office, London; USNA—United States National Archives, Washington, D.C.

Book page numbers refer to editions listed in bibliography.

Introduction

1 Johnson, Eric; *Nazi Terror*.
2 Dörner, Bernward; *Heimtücke. Das Gesetz als Waffe*.
3 Safrian, Hans; *Die Welt*, September 1999.
4 Grunberger, Richard; *A Social History of the Third Reich*, p. 140.

Chapter One: From Cradle to Grave

1 Bajohr, Frank; *Mittelweg 36*, Feb/March 1998.
2 Seydelmann, Getrude; *Gefährdete Balance*.
3 Gurr, Ted; *Why Men Rebel*.
4 Kundrus, Birthe; "Loyal weil satt"; *Mittelweg 36*, Oct/Nov 1997.
5 Letter from IG Farben director in Brandenburg Landeshauptarchiv rep. 75 IGF/Werk Premnitz, 14 June 1942.
6 Klemperer, Victor; *I Shall Bear Witness*.
7 Haffner, Sebastian; *The Meaning of Hitler*.
8 Ibid.
9 Letter from SS Gruppenführer Berger to Himmler, 2 April 1942.
10 "Korruption in Dritten Reich. Zur Lebensmittelversorgung der NS-Führerschaft"; *Jahreshefte für Zeiggeschichte*, No 42, Munich 1944.
11 Kitchen, Martin; *Nazi Germany at War*.

12 Grunberger, ibid.; p. 429. Grunberger's chapter on Nazi humor is also the source for the second opening epigram.
13 Schmidt, Christoph; *Zu den Motiven "alter Kampfer" in der NSDAP*. In Peukert and Reulecke, pp. 21–44.
14 Huntington, Samuel; "Modernization and Corruption"; *Political Corruption*, pp. 377–88.
15 Kitchen, op. cit.

Chapter Two: The Führer and His People
1 *Liebesbriefe an Adolf Hitler—Briefe in den Tod*; Editor Helmut Ulshoefer.
2 Nayhauss quoted in Leeb, Johannes; *Wir waren Hitlers Eliteschuler*.
3 Krüger quoted in Leeb, Johannes; *Wir waren Hitlers Eliteschuler*.
4 Quoted by Alfons Keukmann in his contribution to Wilfried Breyvogel (ed); *Piraten, Swings and Junge Garde: Jungendwiderstand in Nationalsozilismus*.
5 Peukert, Detlev and Jurgen Reulecke; *Die Reihen fast geschlossen, Beiträge zur Geschichte des Alltags unterm Nationalsozialismus*.
6 Mason, Timothy; Introduction to *Angst, Belohnung, Zucht und Ordung*.
7 Professor Ernst Hoffmann; interview with Adam LeBor; Berlin, January 1990.
8 Mason, Timothy, op. cit.
9 Fritzsche, Peter; *Germans into Nazis*, p. 220.
10 Sywottek, Arnold; *Deutsche Volksdemokratie 1935–46*.
11 Mason, Timothy, op. cit.

Chapter Three: The Führer and His Women
1 Stoltzfus, Nathan; *Resistance of the Heart: Intermarriage and the Rosenstrasse Protest in Nazi Germany*, p. 266.
2 Quoted in Gundrun Brockhaus; *Schauder und Idylle*, p. 171.
3 Erdheim, Mario; *Psychoanalyse und Unbewusstheit in der Kultur*, p. 343.
4 Frau Bormann quoted in Hering, Sabine; *Makel, Muhsal, Privileg*, p. 78.

Chapter Four: The Führer and His Generals

1 Überschar, Gert and Vogel Winfried; *Dienen und Verdienen,* p. 72.
2 Ibid, p. 72.
3 General Halder quoted in Baigent, Michael and Richard Leigh; *Secret Germany.*
4 Von Moltke quoted in ibid, p. 26.

Chapter Five: The Triumph of Kitsch

1 Brockhaus, Gudrun; *Schauder und Idylle (Faschismus als Erlebnisangebot).*
2 Bloch, Ernest; *Erbschaft dieser Zeit.*
3 Riefenstahl, Leni; *A Memoir.*
4 Fest, Joachim; *Hitler Eine Biographie.*
5 Mommsen, Hans; "Nationalsozialismus," *Sovietsystem und demokratische Gesellschaft. Eine vergleichende Enzyclopäedie;* Frieburg 1971, vol 4; C.D. Kernig (ed).
6 Bullock, Allan, and Albert Speer; *Die Zeit,* 2 November 1979.
7 Grieswelle, Detlef; *Propaganda der Friedlesigkeit.* Detlef Grisewelle's study of Hitler rhetoric.
8 Ibid.
9 Ibid.
10 Quoted in Kershaw, Ian; *Hitler 1889–1936,* p. 81.
11 Ibid.
12 Ibid.
13 Quoted in Scholdt, Gunter; *Autoren über Hitler,* p. 691.
14 Quoted in White, Ian Boyd; *Kunst und Macht,* p. 43.
15 Nordan, Peter; *Unternehmen Bayreuth,* p. 145.
16 White, op. cit.
17 Reichel, Peter; *Der schöne Schein des Dritten Reichs.*

Chapter Six: From Boardroom to Birkenau

1 Snyder, Louis L.; *Encyclopaedia of the Third Reich,* p. 347.
2 Borkin, Joseph; *The Crime and Punishment of IG Farben.*
3 Ibid, p. 98.
4 Holocaust Educational Trust (HET); *Extermination Through Work: Jewish Slave Labor under the Third Reich,* p. 31.
5 Ibid.
6 Rudy Kennedy; taped telephone interview with Adam LeBor, November 1999.

7 Quoted by Christopher Simpson; *The Splendid Blond Beast: Money, Law and Genocide in the Twentieth Century*, p. 80.

8 Kurt Gurstein quoted in Noakes, Jeremy and G. Pridham; *Nazism 1919–1945, A Documentary Reader, Vol. 3*, p. 1149.

9 Tesch statement, Hamburg, 31 October 1945. PRO file WO 309/626 Zyklon B.

10 Simpson, op. cit., p. 156.

11 Eric Doyle quoted in Borkin, op. cit., p. 143.

12 Charles Coward quoted in ibid, p. 153.

Chapter Seven: Occupiers and Occupied

1 Werner von Grundherr quoted in Noakes and Pridham, op. cit., p. 879.

2 Wistrich, Robert; *Who's Who in Nazi Germany*, p. 12.

3 Wistrich, ibid., p. 13.

4 Goodchild, Sophie; "Queen Mum Wanted Peace with Hitler"; *Independent on Sunday*, 5 March 2000.

5 West, Nigel; *MI5*, p. 91.

6 Marrus and Paxton; *Vichy France and the Jews*, p. 366.

7 Koestler, Arthur; *Scum of the Earth*, p. 97.

8 Dawidowicz, Lucy; *The War Against the Jews, 1933–1945*, p. 433.

9 Pierre Laval quoted in Marrus and Paxton, op. cit., p. 346.

10 Ibid, p. 368.

11 Jean Nodon quoted in "Phantoms Return to Haunt France's Liberation Party"; *Sunday Telegraph*, 28 August 1994. Article by Nicholas Farrell.

12 Gyula Dornbach; interview with Adam LeBor, Budapest, March 2000.

13 Dawidowicz, op. cit., p. 442.

14 Debriefing of Lt. Col. Howie, 2 October 1944. PRO file HS4/108.

15 Marrus and Paxton, op. cit., p. 319.

16 Hugo Bachet's information. PRO file FO 371.

17 Otto Abetz document, 8 April 1942. PRO file FO 371/31939.

18 Conditions in France, British postal interception, May—September 1943. PRO file FO 371/36021, p. 12.

19 PRO file FO 371/36021, p. 13.

20 PRO file FO 371/36021, p. 14.

21 PRO file FO 371/36021, p. 15.

22 Antoine Pereire interview, 14 September 1943. PRO file
    371/36021.

23 Furst, Alan; *Red Gold*, p. 214.

24 Otto Braeutigam memo; Noakes and Pridham, op. cit., p.
    912.

Chapter Eight: Rescuers and Rescued

1 Noakes and Pridham, op. cit., p. 1111.

2 Schneider, Peter; "Saving Konrad Latte"; article in *New York
   Times Magazine*. 13 February 2000.

3 Ursula Meissner quoted in ibid.

4 Edda Göring interview, 3BM television, T*he Real Albert
   Göring*. Broadcast Channel 4, 5 December 1998.

5 Oskar Pilzer; telephone interview with Adam LeBor,
   November 1998. Included in author article on Albert Göring
   in *Sunday Times* magazine, November 1998.

6 Jacques Benbassat, 3BM television, as above.

7 Hans Modry postwar testimony; Skoda archives; Pilsen,
   Czech Republic.

8 Elsa Moravek de Wagner; telephone interviews with Adam
   LeBor, spring 1998.

9 Vladislav Kratky; interview with Adam LeBor, Pilsen, May
   1998.

10 Albert Göring testimony to to Ensign Robert Jackson,
    USNA. Nuremberg, 25 September 1945.

11 Josef Voracek postwar testimony; Skoda archives; Pilsen,
    Czech Republic.

12 British diplomatic cables on Albert Göring's movements
    between Italy and Greece. PRO file FO 371/25110.

13 Noakes and Pridham, op. cit., p. 1123.

14 Ibid, p. 1124.

15 Roberts, Glenys; "Maverick Who Saved Genuises from the
    Gas Chambers"; *Daily Mail*, 6 November 1999, p. 42.

16 Varian Fry quoted in "The Pin-Striped Pimpernel"; *Sunday
    Telegraph Magazine*, 25 May 1997, p. 19. Article by David
    Kerr.

17 Hans Natonek quoted in "The Savior"; *Independent Magazine*,
    11 March 1995, p. 32. Article by Donald Carroll.

18 Charlie Fawcett interview with *Beth Shalom* magazine, included in Varian Fry file at Wiener Library, London.

19 Atchildi, Asaf; *Rescue of Jews of Bukharan, Iranian and Afghan Origin in Occupied France (1940–1944)*; Yad Vashem Studies, Vol. VI, 1967, p. 258.

20 Herbert Pollack quoted in Smith, Michael; *Foley: The Spy Who Saved 10,000 Jews*, p. 65.

Chapter Nine: Neutral Collaboration

1 *Jewish Chronicle*, 5 May 2000. Article by Bernard Josephs.

2 Schellenberg, Walter; *The Labyrinth*, p. 341.

3 Franz von Papen quoted in Kahn, David; *Hitler's Spies*, p. 343.

4 Hitler quoted in ibid, p. 344.

5 See Kahn, David; *Hitler's Spies*; Schellenburg, Walter; *The Labyrinth*; and Rubin, Barry; *Istanbul Intrigues*.

6 Kahn, David, op. cit., p. 185.

7 June 1998 supplement to *Preliminary Study on U.S. and Allied Efforts to Recover and Restore Gold and Other Assets Stolen or Hidden During WWII*, p. 13. Available from: *www.state.gov*.

8 Letter included in PRO file FO115/4008 Bosch 1943–1945.

9 Teddy Kollek quoted in "Istanbul a Centre of Spies, Secrets"; Associated Press report from Istanbul, November 18, 1999. Article by Harmonie Toros.

10 Gilbert, Sir Martin; *Auschwitz and the Allies*, p. 21.

11 Sir Hughe Knatchbull-Hugessen quoted in ibid, p. 22.

12 S.E.V. Luke quoted in ibid, p. 22.

13 Ibid, p. 186.

14 Lipschitz, Chaim U.; *Franco, Spain, the Jews and the Holocaust*.

15 Edward Reichmann; interview with Adam LeBor, Budapest, December 1996.

16 Lipschitz, op. cit., p. 57.

17 Schellenberg, op. cit., p. 344.

18 Doris Pfister; interview with Adam LeBor, Geneva, September 1997.

19 Ben-Tov, Arieh; *Facing the Holocaust in Hungary*, p. 136.

20 ICRC website: *www.icrc.org*

21 Fabrizio Bensi; interview with Adam LeBor, Geneva, September 1997.

22 Rossel report contained in ICRC bound collection: *Documents*

of the ICRC Concerning the Theresienstadt Ghetto, 1990.

23 Extract from Charlotte Opfermann's account of Theresienstadt: *http://history1900s.about.com/education/history* (Guide Jennifer Rosenberg) Charlotte Opfermann's recollection of ICRC visit, contained in email correspondence with Adam LeBor, May 2000.

24 Rossel's visit to Auschwitz. Berlin, 29 September 1944, ICRC archives.

25 Ben-Tov, op. cit., p. 388.

Chapter Ten: Impossible Choices

1 Extract quoted in *New York Times Review of Books*, 26 June 1997. Article by Istvan Deak.

2 Merson, Allen; *Communist Resistance in Nazi Germany*, p. 297.

3 Rabbi Leo Baeck quoted in Braham, Randolph L.; *The Politics of Genocide: The Holocaust in Hungary*, p. 722.

4 Arendt, Hannah; *Eichmann in Jerusalem*, p. 119.

5 Jack Weisblack; interview with Adam LeBor, New York, July 1996.

6 Stanislaw Rozycki quoted in Keller, Ulrich, ed.; *The Warsaw Ghetto in Photographs*, p. 129.

7 Smuggling of food into the Warsaw ghetto: *www.yadvashem.org.il/holocaust/documents/102.html*

8 Judenrat activities: *www.yadvashem.org.il/holocaust/documents/90.html*

9 Chaim Kaplan on the Judenrat: *www.yadvashem.org.il/holocaust/documents/103.html*

10 Dawidowicz, op. cit.

11 Adam Czerniakow on deportation rumors: *www.yadvashem.org.il/holocaust/documents/120.html*

12 Dawidowicz, op. cit., p. 295.

13 General Stefan Rowecki quoted in ibid, p. 385.

14 Zbigniew Wolak; interview with Adam LeBor, Warsaw, December 1998.

15 Gusta Dawidsohn quoted in Dawidowicz, op. cit., p. 376.

16 Merson, op. cit., p. 243.

17 Mordecai Anielewicz's last letter: *www.yadvashem.org.il/holocaust/documents/145.html*

18 German battle report on the Warsaw ghetto uprising:

www.yadvashem.org.il/holocaust/documents/144.html

19 Goebbels on the Warsaw ghetto uprising:
    www.yadvashem.org.il/holocaust/documents/148.html

20 *Life* magazine; "Eichmann Tells His Own Damning Story";
    28 November 1960; Vol. 49, Issue 22.

21 Braham, op. cit., p. 433.

22 Ibid, p. 704.

23 Gilbert, op. cit., p. 204.

24 Ernest Stein; interview with Adam LeBor, New York, July
    1996.

25 Samu Stern quoted in Braham, op. cit., p. 705.

26 Ibid, p. 423.

27 Katalin Csillag; interview with Adam LeBor, Budapest,
    October 1996.

28 Arendt, op. cit., p.124.

29 Gilbert, op. cit., p. 205.

30 Hansi Brand; interview with Adam LeBor, Tel Aviv, March
    1998.

31 Segev, Tom; *The Seventh Million*, p. 32.

32 *Life* magazine, op. cit.

33 Ernest Stein, as above.

34 Laszlo Devecseri; interview with Adam LeBor, Tel Aviv,
    March 1998.

Afterword

1 *Die Welt*, May 2000.

2 *Frankfurter Allgemeine Zeitung*, 1 April 2000.

Bibliography

Aalders, Gerard. Roof, *De Ontvreemding van joods bezit tijdens de Tweede Wereldoorlog*. The Hague: Sdu, 1999.

Aarons, Mark and John Loftus. *Unholy Trinity: The Vatican, the Nazis and the Swiss Banks*. New York: St. Martin's Griffin, 1998.

Abel, Theodore. *Why Hitler Came into Power: An Answer Based on the Original Life Stories of Six Hundred of His Followers*. New York: Prentice Hall, 1938.

Adorno, Theodor W. *Jargon der Eigentlichkeit: Zur deutschen Ideologie*. Frankfurt/M: Suhrkamp, 1964.

Adorno, Theodor W. *Studien zum autoritären Charakter*. Frankfurt/M: Suhrkamp, 1973.

Arendt, Hannah. *Eichmann in Jerusalem*. London: Penguin, 1994.

Arendt, Hannah. *Elemente und Ursprünge totaler Herrschaft*. Munich, Zurich: Piper, 1987 (orig. 1955).

Arnim, Gabriele von. *Das große Schweigen: Von der Schwierigkeit, mit den Schatten der Vergangenheit zu leben*. Munich: Droemersche Verlagsanstalt: Th. Knaur Nachf, 1991.

Ashby Turner Jr., Henry. *German Big Business and the Rise of Hitler*. Oxford: Oxford University Press, 1985.

Atchildi, Asaf. *Rescue of Jews of Bukharan, Iranian and Afghan Origin in Occupied France (1940–1944)*. Jerusalem: Yad Vashem Studies, Vol. VI, 1967.

Auschwitz-Birkenau State Museum (ed). *KL Auschwitz seen by the SS*. Auschwitz-Birkenau State Museum, 1997.

Baigent, Michael and Richard Leigh. *Secret Germany: Claus von Stauffenberg and the Mystical Crusade Against Hitler*. London: Jonathan Cape, 1994.

Bärsch, Claus-Ekkehard. *Erlösung und Vernichtung: Dr. phil. Joseph Goebbels*. Munich: Klaus Boer, 1987.

Bartov, Omer. "Ganz normale Monster." In: Schoeps, 1996, S.63–80.

Bauer, Yehuda. *Jews for Sale? Nazi-Jewish Negotiations, 1933–1945*.

340 \ B<small>IBLIOGRAPHY</small>

New Haven: Yale University Press, 1994.

Beevor, Anthony. *Stalingrad*. London: Penguin, 1999.

Ben-Tov, Arieh. *Facing the Holocaust in Budapest*. Henri-Dunant Institute, Geneva: Dordrecht, Boston and London: Martinus Nuoff, 1988.

Berlekamp, Brigitte and Werner Röhr (eds). *Terror, Herrschaft und Alltag im Nationalsozialismus:. Probleme einer Sozialgeschichte des deutschen Faschimus*. Münster: Westfalisches Dampfboot, 1995.

Bermann, Martin S., Milton E. Jucovy, and Judith S. Klestenberg (eds). *Kinder der Opfer, Kinder der Tater: Psychoanalyse und Holocaust*. Frankfurt/M: Fischer, 1995.

Bessel, Richard, (ed). *Life in the Third Reich*. Oxford: Oxford University Press, 1987.

Binion, Rudolph. "...dass ihr mich gefunden habt." *Hitler und die Deutschen:eine Psychohistorie*. Stuttgart: Klett Cotta, 1978.

Bloch, Ernst. *Erbschaft dieser Zeit*. Frankfurt/M: Suhrkamp, 1985 (orig. 1935).

Bloch, Ernst. *Vom Hazard zur Katastophe: Politische Aufsätze 1934–1939*. Frankfurt/M: Suhrkamp, 1972.

Bock, Gisela. *Zwangssterilisation im Nationalsozialismus: Studien zur Rassenpolitik und Frauenpolitik*. Opladen: Westdeutscher Verlag, 1986.

Borkin, Joseph. *The Crime and Punishment of I.G. Farben*. New York: Free Press, 1978.

Bracher, Karl Dietrich, Manfred Funke, and Hans Adolf Jacobson, (eds). *Nationalsozialistische Diktatur 1933–1945: Eine Bilanz*. Düsseldorf: Droste, 1983.

Braham, Randolph L. *The Politics of Genocide: The Holocaust in Hungary*. New York: Columbia University Press, 1981.

Breyvogel, Wilfried (ed). *Piraten, Swings und Junge Garde: Jugendwiderstand im Nationalsozialismus*. Bonn: 1991.

Brockhaus, Gudrun. *Schauder und Idylle: Faschimus als Erlebnisangebot*. Munich: Kunstmann Verlag, 1997.

Broszat, Martin. *Der Staat Hitlers: Grundlegung und Entwicklung seiner inneren Verfassung*. Munich: Piper, 1987.

Broszat, Martin and Elke Frohlich (eds). *Alltag und Widerstand: Bayern im Nationalsozialismus*. Munich: Piper, 1987.

Browning, Christopher R. *Ordinary Men: Reserve Battalion 101 and the Final Solution in Poland*. New York: HarperPerennial, 1998.

Brückner, Peter. *Das Abseits als sicherer Ort. Kindheit und Jugend zwischen 1933 und 1945.* Berlin: Wagenbach, 1982.

Bullock, Alan. *Hitler and Stalin: Parallel Lives.* London: Fontana, 1993.

Bunting, Madeleine. *The Model Occupation: The Channel Islands Under German Rule 1940–1945.* London: Harper Collins, 1995.

Burleigh, Michael. Ethics and Extermination: Reflections on Nazi Genocide. Cambridge: 1997.

Cole, Tim. Images of the Holocaust: *The Myth of the "Shoah Business."* London: Duckworth, 1999.

Corino, Karl (ed). *Intellektuelle im Bann des Nationalsozialismus.* Hamburg: Hoffmann und Campe, 1980.

Cornwell, John. *Hitler's Pope: The Secret History of Pius XII.* London: Viking, 1999.

Craig, Gordon A. "Germany, 1866–1945," *The Oxford History of Modern Europe.* Oxford: Oxford University Press, 1980.

Crew, David F. (ed). *Nazism and German Society 1933–1945.* London: Routledge, 1994.

Dawidowicz, Lucy S. *The War Against the Jews 1933–1945.* London: Penguin, 1980.

Diner, Dan (ed). *Zivilisationsbruch: Denken nach Auschwitz.* Frankfurt/M: Fischer, 1988.

Dobroszycki, Lucian (ed). *The Chronicle of the Lodz Ghetto, 1941–1944.* New Haven: Yale University Press, 1984.

Dörner, Bernward. "Heimtucke." *Das Gesetz als Waffe.* Paderborn: Schöningh Verlag, 1998.

Drewniak, Boguslaw. *Der deutsche Film 1938–1945: Ein Gesamtüberblick.* Dusseldorf: Droste, 1987.

Ebbinghaus, Angelika (ed). *Opfer und Täterinnen: Frauenbiographien des Nationalsozialismus.* Nördlingen: Greno, 1987.

Ehrlich, Konrad (ed). *Sprache im Faschismus.* Frankfurt/M: Suhrkamp, 1989.

Eramo, Luce d.' *Die Rhetorik der faschistischen Machtausübung oder: Opfern ist Macht.* In: Schaeffer-Hegel, 1988.

Erdheim, Mario. *Psychoanalyse und Unbewusstheit in der Kultur.* Frankfurt/M: Suhrkamp, 1988.

Erikson, Erik H. *Die Legende von Hitlers Kindheit.* In: Dahmer, 1980 (orig. 1942; 1950).

Fest, Joachim. *The Face of the Third Reich.* London: Penguin. 1979.

Fest, Joachim. *Hitler: Eine Biographie.* Frankfurt/M, Berlin: Ullstein,

1987 (orig. 1973).

Fest, Joachim. *Plotting Hitler's Death: The German Resistance to Hitler 1933–1945*. London: Pheonix, 1996.

Fischer, Fritz. *Hitler war kein Betriebsunfall*. Aufsätze, Munich: Beck, 1992.

Fraenkel, Heinrich. *The German People Versus Hitler*. London: George Allen & Unwin, 1940.

Frauengruppe Faschismusforschung (ed). *Mutterkreuz und Arbeitsbuch: Zur Geschichte der Frauen in der Weimare Republik und im Nationalsozialismus*. Frankfurt/M: 1981.

Frei, Norbert. *Vergangenheitspolitik. Die Anfange der Bundesrepublik und die NS-Vergangenheit*. Munchen: Beck, 1996.

Friedlander, Saul. *Kitsch und Tod: Der Widerschein des Nazismus*. Munchen: dtv, 1984.

Friedlander, Saul. *Nazi Germany and the Jews: The Years of Persecution 1933–1939*. London: Phoenix, 1998.

Fritzsche, Peter. *Germans into Nazis*. Cambridge: Harvard University Press, 1999.

Fromm, Erich. *Arbeiter und Angestellte am Vorabend des Dritten Reiches: Eine sozialpsychologische Untersuchung*. Munich: dtv, 1980.

Furst, Alan. *Red Gold*. London: Harper Collins, 1999.

Garton-Ash, Timothy. *The File: A Personal History*. London: Flamingo, 1997.

Gay, Peter. *Weimar Culture: The Outside as Insider*. London: Peregrine, 1988.

Gellately, Robert. *The Gestapo and German Society: Enforcing Racial Policy 1933–1945*. Oxford: Clarendon Press, 1991.

Gerstenberger, Heide and Dorothea Schmidt (eds). *Normalität oder Normalisierung? Geschichtswerkstätten und Faschismusanalyse*. Münster: Westfalisches Dampfboot, 1987.

Geyer, Michael and John W. Boyer. *Resistance Against the Third Reich 1933–1945*. London: University of Chicago Press, 1994.

Gilbert, Martin. Auschwitz and the Allies. London: Mandarin, 1991.

Gilbert, Martin. *Holocaust Journey: Travelling in Search of the Past*. London: Weidenfeld and Nicholson, 1997.

Goebbels, Joseph. *Tagebücher. Band I: 1924–1929*. Ralf Georg Reuth (ed). Munich: Piper, 1992.

Goebbels, Joseph. *Tagebücher. Band I: 1930–1934*. Ralf Georg Reuth (ed). Munich: Piper, 1992.

Goldhagen, Daniel Jonah. *Hitler's Willing Executioners, Ordinary Germans and the Holocaust*. New York: Knopf, 1996.

Grieswelle, Detlev. *Propaganda der Friedlosigkeit. Eine Studie zu Hitlers Rhetorik 1920–1933*. Stuttgart: Ferdinand Enke, 1972.

Gross, Leonard. *The Last Jews in Berlin*. London: Sidgwick and Jackson, 1985.

Grunberger, Richard. *A Social History of the Third Reich*. Penguin, 1974.

Gurr, Tedd. *Why Men Rebel*. Princeton, New Jersey: Princeton University Press, 1970.

Gutman, Israel, (ed). *Encyclopaedia of the Holocaust*. New York: Macmillan, 1989.

Haffner, Sebastian. *Anmerkungen zu Hitler*. Frankfurt/M: Fischer, 1991 (orig. 1978).

Haffner, Sebastian. *The Meaning of Hitler*. Cambridge, Massachusetts: Harvard University Press, 1983.

Hardtmann, Gertrud. "Spuren des Nationalsozialismus bei nicht-jüdischen Kindern, Jugendlichen und ihren Familien." In: Cogoy et al, 1989.

Hering, Sabine. *Makel, Muhsal, Privileg? Eine hundertjahrige Geschichte des Alleinerziehens*. Frankfurt/M: Dipa Verlag, 1998.

Higham, Charles. *Trading with the Enemy: An Expose of the Nazi-American Money Plot*. London: Robert Hale, 1983.

Hilberg, Raul. *Täter, Opfer, Zuschauer: Vernichtung der Juden 1933–1945*. Frankfurt/M: 1999.

Himmler, Heinrich. *Geheimreden 1933 bis 1945*. B F Smith, A F Peterson (ed). Frankfurt/M, Berlin, Vienna: Ullstien Propyläen, 1974.

Hirschfeld, Gerhard and Lothar Kettenacher (eds). *Der "Führerstaat": Mythos und Realität*. Stuttgart: Klett-Cotta, 1981.

"Historikerstreit." *Die Dokumentation der Kontroverse um die Einzigartigkeit der nationalsozialistischen Judenvernichtung*. Munich, Zurich: Piper, 1987.

Hitler, Adolf. *Mein Kampf*. Eidenbändige Volksausgabe. Munich: Eher, 1938.

Holocaust Educational Trust. *Extermination Through Work: Jewish Slave Labor under the Third Reich*. London, 1999.

Houwink ten Cate, J.Th.M and N.K.C.A. In 't Veld. *Fout, Getuigenissen van NSB'ers*. The Hague: Sdu, 1992.

International Committee of the Red Cross. *Documents of the ICRC*

Concerning the Thereisenstadt Ghetto. Geneva: ICRC, 1990.

International Committee of the Red Cross. *The ICRC Infiltrated by the Nazis?* Geneva: ICRC, 1996.

Irving, David. *Göring: A Biography.* London: Grafton, 1991.

Jacobs, Gerald. *Sacred Games.* London: Penguin, 1995.

Johnson, Eric. *Nazi Terror: Gestapo, Jews & Ordinary Germans.* London: John Murray, 2000.

Kahn, David. *Hitler's Spies.* New York: Macmillan, 1978.

Keller, Ulrich, (ed). *The Warsaw Ghetto in Photographs.* New York: Dover Publications, 1984.

Kempowski, Walter. *Haben Sie Hitler gesehen? Deutsche Antworten.* Munich: Goldmann, 1989.

Kershaw, Ian. *Der NS-Staat. Geschichtsinterpretationen und Kontroversen im Überblick.* Reinbek: Rowohlt, 1988.

Kershaw, Ian. *Hitler 1889–1936.* London: Hubris, 1998.

Kershaw, Ian. *Popular Opinion and Political Dissent in the Third Reich: Bavaria 1933–1945.* Oxford: Clarendon, 1983.

Kershaw, Ian. *The "Hitler Myth": Image and Reality in the Third Reich.* Oxford: Oxford University Press, 1989.

Kershaw, Ian. *The Führer Image and Political Integration: The Popular Conception of Hitler in Bavaria during the Third Reich.* In: Hirschfield/Kettenacker, 1981.

Kershaw, Ian. *The Nazi Dictatorship. Problems and Perspectives of Interpretation.* New York: Third Edition, 1993.

Kitchen, Martin. *Nazi Germany at War.* London: Longman, 1995.

Klaus, Martin. *Mädchen im Dritten Reich: Der Bund Deutscher Mädel.* Koln: Pahl-Rugenstein, 1983.

Klemperer, Viktor. *I Shall Bear Witness: The Diaries of Viktor Klemperer 1933–41.* London: Pheonix, 1999.

Koestler, Arthur. *Scum of the Earth.* London: Eland, 1991.

Koonz, Claudia. *Mothers in the Fatherland. Women, the Family and Nazi Politics.* London: Methuen, 1988.

Kotze, Hildegard von, Krausnick, Helmut. *"Es spricht der Führer."* 7 *exemplarische Hitler-Reden.* Gütersloh: Sigbert Mohn, 1966.

Langer, Walter C. *"Das Hitler-Psychogramm." Eine Analyse seiner Person und seines Verhaltens.* Vienna, Munich, Zürich: Moden, 1973.

Lanzmann, Claude. *Shoah.* Munich: dtv, 1988.

LeBor, Adam. *Hitler's Secret Bankers: How Switzerland Profited From*

Nazi Genocide. London: Simon & Schuster, 1997.

Lendvai-Dircksen, Erna. *Reichsautobahn, Mensch und Werk.* Bayreuth: Gauverlag, 1942.

Levy, Alan. *The Wiesenthal File.* Grand Rapids: William B. Eerdmans, 1994.

Lifton, Robert Jay. *The Nazi Doctors: Medical Killing and the Psychology of Genocide.* New York: Basic Books, 1986.

Lipschitz, Chaim U. *Franco, Spain, the Jews and the Holocaust.* New York: Ktav Publishing House, 1984.

Loewy, Ernst. *Literatur unterm Hakenkreuz: Das Dritte Reich und seine Dichtung.* Eine Dokumentation. Frankfurt/M: Hain, 1990.

Loftus, John and Mark Aarons. *The Secret War Against the Jews.* New York: St. Martin's Press, 1994.

Ludwig, Karl-Heinz. *Technik und Ingenieure im Dritten Reich.* Düsseldorf: Droste, 1979.

Lukacs, John. *The Hitler of History.* New York: Vintage Books, 1998.

Maas, Utz. *"Als der Geist der Gemeinschaft eine Sprache fand." Sprache im Nationalsozialismus: Versuch einer historischen Argumentationsanalyse.* Opladen: Westdeutscher Verlag, 1984.

Mak, Geert. *De Eeuw Van Mijn Vader.* Amsterdam/Antwerp: Atlas, 1999.

Marrus, Michael R. and Robert O. Paxton. *Vichy France and the Jews.* Stanford: Stanford University Press, 1995.

Marssolek, Inge. *Bürgerlicher Alltag in Bremen—oder "die zahe Fortdauer der Wonnen der Gewonhnlichkeit" (Christa Wolf).* In: Gerstenberger/Schmidt, 1987.

Marton, Kati. *Wallenberg: Missing Hero.* New York: Arcade, 1995.

Maschmann, Melita. *Fazit: Mein Weg in die Hitler-Jugend.* Munich: dtv, 1979 (orig. 1963).

Mason, Timothy. Introduction to *Angst, Belohnung, Zucht and Ordnung: Herrschaftsmechanismen im Nationalsozialismus,* by Carola Sachse, et al. Opladen: Westdeutscher Verlag, 1982.

Mason, Timothy. *Nazism, Fascism and the Working Class.* Cambridge University Press, 1995.

Mason, Timothy. *The Workers' Opposition in Nazi Germany.* Oxford: History Workshop journal, Spring 1981.

Merson, Allan. *Communist Resistance in Nazi Germany.* London: Lawrence and Wishart, 1985.

Möding, Nori. "Ich muß irgendwo engagiert sein—fragen Sie mich bloß nicht, warum." *Überlegungen zu Sozialisationserfahrungen von Mädchen in NS-Organisationen*. In: Niethammer/von Plato, 1985.

Mommsen, Hans. *Der Nationalsozialismus und die deutsche Gesellschaf: Ausgewählte Aufsätze*. Reinbeck: Rowohlt, 1991.

Mosse, George L. *Der nationalsozialistische Alltag*. Meisenheim: Anton Hain, 1993.

Mosse, George L. *Die Nationalisierung der Massen: Politische Symbolik und Massenbewegungen in Deutschland von den Napoleonischen Kriegen bis zum Dritten Reich*. Frankfurt/M, Berlin: Ullstein, 1976.

Moszkiewiez, Helen. *Inside the Gestapo: A Young Woman's Secret War*. London: Warner, 1998.

Niethammer, Lutz and Alexander von Plato (eds). "Die Jahre weiß man nicht, wo man die heute hinsetzen soll." *Faschismuserfahrungen im Ruhrgebiet*. Berlin, Bonn: Dietz, 1983.

Noakes, Jeremy and G. Pridham (eds). *Nazism 1919–45, A Documentary Reader (Vol. 1: The Rise to Power 1919–1934 [1995] Vol. 2: State, Economy and Society 1933–1939 [1996] Vol. 3: Foreign Policy, War and Racial Extermination [1997] Vol. 4: The German Home Front in World War II [1998])*. Exeter: University of Exeter Press.

Owings, Alison. *Frauen: German Women Recall the Third Reich*. London: Penguin, 1995.

Paloczi-Horvath, George. *The Undefeated*. London: Eland, 1993.

Perrault, Giles. *The Red Orchestra*. New York: Pocket Books, 1970.

Peukert, Detlev and Jürgen Reulecke (eds). *Die Reihen fast geschlossen: Beiträge zur Geschichte des Alltags unterm Nationalsozialismus*. Wuppertal: Hammer, 1981.

Peukert, Detlev. *Inside Nazi Germany: Conformity, Opposition and Racism in Everyday Life*. London: Penguin, 1989.

Peukert, Detlev. *Volksgenossen und Gemeinschaftsfremde: Anpassung, Ausmerze und Aufbegehren unter dem Nationalsozialismus*. Koln: Bund, 1982.

Peukert, Detlev. *Die Weimarer Republik. Krisenjahre der Klassichen Moderne*. Frankfurt/M: Suhrkamp, 1987.

Piper, Franciszek. *Auschwitz: How Many Perished, Jews, Poles, Gypsies*. Auschwitz: Frap-Books, 1996. (First published in Yad Vashem Studies Vol. XXI. Jerusalem 1991)

Pool, James. *Hitler and His Secret Partners: Contributions, Loot and*

Rewards 1933—1945. New York: Pocket Books, 1997.

Presser, Dr. J. *Ondergang. De Vervolging en Verdelging van het Nederlandse Jodendom*. The Hague: Sdu, 1965.

Rees, Laurence. *The Nazis: A Warning from History*. London: BBC Books, 1997.

Reichel, Peter. *Der schöne Schein des Dritten Reiches: Faszination und Gewalt des Faschimus*. Munich, Vienna: Hanser, 1991.

Reichel, Peter. *Politik mit der Erinnerung: Gedächtnisorte im Streit um die nationalsozialistische Vergangenheit*. Munich / Vienna: Hanser, 1995.

Rempel, Gerhard. *Hitler's Children: The Hitler Youth and the SS*. Chapel Hill: The University of North Carolina Press, 1989.

Richie, Alexandra. *Faust's Metropolis: A History of Berlin*. London: 1998.

Richmond, Theo. *Konin*. London: Jonathan Cape, 1995.

Riefenstahl, Leni. *Memoiren 1902–1945*. Frankfurt/M, Berlin: Ullstein, 1990.

Riefenstahl, Leni. *Schönheit im Olympischen Kampf*. Berlin: Deutscher Verlag, 1937.

Ritter, Gerhard. *The German Resistance: Carl Goerdeler's Struggle Against Tyranny*. London: George Allen & Unwin, 1958.

Rosenbaum, Ron. *Explaining Hitler: The Search for the Origins of His Evil*. London: Macmillan, 1998.

Rubin, Barry. *Istanbul Intrigues: A True Life Casablanca*. New York: McGraw-Hill, 1989.

Ruerup, Reinhard (ed). *Topography of Terror: Gestapo, SS and Reichssicherheitshauptamt on the 'Prinz-Albrecht' Terrain, A Documentation*. (English edition) Berlin: Verlag Willmuth Arenhoevel, 1989.

Safrian, Hans. In: *Die Welt*, 1999.

Schellenberg, Walter. *The Labyrinth*. U.S.: Da Capo Press, 2000.

Schmidt, Christoph (1981). *Zu den Motiven 'alter Kampfer' in der NSDAP*. In: Peukert/Reulecke, 1981.

Schmidt, Helmut et al. *Kindheit und Jugend unter Hitler*. Berlin: Siedler, 1992.

Schneider, Christian, Cordelia Stillke, and Bernd Leineweber. *Das Erbe der Napola: Versuch einer Generationengeschichte des Nationalsozialismus*. Hamburg: Hamburger edition, 1996.

Schoeps, Julius H (ed). *Ein Volk von Mördern? Die Dokumentation zur*

Goldhagen-Kontroverse um die Rolle der Deutschen im Holocaust.
Hamburg: Hoffmann und Campe, 1996.

Scholdt, Günter. *Autoren über Hitler: Deutschsprachige Schriftsteller 1919–1945 und ihr Bild vom "Führer."* Bonn: 1993.

Schulte, A. (ed). *Oorlogsreportages uit Nederland en Nederlands-Indië.* Amsterdam: Prometheus, 1995.

Segev, Tom. *The Seventh Million, The Israelis and the Holocaust.* New York: Hill and Wang, 1994.

Sereny, Gita. *Albert Speer: His Battle with Truth.* London: Picador, 1996.

Shirer, William L. *Berlin Diary. The Journal of a Foreign Correspondent 1934–1941.* New York: 1961.

Shirer, William L. *The Rise and Fall of the Third Reich: A History of Nazi Germany* (20th ed.). New York: Simon and Schuster, 1990.

Shirer, William L. *Twentieth Century Journey Vol. II: The Nightmare Years 1930–1940.* Boston: Little, Brown, 1984.

Simpson, Christopher. *The Splendid Blond Beast: Money, Law and Genocide in the Twentieth Century.* Monroe, Maine: Common Courage Press, 1995.

Smith, Michael. *Foley: The Spy Who Saved 10,000 Jews.* London: Coronet, 1999.

Snyder, Louis L. *Encyclopaedia of the Third Reich.* London: Robert Hale, 1998.

Speer, Albert. *Erinnerungen.* Frankfurt/M, Berlin: Ullstein, 1969.

Speer, Albert. *Inside the Third Reich.* London: Pheonix, 1993.

Speer, Albert. *Spandauer Tagebücher.* Frankfurt/M, Berlin, Vienna: Ullstein, 1975.

Stern, Joseph Peter. *Hitler und die Deutschen.* In: Bracher / Funke / Jacobsen, 1983.

Stern, Joseph Peter. *Hitler. Der Führer und das Volk.* Munich: Hanser, 1978.

Sternheim-Peters, Eva. *Die Zeit der großen Täuschungen.* Bielefeld: AJZ, 1987.

Stoltzfus, Nathan. *Resistance of the Heart: Intermarriage and the Rosenstrasse Protest in Nazi Germany.* New York: W.W. Norton, 1996.

Swiebocki, Henryk, (ed). *London Has Been Informed...Reports by Auschwitz Escapees.* Auschwitz: The Auschwitz-Birkenau State Museum, 1997.

Sywottk, Arnold. *Deutsche Volkdemkratie*. Dusseldorf: Bertelsmann Universitätsverlag, 1971.

3BM Television. *The Real Albert Göring*. Broadcast on UK Channel 4, December 1998.

Ueberschar, Gerd and Winifred Vogel. *Dienen und Verdienen, Hitlers Geschenke an seine Eliten*. Frankfurt/M: S.Fischer, 1999.

Vassiltchikov, Marie. *The Berlin Diaries of Marie "Missie" Vassiltchikov 1940–1945*. London: Methuen, 1988.

Webster, Paul. *Pétain's Crime: The Full Story of French Collaboration in the Holocaust*. London: Macmillan, 1990.

Weitz, John. *Hitler's Banker: Hjalmar Horace Greely Schacht*. London: Warner Books, 1999.

Welzer, Harald (ed). *Nationalsozialismus und Moderne*. Tübingen: edition diskord, 1993.

Werkman, Evert E.O. *Dat kan ons niet gebeuren...* Amsterdam: De Bezige Bij, 1980.

West, Nigel. *MI5: British Intelligence Service Operations, 1909–1945*. New York: Random House, 1983.

White, Ian Boyd. *Kunst und Macht im Europa der Diktatoren 1930–1945*. Berlin: Deutsches Historisches Museum, 1996.

Wistrich, Robert S. *Who's Who in Nazi Germany*. London: Routledge, 1995.

Witte, Karsten. *Lachende Erben, Toller Tag: Filmkomödie im Dritten Reich*. Berlin: Vorwerk 8, 1995.

Wyman, David S. *The Abandonment of the Jews*. New York: Pantheon Brooks, 1985.

Zwerin, Mike. *La Tristesse de St. Louis: Swing under the Nazis*. London: Quartet, 1985.

Internet Resources

Holocaust Mailing list: *h-holocaust@h-net.msu.edu*
headlines.yahoo.com.Full_Coverage/World/Holocaust_Assets
history1900s.about.com/library/holocaust
www.cmht.com/slave_labor/fordlabor.htm
www.icrc.orgwww.ushmm.org
www.jchron.co.uk/
www.nizkor.org
www.us-israel.org/jsource/holo.html
www.wiesenthal.com/index.html
www.yadvashem.org.il

Index